INTRODUCING VIGILANT AUDIENCES

Introducing Vigilant Audiences

Edited by
Daniel Trottier, Rashid Gabdulhakov
and Qian Huang

https://www.openbookpublishers.com

ISBN Paperback: 978-1-78374-902-7
ISBN Hardback: 978-1-78374-903-4
ISBN Digital (PDF): 978-1-78374-904-1
ISBN Digital ebook (epub): 978-1-78374-905-8
ISBN Digital ebook (mobi): 978-1-78374-906-5
ISBN XML: 978-1-78374-907-2
DOI: 10.11647/OBP.0200

Cover image: Photo by Vino Li on Unsplash at https://unsplash.com/photos/NpYcvUqx8Go
Cover design: Anna Gatti.

Contents

Acknowledgements

This work was supported by the Netherlands Organisation for Scientific Research (NWO) [276–45–004], as well as by the Erasmus Open Access Fund.

Notes on Contributors

Aurélie Campana is professor of Political Science at Laval University. She held the Canada Research Chair on Conflicts and Terrorism between 2007 and 2017. She is associate director of the Canadian Research Network on Terrorism, Security and Society (TSAS) and member of the Centre International de Criminologie Comparée (Université de Montréal). Her research has focused for years on terrorism in internal conflicts; diffusion of violence across movements and borders and engagement in extremist movements, including Canadian far right groups. Her research appeared in numerous journals, including *Studies in Conflict and Terrorism, Terrorism and Political Violence, International Studies Review, New Media & Society* and *Global Crime*.

Abderrahim Chalfaouat is a media and communication researcher from Morocco. He holds a doctorate in advertising and communication (2019), and an MA in Moroccan American Studies (2011) from Hassan II University of Casablanca. His research interests include media discourse analysis, media policy and digital culture. He is an alumnus of the Annenberg Oxford media policy institute (Oxford, 2015). He also discussed the Arab Barometer findings at the American Institute for Maghrib Studies' annual conference (Tunis, 2015). His publications include book chapters and journal articles, including "Media, freedom of expression and democratisation in post-colonial Morocco" (2015), and "Framing the judiciary in Morocco: The case of Moudawala and Immortal Past" (forthcoming).

Valentine Crosset recently completed her PhD in criminology at Université de Montréal. She is junior research affilitate of the Canadian Network for Research on Terrorism, Security and Society (TSAS), member of the Cybercriminology Laboratory (Université de Montréal) and research assistant at the Cyberjustice Laboratory (Université de

Montréal). Her research examines violent political expression online, content moderation and algorithmic regulation. She has published in several journals such as *New Media & Society* and *Revue Critique Internationale*.

Rianne Dekker is an assistant professor at the Utrecht University School of Governance (USG/USBO). She studies (social) media as modern sources of social pressure within governance in two societal domains: (1) public security and (2) migration and integration. She uses co-design methods, including the living lab methodology as an engaged research practice.

David M. Douglas is a computer ethics researcher based in Australia. He was awarded a PhD in philosophy at the University of Queensland in 2011. He has served as an ethics advisor for the Center of Telematics and Information Technology (CTIT) at the University of Twente in the Netherlands. He has published research papers on free software, Internet regulation, doxing and Internet research ethics.

Simone Driessen is a lecturer and researcher in media and communication at Erasmus University Rotterdam, the Netherlands. In 2017, Simone completed her PhD on popular music fandom, researching how audiences gave meaning to pop music from the recent past (1980s-2000s). She has published her work in e.g. *Participations, Transformative Works and Cultures* and *Popular Music & Society*, and contributed to several edited collections on fandom and pop culture. Her research interests are participatory cultures, (toxic) fandoms, pop culture, and media entertainment at large.

Gilles Favarel-Garrigues holds a PhD in political science (2000) from Sciences Po and a "habilitation à diriger les recherches" (2014) from Ecole des Hautes Etudes en Sciences Sociales (EHESS). He currently works on vigilantism in a comparative perspective, especially in post-Soviet societies. He has recently edited two special issues on this topic: Citizens' Crime Watch and Vigilantism in Post-Soviet Societies, *Laboratorium*, 11, 3, 2019 (with Ioulia Shukan), and Watchful Citizens: Policing from Below and Digital Vigilantism, *Global Crime*, forthcoming, 2020 (with Samuel Tanner and Daniel Trottier).

Rashid Gabdulhakov is a PhD candidate in the Department of Media and Communication at Erasmus University Rotterdam. He is researching digital vigilantism and its manifestation in Russia and other former Soviet republics. Rashid has authored several articles in peer-reviewed journals on this and other topics. He holds a Master of Advanced Studies degree in International and European Security from the University of Geneva, Switzerland and a Master of Arts in Politics and Security from the OSCE Academy in Bishkek, Kyrgyz Republic.

Jiaxi Hou is a PhD candidate at the Graduate School of Interdisciplinary Information Studies of the University of Tokyo, Japan. Her research centers on investigating the intricate relationships between digital technology and its social context, especially on how various digital media platforms contribute to the social class stratification process in Asian societies. She has received her MAS degree from the University of Tokyo, and a BA from the School of Journalism and Communication of Tsinghua University, China. She also works as an independent documentary producer, with a focus on the living conditions of young Chinese migrant workers.

Qian Huang is a PhD candidate in the Department of Media and Communication at Erasmus University Rotterdam. Her current research considers digital vigilantism on the Chinese Internet. Qian has several peer-reviewed publications concerning Chinese online phenomena in relation to the class struggle and nationalism in China. Qian received a Master's degree in Global Communication from Chinese University of Hong Kong in 2014 after a Bachelor's degree in English and International Studies from China Foreign Affairs University.

Albert Meijer is a professor of Public Management at the Utrecht University School of Governance in the Netherlands. His research focuses on new forms of public management and governance in an information age. Professor Meijer is co-editor in chief of the journal *Information Polity* and co-chair of the permanent studygroup on e-government of the European Group for Public Administration.

Tara Milbrandt is an associate professor of Sociology in the Augustana Faculty of the University of Alberta, Canada. She works in the areas of social theory, visual sociology, urban culture and digital media. Her current research explores new and contested ways that photographic images of identifiable strangers are generated and distributed across the contemporary public sphere, raising critical questions about what it means to be a social person, to cohabit and create a world together.

Mojca M. Plesničar is a research associate at the Institute of Criminology in Ljubljana and assistant professor in Criminology and Criminal Law at the University of Ljubljana. She is interested in human behaviour in connection to the criminal justice system. Her research focuses on questions of punishment, sentencing and penal decision-making, but incorporates various strands of related inquiries, such as the role and impact of new technologies on criminal justice, questions of marginal groups in criminal justice (women, minors, migrants), prisons, sexual and violent crime, etc. Mojca has published nationally and internationally and has held visiting positions at Universities in Trieste, Cambridge and Warwick. She is currently heading a three-year research project on objectivity and subjectivity in criminal justice, financed by the Slovenian research agency. In her future research, she plans to explore the roles and decision-making strategies of professionals in the criminal justice system (judges, prosecutors, attorneys), especially in light of the changing nature of criminal justice in recent decades.

Pika Šarf is a junior researcher at the Institute of Criminology and a PhD student of Criminology at the Faculty of Law, Ljubljana. In her doctoral thesis she is exploring the interoperbility of information systems in the Area of Freedom, Security and Justice (AFSJ) in light of data protection law. Pika is interested in questions of law and technology, with a special focus on regulation of cyberspace, cybercrime, cyber war, cyber espionage and privacy in the digital age.

Samuel Tanner is an associate professor at the School of Criminology, Université de Montréal. He is also a member of the International Center for Comparative Criminology (ICCC) and the International Studies and Research Center (CÉRIUM) of the Université de Montréal. His research focuses on the impact of technology on policing and activism, and on digital vigilantism. His work has been published in *Security Dialogue*, *Global Crime* and *New Media & Society*.

Daniel Trottier is an associate professor at the Department of Media and Communication of Erasmus University Rotterdam. His current research considers the use of digital media for the purposes of scrutiny, denunciation and shaming. Daniel is the PI of a five-year NWO-funded project on this topic. He has authored several articles in peer-reviewed journals on this and other topics, as well as *Social Media as Surveillance* in 2012, *Identity Problems in the Facebook Era* in 2013, and *Social Media, Politics and the State* (co-edited with Christian Fuchs) in 2014. Daniel completed a PhD in Sociology at Queen's University in Kingston, Canada.

Isabel Linton is a PhD candidate at Bangor University, conducting practice-based research on transmedia storytelling and digital fiction. Her research interests include creative writing, fandom and digital fiction. She has taught modules on transmedia storytelling and game design.

Sarah Young is a Marie Skłodowska-Curie LEaDing Fellows postdoc at Erasmus University in Rotterdam, The Netherlands. She researches surveillance, technical communication, information and rhetoric especially in the law enforcement and investigation context. She previously worked as a lecturer at the School of Information at the University of Arizona and spent over eleven years contracted as an investigator for the US government.

Introducing Vigilant Audiences

Daniel Trottier, Rashid Gabdulhakov and Qian Huang

In nearly any context, people are attentive and judgemental when it comes to the affairs of others. Vigilant audiences entail a range of phenomena, span geographic areas and vary in their motivations as well as their affiliations. This watching can escalate to vigilantism if audiences witness something that demands a response. We understand digitally mediated vigilantism to include practices where citizens (or digital media users more generally) are offended by other citizen actions, and retaliate through practices and repertoires that include mobile devices and social platforms (Trottier, 2017). As a global development, digital media audiences denounce and bear witness to criminal and moral offences. They consume footage of these events, but also take a collective role in scrutinising and seeking retribution against targets. Two examples illustrate some of the concerns explored in this edited volume.

First, consider the global response to the Charlottesville 'Unite the Right' rally in 2017 (covered in Milbrandt's chapter in this volume). In response to images of torch-bearing crowds chanting racist and anti-Semitic slogans, it is not difficult to imagine why witnesses denounced these participants, and sought to hold them accountable by any available means. Here, digital media audiences felt compelled to bear witness to racial hatred, in order to prevent future rallies and comparable incidents. As we shall see in later chapters, audiences were asked to share information about the participants, as well as to join in denouncing them. Yet even consuming these images appears to carry social importance, as it involves recognising political developments for what

  https://doi.org/10.11647/OBP.0200.01

they are, and recognising white nationalists for who they are, in order to assert that they will not be accepted in society. The backlash against these images can be understood as positive developments as they call out — or openly denounce — troubling instances of racial hatred that could otherwise be normalised and accepted.

We can contrast this case to a second instance of mediated denunciation. Roughly six months before Charlottesville, a sixty-eight-year-old woman in the Netherlands was caught on camera pocketing someone else's wallet. Camera footage of the incident circulated on a regional crime-fighting programme, and the woman turned herself in to the police. The footage continued to circulate, and ended up on a local video hosting site where it garnered an additional half-a-million views (Baard, 2017; Trottier, 2018). The website includes a comments section where the audience published vitriolic and malicious comments. Shortly afterwards, the woman took her own life. Mediated scrutiny and denunciation led to an outcome that defies any sense of justice or proportionality. Even relatively minor forms of ridicule and shaming can culminate in insurmountable harm, especially for those who may be marginalised or otherwise vulnerable. Shaming in particular is a collective assault on a target's social standing and self-worth. Much like the Charlottesville backlash, audiences varied in the extent of their engagement with mediated coverage. Yet simply having watched the video contributes to its metrics on the Internet, and contributes to an imagined audience-cum-jury of peers. In both cases, people are consuming images and responding to them in a way that may seem just or at least minimally harmful at the level of any single person's actions. Cumulatively, they serve a powerful and pivotal role in terms of scrutinising the worth of a fellow citizen.

While these incidents emerged in response to particular events, ranging from shoplifting to white-nationalist rallies, vigilantism may persist through pre-existing groups. Despite the seemingly 'disruptive' nature of digital technologies, those who experience the greatest harm may be those who have historically faced social disadvantages and vulnerabilities. Consider the plight of Kyrgyz migrant workers in Russia, notably the scrutiny and violence leveraged against women by their families and peers (Gabdulhakov, 2019). Local communities back home consume footage of the abuse of female migrants abroad in response to accusations that they were seen interacting with non-Kyrgyz men. While digital media technologies allow this harmful and denunciatory content to circulate globally, they also mobilise communities that are locally entrenched. Other examples of such vulnerabilities include the case of sexual minorities who fall target to vigilantes amid a broader social stigma. In Russia, non-heterosexual relations are interpreted as perversion, generating a 'ripe' atmosphere 'for opportunistic uses' when it comes to 'moral entrepreneurship' in vigilante practices (Favarel-Garrigues, 2019, pp. 4, 6).

Longstanding forms of moral scrutiny and justice-seeking are linked up with a connected and pervasive media landscape. It is possible to focus on emerging developments, including large-scale decentralised social coordination among digital media users, as well as the reach of wearable and otherwise socially embedded technologies. These novelties may lead us to believe that users are uniquely empowered through new media practices. Yet we are also witnessing the reproduction and furthering of existing relations and behaviours. Vigilant audiences are an extension of public and pre-digital gatherings like Russia's comrades' courts (Gabdulhakov, 2018) and China's village pact or 'pidou' during the Cultural Revolution (Huang et al., 2020), but also other contemporary mediated publics assembled by crime-based reality television (Schlesinger & Tumber, 1993), and a denunciatory tabloid press (Johansson, 2007). We need to consider how these inform and shape citizen-led scrutiny and denunciation through digital media, especially when formal media actors like newspapers and broadcast media also increasingly maintain an audience base on platforms like Twitter and Facebook (Chadwick, 2017).

Digital vigilantes seek job losses and embodied interventions against their targets, and typically express their disapproval through denunciation, shaming and doxing (sourcing and circulating any available information about them, see Douglas' chapter in this volume). In using the term vigilantism to describe these digitally mediated practices, we draw upon scholarly perspectives that conceptualise an otherwise value-laden label. Moncada points to five core dimensions when speaking about vigilantism, including 'social organisation, target, repertoire, justification and motivation' (2017, p. 407). Each of these raises complexities that we will briefly address.

First, vigilantes may be either individually or collectively organised, and as a collective can be formalised or relatively informal (ibid.). Although earlier definitions treated spontaneous forms of self-defence as distinct from vigilantism, the kinds of connectivity afforded to digital media users (van Dijck & Poell, 2013) complicate this distinction. For example, an individual can spontaneously upload footage of racial abuse to their Twitter account, without much forethought about desired audiences or intended outcomes. Yet intended outcomes may be determined later on by an assembly of users who coalesce around this incident. When it comes to gathering an audience around an actionable event, we can consider instances where an audience is pre-assembled in relation to a media franchise (as Driessen does in her contribution to this book), as well as cases like the Charlottesville rally where an audience is brought together afterwards.

Second, (digital) vigilantism is centred on a target, who is deemed to have violated a certain social order. As Moncada (2017) points out, this may involve criminal acts as well as actions and utterances that are morally offensive. It bears noting that the ease with which offending images and videos can circulate online means that these manifestations occur largely outside any single jurisdiction. Moreover, moral denunciations can be an opportunity to seek legal and institutional reform, as has been the case in the #metoo movement (North, 2019). When it comes to selecting a target of denunciation, it is not just the specific individual who may come under scrutiny. Rather, this can spread to a broader category of target. This is once again evident in light of #metoo, where the denunciatory focus includes not only the alleged predator, but also norms and beliefs that serve to tolerate sexual abuse. Yet vigilante acts against members of vulnerable and marginalised communities more broadly can also serve to increase the scrutiny and repression conducted by the community at large.

Third, vigilantes make use of repertoires that 'range from lethal to non-lethal' (ibid.). While embodied vigilantism primarily involves physical forms of violence, digitally mediated cases may touch upon cultural or institutional forms of violence (Galtung, 1990) that may severely compromise subsequent life chances for the target as well as those affiliated with them. Here we can consider job loss as a central part of the digital vigilante's repertoire, which aims to place the target and their dependents in an economically and socially precarious position. Fourth, vigilantes and their supporters invoke justifications for their activities in order to seek broader legitimation. As they are able to attract a geographically and ideologically dispersed audience, digital vigilantes in particular may fail in convincing these audiences with their justifications, and may in turn trigger counter-denunciations against themselves and their actions. In considering cultural polarisation in the Anglo-American context and elsewhere, certain denunciations and calls for action may be rebuked on ideological grounds, with a sizeable audience turning to the initiators' Twitter feed in order to call attention to (for instance) 'problematic' content. Here too we can consider how categorical affiliations such as gender and ethnicity may enable or constrain attempts to justify vigilantism to a broader audience.

Finally, vigilantes are compelled by motivations that 'cannot be assumed to align neatly' with stated justifications (Moncada, 2017, p. 408). These may include closely held values linked to criminal justice, but participants may also seek financial gain (through merchandise sales or ad revenue on their social media accounts). Likewise, one of the key tensions that informs this book lies in the motivations of the wider audiences that participate in vigilant denunciations. We may consider whether there are connections between a desire to seek retribution, and a desire to consume entertaining footage. Put simply, vigilant audiences are characterised by a confluence of entertainment and criminal justice.

We should therefore consider the notion of the audience, especially when highlighting the shift from embodied to digitally mediated practices. We can begin by considering how the audience is understood in contemporary media and cultural studies literature, notably how they may endorse, resist or negotiate with vigilant discourses (Hall, 2001). As stated above, audiences may be ideologically aligned with an attempt to seek (social or criminal) justice, but such events are just as likely to attract bystanders that either reinterpret the meaning or deny the legitimacy of these events. Prior studies on television audiences stress the active role viewers take in ascribing meaning to content (Ang, 2013). In principle, such abilities have only been enhanced by the emergence and popularisation of social media platforms that solicit input and engagement from their users. Not only are digital media users more engaged in domains such as political campaigns (Vitak et al., 2011) and journalism (Braun & Gillespie, 2011), but it has arguably never been easier for users to watch over and express their opinions about their peers (Andrejevic, 2004). Such scrutiny occurs in real time, for instance when a livestream triggers both supportive and critical comments (see Tanner et al.'s contribution to this volume), but also through the retrospective scrutiny of user-generated content that may span years and transcend any individual context (Trottier, 2012).

Peer-to-peer scrutiny may be manifest in the form of harassment and stalking, but must also be recognised in more innocuous and acceptable forms of listening, lurking (Crawford, 2011) and even orbiting (Stauffer, 2018) that may serve to normalise asymmetrical relations of visibility. In other words, we should be attentive to the range of contexts where digital media users are compelled to make themselves publicly visible (either for intrinsic reasons, such as self-expression, or more tangible goals such as gainful employment), if only because of the kinds of audiences and scrutiny that may emerge in consequence. A personal Twitter account can end up harming its owner if opponents use it to locate and republish discrediting statements. Likewise, review platforms like Yelp or Tripadvisor may be weaponised to denounce and harm the public standing of individuals (Finley, 2015). Digitally mediated scrutiny and denunciation necessarily involve an assemblage of human and non-human actors (Haggerty & Ericson, 2000; Trottier, 2018). While users may temporarily coalesce around an offensive event, we must acknowledge that specific media platforms frequently serve as hubs to coordinate and host such coalescence. Platforms like 4chan and 8chan, specific sub-communities like the Reddit Bureau of Investigation (Myles et al., 2020) and culturally specific news sites like *GeenStijl* in the Netherlands are closely linked to open denunciations. Although these groups evoke a 'viral' reaction among a greater public, they also rely on a core of more closely affiliated users who may invest more time and be more explicitly ideologically aligned.

Contributions to this edited collection address contemporary digital media practices involving users both consuming and participating in the denunciation of other individuals. These engage with a range of (cross-)disciplinary perspectives, including but not limited to sociology, criminology, philosophy, legal, cultural and media studies. While drawing upon cases in the Anglo-American context, this collection also endeavours to consider developments in regions that have received less coverage in English-language scholarship. These cases often transcend the boundary between policing and entertainment, and one of our goals is to call attention to the confluence between these practices in dispersed contexts. Remaining attentive to social harms that may arise, we seek to privilege the particular contexts when exploring cases. As the opening examples clearly show, what may be considered appropriate or ethical in one context would be inconceivable in another.

In particular, we seek to make theoretical and empirical contributions by considering how particular cases and more general practices are made meaningful. This includes taking into account how digital media users develop denunciatory and shaming practices as well as how the press and other public figures may support or contest them. Because the incidents themselves are by definition mediated, it is important to consider the distinction between providing coverage of a vigilante campaign, and contributing to its ends by invoking a greater audience. We are also concerned with the role that digital vigilantism can play in either contesting or reinforcing categorical forms of discrimination and violence, and how such possibilities are shaped by local cultural contexts. Finally, we consider how vigilante audiences either challenge or further support criminal justice practices such as police investigations.

Exploring Local/Global Tensions in Class-Based Scrutiny and Denunciations

When looking broadly at cases of justice-seeking through digital media, this book is especially concerned with the relations between global developments and local conditions. On the one hand, we are witnessing the use of similar digital practices across cultural contexts. Not only do these practices make use of the same platforms (such as Facebook or Twitter), but they also mobilise comparable discourses or repertoires, including linking instances of sexual violence across countries and industries with the #metoo hashtag (Mendes et al., 2018), as well as connecting accusations that political opponents are funded by George Soros (Weaver & Hopkins, 2018). Paradoxically, despite seemingly greater cultural polarisation, fragmentation and a more inward-looking Internet, recent mediated expressions of nationalism and nationhood seem in some ways interchangeable. As one example, national identities online draw upon a globalised repertoire when repurposing image macros (memes) across national or ideological lines.

Fig. 1.1 Local Adaptations of a Global Meme (unknown creators, unknown dates of creation, published under fair use)

The cases this book considers are also shaped by local circumstances, and are best understood with at least some consideration of local governments, local press and local values. While having to account for emerging technologies and practices, states may still assert some degree of sovereignty over global information flows. This is partly to make Silicon Valley platforms accountable to local (tax) laws, but also to have some control over those information flows. Recent examples include Russia's Internet-governing laws, such as the 'Yarovaya law package' that expanded anti-extremism legislation to the digital domain; the law on 'fake news' that made online criticism of the state a legal offence (*The Moscow Times*, 2018; 2019); as well as tje 'Great Firewall of China' that restricts access to American platforms (Xiao, 2019). Governments also shape what is considered legally and morally acceptable, for instance when the UK sought to address 'social harms' associated with digital media (Volpicelli, 2019). And while platforms like Orkut and Instagram have steadily been acquired by tech giants like Google and Facebook, in Russia, VKontakte (a social network comparable to Facebook) and Yandex (a search engine comparable to Google) have not only resisted such takeovers, but also appear to flourish (Yegorov, 2019) under what we may consider a kind of digital nationalism. Although domestic platforms in Russia are more appealing to users due to simplicity and content diversity (ibid.), they are also closely collaborating with Russia's security forces in compliance with the above-mentioned legislation. Even global forms of justice-seeking may be interpreted differently in local contexts. The call to denounce sexual abuse of children is near universal, yet Russia's Occupy Paedophilia has mobilised under this banner to assault sexual minorities. And while developments in one context can resemble or provide insights for digitally mediated denunciations elsewhere, vigilant audiences are necessarily shaped by local circumstances.

As an example of this, consider the discursive notion of the 'nice car' (typically a late-model and high-end foreign vehicle). Drawing from a comparative study that the editors of this book have recently carried out (Huang et al., 2020), nice cars are manifest as an abstract trope that can in turn be spotted and even photographed or filmed in one's neighbourhood. If that footage is publicly shared, it can serve as an opportunity to denounce the owner, but also a broader category of individual such as 'the wealthy'. This may become an opportunity to address misdeeds such as bad parking or aggressive driving, and we might expect that it also becomes a moment to air more general concerns such as growing wealth disparities and abuses of economic privilege. Looking at comparable incidents in Russia, China and Anglo-American countries, we see comparable denunciations shaped both by the affordances of digital media tools, but also by regional factors such as the press and civil society, which may or may not be willing to further mobilise denunciations against drivers of luxury vehicles.

In Russia, mediated scrutiny, shaming and exposure of citizens by fellow citizens are deeply rooted in the country's history (Gabdulhakov, 2018). In the 1970s and 1980s, amid severe production shortfalls, Soviet society developed a privileged stratum of citizens who could access goods and services through the system of *blat* — a web of strategic connections and mutually beneficial favours (Ledeneva, 1999). Through social connections of *blat* socialist citizens could even acquire a foreign-brand (*'inomarka'*) vehicle. Such privileges of the select few served as irritants for the greater masses, deepening socio-economic tensions in a state that grounded its credo on principles of egalitarianism.

In contemporary Russia, inequality on the roads remains a pressing issue, though it is possible to distinguish unique features of post-Soviet vigilante justice, characterised by mediated visibility afforded by social media, distrust in police and the prevalence of moral crusades (Favarel-Garrigues & Shukan, 2020, p. 6). In 2010 Russia's pro-Kremlin youth commissars from the nation-wide *Nashi* [Ours] youth movement founded several vigilante projects, including *StopXam* [Stop a Douchebag].[1] StopXam launched its fight against "traffic violations and arrogance on the road" (stopadouchebag.org, n.d.) and quickly gained popularity across the country and in other former Soviet states. Participants approach perceived traffic violators and place stickers on their windshields, reading "I spit on everyone, I drive where I want"; the process of retaliation is filmed, edited and uploaded on the group's YouTube channels (Gabdulhakov, 2020). StopXam claims to be indiscriminate in who they approach with retaliation; however,

---

1   Pronounced as 'Stop Kham'. Orthography and translation used by the groups is preserved.

participants often feature the 'rich and famous', ensuring the popularity of the episodes.

Confrontations between participants and the drivers escalate to verbal and physical altercations, generating added entertainment for the audience. The message that participants send through their practices is that unlike Russia's police, they are not afraid to approach people who otherwise feel immune on the roads. When marking luxurious vehicles with stickers, participants engage in a performance of class-struggle in which the fearless youth bring to justice those who are used to getting away with misdeeds. Picking up on the cases, traditional media outlets engage in framing of StopXam, law enforcement and other relevant actors, while further exposing the targets (Gabdulhakov, 2020). Additionally, when addressing such phenomena as citizen-led justice movements that instrumentalise social media, platforms such as YouTube enable the circulation of denunciatory videos, making them continuously available to wider audiences. Audience members perpetuate the circulation by sharing content and otherwise reacting to it (comments, emojis, 'dis/likes'). While StopXam's retaliatory repertoire is intensified and amplified through (edited) exposure of targets online, YouTube episodes can be monetised to generate an income. Additional funds can be generated through merchandise sales and via state subsidies. StopXam and other vigilante groups in Russia have turned into brands with their own online stores; they have been endorsed by the state through presidential grants in support of their activities (Gabdulhakov, 2018, p. 326). The relationship between vigilante formations and the state, however, should not be perceived as monotonous. Here we can differentiate between state-loyal participants (former Nashi members), state-targeting participants (investigations exposing corrupt officials, etc.) and openly criminal participants (moral police targeting women, migrants and sexual and other minorities). Each cluster varies in their application of legal frameworks; yet even the relationship between StopXam and the state has not been entirely smooth. Over the years of their operation, the framing of StopXam participants by state media evolved from "heroes" to "hooligans" (Gabdulhakov, 2020). The negotiation of trust, support and interests between state authorities and vigilantes are temporally dynamic.

In contrast, the meaning that 'nice cars' bear in contemporary China reflects a different context. Before the Opening and Reform, it was considered a 'bourgeois lifestyle' to own a private car and only top government officials were equipped with passenger cars (Barme, 2002). Therefore, the word 'gongche', which means 'public service car', had a connotation of governmental privilege and political power that lingered in Chinese society during the following decade. In addition, to own a private car signifies a better economic status because it requires resources beyond the reach of most citizens (Zhang, 2017). Despite recent economic growth coupled with a growing domestic car market (Wu, Zhao & Ou, 2014), foreign brands such as Audi and Mercedes-Benz are still regarded as privileged commodities. Meanwhile, growing economic disparity also furthers conflicts between social strata in China (Anagnost, 2008).

Such social conflicts are manifest through cases where a vigilant audience scrutinises individuals with 'nice cars'. Offences typically stem from traffic conflicts, among which cases involving 'nice cars' usually solicit a larger degree of attention and denunciation. Such scrutiny is often picked up by mass media and reported with titles that feature a typical pattern: A woman/man (of a certain social identity) + who drives + a 'nice car' brand + scratched/hit/injured/beat/ran over/killed + a socially disadvantaged individual. Such titles serve to frame these incidents into conflicts between social strata (Huang et al., 2020). Audiences are also offended when people publicly show off their luxurious cars, even though the target might not have broken any law. Potentially, questions about the legality of their achieved wealth will be raised and crowdsourced investigation will follow. Thirdly (and relatedly), corruption and government-related privilege are linked to 'nice cars' due to the enduring connotations evoked by public service cars. The third type of incident has decreased dramatically since Xi Jinping took power, due to the reformation of the public-service car system (Xinhua News Agency, 2014) and the party's internal anti-corruption campaign.

In these cases, one struggles to distinguish between participants and audience, due to the lack of formal organisation coupled with the interchangeability between these roles when an audience shifts from lurking to reposting and vice versa. As a result, the Chinese mass media normally refer to the participants/audience as 'netizens', or as a faceless mass who are 'concerned' or 'angry'. The media often spotlight the identity of the targets and the social group they belong to, which shapes the public discussion of such incidents. The scrutiny of people who drive nice cars can help expose, punish and deter individuals who either transgress traffic laws or are compromised through corruption, alongside other social injustices in China. However, it can also harm people if the accusation is unsubstantiated, or when a disproportionate punishment results from the incident being framed as class conflict. Interestingly, in recent years, audiences in China have raised questions about mass-media framing when such incidents happen (Ji, 2019).

In Anglo-American countries, class awareness has recently manifested through critical discourses about billionaires and the so-called "1%" in the context of the Occupy movement (Breau, 2014). While roadside offences like bad parking are captured and discussed in localised Facebook groups, there is a curious absence of concern for the political and economic conditions that shape ownership of 'nice cars'. Upmarket and foreign brands of vehicles are often acknowledged in these groups, and it may be inferred that their owners perceive themselves as above the law. Yet in comparison to China and Russia, there is no broader class-based mobilisation. Discourse on these groups remains localised to specific neighbourhoods, and denunciations against nice cars pertain more to brand preference, rather than social strata. Beyond references to neighbourhoods, vigilant audiences are not mobilised based on perceived economic disparities. Likewise, press coverage of so-called 'crap parking' groups focuses more on the novelty of the groups themselves, rather than embracing the class-based framing of their activities as seen in China.

Through these cases we can begin to ascertain a seemingly global pattern of scrutiny and denunciation of the wealthy, by way of their vehicles. These different instances reflect a common desire to express frustration with the owners of luxury vehicles when they breach traffic laws. They also reflect the manner in which public roadways can be contested and politicised spaces (Nikiforov, forthcoming). Yet, in each country, we see socio-political circumstances shaping digitally mediated cultural practices. In Russia and China, user-led denunciations and targeted visibility can escalate into a more cohesive and culturally significant event, and receive greater public support as well as attention from the press. In countries like the United Kingdom and the United States, similar offences receive negligible attention from a national digital media audience, and typically fail to culminate in something more collectively significant. They may simply be manifest as a series of badly parked luxury vehicles, rather than mobilise a more enduring campaign or attempt at social reform.

Section and Chapter Overview

The following chapters consider cases that appear to involve both justice-seeking and entertainment-seeking. Indeed, the confluence between these desires is a troubling development in citizen use of digital media. Yet it is possible to identify cases where there is a deliberate foregrounding of entertainment as an intended outcome of scrutiny, as well as vigilant audiences that may have already converged around a television programme or movie franchise. In the next chapter, Driessen addresses fandoms as 'pre-existing collectives' that hold actors and authors accountable for offences that take place both within and beyond the screen. Such communities are centred around a set of beliefs that may concern casting decisions and issues of representation on screen, but also call attention to the conduct of actors in their private lives. Thus, vigilant scrutiny among audiences spills over from on-screen to off-screen, but also spreads from public figures to less prominent members of the public including critics who may challenge these beliefs. The following chapter by Linton picks up on these themes in considering offence-taking and mobilisation in the context of comedic performances. While all of the cases covered in this book consider offence-taking to some degree, comedy-based forms of entertainment are unique in the sense that they are typically seeking to transgress or at least unsettle moral boundaries. Here, too, scrutiny and denunciation can transcend the boundary between fiction and real life, and, in so doing, reach a broader audience who is not acquainted with the original context of the comedic work.

Culture and class stratifications are reproduced through content that circulates on digital platforms, and these platforms may be compelled to undergo transformations as a result of their association with this content. Jiaxi Hou's chapter considers the prominence and scrutiny of an underclass subculture in China, and how its visibility led to denunciations by other communities. Here, the mediated visibility brought about by social media platforms serves both to affirm a community of supporters as well as to incite scrutiny and rebuke from a broader audience. In considering the role of the state and platform in the context of broader socio-cultural circumstances, this chapter presents vigilant audiences as shaped by a multiplicity of actors. Even a denunciatory label like 'vulgarity' can be unpacked to refer to a range of offences, targeting not just individual artists but a broader social underclass in the name of collective morality.

A second set of chapters considers how citizenship and broader notions of national identity are produced and expressed through mediated denunciation. National identities are often expressed through exclusionary rhetoric and practices, where outsiders and critical voices are met with retaliation. Likewise, we find instances where shared morality is defended among an online audience that largely corresponds to a national population. Tanner et al.'s chapter considers far-right vigilantism as a transnational manifestation with an emphasis on the tenuous and contested process of technical mediation. By looking at a Canadian alt-right figure's vigilante activities in Europe, they provide a detailed account of the technical and mediated conditions through which an audience is produced. Audiences are assembled through a range of readily available technologies and practices, yet this process of assembling is tenuous and contested. Even an incendiary media artefact such as a so-called "Molotov JPEG" (Hawley, 2017) is tentative, and may provoke unanticipated outcomes.

Incidents that reinforce commonly held values may be contentious in their execution, provoking controversies and even counter-denunciations. Favarel-Garrigues' chapter considers how the Russian group *Lev Protiv* asserts a social order in public spaces, and in turn becomes subject to public scrutiny and controversy. While patrolling and confronting those consuming drugs or alcohol in public spaces, Lev Protiv members bring these offences to a wider public. As such, conventional vigilantism is positioned "in front of a permanent audience" (Favarel-Garrigues, this volume, p. 125), that enhances the scope of the group but also appears to generate a critical backlash. Such controversies appear to fuel the group's prominence, a striking development even within the post-Soviet context.

Chalfaouat's chapter addresses digital vigilantism as citizen-led justice-seeking in the Moroccan context. In spite of the potential for mob justice, he considers how citizens can be empowered as a result of recording and denouncing misconduct. In the case of an assault of a teacher by a student, the viral circulation of the footage is both shaped by and acts as a catalyst in struggles between educators, citizens and the government. Local and online media venues also play a pivotal role in circulating and facilitating outrage as well as conflicting accounts of the offence under scrutiny. Of particular interest in this study is the degree to which citizens are compelled to co-produce security as a result of emerging technological affordances, but also through relations with state authorities.

While vigilant audiences may often be associated with social harms and regressive politics, recent examples including the backlash to the white supremacist rally in Charlottesville appear to support more progressive causes. The next set of chapters considers scrutiny and denunciation of hate speech and populism by vigilant audiences. In doing so, these works address an ambivalence whereby otherwise troubling forms of citizen-led justice may be considered acceptable by a wider public. These contributions consider recent cases in order to work towards an understanding of the potential acceptability of these practices in various contexts and circumstances.

Plesničar and Šarf's chapter considers the backlash to hate speech occurring on social media in the Slovenian context. When seemingly public content on Facebook was republished on a denunciatory Tumblr page, it was re-contextualised, and its authors came under greater public scrutiny. Yet when physical posters of the denunciations appeared in the nation's capital, a counter-denunciation arose against the anonymous authors of the Tumblr page, and a broader debate emerged about the appropriateness of these tactics. This chapter draws upon a range of data to consider the socio-cultural as well as legal contexts of republishing as weaponised visibility. Not only does this case raise the issue of who is entitled to denounce, but also how the notion of 'the public' itself may be context-specific and contested.

Many prominent cases of hate speech are manifest as collective and largely anonymous incidents. Denunciations of events like Charlottesville appropriate images of these events, not only to deanonymise participants, but also to deny the legitimacy of racist and nationalist discourses in public life. Milbrandt unpacks the call for action put forth by Twitter account @yesyoureracist, as well as the audience that emerges in consequence of that call. Her analysis evokes asymmetrical relations of visibility that appear to be normalised in Anglo-American contexts, among others. The notion that it is "merely a matter of time before anonymous faces are rendered identifiable" (Milbrandt, this volume, p. 234) suggests a surveillant imaginary (Lyon, 2018) about not only what can be achieved by vigilant audiences, but also the conditions in which this may be permissible.

Douglas' chapter further explores these conditions in relation to the possibility of Hine's (1998) understanding of non-violent vigilantism. Deanonymisation of hate speech through doxing is presented as a viable practice, notably when coupled with de-radicalisation programmes and other forms of the potential reintegration of the target. Vigilantism is always context-specific, and even progressive forms of engagement may raise unanticipated outcomes. Yet the arguments considered in this section are especially helpful in beginning to decouple acceptable from unacceptable forms of denunciation.

Finally, vigilant audiences may complicate or otherwise impact police work. Dekker and Meijer provide an account of how European law-enforcement professionals negotiate the boundaries between accepted and unsanctioned online engagements among digital media audiences. These developments are largely made meaningful by notions of community policing, in which local context and collaboration with the authorities are pivotal factors. Established principles of police work are troubled by what is easily available to digital media users. By raising questions of legality and acceptability, these practices reopen debates about the role of citizens in policing, as well as the demands for police accountability that underpin vigilant engagements (Johnston, 1996). Police may generally consider vigilant citizens as an added burden, yet they may also engage in mediated practices that inform and encourage audiences' sense of criminal justice. Young's chapter in this section considers mugshot websites in the United States, and in particular the apparent contradictions between shaming arrestees for crime-prevention purposes, and shaming for amusement. Although such initiatives may be state-funded, by making mugshots digitally accessible they facilitate unanticipated and unwanted actions by citizens and other private actors. As such, Young's focus on new policing initiatives brings us back full circle to entertainment as a mobilising force in citizen justice and shaming, even among formal agencies.

Ethical Concerns of Researchers Studying Mediated Visibility

The contributors and editors of this collection share concerns over mediated visibility and related social harms. This is a tangible issue for those who experience unwanted scrutiny, and is linked to troubling practices such as harassment, stalking, discrimination and unjust punishment. In studying and directing attention to these practices, we hope for a better understanding of their emergence in order to begin to alleviate related harms. Yet as researchers we also have to be aware of and acknowledge our potential role in producing and reproducing such harms. This involves being mindful of our research data, including how it is gathered and retained, but also how such data can be repurposed. As an outcome of this collection, we hope to draw attention to asymmetrical relations of visibility between social actors. In some cases, these efforts will involve making under-studied practices, actors, negotiations and decisions more visible to our readership. Yet this is not a one-size-fits-all approach, and some aspects of social life are obscured for a reason. As we seek to understand how these cases are publicly manifest, it seems appropriate to direct our attention to press reports and other seemingly 'official' channels, but also social media posts and other content that may be publicly available, at least for a limited period of time.

When interpreting such social media data one of the first observations a researcher will make is its volatility. Text, image and video content may circulate widely one day, only to be removed from all public sources shortly thereafter. This is due to various reasons, including targets of harassment requesting the data is removed, social media platforms removing it for violation of terms of service, vigilantes themselves not wanting to attract any further attention, or simply because the hosting website has been neglected. In many cases it would appear that actionable and stigmatising content — and the denunciations that surround them — are invoked and then revoked in a strategic manner. In response to such volatility, it may be tempting for researchers to purposively and aggressively seek out and retain this data. Indeed, this is a practice that has gained cultural traction through the use of the term 'receipts', whereby digital media users take screenshots of others' offences, and retain them for subsequent judgements (Waldman, 2016). Whether researcher or concerned citizen, it is understandable why we may wish to capture and retain evidence of criminal or moral offences, as well as the public outrage that may follow. Yet in (re)publishing this data, we risk bringing further unwanted visibility to those who have already suffered excessively in this regard. While we may otherwise see no trouble in collecting data that are considered public or open source, Young's chapter on mugshot photography covers one of many examples of supposedly public data being repurposed for troubling ends (see also Zimmer, 2010).

As such, we must consider the possibility of unwanted or otherwise harmful forms of visibility against the targets of, and participants in, digital vigilantism. The term 'target' here should be understood in broad terms: not just those originally denounced, but also those who may experience categorical discrimination as a result of the open circulation of these cases. In order to prevent further unwanted scrutiny of private citizens, at times we chose not to include names or other personal information in our reporting, even if this already appeared in the press or elsewhere. This amounts to deciding not to republish names and identities that may otherwise remain searchable. However, this approach is called into question when considering the status of public and quasi-public figures. Both Favarel-Garrigues and Linton's chapters include the names of members of civil society and comedians who can clearly be understood as public figures. Such decisions are not always straightforward, as even public figures can be subject to unwanted forms of visibility, for example, when details of their private lives are leaked to the public. Moreover, if we treat a YouTube celebrity with one hundred million subscribers as a public figure, how should we approach an aspiring star with a more modest following?

As a result of our concerns with mediated harm, we aim to be careful about what we make visible in this collection. In taking a global approach, we are necessarily calling attention to cases and targets that were previously unknown to at least a part of our readership. Yet in reflecting on these concerns and guidelines, we do not intend to develop an approach that collapses the moral implications of the cases considered in the following chapters. To be clear, there is no moral equivalence between doxing Nazis, and Nazis doxing.

References

Anagnost, A. (2008). From 'class' to 'social strata': Grasping the social totality in reform-era China. *Third World Quarterly* 29(3), 497–519, https://doi.org/10.1080/01436590801931488

Andrejevic, M. (2004). The work of watching one another: Lateral surveillance, risk, and governance. *Surveillance & Society*, 2(4), 479–97, https://doi.org/10.24908/ss.v2i4.3359

Ang, I. (2013). *Watching Dallas: Soap Opera and the Melodramatic Imagination*. London: Routledge, https://doi.org/10.4324/9781315002477

Baard, L. (2017 January 28). Vrouw pleegt zelfmoord na tonen beelden diefstal. *AD.nl*, http://www.ad.nl/nieuws/vrouw-pleegt-zelfmoord-na-tonen-beelden-diefstal~ae217dc1

Barme, G. (2002). Engines of revolution: car cultures in China. *Autopia: Car and Culture*. Eds Wollen, P. & Kerr, J. London: Reaktion.

Braun, J., & Gillespie, T. (2011). Hosting the public discourse, hosting the public: When online news and social media converge. *Journalism Practice* 5(4), 383–98, https://doi.org/10.1080/17512786.2011.557560

Breau, S. (2014). The Occupy Movement and the top 1% in Canada. *Antipode* 46(1), 13–33, https://doi.org/10.1111/anti.12044

Chadwick, A. (2017). *The Hybrid Media System: Politics and Power*. Oxford: Oxford University Press, https://doi.org/10.1093/oso/9780190696726.001.0001

Crawford, K. (2011). Listening, not lurking: The neglected form of participation. In H. Greif, A. Lasen, L. Hjorth and C. Lorbet-Maris (eds), *Cultures of Participation* (pp. 63–74). Berlin: Peter Lang, https://doi.org/10.3726/978-3-653-01238-5

Favarel-Garrigues, G. (2019). Digital vigilantism and anti-paedophile activism in Russia. Between civic involvement in law enforcement, moral policing and business venture. *Global Crime* (online first), https://doi.org/10.1080/17440572.2019.1676738

Favarel-Garrigues, G., & Shukan, I. (2020). Perspectives on post-Soviet vigilantism. Introduction. *Laboratorium: Russian Review of Social Research* 3(3), 4–15, https://doi.org/10.25285/2078-1938-2019-11-3-4-15

Finley, K. (2015 July 28). Internet Attacks Lion Killer with Poisoned Yelp Reviews. *Wired.com*, https://www.wired.com/2015/07/yelp-poacher

Gabdulhakov, R. (2018). Citizen-led justice in post-Communist Russia: From comrades' courts to dotcomrade vigilantism, *Surveillance & Society*, 16(3), 314–31, httcs://doi.org/10.24908/ss.v16i3.6952

Gabdulhakov, R. (2019). In the bullseye of vigilantes: Mediated vulnerabilities of Kyrgyz labour migrants in Russia. *Media and Communication,* 7(2), 230–41, https://doi.org/10.17645/mac.v7i2.1927

Gabdulhakov, R. (2020). Heroes or hooligans? Media portrayal of StopXam [Stop a Douchebag] vigilantes in Russia. *Laboratorium: Russian Review of Social Research,* 11(3), 16–45, https://doi.org/10.25285/2078-1938-2019-11-3-16-45

Galtung, J. (1990). Cultural violence. *Journal of Peace Research,* 27(3), 291–305, https://doi.org/10.1177/0022343390027003005

Haggerty, K. D., & Ericson, R. V. (2000). The surveillant assemblage. *The British Journal of Sociology,* 51(4), 605–22, https://doi.org/10.1080/00071310020015280

Hall, S. (1973). Encoding and decoding in the television discourse. In M. G. Durham and D. M. Kellner (eds), *Media and Cultural Studies: Keyworks* (pp. 163–73). Oxford: Blackwell.

Hawley, G. (2017). *Making sense of the alt-right.* New York: Oxford University Press, https://doi.org/10.7312/hawl18512

Huang, Q., Gabdulhakov, R., & Trottier, D. (2020). Online scrutiny of people with 'nice cars': The class struggle in China and beyond. *Global Media and China* (online first), https://doi.org/10.1177/2059436420901818

Ji, P. (2019). Nvzi zuijia mashaladi Shijian: weihe 'haoche he nvsiji' huibei fengwei yuanzui [Drunk Maserati female driver incident: why are 'nice car and female driver' original sins? Sina.com, https://k.sina.com.cn/article_15 66609257_5d608f6900100guz0.html

Johansson, S. (2007). *Reading Tabloids: Tabloid Newspapers and their Readers.* Stockholm: Södertörns Högskola.

Johnston, L. (1996). What is vigilantism? *The British Journal of Criminology,* 36(2), 220–36, https://doi.org/10.1093/oxfordjournals.bjc.a014083

Lyon, D. (2018). *The Culture of Surveillance: Watching as a Way of Life.* Cambridge: Polity.

Mendes, K., Ringrose, J., & Keller, J. (2018). #MeToo and the promise and pitfalls of challenging rape culture through digital feminist activism. *European Journal of Women's Studies,* 25(2), 236–46, https://doi.org/10.1177/1350506818765318

Moncada, E. (2017). Varieties of vigilantism: conceptual discord, meaning and strategies. *Global Crime,* 18(4), 403–23, https://doi.org/10.1080/17440572.2017.1374183

Myles, D., Benoit-Barné, C., & Millerand, F. (2020). 'Not your personal army!' Investigating the organizing property of retributive vigilantism in a Reddit collective of websleuths. *Information, Communication & Society,* 23(3), 317–36, https://doi.org/10.1080/1369118x.2018.1502336

Nikiforov, A. (forthcoming). Road traffic as a framework for politicization of an apolitical society in Russia.

North, A. (2019 October 4). 7 positive changes that have come from the #MeToo movement. *Vox.com*, https://www.vox.com/identities/2019/10/4/20852639/me-too-movement-sexual-harassment-law-2019

Schlesinger, P., & Tumber, H. (1993). Fighting the war against crime: Television, police, and audience. *The British Journal of Criminology*, 33(1), 19–32, https://doi.org/10.1093/oxfordjournals.bjc.a048288

Stauffer, R. (2018 December 8). Orbiting, another thing for online daters to worry about. *The New York Times*, https://www.nytimes.com/2018/12/08/style/orbiting-dating.html

The Moscow Times. (2018, July 1). Russia's 'Big Brother' law enters into force, https://www.themoscowtimes.com/2018/07/01/russias-big-brother-law-enters-into-force-a62066

The Moscow Times. (2019, March 18). Putin signs 'fake news', 'internet insults' bills into law, https://www.themoscowtimes.com/2019/03/18/putin-signs-fake-news-internet-insults-bills-into-law-a64850

Trottier, D. (2012). *Social Media as Surveillance: Rethinking Visibility in a Converging World*. Farnham: Ashgate, https://doi.org/10.4324/9781315609508

Trottier, D. (2017). Digital vigilantism as weaponisation of visibility. *Philosophy & Technology*, 30(1), 55–72, https://doi.org/10.1007/s13347-016-0216-4

Trottier, D. (2018). Coming to terms with shame: Exploring mediated visibility against transgressions. *Surveillance and Society*, 16(2), 170–82, https://doi.org/10.24908/ss.v16i2.6811

Van Dijck, J., & Poell, T. (2013). Understanding social media logic. *Media and communication*, 1(1), 2–14, https://doi.org/10.17645/mac.v1i1.70

Vitak, J., Zube, P., Smock, A., Carr, C. T., Ellison, N., & Lampe, C. (2011). It's complicated: Facebook users' political participation in the 2008 election. *Cyberpsychology, Behavior, and Social Networking*, 14(3), 107–14, https://doi.org/10.1089/cyber.2009.0226

Volpicelli, G. (2019, April 9). All that's wrong with the UK's crusade against online harms. *Wired.co.uk*, https://www.wired.co.uk/article/online-harms-white-paper-uk-analysis

Waldman, K. (2016, July 21). How 'show me the receipts' became a catchphrase for holding the powerful accountable. *Slate.com*, https://slate.com/human-interest/2016/07/how-show-me-the-receipts-became-a-catchphrase-for-holding-the-powerful-accountable.html

Weaver, C., & Hopins, V. (2018, November 4). The Soros conspiracy theory goes global. *The Financial Times*, https://www.ft.com/content/e2a1ecb0-dc0d-11e8-9f04-38d397e6661c

Wu, T., Zhao, H., & Ou, X. (2014). Vehicle ownership analysis based on GDP per capita in China: 1963–2050. *Sustainability, 6*(8), 4877–99, https://doi.org/10.3390/su6084877

Xiao, B. (2018, November 10). 'I don't know Facebook or Twitter': China's Great Firewall Generation Z cut off from the West. *ABC.net.au*, https://www.abc.net.au/news/2018-11-10/chinas-great-firewall-generation-who-dont-know-facebook/10479098

Xinhua News Agency (2014). Zhongyang he guojia jiguan gongwu yongche zhidu gaige fangan [Reform plan for the public service car system of the central and state agencies], http://www.gov.cn/zhengce/2014-07/16/content_2718785.htm

Yegorov, O. (2018, February 12). Facebook and Google's Russian rivals: Why are they winning? *Russia Beyond*, https://www.rbth.com/science-and-tech/329970-russian-facebook-vk-russian-google-yandex

Zhang, J. (2017). (Extended) Family car, filial consumer-citizens: becoming properly middle class in post-Socialist South China. *Modern China, 43*(1), 36–65, https://doi.org/10.1177/0097700416645138

Zimmer, M. (2010). 'But the data is already public': On the ethics of research in Facebook. *Ethics and Information Technology, 12*(4), 313–25, https://doi.org/10.1007/s10676-010-9227-5

'For the Greater Good?' Vigilantism in Online Pop Culture Fandoms

Simone Driessen

Introduction

Over the past few years, various movie prequels, sequels and reboots have occupied cinemas. Most of these, like *Star Wars* and *Ghostbusters*, continued their original storylines in new, innovative ways. Although this led to praise from fans and movie critics, it also prompted critique. Take for example the debates that followed the releases of the Star Wars instalments *The Force Awakens* (2015) and *The Last Jedi* (2017). Both received a lot of criticism about their storylines and casting choices, particularly from a vocal minority of fans who were upset about the movies' casting decisions. The protagonist of the saga, Rey (portrayed by Daisy Ridley) was female, which did not fit the typical 'male-hero' trope of the previous movies. Furthermore, adventurous companion Rose (portrayed by Asian-American actress Kelly Marie Tran) did not have the typical looks or body type of a Hollywood actress. Both Ridley and Tran (Rey and Rose) took their Instagram profiles offline due to criticisms and comments received by alleged Star Wars fans who heartily disagreed with their roles in the franchise.

These actresses going offline due to online harassment was not a stand-alone incident and seems to fit a trend of bullying celebrities on social media (cf. Condis, 2018 and Massanari, 2017). The harassment of *Ghostbusters* actress Leslie Jones in 2016 is another example: Jones

     https://doi.org/10.11647/OBP.0200.02

decided to (temporarily) remove her Twitter profile after she was repeatedly pestered by conservative writer and professional troll Milo Yiannopoulos and his followers. Twitter decided to ban Yiannopoulos from the platform, but the damage had already been done (see Proctor, 2017; Johnson, 2018; Blodgett & Salter, 2018 for detailed discussions of the *Ghostbusters* case). These diverse cases illustrate so-called toxic fandom (cf. Hills, 2018): harmful practices driven by fans' feelings of entitlement, possessiveness or superiority, which enable them to make claims about their favourite franchise.

The growth of this phenomenon, perpetuated by an allegedly small group of fans who feel entitled to make these harmful claims, seems to align with a current trend in Western media, namely that of reboots, prequels, sequels or re-releases of formerly popular cultural products. *Star Wars* originated in the seventies, *Ghostbusters* in the eighties. The fans seemed to be split between either clinging to past portrayals or demanding for more faithful representations of today's world. In other words, the fans seemed to hijack the narratives surrounding these franchises; for example, by publicly criticising casting choices and the film's writer and director, or by objecting to the development of the film's or a character's storyline. Consequently, the group of unhappy fans has become (more) vigilant towards the story and character development of the franchise they enjoy. This vigilance leads to opposing viewpoints within these fandoms, which is predominantly visible online, where audiences express their love or hate for the franchise's new developments on various social media platforms (Johnson, 2018). These strong differences *within* the pre-existing community of a fandom is a topic that has thus far gained little academic attention, whilst rivalry *between* different fandoms — particularly present in sports (Gushwan, 2012) — has received greater coverage.

This study aims to better understand this phenomenon of vigilance in fandoms by examining the interplay between fans, celebrities and producers. It will do so by exploring the different practices fans employ to 'hijack' franchise narratives using digital vigilantism (DV). DV is defined by Trottier (2017, p. 55) as the process whereby citizens collectively take action, in the online realm, against other citizens they feel offended by or who have opposing views about an issue. This resonates with Scott's notion of toxic fan subcultures, which tend to be "...instances of coordinated harassment on social media platforms against content creators, celebrities, and other fans" (2018, p. 144). Social media platforms are key to this phenomenon, as in practice they enable access to other fans, celebrities and content creators. Scott's (2018) toxic fan subcultures can publicly express oppositional and otherwise hostile sentiment and are further legitimised by these content creators' and celebrities' direct responses (e.g. J.K. Rowling's responses to fans via Twitter). In this way, fandoms and producers alike use (unwanted) exposure as an overt strategy. Visibility becomes a "weapon in the struggles they wage in their day-to-day lives" (Thompson, 2005, p. 31). More particularly, visibility plays the most significant role in those cases in which celebrities and their private lives are scrutinised, and when these fandoms engage in the practice of mediated shaming: a "user-led surveillance practice to render other social actors visible in a punitive and denunciatory light" (Trottier, 2018, p. 171).

Purpose

To examine how DV plays a role in pre-existing communities, the purpose of this study is twofold: First, it aims to bring vigilantism and fan studies together by offering an understanding of online fan practices through the lens of digital vigilantism. Secondly, it provides an exploration of how DV is empirically manifest in pop-culture fandom, by providing examples from the fandom of the Harry Potter spin-off movie series *Fantastic Beasts and Where to Find Them* (2016–current). The different ways in which the fans hijacked narratives (e.g. related to character or story development) are discussed. First, I highlight how fans denounced the involvement of actor Johnny Depp and campaigned for him to be removed from the film. Second, the fans criticised film producer David Yates and author J.K. Rowling for not taking a stand against Depp's involvement. Third, following Rowling's continued lack of opposition to Depp's inclusion, fans continued to hijack the franchise narrative by shaming Rowling. Fourth, this chapter exposes how these escalating situations surrounding the franchise challenged the norms and values of the fandom. Although this particular case is selected here, the phenomenon of vigilant fandoms reaches beyond new or old franchises, or movie fandoms solely, as mentioned in the introduction.

This chapter brings together two different fields that have a strong focus on active, resistant audiences. First, fan studies considers fans as active, participatory audiences that have a high affective investment in an object (cf. Jenkins, 1992). Second, digital vigilantism studies (cf. Trottier, 2017) considers how collectives turn to mediated tools to take action against something or someone. Digital vigilantism has its roots in the broad field of surveillance studies, which interprets 'surveillance' as a mode of organisation and behaviour, e.g. how to conduct oneself relative to the norms of society or online (cf. Lyon, 2017; Andrejevic, 2007). What makes this work different in comparison to other studies on vigilantes, which often tackle political or legal issues, is that fandoms form a pre-existing collective. Vigilant audiences are commonly theorised as spontaneous yet coordinated groups taking action (Trottier, 2017). Fandoms are a pre-existing group (though comparable to religious or political groups) of which a small cluster has become vigilant due to new developments surrounding their object of affection. Additionally, this sheds new light on the policing of 'good vs. bad' fans; a topic scarcely discussed in fan studies (notable exceptions are, for example, *Twilight* fans not being proper Comic-Con geeks, see Busse, 2013; or *Twilight* fans being interlopers in the Muse fandom, see Williams, 2013).

What follows is an overview of how studies on fans and DV offer a theoretical framework to understand resistant, active audiences. Then, a description of different online fan practices resonating with vigilantism is offered. Next, I examine the different ways in which fans hijacked narratives surrounding *Fantastic Beasts* by analysing online material (articles and tweets) and thus revealing instances of unwanted exposure, mediated shaming, denunciation, online campaigning and calling people out within pre-existing communities, like a fandom. The conclusion considers this study's implications with suggestions for future work.

Understanding Fan Practices as Modes of Vigilantism

Fandom and vigilantism are united by the fact that both groups are participatory audiences. In his seminal work on fans, Henry Jenkins (1992) defined them as textual poachers: appropriating those bits of a storyline that are interesting to them, or re-creating the story by building on poached elements, retelling the story with their own emphasis or adjustments. This implies that fans (although not all) have a tendency to go against dominant readings of certain narratives, or at least to negotiate their interpretation of a media text (e.g. a film, book or TV show). This also implies that fans have grown accustomed to re-appropriating or running afoul of the traditional canon of a story: they can add their own twist to it. But this is also a way to offer criticism of the original text, particularly if the fans consider it unsatisfactory. Jenkins' work fits the so-called "'fandom is beautiful' phase" (Gray et al., 2007, p. 3), a categorisation of early studies on fan cultures that often focus on how fan audiences are indeed resistant and creative. While fandom is an important aspect of popular culture, there is still a need to consider notions of resistance and creativity with nuance, particularly when looking at recent toxic fan practices (Proctor, 2017; Hills, 2018; Scott, 2018).

Nowadays, via social media particularly, fans can poach material and render visible their re-appropriations more easily, which suggests that fans are also potentially more easily confronted with other interpretations of the original text. According to Barnes (2018), the emotions that these adaptations elicit might invite fans to comment on the adaptations. Besides, because of social media, fans' objects of fandom are more accessible and visible than before (cf. Thompson, 2005), which also makes it easier to critique them. Barnes (2018) argues that this 'commenting culture' (fans' expressions of (dis)like or (dis)agreement) is grounded in affective investment. That might also explain why fans respond so strongly to each other when a commenter is vicious or angry, as this inspires a feedback loop (cf. Barnes, 2018) of similar comments.

Challenged Doxas and Fan Policing

To understand this group of vocal fans, the so-called toxic fans, Hills (2018) takes a Bourdieusian position in defining them by drawing on field theory. He argues "what has been journalistically and academically identified as 'toxic' online behaviour emerges precisely when a field's previously stable doxa has been disrupted and called into question by heterodox forces" (Hills, 2018, p. 107). For example, if new fans enter a pre-existing fandom like *Star Wars* then the older group's doxa (the composition of the collective that has been taken for granted) is challenged (i.e. 'these newbies cannot become as knowledgeable as the older fans'). Or, if a movie previously featuring an all-male cast (like *Ghostbusters*) is remade with a female cast, a doxa (the belief about who is best at portraying the story) is challenged. Hills continues by explaining that not all fandoms are toxic, but he does suggest that fandoms are always "*doxic* in specific ways that tend to exclude certain kinds of fans" (2018, p. 111). These conceptions of exclusion, policing or protecting one's doxas resonate with the behaviour and practices of digital vigilantes (cf. Andrejevic, 2007; Trottier, 2018).

Notions of exclusion and belonging have often played a role in fan studies (cf. Sandvoss, 2005). Busse, for example, examined how fans practice an "internal fannish dismissal" (2013, p. 73) of new fans entering a fandom. When the popular teen series *Twilight* became part of the Comic-Con (CC) convention, the CC fans dismissed the *Twilight* teens attending the event. The CC fans felt that they were higher up the ladder of cultural hierarchies (a legitimate, longstanding convention versus a mainstream, fleeting, 'smut' success). By policing who is a 'rightful' attendee of Comic-Con, the CC fans aimed to protect their own sense of community (Busse, 2013). Peculiar to this instance of policing is its revelation of a gender bias: the largely female fan base of *Twilight* attending a male-dominated space such as Comic-Con did not fit the doxa of the conference's regular "geek hierarchy" (Busse, 2013). Similarly, Stanfill (2013) examined how fans of the series *Xena: Warrior Princess* stereotype each other by denoting their activities as peculiar, stigmatised or simply a bit too much (e.g. a fan getting a back-piece tattoo of a particular scene from *Xena*). These previous works expose how fans have a tendency to create their own boundaries around the fan community and who can join it, as well as what constitutes the doxa of a 'good' fan (behaviour).

The doxic character of fandom confirms that exclusion, creating a hierarchy and policing are not new to fandom. Furthermore, fans themselves appear to be vigilant about who enters or is part of their community. Yet this denunciation of other fans or the franchise's producers (e.g. *Ghostbusters*' strategy of employing a diverse cast instead of creating a nostalgic reboot of the old product) seems to have become more visible due to social media. Some have even gone as far as shaming other fans or celebrities involved in the franchises they care about, including the cases of Rey and Rose mentioned at the beginning of this chapter. The fans seem to watch and control who holds the right views, thus the right doxas. That turns this type of surveillance amongst these groups into a cultural practice (Monahan, 2011). Surveillance according to Monahan involves "exercises of power and the performance of power relationships" (2011, p. 495), which is present in these previous examples. As Monahan interprets Lyon (2001): "different forms of surveillance could be positioned along a spectrum from 'care' to 'control'" (2011, p. 497). In other words, fans can go from watching over each other for protection to enforcing particular behaviour.

Fans seem to have grown more vocal and concerned about changing doxas (see Proctor, 2017; Scott, 2018; Barnes, 2018). Moreover, publicly expressing such comments online makes their criticism and concern visible to all. This in turn can lead to other fans joining in this practice of expressing their (dis)agreements and might potentially result in demands from the disgruntled fans that the doxas should continue unchanged. I thus propose that we can also consider them as (digital) vigilantes (Trottier, 2017): a loose, yet organised collective that takes deliberate action against an offence. Nowadays, the changing doxas of fandoms are rendered visible through online communication via various social media platforms (Thompson, 2005; Barnes, 2018). However, this development also needs to be nuanced. It is questionable if these people are fans at all, or whether they are just social actors that use fandom to pester others (Proctor, 2017; Hills, 2018). Likewise, those involved in practices like DV might also temporarily come together as a loose and spontaneous network of people (Trottier, 2018) who leave the discussion after the hype is over.

Bringing surveillance and fan studies together, by approaching fans' online practices as modes of vigilantism, helps to explore how shared values and norms are debated. According to Trottier, DV campaigns express a form of collective identity based on, for instance, "national, religious or ethnic forms of solidarity" (2017, p. 57). The campaigns in fandoms against producers or franchise developments might express a form of *affective* solidarity building on a (former) mutual love and understanding for the media text and fandom that is now challenged and negotiated. The fandom and their beloved celebrities (and the private lives of these celebrities) are placed under public scrutiny, and discussions are intense and enduring (Thompson, 2005; Trottier, 2017). This suggests that these franchise audiences also become more polarised, which is an interesting aspect to explore at a time when fandom can be considered a proven aspect of contemporary politics (Dean, 2017).

Trolling

In today's world, due to the increase of social media platforms, it is possible for fans, stars and producers to (parasocially) interact. As Proctor states: "[f]an quarrels and conflicts are not a new phenomenon either, but the migration from the (analogue) margins into the (digital) mainstream has exposed the various operations of fan cultures to the larger online public..." (2017, p. 1124). That is, fans now have the (digital) tools to go beyond mere poaching, the typical way to re-appropriate or express criticism of the original media text. Now, the fans can reach out to producers, and express their criticism more visibly, thus more publicly than before.

The vocal criticism expressed by some of the fans within a fandom can be defined as trolling, a now polarised term often used in the public sphere for anything related to having fun at the distress of others. To clarify, I draw on Phillips' (2015) definition, which conceptualises trolling as a form of amusement that one might have at someone else's expense.[1] Unlike demanding change for affective reasons, trolling is often purposefully harmful or intended to upset media creators or other fans rather than elicit a sincere response. Yet, to troll, one needs to possess a certain amount of knowledge to make fun of that person, or to know when trolling becomes amusing for a wider audience. The humour of these trolls therefore leads to in-or exclusion: those in on the joke and those who are not. My use of the term then avows the idea that this group of fans who trolls also needs to have knowledge of their 'target'. When Gamergate happened, the trolls were keen to release personal information (doxing) and chose their subjects based on their close involvement and (known) positions in the gaming subculture (Condis,

---

1   Phillips, in Phillips & Milner (2017) indicates that the use of 'trolling' is ever-changing, and that the 2015 definition might already be outdated. Yet the overall sentiment that trolling is a practice that requires one to offend or be humorous at somebody else's expense remains.

2018; Barnes, 2018). Phillips (2015) argues that trolling can amplify certain issues or challenges at stake in society. Trolls are metaphorically starting a fire and walking away from it. The actual fire is not the 'lulz' (the fun or laughter at someone else's expense), but the build-up to the action.

In asserting how trolling connects to fan studies, Scott clarifies why and when fans or producers can be labelled trolls:

> When [...] they have become *too aggressive in their affective claims to textual ownership*, manifested in actively attempting to *sway or collectively criticize* particular representational choices. Producers are situated as trolls when they, for either industrial or personal reasons, *insert themselves into fan communities* of practices or actively attempt to contain particular forms of fannish reading (2018, p. 146, emphasis added).

So, trolling fans are perhaps not so much in it for the 'lulz' as argued by Phillips (2015), but rather are too *passionate* or too concerned about changes happening to their beloved object of fandom. Therewith they exclude or are vigilant of those who do not follow their 'textual ownership', or who do not accept or agree with their doxa. Scott (2018) clarifies her assertion of trolling by using the case of headmaster Albus Dumbledore's unspecified sexuality in the Harry Potter franchise. Although J.K. Rowling has stated she envisions Dumbledore as gay, he is not (explicitly) portrayed as such in the existing movies or in the *Fantastic Beasts and Where to Find Them* spin-off. The fans however, ever since learning about Dumbledore's sexuality, were also left divided: some fans objected to the idea, while other fans have regularly attempted via Twitter and various social media campaigns to make this more explicit. Yet neither the movie producers nor J.K. Rowling considered this an element that should be explicitly mentioned. That fans organised such actions does not per se mean that they are trolling (nor does it imply that movie producer David Yates does),[2] yet there are resemblances with the vigilante mindset: fans organise themselves actively as a collective against a particular person or happening they were offended by (either Yates not willing to make Dumbledore's sexuality explicit, or the thought of Dumbledore as gay).

---

2   See the full article here: https://edition.cnn.com/2018/02/01/entertainment/jk-rowling-dumbledore-gay/index.html

Totemic Nostalgia

On the other hand, if the filmmakers were to portray Dumbledore as homosexual, some fans might genuinely feel hurt by this change made by the adaptation. Proctor (2017), in his study of the *Ghostbusters* fandom who reacted toxically to the all-female reboot, describes this genuine pain as "totemic nostalgia [...] a fan protectionism, which is not toxic, centred on an affective relationship with a fan object, usually forged in childhood" (Proctor, 2017, p. 1122) and which should be read as "innocuous rather than explicitly toxic" (ibid, p. 1129). In other words, Proctor makes an argument that we should not refer to all fan behaviour as toxic.

The media often cherry-pick the worst cases of toxic fan behaviour, thus amplifying them. Yet some of the fans that denounced the casting of the all-female *Ghostbusters* reboot because of childhood nostalgia might also be those who engaged in the bullying of actress Leslie Jones. This leads us to question what the dominant doxa of a fandom is, and who determines this doxa.

Still, not all fans participate in these practices of trolling, totemic nostalgia or other ways of expressing their criticism. Yet these can be examined because fans, as Proctor (2017) argues, now quarrel online. Fan practices have gained more visibility (cf. Thompson, 2005; 2011), and are amplified more easily through the online reach of social media platforms. Moreover, they are no longer confined to fan-only spaces (e.g. secluded fora or fan conventions).

Case Study: Controversies Surrounding *Fantastic Beasts*

This chapter offers an empirical snapshot of vigilantism in an Anglo-American pop culture fandom, namely that of *Fantastic Beasts and Where to Find Them* (*Fantastic Beasts* or *FB* from hereon). These fans are not drawn together because of an event that happened; they were already formed as a collective. Yet they have been divided by new developments in the fandom and franchise they care so much about.

Fantastic Beasts is a spin-off series of the Harry Potter franchise. The series is created and written by author J.K. Rowling, and produced by Warner Brothers. *FB* was first mentioned in the Harry Potter series as a popular book that the wizards read to learn about fantastic beasts, written by Newt Scamander, who is the main protagonist of the movies. Due to the enormous popularity of the Harry Potter franchise, the *Fantastic Beasts* mentioned in the original books turned into an actual published book of its own. A movie based on the adventures of Newt Scamander followed in 2016 (directed by David Yates, who had previously been involved in the Potter franchise as director of several of its films).

A second *FB* film was released in 2018, as part of a planned total of five. *The Crimes of Grindelwald* (shortened to *Grindelwald*), has stirred up commotion in the fandom because of its casting choices. Particularly controversial were the casting of Johnny Depp as Grindelwald, a powerful, dark wizard, and the involvement of South Korean actress Claudia Kim as Nagini, a woman/snake-like creature who later turns into the dark wizard Voldemort's pet and horcrux (an object that stores part of Voldemort's soul so he can return to power). Fans also condemned the lack of emphasis on Dumbledore's sexuality. As a result of these controversies, several issues were highlighted in traditional media. Venues like *The Guardian*, *USA Today* and *Vice* criticised the lack of diverse ethnic voices shaping the wizarding world of *Fantastic Beasts*. According to these media, decisions about casting or (what is not included in) the narratives of the movies were made because J.K. Rowling and Warner Brothers sought to keep the movies accessible to all age groups, and did not want them to be rated PG (a more restrictive rating than the child-friendly U).

For this study, I looked at the controversies surrounding *Fantastic Beasts*. These controversies have their roots in fans' tweets, but got picked up by members of the news and entertainment media. To analyse these controversies, a snapshot sample of fifteen articles was selected.[3] The articles offered a more opinionated perspective on the franchise and contained tweets (N=56) from fans about the franchise. Although I will not refer to specific Twitter handles, the tweets can still be traced back to their origins (cf. Zimmer, 2010). I considered it a prerequisite that the tweets discussed in this chapter appeared online as part of a

---

3   In total, searching for all news related to Johnny Depp's involvement in *Fantastic Beasts* in the Nexis database yielded 263 articles between January 2016 and December 2018. Articles on Claudia Kim's casting as Nagini over the same time period offered 369 results.

news or entertainment media article, which implies that they have been taken from a public(ly accessible) account. However, this also might bring about a bias in the data: these media outlets might have selected cases they found most interesting (cf. Proctor, 2017). The tweets have, through this pre-selection, gained visibility, prominence and endurance by being part of a publication. However, I aim to overcome this bias by contextualising and analysing them in connection to each other, and not as sole expressions of criticism or dissatisfaction.

The articles selected all covered one of the controversial topics surrounding *FB*, with a particular focus on the casting of Johnny Depp as Grindelwald and the decision to cast South Korean actress Claudia Kim as Nagini. Articles included are from the online platforms of news and entertainment outlets *NME, Buzzfeed, Slate, Floor 8, ELLE (Dutch version), Yahoo (Lifestyle)* and *Vice* and the websites of British media *BBC, The Independent* and *The Guardian*. All were published between 2016 and 2018. These outlets (and articles) were chosen because of their accessibility and fit with the (adult) target audience of *Fantastic Beasts*.

To uncover these empirical manifestations related to the various controversies surrounding the *FB* movies, I conducted a thematic analysis (see Braun & Clarke, 2006). That means I aimed to identify patterns by assigning codes to the material, followed by grouping these codes together into overarching themes that summarise these patterns. Although these materials only form a snapshot of the vast amount of articles on these different controversies, they are by no means cherry-picked (cf. Proctor, 2017), nor do these practices only happen in popular culture fandoms. Sports fandoms thrive by cultivating rivalries, yet are considered a different type of fandom to study in comparison to pop-culture fandoms (cf. Gushwan, 2012).

Results

This section presents four patterns related to digital vigilantism in the fandom of *Fantastic Beasts*. The different steps discussed show how different narratives surrounding *Fantastic Beasts* (e.g. casting choices, story development) are hijacked by its fans, who engage in practices like denunciation, calling out and shaming actors and producers. These practices reveal how grievances escalated within the fandom (and in the media) surrounding the development of the movie. First, I briefly discuss the unwanted exposure of the lead actor in Grindelwald, namely the fandom denouncing Johnny Depp as an abuser; second, following this casting choice the fans organised a campaign to remove Depp from the film and fans called out and shamed — meaning they publicly denounced and stigmatised (cf. Trottier, 2018)—the movie's director, Yates, for casting him; third, the shaming of Rowling by fans, both for Depp's involvement and for casting Kim as Nagini; finally, I illustrate how the fan doxas are challenged by changes in the franchise.

Unwanted Exposure

The first step in the 'hijacking' of *Fantastic Beasts* came after the alleged accusations, influenced by the #MeToo movement, against lead actor Johnny Depp. Fans started petitioning to remove him from the movie, condemning his involvement. Depp has a notorious reputation (accused by ex-partner Amber Heard of domestic abuse, see Rao, 2020) and was seen as a poor fit for the child-friendly and inclusive franchise. This generated unwanted exposure (Thompson, 2005; 2011) for the movie, but also for Depp. Comments like this one made by a Twitter user cited by *NME* "it really isn't too late to replace Johnny Depp, guys" (*NME*, 2017) are exemplary. Another person expressed their excitement about the main character, Newt Scamander, but states "then I remember we'll see more of johnny depp [sic]" (*Independent*). When the trailer appeared online, comments like this materialised again; one fan said "I legitimately love everything about this. Except the fact that Johnny Depp is still Grindelwald" (*ELLE*, 2017). In sum, they all contain phrases that denounce Depp, with the result that his involvement was heavily criticised. Madianou has described how such unwanted and unexpected exposure often reveals the "power asymmetries of shame" (2011, p. 5). Both Depp and the franchise itself were unable to control this sudden backlash. According to an article in *People* ('Johnny Depp Sues UK Tabloid for Defamation over Story Slamming Him and J.K. Rowling' by Ale Russian, published in June 2018), Depp even sued a British tabloid for libel over a story in which the actor was denounced as a "wife-beater".

Rowling defended Depp's casting, trying to make the fans see why keeping him in the movie was justified after he and Heard settled in court. She is cited in an interview with *Variety* (Clarke, 2017) stating that she accepts that some fans will not be satisfied "however, conscience isn't governable by committee. Within the fictional world and outside it, we all have to do what we believe to be the right thing". By expressing her opinion publicly, Rowling might attempt to "contribute to the audience's sense of acceptable social norms and thus, to the awareness of other's regard" (Madianou, 2011, p. 6) and try to influence the outlook the fans have on the casting. To put it bluntly, she seems to argue that the case is settled and that it is not up to her or the fans to make judgements, and therewith commands the fandom to move on.

Online Campaigns

The second moment of escalation in which the fans were involved, and the second trend identified, is related to the continuing vigilantism of the fandom in the Depp case. They made an active comparison and initiated an online campaign (Trottier, 2017) for director David Yates to follow the example of Ridley Scott, who fired Kevin Spacey from *All the Money in the World* after several sexual assault allegations were made against the actor.[4] Ridley decided to cease working with Spacey and even reshot the movie with another performer in the role, completely erasing Spacey from the project. Tweets like the following demonstrate how fans considered this situation as exemplary for Depp's position and future in the franchise: "If Ridley Scott fire Kevin Spacey after filming an entire movie with him and voluntary reshooting it a month before release, then y'all can do the same thing w Johnny Depp bc you still have a year to go [sic]" (*NME*, 2017). Likewise, another fan remarks,

> If Kevin spacey can get ditched last minute from a movie they can recast johnny depp in fantastic beasts, his character canonically already changed his face so how about perhaps recasting with someone who's not an abuser maybe [sic] (*ELLE*, 2017).

---

4   See this article in *The Guardian*: https://www.theguardian.com/culture/2017/ nov/09/kevin-spacey-cut-out-of-film-and-replaced-by-christopher-plummer

This fan also mentions how the story of *Fantastic Beasts* would lend itself for a recasting, more so than the situation Ridley Scott had to deal with for his movie.

The choice to keep Depp in the movie led to the calling out and shaming of Yates as producer, but also to the denunciation of Rowling as writer: jokingly, one fan commented that "David Yates' justification for having Johnny Depp in *Fantastic Beasts 2* is every bit as weak as Ron Weasley's magic skills" (*Independent*, 2017). Another fan states more seriously: "[...] there's Johnny Depp in it and I promised myself I would boycott all of his films. I just don't get *why someone as vocal as J.K. Rowling accepted* that he play in the film [sic]" (*NME*, 2017, emphasis added). Similarly, another fan tweeted: "The only thing I really need to know is how @jk_rowling is so *vocal on feminism and women's issues*, yet is willing to turn a blind eye to actual domestic abuser Jonny Depp starring in one of her book adaptions?" (*ELLE*, 2017, emphasis added). Rowling is denounced by these fans who shame her by pointing out the hypocrisy of her own behaviour — also a signal of totemic nostalgia, commenting on how Rowling 'used to be' (cf. Proctor, 2017; Barnes, 2018). Drawing on that past image of Rowling, as someone who usually advocates for women's issues, was intended to highlight the apparent contradiction of her decision not to take action against an alleged abuser who was part of her own project.

Shaming and Denouncing Rowling

The situation escalated further thanks to fans' continued shaming of Rowling, which intensified when the casting of South Korean actress Claudia Kim as Nagini was announced. Nagini never received much of a backstory in the original Harry Potter books, but was mostly known as Voldemort's pet. Therefore, the reveal of Nagini as a woman of Asian heritage was remarkable. One fan denounced Rowling as follows "Apparently JK Rowling decided that Nagini (volemort's pet snake) is a Korean woman and I am so sad that so much of my childhood was wasted on such an unsurprisingly racist white woman [sic]" (*Yahoo*, 2018). Another phrases their denunciation even more strongly: "JK Rowling is trash [...] If you don't see anything racist about an Asian woman being the pet of a white man — who is basically magic hitler, I don't know what to say [sic]" (*Floor8*, 2018). Or as another commenter indicated "listen Joanne, we get it, you didn't include enough representation when you wrote the books. But suddenly making Nagini into a Korean woman is garbage. Representation as an afterthought for more woke points is not good representation" (*BBC*, 2018). Another fan puts the discussion in relation to the Harry Potter movies, where another Asian actress/character (Cho Chang) was portrayed stereotypically: "I just want to say I'm impressed with JK Rowling. It takes a LOT of confidence to go 2/2 on racist Asian stereotypes. Cho Chang being the demure 'gentle flower' and #Nagini being the sexually attractive dragon lady" (*Yahoo*, 2018).

Rowling reacted with an explanation of why the character Nagini in the film is Asian: allegedly, the snake-like creature has its roots in Indonesian mythology. Journalist Hanna Flint, in her articles for *The Guardian* (2018b) and *Yahoo News* (2018a) marks this "constant rejigging of the original narrative furniture" as "retcon", meaning retroactive continuity. This is a strategy or phenomenon that might (help to) overcome totemic nostalgia, as it enables new developments by creating a timeline that is already a part of the story, yet this might lead to dissatisfaction for some fans. As with the Depp controversy, the Nagini episode again exposed how fans "police" the norms and values of their fandom, and the franchise and its creators (cf. Busse, 2013; Scott, 2018). As is also illustrated in articles by author Nicole Clark (2018) for online platform *Vice*, Rowling has always been admired for her vocal attitude against inequality and injustice with regard to certain issues, for example, homosexuality, yet she was now (in the cases of the Depp and Nagini controversies) criticised for apparently not living up to these values, and she was consequently shamed for this change in behaviour and mindset. Nicole Clark (2018) illustrates this by bringing in Dumbledore's alleged sexuality, noting that "there were no solid markers to confirm a lived experience of homosexuality" and "no representation that might suggest to young, gay readers that they too could grow up to be the world's most powerful wizard". She concluded that "[t]o claim that kind of power in retrospect is not only goofy, but deeply disrespectful". Reporting on the case by *Vice* (Clark, 2018) further amplified the visibility of the dispute and seemed to support the practices of shaming and calling out that fans engaged in via social media.

Likewise, Terry Nguyen (published in *Vice*, 2018) argued that Rowling glosses over the racist and colonialist histories that inspired the backstories for some other characters in *Fantastic Beasts*. He stated: "[t]hat ignorance effectively destroys Rowling's progressive mirage and the significance of her characters of color [...]". Here too, the practices of fans are amplified through, or resonate with, the arguments of the journalist. The denunciation of Rowling suggests that fans do not always agree with her. Moreover, the fans render Rowling's conflicting opinions and decisions more visible by calling attention to and shaming these instances online.

The Challenged Doxa

The fourth pattern identified in fans' reactions is illustrative of the challenged and changing doxas (cf. Hills, 2018) of the fandom. In the Depp controversy, this relates closely to the topic of abuse, a topic brought up in 2017 by journalist Alanna Bennett from *Buzzfeed*, whose article generated another wave of condemnation towards Depp and his involvement in the film. She argued that abuse has always been a central theme in the franchise itself: "That was a big part of what made Harry's escape into the wizarding world feel impactful — he was finally granted a reprieve from life with his abusers". Abuse thus became the central theme these vigilant fans focused on in their online campaign against Depp. As one fan explained: "The Harry Potter universe is all about being against the abuse of power and yet you cast a known abuser?" (*Buzzfeed*, 2017). Similarly, another fan remarked: "What really gets me, is how many victims of abuse have used the Harry Potter franchise as a means to heal. How must they feel now?" (*Buzzfeed*, 2017). This also gives an insight into why the fans were surprised that Rowling did not challenge the casting of Depp. As one fan put it: "[...] the danger in looking the other way bc the truth is inconvenient. Jk rowling saying she doesn't believe amber heard and is happy to keep a wife beater employed is disgusting. F*ck her [sic]" (*Buzzfeed*, 2017). Fans are making visible (cf. Thompson, 2005) and commenting (cf. Barnes, 2018) on what is wrong with the path the franchise took, and particularly with this not having been challenged by its creators.

What these different modes (shaming, denunciation etc.) and the examples regarding *Fantastic Beasts* illustrate is that, when considering these fan practices, it is necessary to look at the different power relations at stake. Again, this highlights how the doxa of fandom is challenged, and what being a "good" fan (a contested notion: see Busse, 2013; Hills, 2018) entails: is it the fan defending Depp's casting because J.K. Rowling approves, or the fan seeking social justice because Depp is an alleged domestic abuser?

The Nagini controversy is encapsulated by tweets like the following: "How did nobody involved in Fantastic Beasts 2 look at this Nagini situation and think, 'huh, this sounds problematic...'?" (*USA Today*, 2018). However, some fans suggested that this clinging to the past by some fans is limiting for the franchise and fandom at large. For example, this comment illustrates such a sentiment: "So...Jk Rowling is racist now for casting a POC as a villain? What has this world gone to... People need to stop attacking their own allies for no reason [sic]" (*BBC*, 2018). Or this one: "jk rowling is not a racist by making Asian woman as nagini's true form. I believe it's just an act of bringing up some race diversity to the movie [sic]" (*Yahoo*, 2018), which then continues with "nagini is not a 'white man's pet', she so precious to Voldemort he turned her into his closes horcrux [sic]". Although these two comments resemble claims about the diversity of the franchise, they could likewise be interpreted as trolling other fans: they suggest that those fans concerned about Nagini's casting should not be so easily offended by these "retcon developments". Twitter comments mostly do not offer much context or space to further clarify these opinions. However, this fan provides some background as to why she has a particular opinion on Nagini's casting "as an Asian woman I'm not particularly offended about Claudia being nagini [...] people are just so easily offended these days, you can't enjoy anything without it having some sort of racist deeper meaning [sic]" (*Yahoo*, 2018). She also criticises the fans who are offended for over-analysing or being judgmental about the meaning behind this casting choice.

Conclusion and Recommendations

This chapter illustrates how a combination of fan and surveillance studies offers tools to understand vigilant, sometimes toxic practices that fans engage in. It has done so through looking at the fandom of *Fantastic Beasts* and various controversies surrounding the franchise that led to the hijacking and escalation of its narratives, as well as disagreements within this pre-existing community.

For the *Fantastic Beasts* fans, it might be argued that the fans gave greater visibility to the stories about Johnny Depp as an (alleged) domestic abuser, generating unwanted exposure for him and the franchise. They continued to amplify this allegation by campaigning for his removal from the film, and calling out David Yates and J.K. Rowling for not taking action. The fans organised themselves collectively against this casting decision, yet to no avail. Consequently, this episode spilled over into anger about the other controversy, and the two fuelled each other, with Rowling becoming the target of the Nagini casting controversy and being denounced as racist, and as an author who sought to pay lip service to diversity without properly engaging with what diverse representation in her books and films would involve. Again, this escalation illustrated the affective ownership of fans, but also indicated how these fans found it unacceptable to retro-con Nagini's identity as an Asian woman prior to her transformation into a snake. The Depp and Nagini controversies are examples of how the fandom hijacked the franchise's narrative, while also exposing fans' reactions to changes in the doxa of the fandom and the franchise. The fans were asked to include and embrace these characters, but some fans considered the way these characters were introduced to be wrongful, and this led to conflicting views within the fandom.

This chapter demonstrates how the framework of vigilantism is applicable to and is present in fan studies. The 'policing' behaviour of fans, be it out of affection or totemic nostalgia, might influence surveillance studies to consider further the *affective* dimension of vigilant practices, in addition to looking at surveillance as a cultural practice (Madianou, 2011). Moreover, albeit on a micro level, the challenged doxas offer strong indications of how using visibility as a weapon (cf. Thompson, 2005; Trottier, 2017) might result in the inclusion or exclusion of individuals in such strong pre-existing entities as fandoms. These vigilant practices can move beyond the practice of trolling (cf. Scott, 2018) or policing good or bad fans. We must examine these practices by looking at the role affection plays in these doxas of communities, and what might be the consequences when these doxas change. Small shifts in the doxa can lead to significant (perhaps not always intended) implications that might be challenging for groups known for coherence and belonging (Barnes, 2018). Moreover, these challenged doxas also inform us about the cultural norms and values that those involved with these groups are so passionate about. Understanding these challenges on a micro level might help us to understand them on a macro or societal level.

The case examined here is a brief exploration of vigilantism in pop-culture fandoms (also present in the fandoms of *Ghostbusters*, and *Star Wars* mentioned previously). Yet, the schisms within a fandom illustrated on this micro level — between 'good' and 'bad' fans, and the involvement of 'toxic' or 'vigilant' fans — might be a helpful framework in understanding the polarisation of contemporary politics (Dean, 2017), or the so-called 'culture wars'. Future work could look at political groups, and the practices they engage in to campaign for or against someone. Yet to better understand this phenomenon, such research would also need to consider these vigilant-fan practices globally, as this analysis offers an Anglo-American perspective. The current discourse of labelling these audiences as toxic or trolls needs to be carefully (re-)examined: what makes one toxic, totemically nostalgic, too affective or a troll? And would these fans consider themselves vigilant or rather affective fans? Due to the scope of this study, the different terminologies have been briefly characterised, yet it would be valuable to explore this further (see also Proctor et al., 2018).

To conclude, much like vigilantes, fans form communities defending what they stand for. This interdisciplinary framework of fandom and vigilantism then offers a point of departure to understand other socio-cultural challenges.

References

Andrejevic, M. (2007). Surveillance in the digital enclosure. *The Communication Review* 10, 295–317, https://doi.org/10.1080/10714420701715365

Barasch, A. (2018, September 25). Why *Harry Potter* fans are so upset about a twist in the new *Fantastic Beasts* trailer (and Also Snake Milking). *Slate*, https://slate.com/culture/2018/09/fantastic-beasts-trailer-controversy-nagini-snake-milking.html

Barnes, R. (2019). *Uncovering Online Commenting Culture. Trolls, Fanboys, and Lurkers*. Cham, Switzerland: Palgrave Macmillan, https://doi.org/10.1007/978-3-319-70235-3

BBC (2018, September 27). JK Rowling defends Nagini casting in *Fantastic Beasts*. BBC, Entertainment and Arts, https://www.bbc.com/news/entertainment-arts-45666350

Bennett, A. (2017, December 9). Johnny Depp's continued presence is slowly poisoning "Fantastic Beasts". *Buzzfeed*, https://www.buzzfeednews.com/article/alannabennett/johnny-depp-poisoning-fantastic-beasts?bfsource=relatedmanual

Blodgett, B., & Salter, A. (2018). Ghostbusters is for boys: Understanding the geek masculinity's role in the Alt-right. *Communication, Culture & Critique*, 11, 133–46, https://doi.org/10.1093/ccc/tcx003

Braun, V., & Clarke, V. (2006). Using thematic analysis in psychology. *Qualitative Research in Psychology*, 3(2), 77–101, https://doi.org/10.1191/1478088706qp063oa

Busse, K. (2013). Geek hierarchies, boundary policing, and the gendering of the good fan. *Participations: Journal of Audience & Reception Studies*, 10(1), 73–91.

Clark, N. (2018, September 27). Why casting Nagini as an Asian Woman in "Fantastic Beasts" is so offensive. *Vice*, https://www.vice.com/en_us/article/d3jybm/why-the-casting-of-nagini-as-an-asian-woman-in-fantastic-beasts-is-so-offensive

Clarke, S. (2017). J.K. Rowling and Warner Bros defend Johnny Depp as Grindelwald in *Fantastic Beasts*. *Variety*, https://variety.com/2017/film/news/j-k-rowling-warner-bros-defend-johnny-depp-grindelwald-fantastic-beasts-1202632964

Condis, M. (2018). *Gaming Masculinity: Trolls, Fake Geeks and the Gendered Battle for Online Culture*. Iowa City: Iowa University Press, https://doi.org/10.2307/j.ctv3dnq9f

Dean, J. (2017). Politicising fandom. *The British Journal of Politics and International Relations*, 19(2), 408–24, https://doi.org/10.1177/1369148117701754

Fiske, J. (1992). The cultural economy of fandom. In J. Jensen (ed.), *The Adoring Audience: Fan Cultures and Popular Media* (pp. 30–49). London: Routledge.

Flint, H. (2018a, September 26). JK Rowling accused of racism of Nagini portrayal in 'Fantatic Beasts: The Crimes of Grindelwald'. *Yahoo News,* https://www.yahoo.com/lifestyle/jk-rowling-accused-racism-nagini-portrayal-fantastic-beasts-crimes-grindelwald-142415625.html?guccounter=1

Flint, H. (2018b, September 28) *Fantastic Beasts* isn't racist, but JK Rowling should stop tweaking the source material. *The Guardian,* https://www.theguardian.com/film/2018/sep/28/fantastic-beasts-isnt-racist-jk-rowling-source-character-claudia-kim-nagini

Gray, J., Sandvoss, C., & Harrington, C. L. (eds) (2007) *Fandom. Identities and Communities in a Mediated World.* New York: New York University Press.

Gushwan, M. (2012). Fandom, brandom and the limits of participatory culture. *Journal of Consumer Culture,* 12(1), 19–40, https://doi.org/10.1177/1469540512438154

Hills, M. (2018). An extended foreword: From fan doxa to toxic fan practices? *Participations: Journal of Audience & Reception Studies,* 15(1), 105–26.

Jenkins, H. (1992). *Textual Poachers. Television Fans and Participatory Culture.* New York, NY: Routledge.

Jensen, E. (2018, September 28). "A racist, misogynist disaster": Twitter slams Claudia Kim's "Fantastic Beasts" casting. *USA Today,* https://eu.usatoday.com/story/life/entertainthis/2018/09/27/fantastic-beasts-casting-claudia-kim-nagini-2/1440752002

Johnson, D. (2018). From the ruins: Neomasculinity, media franchising, and struggles over industrial reproduction of culture. *Communication, Culture & Critique,* 11, 85–99, https://doi.org/10.1093/ccc/tcx013

Lyon, D. (2017) Surveillance culture: engagement, exposure, and ethics in digital modernity. *International Journal of Communication,* 11, 824–42.

Madianou, M. (2011). News as a looking-glass: Shame and the symbolic power of mediation. *International Journal of Cultural Studies,* 15(1), 3–16, https://doi.org/10.1177/1367877911411795

Massanari, A. (2017). #Gamergate and The Fappening: How Reddit's algorithm, governance, and culture support toxic technocultures. *New Media & Society,* 19(3), 329–46, https://doi.org/10.1177/1461444815608807

Meijer, A. (2017, November 17). *Harry Potter*-fans dreigen *Fantastic Beasts 2* te boycotten vanwege Johnny Depp. *ELLE* (Dutch website), https://www.elle.com/nl/lifestyle/films-tv/a569786/harry-potter-fans-dreigen-fantastic-beasts-2-te-boycotten-vanwege-johnny-depp

Monahan, T. (2011). Surveillance as cultural practice. *The Sociological Quarterly,* 52(4), 495–508, https://doi.org/10.1111/j.1533-8525.2011.01216.x

Nguyen, T. (2018, November 26). In "Fantastic Beasts", J.K. Rowling fails at writing characters of color. *Vice*, https://broadly.vice.com/en_us/article/vba7yj/harry-potter-fantastic-beasts-movie-diversity?utm_source=vicefbus&fbclid=IwAR0PZmQTO7VMphtLYrlp1Pn_Ha-xyTqUEIMsY_NF_IOkSXkeTOLKQNy_4dM

Phillips, W. (2015). *This is Why We Can't Have Nice Things: Mapping the Relationship between Online Trolling and Mainstream Culture*. Cambridge, MA: MIT Press, https://doi.org/10.7551/mitpress/10288.001.0001

Phillips, W., & Milner, R. (2017) *The Ambivalent Internet. Mischief, Oddity and Antagonism Online*. Cambridge: Polity Press.

Proctor, W. (2017). "Bitches ain't gonna hunt no ghosts": Totemic nostalgia, toxic fandom and the ghostbusters platonic. *Palabra Clave*, 20(4), 1105–41.

Proctor, W., Kies, B., Chin, B., Larsen, K., McCulloch, R., Pande, R., and Stanfill, M. (2018). On toxic fan practices: a round-table. *Participations: Journal of Audience & Reception Studies*, 15(1), 370–93.

Pulliam-Moore, C. (2018, June 5). People in positions of power need to help shut down vitriolic fan behavior. *IO9*, https://io9.gizmodo.com/people-in-positions-of-power-need-to-help-shut-down-vit-1826575769

Rao, S. (2019, May 22). A timeline of Johnny Depp and Amber Heard's ongoing legal battle. *Washington Post*, https://www.washingtonpost.com/arts-entertainment/2019/05/22/timeline-johnny-depp-amber-heards-ongoing-legal-battle

Reilly, N. (2017, November 17). People aren't happy with Johnny Depp's casting in 'Fantastic Beasts 2'. *NME*, https://www.nme.com/news/film/people-arent-happy-johnny-depp-starring-fantastic-beasts-2-2160361#yLTUczUlJOrf2POu.99

Samuel, D. (2018, September 27). JK Rowling responds to fans calling out 'Fantastic Beasts' for 'racist' Nagini casting. *Floor 8*, https://www.floor8.com/posts/14624-jk-rowling-responds-to-fans-calling-out-fantastic-beasts-for-racist-nagini-casting

Sandvoss, C. (2005). *Fans. The Mirror of Consumption*. Cambridge, UK: Polity Press.

Scott, S. (2018). Towards a theory of producer/fan trolling. *Participations: Journal of Audience & Reception Studies*, 15(1), 143–59.

Stanfill, M. (2013). "They're losers, but I know better": Intra-fandom stereotyping and the normalization of the fan subject. *Critical Studies in Media Communication*, 30(2), 117–34, https://doi.org/10.1080/15295036.2012.755053

Stolworthy, J. (2017, November 29). Fantastic Beasts sequel should be cancelled following David Yates defence of Johnny Depp, say fans. *The Independent*, https://www.independent.co.uk/arts-entertainment/

fantastic-beasts-2-johnny-depp-director-david-yates-cancelled-defence-backlash-amber-heard-twitter-a8081796.html

Thompson, J. (2005). The new visibility. *Theory, Culture & Society,* 22(6), 31–51, https://doi.org/10.1177/0263276405059413

Thompson, J. (2011). Shifting boundaries of public and private life. *Theory, Culture & Society,* 28(4), 49–70, https://doi.org/10.1177/0263276411408446

Trottier, D. (2017). Digital vigilantism as weaponisation of visibility. *Philosophy & Technology,* 30(1), 55–72, https://doi.org/10.1007/s13347-016-0216-4

Trottier, D. (2018). Coming to terms with shame: Exploring mediated visibility against transgressions. *Surveillance & Society,* 16(2), 170–82, https://doi.org/10.24908/ss.v16i2.6811

Williams, R. (2013). "Anyone who calls muse a *Twilight* band will be shot on sight": Music, distinction, and the "interloping fan" in the *Twilight* franchise. *Popular Music and Society,* 36(3), 327–42, https://doi.org/10.1080/03007766.2013.798543

Zimmer, M. (2010). "But the data is already public": on the ethics of research in Facebook. *Ethics Information Technology,* 12, 313–25, https://doi.org/10.1007/s10676-010-9227-5

Contesting the Vulgar *Hanmai* Performance from Kuaishou: Online Vigilantism toward Chinese Underclass Youths on Social Media Platforms

Jiaxi Hou

Introduction

In November 2017, Chinese cyberspace was outraged after a group of middle-class parents alleged that their children were forced to strip naked and jabbed with needles in a Beijing kindergarten. Since 2010, more than sixty similar cases of child abuse have been reported in news media and Internet sites, not including other incidents concerning children's well-being, such as food or vaccine safety issues.[1] This outrage was prevalent on various social media platforms, including the dominant Sina Weibo[2] and WeChat[3] and other platforms more popular

---

1   English reports of the news can be found at: https://www.nytimes. com/2017/11/24/world/asia/beijing-kindergarten-abuse.html, or https://www. bbc.com/news/world-asia-china-42105443

2   Though with significant differences in user behaviors (Gao et al., 2012), Sina Weibo and Twitter are two comparable micro-blogging platforms, where public discussions occur. The monthly active users of Sina Weibo reached 462 million by the end of 2018. The data can be retrieved from its business report at https://tech.sina.com. cn/i/2019-03-05/doc-ihsxncvh0033063.shtml

3   WeChat is a mobile application with multiple functions: instant messaging, voice and video call, social networking, gaming and mobile commerce. 86.9% of China's

    https://doi.org/10.11647/OBP.0200.03

with the middle class, such as Zhihu and Douban.[4] In the widespread agitation against the suspected teacher and the related institutions, an underclass[5] *hanmai* [shouting with a microphone] performer, Tianyou, also expressed his anger in a short music video that he produced. Yet comments about Tianyou's work were extremely polarised compared to the contributions of other participants in the general outrage. On Kuaishou, the video-clip-sharing platform where the *hanmai* video was initially circulated, Tianyou was greeted with applause. However, when the video was shared on other social media platforms, their comment sections were filled with insults and rebukes, such as: "you should graduate from primary school first before you dare to say anything" or "do not show off your disgusting vulgarity in front of the public".[6]

Why were opinions so divided on different social media platforms? Why was Tianyou treated as unqualified to participate in online public discussions through *hanmai* videos and why did people transform him into an object of denunciation? These were the first empirical questions of the study. Firstly, it is necessary to have a basic understanding about what *hanmai* is, its connection with the platform Kuaishou and its place in contemporary Chinese digital culture. A vocal performance with

---

802 million Internet users used *Pengyouquan* [Moments], the social networking function of WeChat, while the Subscription Accounts function allows individuals, media institutions, enterprises and the government to establish their own official account. The data can be retrieved from the 42nd China Statistical Report on Internet Development by China Internet Network Information Centre in July 2018 from http://www.cnnic.cn/hlwfzyj/hlwxzbg/

4   From a Western perspective, Zhihu looks like a Chinese version of Quora and Douban shares some similarities with IMDb. Though official user data is lacking, the two platforms are perceived as attractive to urban middle-class users, especially those who have received a high level of education. Descriptions and individual analysis about the characteristics of users of Zhihu or Douban can be found in online discussion posts such as https://zhuanlan.zhihu.com/p/51561339, or blogs https://news.newseed.cn/p/1336055

5   The term underclass in this study includes various social groups, from peasants to rural migrant workers and from laid-off workers in small towns to youth with limited educational resources. In general, it refers to the disadvantaged social groups in transitional China. Rather than referring to a social group of restricted scale, the term underclass might cover over half the general population of China (Li 2005).

6   These comments were posted when Tianyou's video was shared on Bilibili.com, another large video sharing social media platform in China. These comments are no longer available online now because the video was deleted, but they were recorded in the fieldnotes of the researcher on February 14, 2018.

musical accompaniment, *hanmai* is usually circulated through online video clips. The characteristics of *hanmai*, including the emphasis on the rhyming lyrics, the rhythmic background music and frequent use of MC as the title of the performers, might remind an unfamiliar spectator of the style of rapping in African-American hip-hop culture, though both the *hanmai* community and the Chinese hip-hop community refuse to admit the similarities. *Hanmai* was first generated and mainly circulated on Kuaishou, one of the largest social media platforms in China with over 700 million registered users, characterised by a video sharing function. Because of the large user base of the video-centric platform, the user-generated visual artefacts on Kuaishou are highly diversified. Nonetheless, *hanmai* is the only genre that co-evolved with the platform since its launch in 2014; it is barely tolerated on other social media platforms because of its 'vulgarity'.

This study attempts to examine not only what is expressed in *hanmai* videos by the young Chinese underclass today, but also why and how *hanmai* was collectively resisted as vulgar by vigilant audiences from other social groups. Through empirical exploration, it tries to explain how vigilant practices, including denunciating, shaming and humiliating, can be utilised to exercise disciplinary force and contribute to the class-stratifying process. The study should be understood in the contemporary Chinese context, where not only was consensus around values and principles absent from a society undergoing drastic change, but digital technologies, especially social media platforms, were deeply embedded in these dynamic social changes. The study identifies different forms of online denunciations in the class-stratified public dialogue: underclass youths utilised affective and rhetorical denunciations of the upper social classes to construct their social identities; and the middle-class condemned the aesthetic and moral inferiority indicated by the 'vulgar' *hanmai* videos. The visibility of *hanmai* had once empowered the previously silent underclass group, but it was also utilised by the middle-class audience as a weapon in user-led vigilantism, triggering cooperation between the government and private corporations to formulate a new form of visibility for underclass youths to replace the 'vulgar' *hanmai* culture.

The study uses digital ethnographic methods to track the developments of the *hanmai* culture on Kuaishou, from its emergence as the collective self-representation of the young Chinese underclass, to the explosive denunciations it received and eventually its gradual disappearance under the cooperative surveillance of the state, the platform and society as a whole. I obtained the data for this research during a two-year observation period from December 2016 to December 2018, from four primary sources around the assemblage of Kuaishou and *hanmai*. This intentional integration of varied or even conflicting sources of data followed the principles suggested by multimodal ethnography, in order to provide a more comprehensive understanding of how meanings are constructed in the multimedia world (Dicks et al., 2006). The first component of the data was collected through a repetitive "walkthrough" of Kuaishou, in order to identify the application (app)'s relatively closed technical system and how users interact on it (Light et al., 2018).[7] Secondly, I collected forty-eight videos of *hanmai* works with their lyrics transcribed, in order to find out how the underclass youth actually expressed themselves using *hanmai* videos and what they said. Thirdly, I sought out different forms of online discussions related to *hanmai*, especially those containing denunciative discourses, including blogs and posts on Sina Weibo, WeChat, Zhihu and Douban. These data did not just reflect the realities of digital denunciation; they could also help to capture the imbrication between the technologically mediated and the physical worlds (Murthy, 2008). Fourth, I conducted semi-structured interviews with sixteen individuals from related groups who participated in this *hanmai* culture and the online vigilantism that targeted it, including the performers and spectators of *hanmai*, hip-hop followers, users of the other social media platforms who posted comments about *hanmai* and programmers from the Kuaishou company.[8]

---

7   "The walkthrough method is a way of engaging directly with an app's interface to examine its technological mechanisms and embedded cultural references to understand how it guides users and shapes their experiences. The core of this method involves the step-by-step observation and documentation of an app's screens, features and flows of activity — slowing down the mundane actions and interactions that form part of normal app use in order to make them salient and therefore available for critical analysis" (Light, Burgess, & Duguay, 2018, p. 882).

8   In the following sections, thirteen of the interviewees allowed me to translate their Chinese Internet pseudonym into English; the other three preferred a completely new pseudonym.

The Social and Cultural Context of the Underclass *Hanmai* Culture

First, it is essential to clarify the position and social significance of *hanmai* culture in the contemporary Chinese context. For both their lovers and their haters, *hanmai* videos were the first prevalent format for the self-representation of the young Chinese underclass. During the last decade (as of June 2018) Chinese mobile Internet users have increased to 98.3% of the overall 802 million people who are able to access the Internet,[9] thanks to the availability of low-end smartphones with cameras and the gradually decreasing telecommunication tariffs. Access to the Internet is no longer the privilege of college students, or the middle class who live in the metropolis. Technological progress has provided the basis for the visibility of disadvantaged social groups that were previously silent in Chinese cyberspace.

What identifies the underclass is not a straightforward question that can be easily answered with census statistics of the population's income, ethnicities, occupations, educational backgrounds or origins; it is much more complicated than that. One finds discrepancies between realities and imaginations, between a person's own sense of their (multiple) identities and how they are perceived by others. Moreover, the situation may be further complicated as China is still a drastically transitioning society, where there is hardly any consensus about either the standards of social class stratification or the norms of each specific social group. One possible solution might be to differentiate the two terms about class most commonly used in the Chinese language. One is *jieji*, which evokes particular concepts such as peasants, workers and capitalists within the Chinese Communist Party's Marxist-Leninist ideology (Goodman, 2014). The other is *jieceng*, which denotes stratum or strata and has been adopted in the twenty-first century to describe social stratification after the recent economic reforms (Lu, 2002). Though the latter is more resonant today, the historical legacies of *jieji* must not be overlooked, the most significant being the strictly enforced house registration system — to give it its Chinese term, *hukou*. From 1955 until today, the *hukou* system segregates the general population

---

9   The data can also be accessed at http://www.cnnic.cn/hlwfzyj/hlwxzbg/

into two groups of residents, the rural and the urban, according to their birth places and family locations. The rural/urban division in the *hukou* system still plays an important role, not only in contributing to general income inequalities (Xie & Zhou, 2014), but also in framing people's identities and perceptions within the class system (Afridi et al., 2015).

Mobility used to occur mostly within each of the two groups before the 1980s. The forty-year economic reform transformed the geographical and temporal migration between the countryside and city with great ease. However, it is still difficult to change the attribute of one's *hukou* within the strict binary of the rural/urban system. In general, rural populations might have enjoyed reputational prestige during the communist experiment, but they were inferior in economic and material aspects compared to the urban citizens (Li, 2004a). As a result, while the rural residents (and especially the peasants) might nominally rank high in the *jieji* system, the forty-year economic reforms saw them decline to the level of the underclass under the concept of *jieceng*. Until the end of 2018, over 288 million people with rural *hukou* were working in cities.[10] These elites from the rural region not only faced exclusion from the primary labour market, the welfare system and the social networks of the cities, but they also lived in a precarious rift between the two reconstructed social stratification systems because they were perceived as an underclass in their new surroundings (Li, 2004a).

Nonetheless, although they are an essential aspect of the Chinese underclass, rural migrant workers are not the only component. Much more diversified social groups are closely connected to the Chinese underclass, thanks to the enlarging inequalities in contemporary Chinese society (Sun, 2003). For example, rapid urbanisation has uprooted numerous rural residents and transplanted them to newly constructed towns and cities by directly issuing them with the urban *hukou*.[11] These passive immigrants are often unable to adjust immediately

---

10 The data can be retrieved from the National Bureau of Statistics of China, http://www.stats.gov.cn/tjsj/zxfb/201902/t20190228_1651265.html

11 To better facilitate economic development, the Chinese government has been working to replace hundreds of millions of small rural homes with newly constructed high-rises in towns and cities so as to improve the general population's living standards and also enlarge the consuming class of city dwellers. Related reports can be accessed from https://www.nytimes.com/2013/06/16/world/asia/chinas-great-uprooting-moving-250-million-into-cities.html

to their new urban surroundings and find it difficult to establish themselves, even with the financial compensation from the government (Li, 2004a).

Secondly, the drastic economic reform among state-owned enterprises since the 1990s has created over ten million unemployed workers, who form part of the impoverished urban population. Being laid off from the state-owned factories and businesses does not simply mean losing a stable job, but also the sudden loss of access to the welfare system, ranging from healthcare to a child's education. Thirdly, the forty-year-long economic reform has anchored part of the class stratification in Chinese transitional society (Li, 2004b) and therefore this period has witnessed inherited poverty and marginalisation among the younger generation. For example, the migrant workers' temporary working status has divided millions of rural families, as most of the children are left in the village alone or with their grandparents while their parents work thousands of miles away, providing only financial support during their childhood. These children eventually come to face their own life choice: whether or not to join a new generation of rural migrant workers.

These different groups used to be regarded as unrelated categories within the larger framework of the underclass (Lu, 2002) or subordinate class (Goodman, 2014). Though these different groups shared commonalities in economic status such as monthly income, they hardly constructed a collective class consciousness (Solinger, 2012). In the media, they are usually depicted distinctly, with a different focus depending on the context. For example, the rural migrant workers, the most central group within the underclass, are usually presented as the laughable 'other' in urban cinemas, avoiding any discussion about the structural inequalities, in order not only to pursue commercial success among the urban audience, but also to accord with the state's media policy to represent a harmonious society (Sun, 2014). On the other hand, the laid-off workers are depicted more as the pathetic 'others,' as their suffering is perceived as a direct consequence of the structural social transitions (Liu, 2016).

The prevalent access to social media platforms such as Kuaishou emerged in this social context, when the younger members of the underclass could, for the first time, take out their mobile phones, record themselves and publicise their own videos online. This process also contributed to the emergence of collective identities that were no longer shaped by the boundaries among different groups within the underclass. Contradicting the stereotypes in traditional media, the young underclass concentrated on themselves, their social realities and recorded their dreams and ambitions in the *hanmai* videos. At its peak, tens of thousands of *hanmai* videos were created and shared on Kuaishou, while many more spectators were viewing, liking, commenting and tipping[12] each other within the community. As the superstar of *hanmai*, MC Tianyou used to have over forty million followers on Kuaishou, who called themselves soldiers in his army. However, the explosive visibility of this subculture among the young underclass also attracted attention and opprobrium from other social groups, especially urban, middle-class Internet users.

Reconstructing the Underclass on Social Media Platforms

Though the technological foundations for the visibility of the underclass can hardly be neglected, the current study assumes that the Internet technology and social media in particular, is created, configured and used by human beings in specific social contexts (Fuchs, 2014). Meanwhile, the process of supporting daily activities online is so complicated that these things should be interpreted as mediators rather than intermediaries (Latour, 2005), which profoundly contribute to affecting our imagined perception of the differences between the online and offline world. In other words, the main theoretical concern of this study is to investigate how the Internet, with its platform characteristics and the Chinese class-based society are mutually shaping and shaped by each other within an intricate network, using the empirical case of *hanmai* videos on the Kuaishou social media platform and the vigilante

---

12 Tipping, or *dashang* in Chinese, refers to viewers buying virtual gifts to reward the creators. The specific affordance and behaviour on Chinese social media platforms not only largely affects the social interactions between the viewers and creators (Lee et al., 2018), but also contributes to changed business models, as the donations form a large proportion of the revenues of social media companies. Related reports can be found at https://www.abc.net.au/news/2019-02-17/inside-chinas-lucrative-livestreaming-industry/10810788 and https://view.inews.qq.com/a/20170706A06C2200 (in Chinese).

practices that followed. Refusing the platform's claim to be a neutral, objective and reliable "mirror of the authentic world" (Zhang & Zhou, 2017), I interpreted this claim as a strategic metaphor that aimed not only to circumvent any obligations to answer to regulatory demands, but also to justify their services in negotiation with different types of users and government departments: in other words, to suggest that, as a platform, Kuaishou simply facilitated users' online expressions without intervention.

The paradigm that neutral social media platforms reflect social realties fails to capture the dialectical relationship between technology and society. Moreover, it is especially contested in the case of Kuaishou and its use in a transitional Chinese society that is characterised by economic as well as ideological cleavages (Sun, 2003). By regarding Internet technology as socially constructed, the current study assumes different social media platforms with various technological affordances (Bucher & Helmond, 2018) are gaining implicit power in assembling different online communities and facilitating cultural activities. Therefore, different platforms attract users with different backgrounds, with the result that various values and principles are cultivated in the vigilant practices targeting *hanmai*.

On the other hand, the study also refuses to regard the identities of the underclass as reflections of objective social positions, but assumes that such identities are conferred on subjects (Lawler, 2004). Some literature addresses the engagement of the Chinese underclass with digital technology by concentrating on how disadvantaged social groups might be empowered by the Internet. For example, as a result of the annual commute among rural migrant workers between cities and villages, mobile devices are brought back to the villages. These not only construct new social ties among the rural residents but also provide benefits by connecting them with the resource-rich urban areas (Oreglia, 2013). Besides these material advances, previously disadvantaged rural workers can also use the mobile phones to "see the world" and gain an imagined sense of mobility by being online with some level of autonomy (Wallis, 2013, p. 3). However, my study is not restricted to the specific underclass group of rural migrant workers but is framed by the notion that the identities of the underclass are reconstructed in the dynamic negotiations between themselves, others and technological platforms. It relies on the Bourdieu's theoretical basis that classifying operations are dynamically classifiable practices rather than objective actions (Bourdieu, 1984). Expanding from Bourdieu's analysis in fields such as education, lifestyles and cultural tastes, the integrated concepts of capital, field and habitus could be applied in the realm of online space (Ignatow & Robinson, 2017).

This research regards the members of the *hanmai* community as taking part in a dynamic process of self-construction, being recognised, in particular by middle-class Internet users, as having emerging collective identities as underclass youths. Such a process is not only made visible in the production and circulation of *hanmai* videos, but also through the online denunciations targeting them. The precarious situation that the young Chinese underclass are facing is significant, both in itself and as an insightful empirical context to understand how digital technology contributes powerfully to class stratification (Sterne, 2003). Moreover, this study also examines Kuaishou and other social media platforms as a digitally mediated field with implicit values, norms and rules embedded in its technological affordances. Habitus, in this study, refers not only to our ways of being in the world (Bourdieu, 1984); it also takes humans' perceptions of technology into consideration. Visual materials have always been important to understand how habitus affects people, because elements that are hard to verbalise or articulate are contained there (Sweetman, 2009). Thus, the platform of Kuaishou concentrating on the creation and spread of videos can serve as a good field for us to understand the nuances and complexities of habitus in the Chinese class-stratifying process.

More specifically, this chapter departs from previous literature in its attention to the practices of vigilantism in the process of class stratification. The theoretical basis of digital vigilantism in this study is consistent with the definition that it is an ongoing process, in which people are collectively offended by others and respond by collaborative revenge, with certain patterns of actions afforded by digital technology (Trottier, 2017). In this case, the vigilant audiences, mostly composed of middle-class Internet users, were offended by the visibility and 'vulgarity' of the underclass youths in the virtual space. Therefore, practices of shaming, denunciations and humiliations were widely utilised in the dialogue among the different social groups, in order to exercise disciplinary force and social control (Kasra, 2017). In particular, the sudden visibility of an underclass with their own agency did not necessarily serve to empower a previously disadvantaged social group, but might also lead to misrepresentation, denunciation and regulation (in the Foucauldian sense of surveillance) of the original visual expressions due to the dynamic power structure (Brighenti, 2007). Moreover, the underclass youth (rather than any specific individuals) were the collective target of the online vigilantism in this case, which differs from other studies (cf. Cheong & Gong, 2010). When the targets of collective denunciations shift from specific individuals to categorised social groups, the mechanisms of the vigilant practices and the power negotiations behind them also change.

The Affective and Rhetorical Denunciations in *Hanmai*

Although it is widely recognised as a result of social media platforms, in the eyes of many *hanmai* followers, *hanmai* is consistent with various cultural practices from the pre-digital age. The essential characteristic of online *hanmai* videos is the reading or recitation of improvised rhymed lyrics with musical accompaniment. Not all *hanmai* performers necessarily shout into their microphone according to the term's literal meaning; nonetheless, the term 'shouting' underscores that the lyrics are of greater importance than the other musical or visual elements in *hanmai* videos. Concentrating on this feature, some *hanmai* followers, such as Jia (2017) and Zhong, interpret current *hanmai* culture as an adaptation of traditional Chinese oral storytelling performance, especially the form that arose from the folk cultures popular in North China. Comprising a wide variety of speaking and singing arts, Chinese oral narrative entertainment has not only survived for more than a millennium, but possesses specific features in local dialects from various regions (Boerdahl, 2013). In particular, the frequent use of playful doggerel in *hanmai* lyrics shares significant commonalities with *errenzhuan* [the rotation of two people], the ancient telling and singing art form that still plays an important role in the entertainment of Northeast rural residents (Ma, 2019).

Others, such as Tang (2017), propose that online *hanmai* performance actually evolved from its offline origins in the 1990s, when nightclubs gained popularity among the younger generations. Unlike the nightlife hotspots intended for the benefit of overseas tourists and investors in metropolises such as Beijing and Shanghai (Farrer, 2008), the nightlife spaces in small cities and rural regions were characterised by a hybridity of karaoke, dancing and DIY (Do-It-Yourself) elements (Chew, 2010), so that it was necessary for microphone controllers, or MCs, to excite the crowd with improvised and playful rhymed words in the gaps between different songs. Despite the divergences in exploring the origins of *hanmai* culture, the fact that its offline basis is closely connected to the social and cultural atmosphere of rural and small city residents from the north cannot be neglected, even though digital technologies have largely enhanced its range of circulation and might also have altered its elements, notably from the perspective of *hanmai* followers.

Either the traditional *errenzhuan* art form or the nightlife in rural regions have embedded *hanmai* performance in underclass culture, and such connections are also articulated by both *hanmai* creators and its audience. At the beginning of many *hanmai* videos, or in the comments at the bottom of these videos, it is repeatedly mentioned that only *laobaixing* [people with hundreds of surnames] can understand the real meanings of the *hanmai* lyrics. According to the *Modern Chinese Dictionary*, *laobaixing* refers to ordinary people who are not soldiers or government officials, but the *hanmai* community reclaimed this term for themselves. MC Changjiang described himself as a *laobaixing* because he quit school at the age of twelve and used to work twenty-one hours a day as a construction worker and a dishwasher in order to survive. MC Yushao characterised the *laobaixing* using the true story of one of his followers who had to break up with his fiancée because he could not offer 500 thousand Chinese yuan as the betrothal gift. However, *laobaixing* is not used only by the *hanmai* community. Diverse social groups can use this term self-referentially, or they can be described as *laobaixing* by actors in the media landscape, ranging from the cosmopolitan middle class, to rural migrant workers and to Chinese emigrants living overseas. The significance of how the *hanmai* community interprets the word is that they add a sense of relatively lower economic and reputational status to the original meaning, to emphasise themselves being powerless in contemporary Chinese society. Nonetheless, even within the *hanmai* community there are differences in understanding about exactly what constitutes the underclass from the perspective of employment, the economy or respectability.

Identifying themselves as a collective group of *laobaixing*, *hanmai* creators usually incorporate denunciations toward other social groups in their lyrics. Particularly the upper social class, composed of government officials, the rich and some morally degraded intellectuals, are constructed as the imagined objects deserving censure. In MC Tianyou's *hanmai* video, "*Laobaixing* Has A Word to Say", which triggered the middle-class denunciations in the Beijing kindergarten case described in the introduction, he severely condemned the suspect teacher in his lyrics:

> You were the hope for our national rejuvenation
> These young flowers once sang for you
> But now you abuse them, assault them and torture them
> Without any hesitation
> [...]
> I am not a good person, but I am human
> Your hypocrisy has made you lose your soul[13]

A clear distinction has been drawn between *laobaixing* and the stigmatised upper class. Consistent with how pop music may affect the identities of young people in the other social contexts (Frith, 1996), the emphasis on social class in *hanmai* lyrics reproduces differences in identities. Röttger-Rössler et al. (2019) argued in their study that visual artefacts were particularly effective at representing young people's affective relationships and emotional feelings, especially when the youths felt that it was difficult to verbalise these experiences. Similarly, participating in *hanmai* culture by either performing or viewing these videos constructed the collective consciousness of the underclass on the basis of affection rather than rationality. The young underclass expressed hardly any clear expectations for structural reform, or practical strategies for social change, in order to defend their own rights, topics that were relatively prevalent in young middle-class Chinese online discussions (Fu, 2019). The young underclass chose to underline their intensified emotional feelings, such as anger, yearning and desperation, in their *hanmai* culture, and never talked about how their situation could be improved.

---

13   The original video is no longer available online. However, thanks to YouTube user Bee at Kwai's efforts in making an archive of *hanmai* videos, we can still see the reposted video: https://www.youtube.com/watch?v=SryWoHxqpH8&

Moreover, as a user-generated genre, participation in *hanmai* culture is not limited to viewing the videos, but also includes the interactions within the community and a flexible shift between being a creator and a spectator, as barriers to participation have broken down. This active participation contributes to the sense of belonging inherent in this new identity, which renders the group distinct from those they criticise in their lyrics. Regarding *hanmai* as a vernacular creation embedded in their real-life experiences, the community weighs social class as the more significant distinguisher to construct their identity, rather than gender or sexuality (Whiteley, 2013) or ethnicity (Grgurić & Janković-Paus, 2018), which dominate in other global contexts.

The difference of identities between the powerful and the powerless is sometimes conveyed rhetorically. Authority is usually portrayed using iconic symbols such as the Buddha or an emperor, fictional or distant figures in traditional Chinese culture, rather than current government officials or the rich. To symbolise themselves, the community idolise Monkey King as the representative of *laobaixing*. The main character in the sixteenth-century Chinese classical novel *Journey to the West*, Monkey King has always been an important rebel figure because his experiences in challenging the Buddha and the Jade Emperor and pursuing personal freedom have been retold many times in popular adaptations in film, anime or TV series. The importance of Monkey King is so significant in *hanmai* culture that there is even one specific Monkey-King voice within the vocal styles of *hanmai*; a beastial, hoarse and sharp voice in a particularly high tone. In MC Qixing's work, "Buddha Says", this vocal style was utilised organically together with the lyrics to express the anger and confusion of Monkey King, a protector and also a spokesperson of *laobaixing*, when he tried to challenge the authority of the Buddha.

> Buddha, open your eyes and see these ugly faces
> The evil are waiting for reward but the good are begging for forgiveness
> Buddha, I believe in you but where on earth are you
> I have walked for hundreds of thousands of miles
> You tell me you are in my heart
> Buddha says turning back and I can see the shore
> I go back but I don't have a home anymore[14]

---

14 Again, the original video is no longer available but the reposted version can be accessed at https://www.youtube.com/watch?v=6cyOdouZ48o

Through the affective and rhetorical criticisms of the upper class, the imagined adversary of *laobaixing*, underclass youths' anger and confusion were expressed in the lyrics and cherished by the online audience. The audience understood that these lyrics spoke out the innermost feelings of Monkey King, whereas in the original work, it is well known that Monkey King was gradually disciplined by his master during the arduous journey from China to India to search for the truth of Buddhism. The comment section of *hanmai* videos on Kuaishou was usually suffused with praise, acknowledgement and support. The most frequent remark is either 666, a popular Internet slang term on Kuaishou that means 'awesome', or *laotie* [buddies], an intra-community appellation indicating the intimate relationships among the users. Even though some MCs mark their videos as 'original' if they write the lyrics by themselves, they always encourage other competing MCs or the viewers to perform the song freely themselves or to paraphrase the lyrics. The distinction between the upper class, depicted as the blameable 'others' in the lyrics of *hanmai*, and the *laobaixing* themselves, are further reinforced by the affective interactions within the community.

Besides the Monkey-King voice, other popular vocal styles indicate the different categories of the content and also different ideologies behind the lyrics. For example, the 'emperor' voice is usually used in a *hanmai* work when the ambition of social mobility is underlined, while the 'alcohol and tobacco' voice usually emphasises the sufferings from intimate relationships caused by class boundaries. Creating, performing and viewing *hanmai* videos have transformed their exploration of the emerging underclass identity into a constantly changing process of performativity. Moreover, the lack of dialogue between the *hanmai* community and an imagined upper class has deflated the denunciative discourses in *hanmai* lyrics, and at the same time, positions *hanmai* as self-referential, and as something that entertains its own group. However, the rapidly increasing visibility of both *hanmai* and Kuaishou has evoked antagonism among other social groups, which means that the previously non-vigilante denunciations in *hanmai* lyrics have transformed the *hanmai* community into the subjects of large-scale online vigilantism led by middle-class Internet users.

Hanmai Being Denunciated: from Ignorance to Multifaceted Vulgarity

The similarities between *hanmai* performances and rapping in African American hip-hop culture boosted the former's visibility. Neglecting the *hanmai* community's identity as a local culture rooted in underclass lives in rural regions of North China, some hip-hop lovers identified *hanmai* as a localised Chinese hip-hop culture. For example, one hip-hop fan, Xiao, compared MC Tianyou with a popular Chinese rapper, GAI, arguing that both of them have depicted the street life of the young underclass based on their real experiences.[15] A music critic and producer, Liang (2017), also argued that *hanmai* might be closer to the initial spirit of authenticity in African American hip-hop culture, compared to Chinese hip-hop, because *hanmai* was actually generated by the underclass, while contemporary hip-hop culture was more attractive to urban middle-class youths as it resonated with their cosmopolitan lifestyles (Kloet, 2010). The identification of the similarities between *hanmai* and hip-hop rapping, rather than the denunciations in the lyrics of *hanmai*, infuriated the Chinese hip-hop community. Xiao's personal page on Douban was soon inundated with comments stating *"Hanmai* Is Not Hip-hop" together with insults towards Xiao, MC Tianyou and the whole *hanmai* community. Similar offensive discourses toward *hanmai* arose on platforms like Sina Weibo, Zhihu and Douban.

The hip-hop community originally began to denounce *hanmai* performers because of the lack of originality in their music, the simplicity of their 'flow',[16] and their ignorance of intellectual property protection. A hip-hop group, Xinjiekou, accused the whole *hanmai* community of plagiarising flows from Chinese hip-hop musicians. They created a rap song entiteld "Fuck *Hanmai*", on Sina Weibo in order to provoke collective resistance against *hanmai*. By denouncing the supposed offences carried out by the *hanmai* community (which included not only plagiarism, but also their rural backgrounds and their rustic tastes) the previously

---

15 Xiao shared the experience with the researcher in an interview held on February 2, 2018.

16 Though rappers seldom define the term, 'flow' is an important element for the audience to judge the qualities of hip-hop music. It usually describes the rhythm of the music and the rhymes of the lyrics and how well the two elements interact.

unknown hip-hop group gained popularity and reaffirmed the class differences between *hanmai* and rapping. Ironically, when the fact that Xinjiekou itself had also been involved in dozens of copyright disputes was disclosed by hip-hop fans, the hip-hop community was not collectively mobilised to reach a consensus in resisting *hanmai* using vigilante rap, as Xinjiekou had expected. Xinjiekou is not an exclusive case, as hip-hop culture has evoked legal and intellectual property controversies from its very beginning due to its sampling practices (Self, 2001). Nonetheless, ignorance of copyright was the initial cause of the hip-hop community's denunciations of *hanmai* culture. Vigilant practices have served as one of the key distinctions with which the middle-class hip-hop community differentiate themselves from the underclass *hanmai*.

This denunciation of *hanmai* attracted wider public attention from more diverse middle-class Internet users. Unlike the hip-hop community's anxiety to differentiate themselves from the *hanmai* community, the wider middle-class public was astonished by the extent of vulgarity in *hanmai* videos. On Zhihu, thousands of questions and answers were posted to discuss why *hanmai* was so vulgar and what consequences would emerge if these vulgar works continued to be popular among the younger generations, in order to provoke collective resistance to *hanmai*. Interestingly, the content of *hanmai* actually contained much less profanity or vulgarity compared to American hip-hop culture (Taylor & Taylor, 2007). We may ask what 'vulgarity' means when the word is prevalently used in the public denunciations targeting *hanmai* culture and community. This study identifies three layers of meaning intended by different users of the term 'vulgarity': the aesthetic, the moral and the technological.

Aesthetic Vulgarity

The immature vocal style, the monotonous rhythm, the substandard recording facilities and the garish filters together constituted the reasons that middle-class Internet users' denounced *hanmai*. One of the most unacceptable features was therefore its low quality from an aesthetic perspective, especially when compared with global hip-hop culture. Preference for the latter indicated a modern and cosmopolitan cultural taste that could always keep up with the global trends (Kloet, 2010), while being a *hanmai* follower was denounced using terms like 'rustic' and 'vulgar'. Such comparisons between *hanmai* and hip-hop could be particularly popular in shaming and humiliating discourses. For example, to answer the question what is the difference between *hanmai* and rapping, answers such as "hip-hop is like the food you eat for dinner but *hanmai* is like the shit you try to get rid of after you eat" or "hip-hop is a genre of modern music but *hanmai* is what the ancient homeless say when begging" received hundreds or even thousands of likes and supportive comments. Denunciations of *hanmai* in the name of vulgarity could be interpreted as a class-stratifying practice in Bourdieu's sense of the distinction through cultural tastes (Bourdieu, 1984).

However, from the perspective of a *hanmai* lover, it was the simplicity of *hanmai* that attracted *laobaixing* to participate in this online culture, because all it required was to write what they wanted to say, organise the words using rhymes and recite them before a webcam with a musical accompaniment. For those who did not want to write their own lyrics, all the lyrics written by acknowledged MCs were ready-made and openly shared within the community for everyone to use. The *hanmai* community did not even feel the aesthetic humiliations as the middle-class vigilant audience expected. When asked about how he felt about being compared to a beggar, MC Tianyou answered from a different perspective: "[Beggars] work hard to create the rhymes, get some praise and also receive some money from the audience. What is wrong with being a beggar?" The aesthetic denunciations seemed to miss their destination, as the *hanmai* community perceived their vernacular creations as closely connected to the traditional Chinese folk culture within their own context. Nonetheless, the denunciations not only further reinforced the boundary between different social classes with different cultural tastes, but also increased the visibility of *hanmai* culture in public discussions.

Moral Vulgarity

The visibility of *hanmai*, escalated by increasingly widespread public denunciations, triggered more attention from a middle-class, vigilant audience, who later regarded these videos as proof of the moral degradation among the underclass youths and worried about their social influence. Although *hanmai* videos lacked straightforward profanity or offensive language, they were still perceived as vulgar for being a potential threat to existing moral values and public interests. Rather than directly condemning the aesthetic inferiority of *hanmai*, denunciatory discourses about the moral aspects of *hanmai*'s vulgarity were combined with disgust, but also sympathy. For example, a freelance columnist with the pseudonym Crocodile argued that the vulgarity of *hanmai* was socially constructed, as a reaction to the fact that upward mobility was highly restricted for the underclass youths: "[y]ou will feel helpless when you watch these *hanmai* videos, you know? You can do nothing, and they can do nothing either, because they don't have any hope in their life. You can just feel it from their vulgar lyrics".[17]

Denunciations also indicate conflicting expectations and values about how the underclass youths should behave among the middle-class vigilant audiences themselves. For example, Liu, a Sina Weibo user, argued that current *hanmai* works indicated the loss of traditional values such as diligence and endurance, which were cherished among the older generation of rural migrant workers, because the underclass youth now spend too much time dreaming about defeating fictional emperors and replacing them. Elsewhere Tong expressed her particular dislike of the intense yearning for upward social mobility expressed by the young underclass using symbols of traditional Chinese culture on WeChat. The appropriation of symbols and languages from traditional Chinese culture was either considered as disrespectful and ignorant towards the orthodoxy of traditional culture, or as a refusal of modern values. These different or even contradictory perspectives contributed to the multi-layered meanings of vulgarity in condemning the whole *hanmai* culture, as the term might have different meanings for different members of the vigilant audience. The lack of proper moral values was the significant charge in this case of public vigilantism against *hanmai* culture. This echoes with certain characteristics of contemporary Chinese society (Sun, 2003), in which no single value system, either traditional Chinese, socialist, or neoliberal, is dominant among the public.

---

17 From the researcher's interview with Crocodile on 2018, June 27.

Technological Vulgarity

Moreover, the aesthetic and moral denunciations were always intertwined with technological concern, especially referring to the recommendation algorithm that characterised the Kuaishou platform. The use of recommendation algorithms to provide customised content had been the underlying principle of Kuaishou from its launch. Users were assumed to restrict their behaviours to simply scrolling through and watching videos without performing additional actions. This naturalised process was constructed through the combination of the concise user interface, particular strategies in content distribution and the refining algorithm. Kuaishou also established a particular strategy to exclude videos generated by celebrities or top users from being distributed in the recommendation system. The technological affordances of the platform had attracted new Internet users and empowered previously silent groups by augmenting their visibility. However, these affordances also contributed to public denunciations when the social impacts of the algorithm were repeatedly mentioned.

In particular, the unpredictability and intricacy of the recommendation system, as well as the traffic-centric logic used in designing its algorithm, provoked most criticism from the vigilant audience, which blamed Kuaishou alongside *hanmai* culture. For example, Yan strongly opposed Crocodile's expression of the hopelessness of the underclass youths by arguing that:

> The frightening thing is its recommendation system. If you see one vulgar video, like a teenage mother, the system will push you much more. But are there so many teenage mothers in real life? The system only cares about the traffic. This can exemplify social problems, but it will also harm the young people, especially teenagers, because they have not got the ability to correctly understand things.[18]

In arguing over who should take responsibility for spreading the vulgarity of *hanmai* culture — the algorithm, underclass youths or social structures — the middle-class vigilante audience had not arrived at a consensus. Nonetheless, the middle-class, user-led vigilantism against the vulgarity of *hanmai* culture appropriated its visibility, which might

---

18   Yan expressed this in an interview with the researcher on January 17, 2018.

once have empowered the previously silent young underclass. Finally, it succeeded in objectifying *hanmai* videos as a visual resource, triggering more powerful social sectors to surveil and regulate the young underclass. By condemning the vulgarity of *hanmai*, the middle class reinforced their perceived aesthetic and moral superiority compared to the underclass youths, as well as their ability to recognise the risks of new technological affordances.

From User-led Vigilantism to Institutional Surveillance

The user-led vigilantism among middle-class Internet users did not develop into organised action against the underclass youths' *hanmai* culture, though shaming, condemning and humiliating discourses were prevalent in public discussions. However, it triggered the state and the platform, two powerful social institutions, to rethink what kind of representations of underclass youth should be visible in the virtual world. In April 2018, Chinese Central Television, which served not only as a media organisation but also as a branch of state authority, criticised Kuaishou for providing vulgar and harmful information to younger generations. The State Administration of Radio and Television soon required Kuaishou to examine its existing online content and stop uploading new videos, and the app was forcibly removed from the Android app store.[19] Besides these punishments, it was also disclosed that the authorities summoned Kuaishou's administrators for a face-to-face meeting, after which they were required to hire a larger censorship team of at least 3,000 new employees to manually review all the user-generated videos before they were distributed automatically using the algorithm.[20]

At the same time, a new round of the *Jingwang* [Purifying the Internet] campaign was launched: several state-level institutions collaborated in order to crack down on vulgar and obscene content online. The national *Jingwang* campaign never claimed it was targeting either Kuaishou or

---

19   The announcement was publicised through the State Administration of Radio's WeChat account on April 4, 2018: https://mp.weixin.qq.com/s/jnn-uMPl_uPaFbunaE4Kgg

20   The transcript report can still be accessed from the following URL, though the originals were deleted: https://36kr.com/p/5127645

the *hanmai* culture;[21] nevertheless, the state's intervention in the name of protecting juveniles from vulgar online content had significant impacts on Kuaishou. For example, in the end of May, Kuaishou publicised an announcement indicating that they had removed nearly 700,000 video clips and blocked almost 200 accounts every day from early April in the name of combatting vulgarity.[22] Under these conditions, *hanmai* videos gradually disappeared from the platform. It was transformed from a genre with tens of thousands of updates every day, to nothing; no one was performing any longer, no videos were being shared, and no more public discussions about it were raised.

On the other hand, Kuaishou actively cooperated with the state to create new sets of algorithms and surveillance rules to purify the online expressions of the young underclass. In the letter of apology posted by Kuaishou, Su Hua, its CEO, claimed that "the algorithm will be optimised with a healthy and positive value" that "strictly complies with the national regulations and common ethics and morals".[23] The changed algorithm not only excluded *hanmai* videos, but also gave more weight to underclass videos with so-called "healthy and positive values", such as the magnificent Chinese farmland or the happily singing rural migrant workers on construction sites. The underclass youths' anger and confusion was erased together with *hanmai*; the ambitions they once articulated were no longer visible, and neither were the formerly enthusiastic public denunciations about the vulgarity of *hanmai*, especially those discourses that interpreted this vulgarity as the result of powerlessness and social inequalities that the underclass youths encountered. Few participants in the online denunciations were willing or able to share their opinions any longer,

---

21 The *Jingwang* campaign was initiated after the establishment of the Cyberspace Administration of China in 2014, led by Chinese president Xi Jinping, which was to pay special attention to the regulation and management of online information. *Jingwang* campaigns were co-organised by the National Office against Pornographic and Illegal Publications, the Cyberspace Administration of China, the Ministry of Industry and Information Technology and the Ministry of Public Security.

22 The announcement was publicised through Kuaishou's WeChat account on May 27, 2018: https://mp.weixin.qq.com/s/UzX0vwI01MJo9olu27K4MA

23 This is taken from the letter of apology that was publicised in the form of banner on Kuaishou in April 2018. There is no available link since it is shared only within Kuaishou app. The researcher kept the snapshot of the letter in her fieldnotes on April 8, 2018.

except to support effective acts of the state. While new technology can be utilised by civil participants, either to improve a previously disadvantaged social group's visibility or provoke public discussions in the form of denunciations, it is also harnessed by the authorities, with cooperation from the platforms themselves, to scrutinise the mediated image of the underclass youths.

Conclusion

By tracing the evolution of *hanmai* culture and related online vigilante practices, this study examined how the use of social media platforms is a significant aspect of the Chinese class-stratifying process. *Hanmai* videos, on the one hand, were utilised to express not only the emerging collective identity of the underclass youths, but also their social visibility in the digital public sphere. However, they also served to reinforce middle-class identity when vigilant middle-class audiences denounced the aesthetic and moral vulgarity of *hanmai*, using technological concerns as a weapon. The technologically mediated visibility of Chinese underclass youths in the form of *hanmai* videos transformed from a force that empowered social recognition to a trigger for various disciplinary forces, both from the middle-class audiences and from state power, in cooperation with social media platforms.

References

Afridi, F., Li, S. X., & Ren, Y. (2015). Social identity and inequality: The impact of China's *Hukou* System. *Journal of Public Economics*, 123, 17–29, https://doi.org/10.1016/j.jpubeco.2014.12.011

Boerdahl, V. (2013). *The Eternal Storyteller: Oral Literature in Modern China*. Oxon: Routledge, https://doi.org/10.4324/9780203036761

Bourdieu, P. (1984). *Distinction: A Social Critique of the Judgement of Taste*. Cambridge, MA: Harvard University Press.

Brighenti, A. (2007). Visibility: A category for the social sciences. *Current Sociology*, 55(3), 323–42, https://doi.org/10.1177/0011392107076079

Bucher, T., & Helmond, A. (2018). The affordances of social media platforms. *The SAGE Handbook of Social Media* (pp. 223–53). London: Sage, https://doi.org/10.4135/9781473984066.n14

Cheong, P. H., & Gong, J. (2010). Cyber vigilantism, transmedia collective intelligence, and civic participation. *Chinese Journal of Communication, 3*(4), 471–87, https://doi.org/10.1080/17544750.2010.516580

Chew, M. M. (2010). Hybridization of karaoke and dance clubbing practices in Chinese nightlife. In Y. Chu, & K. E. Man (eds), *Contemporary Asian Modernities: Transnationality, Interculturality and Hybridity* (pp. 287–307). Bern: Peter Lang, https://doi.org/10.3726/978-3-0351-0035-8

Dicks, B., Soyinka, B., & Coffey, A. (2006). Multimodal ethnography. *Qualitative Research, 6*(1), 77–96, https://doi.org/10.1177/1468794106058876

Farrer, J. (2008). Play and power in Chinese nightlife spaces. *China: An International Journal, 06*(01), 1–17, https://doi.org/10.1142/S0219747208000034

Frith, S. (1996). Music and identity. In S. Hall & P. du Gay (eds), *Questions of Cultural Identity 1* (pp. 108–28). London: Sage, http://dx.doi.org/10.4135/9781446221907.n7

Fu, J. (2019). Prefigurative politics in Chinese young people's online social participation. In H. Cuervo & A. Miranda (eds), *Youth, Inequality and Social Change in the Global South* (pp. 255–68). Singapore: Springer, https://doi.org/10.1007/978-981-13-3750-5_17

Fuchs, C. (2014). *Social Media: A Critical Introduction.* Los Angeles: Sage, https://doi.org/10.4135/9781446270066.n1

Goodman, D. S. (2014). *Class in Contemporary China.* Cambridge: Polity Press.

Gao, Q., Abel, F., Houben, G.-J., & Yu, Y. (2012). A comparative study of users' microblogging behavior on Sina Weibo and Twitter. In J. Masthoff, B. Mobasher, M. C. Desmarais, & R. Nkambou (eds), *User Modeling, Adaptation, and Personalization* (pp. 88–101). Berlin Heidelberg: Springer, https://doi.org/10.1007/978-3-642-31454-4_8

Grgurić, D., & Janković-Paus, S. (2018). A popular music form in the construction of identity: Historical discourse analysis of canzonetta fiumana. *International Review of the Aesthetics & Sociology of Music, 49*(2), 295–310

Ignatow, G., & Robinson, L. (2017). Pierre bourdieu: Theorizing the digital. *Information, Communication & Society, 20*(7), 950–66, https://doi.org/10.1080/1369118X.2017.1301519

Jia, Y. (2017, August 22). Ruhe pingjia hanmai zhe yi wenhua xianxiang? Hui xiang xiha yiyang chengwei yizhong wenhua ma? [How to evaluate *hanmai* as a cultural phenomenon? Will it develop to hip-hop?], https://www.jianshu.com/p/e2e87ba96283

Kasra, M. (2017). Vigilantism, public shaming, and social media hegemony: the role of digital-networked images in humiliation and sociopolitical Control. *The Communication Review, 20*(3), 172–88, https://doi.org/10.1080/10714421.2017.1343068

Kloet, J. de. (2010). *China with a Cut: Globalisation, Urban Youth and Popular Music.* Amsterdam: Amsterdam University Press, https://doi.org/10.5117/9789089641625

Latour, B. (2005). *Reassembling the Social: An Introduction to Actor-network-theory.* New York: Oxford University Press.

Lawler, S. (2004). Rules of engagement: Habitus, power and resistance. *The Sociological Review,* 52(2), 110–28, https://doi.org/10.1111/j.1467-954x.2005.00527.x

Lee, Y.-C., Yen, C.-H., Chiu, P.-T., King, J.-T., & Fu, W.-T. (2018). Tip me!: Tipping is changing social interactions on live streams in China. *2018 CHI Conference on Human Factors in Computing Systems,* https://doi.org/10.1145/3170427.3188543

Li, Q. (2004a). *Nongmingong yu zhongguo shehui fenceng* [*Rural Migrant Workers and Chinese Social Stratification.*] Beijing: Shehui kexue wenxian chubanshe. [Social Sciences Academic Press].

Li, Q. (2004b). *Zhuanxing shiqi zhongguo shehui fenceng.* [*Social Stratification in Chinese Transitional Society.*] Beijing: Shehui kexue wenxian chubanshe. [Social Sciences Academic Press].

Li, Q. (2005). *Dingzixing shehui jiegou yu jiegou jinzhang.* [The Inverted T-shape social structure and structural strain.] Shehuixue yanjiu [Sociological Research] (2), 55–73.

Liang, H. (2017, March 24). Hanmai yu shuochang: Yichang wukebimian de jieji BATTLE. [*Hanmai* and Hip-hop: An inevitable BATTLE between social classes]. (Interview by Tang Bo. for VICE China), https://daily.zhihu.com/story/9317114

Light, B., Burgess, J., & Duguay, S. (2018). The Walkthrough method: An approach to the study of apps. *New Media & Society,* 20(3), 881–900, https://doi.org/10.1177/1461444816675438

Liu, Y. (2016). *Lishi, Jiyi, Shengchan: Dongbei laogongye jidi wenhua yanjiu* [*History, Memory, Production: Cultural Studies of the Industrial Region in Northeast China*]. Beijing: Zhongguo yanshi chubanshe [China Yan Shi Press].

Lu, X. (2002). *Dangdai zhongguo jieceng yanjiu baogao.* [*Social Stratification in Contemporary China*]. Beijing: Shehui kexue wenxian chubanshe. [Social Sciences Academic Press].

Ma, H. (2019). Chinese entertainment industry: The case of folk *Errenzhuan. Asian Theatre Journal,* 36(1), 79–100, https://doi.org/10.1353/atj.2019.0004

Murthy, D. (2008). Digital ethnography: An examination of the use of new technologies for social research. *Sociology,* 42(5), 837–55, https://doi.org/10.1177/0038038508094565

Oreglia, E. (2013). *From Farm to Farmville: Circulation, Adoption, and Use of ICT between Urban and Rural China* (Doctoral dissertation, The University of California, Berkeley, United States), https://escholarship.org/uc/item/68s0x1r3

Röttger-Rössler, B., Scheidecker, G., & Lam, A. T. A. (2019). Narrating visualized feelings: Photovoice as a tool for researching affects and emotions among school students. In A. Kahl (ed.), *Analyzing Affective Societies: Methods and Methodologies* (pp. 78–97). Oxon: Routledge, https://doi.org/10.4324/9780429424366-5

Self, H. (2001). Digital sampling: A cultural perspective. *UCLA Entertainment Law Review,* 9, 347–59, https://heinonline.org/HOL/Page?handle=hein.journals/uclaetrlr9&id=363&collection=journals&index=

Solinger, D. J. (2012). The new urban underclass and its consciousness: Is it a class? *Journal of Contemporary China,* 21(78), 1011–28, https://doi.org/10.1080/10670564.2012.701037

Sterne, J. (2003). Bourdieu, technique and technology. *Cultural Studies,* 17(3–4), 367–89, https://doi.org/10.1080/0950238032000083863a

Su, H. (2018, May 24). "Baman" chuangyezhe Su Hua: Kuaishou qinian yijian beihou de chuxin. [A determined start-up entrepreneur Su Hua: Kuaishou has never forgot why we started after seven years since launch]. Interview by Fang Li for *Tencent University,* https://mp.weixin.qq.com/s/lZMDl8TPlTlHl2Tf1qv4xg

Sun, L. (2003). *Duanlie: Ershi shiji yilai de zhongguo shehui.* [*Cleavage: Chinese Society after the 1990s.*] Beijing: Shehui kexue wenxian chubanshe. [Social Sciences Academic Press].

Sun, W. (2014). *Subaltern China: Rural Migrants, Media, and Cultural Practices.* Lanham, Maryland: Rowman & Littlefield.

Sweetman, P. (2009). Revealing habitus, illuminating practice: Bourdieu, photography and visual methods. *The Sociological Review,* 57(3), 491–511, https://doi.org/10.1111/j.1467-954x.2009.01851.x

Tang, Z. (2017, November 7). Hanmai zigu yilai jiushi dongbei de wenhua chuantong. [*Hanmai* has always been part of the tradition of North-east local culture],https://new.qq.com/omn/20171107/20171107A0JUBX.html

Taylor, C., & Taylor, V. (2007). Hip Hop is now: An evolving youth culture. *Reclaiming Children and Youth,* 15(4), 210–13, https://search.proquest.com/docview/214193352?accountid=14357

Trottier, D. (2017). Digital vigilantism as weaponisation of visibility. *Philosophy & Technology,* 30(1), 55–72, https://doi.org/10.1007/s13347-016-0216-4

Wallis, C. (2013). *Technomobility in China: Young Migrant Women and Mobile Phones.* New York: New York University Press, https://doi.org/10.18574/nyu/9780814795262.001.0001

Whiteley, S. (2013). *Sexing the Groove: Popular Music and Gender.* Oxon: Routledge, https://doi.org/10.4324/9780203351338

Xie, Y., & Zhou, X. (2014). Income inequality in today's China. *Proceedings of the National Academy of Sciences,* 111(19), 6928–33, https://doi.org/10.1073/pnas.1403158111

Zhang, W., & Zhou, X. (2017, November 7). Kuaishou CEO Su Hua: Zuo zhenshi shijie de yimian jingzi. [Kuaishou CEO Su Hua: Be a Mirror of the Real World]. *The Beijing News,* http://www.bjnews.com.cn/news/2017/11/07/463202.html

Zhong, S. (2019, January 4). Lun hanmai tong errenzhuan he dongbei samanjiao de neizaiyizhi. [Hanmai has common origins with errenzhuan from Shamanism], https://site.douban.com/301865/widget/notes/194102538/note/702564962/

'I don't think that's very funny': Scrutiny of Comedy in the Digital Age

Isabel Linton

Introduction

Comedy evokes strong emotions, and though it is generally intended to create a positive response, jokes can sometimes cause offence or other harmful effects. This chapter will investigate the line between what is tasteful and what is not — and, of course, who has the right to decide this. Due to the subjective nature of comedy, it is possible to create distasteful comedy without it being intentionally harmful, but audiences may take issue with work in which they consider the lack of taste to be harmful or potentially harmful, either to themselves or to others. This chapter discusses examples of when audiences have acted as digital vigilantes towards comedy, particularly in online spaces, and it questions when it is appropriate for audiences to react in this way. The debate is not a new phenomenon, but with the rise of social media and the ease with which information and vitriol can be shared and de-contextualised, it is now becoming an even more important topic to address. Audiences can easily take to the Internet and air their grievances about a snippet of comedy, and this can often spread faster than the initial text (for the purpose of this chapter, 'text' will refer to a performance, video, joke or event). This can then lead to audiences forming an opinion about it, and potentially feeling outrage towards it, having never experienced it first-hand. Due to the way that information is shared, digital audiences

 https://doi.org/10.11647/OBP.0200.04

are increasingly engaging in commentary on a subject to which they were not originally exposed. Audiences, and therefore digital vigilantes, can criticise something that did not originally concern them, or has been taken out of context, and this can be problematic for both audiences and comedians/creators.

The majority of cases discussed in this chapter focus on satire, attempted satire, or events that were framed as satire after the event. An early example relevant to this research is *The Great Dictator* (dir. Chaplin, 1940). The film was critically received but years after its release, Chaplin stated that "Had I known of the actual horrors of the German concentration camps, I could not have [...] made fun of the homicidal insanity of the Nazis" (Chaplin, 1964, p. 392). Though there was no digital media at the time, Chaplin went through a similar type of self-reflection as that which will be discussed in many of the examples in this chapter. In modern times, practitioners cannot have this delayed response to their text, and as such often become engaged in discussions with fans, audiences and digital vigilantes directly following the release of the text, with no significant delay between the performance and the discussion. This limits the opportunity for self-reflection on the part of the practitioner. However, due to social media, and the opportunities created by the Internet more generally, practitioners now also have the ability, and responsibility, to be aware of the cultural significance and connotations of their work. To be able to engage in media, they must also be able to access and experience it, and therefore have an awareness of the implications of their work. This awareness of current events is often the basis of their comedy but can lead to a negative response from audiences when the practitioner appears under-researched or of improper agency to discuss the issue. If a reader of the text (e.g., an audience member) cannot see that the practitioner has direct experience of the issue they are discussing, the reader will be hesitant to engage with the discourse, and this can lead to audiences feeling uncomfortable, or offended, as will be outlined in this chapter. If the practitioner is considered to be more powerful than the subject of the joke, they lack the agency to make certain jokes as audiences are likely to object if they feel that the comedian is 'punching down' rather than 'punching up'.[1]

---

1   The concept of 'punching down/up', although idiomatic, is a comedic term
    regarding the perceived power dynamics between the individual making the joke

Digital vigilantism (DV) "is a process where citizens are collectively offended by other citizen activity, and respond through coordinated retaliation on digital media" (Trottier, 2017, p. 55). This chapter discusses how comedy practitioners, in particular those who publish their work online, are viewed as citizens, and therefore can be subject to digital vigilantism towards their work. When considering comedy, "factors which can influence humour appreciation are such things as religious beliefs, political convictions, and sexual orientation" (Lockyer & Pickering, 2009, p. 128), and this raises issues of agency, ethics and morality, when writing and producing comedy.

In this chapter it is important to consider the cultural capital of comedy. "The tastes actually realized depend on the state of the system of goods offered" (Bourdieu, 1984, p. 228): the issue of taste, and reactions to it, are dependent on the state of capital of the good. Bourdieu argued that the bourgeois theatre is a respectable and enjoyable place to visit "because it only asks questions which 'everyone asks himself', from which 'the only escape' is 'humour and incurable optimism'" (Bourdieu, 1984. p. 267). He then described how, although the theatre and its comedy is relatively accessible to those with the means, the next stratum — visiting the opera, galas, etc. — expressed an accordance with being part of high society (Bourdieu, 1984, p. 269). Visitors to a comedy show would generally be of lower capital "culturally or economically" (Bourdieu, 1984, p. 283), and this lowers the capital of entertainment such as the theatre, and, when applied to more modern entertainment, comedy. Comedy has never been considered to have a high cultural capital, and as such has, so far, been given leeway to discuss human experiences that may be considered inappropriate for other genres. It is worth noting that this chapter is written from an Anglo-American perspective, and that in different cultures and countries opinions of comedy and comedy laws can differ.

In fictional comedy, the audience is generally separated from potentially offensive jokes as they understand that the narrative is imagined. However, fictional comedy based on real-world events can be more problematic. Producer Amy Poehler faced backlash for the show

---

and the subject matter of the joke. It is generally agreed by practitioners that it is appropriate to 'punch up' by making jokes about those in higher power, but not to 'punch down' on those who are in a lower position.

Difficult People (dir. Klausner, 2015–2017) when audiences considered a joke made by a character to be a step too far. A character within the show tweeted "I can't wait for Blue Ivy to be 18-year-old so R Kelly can piss on her", causing uproar on real-world Twitter. Here viewers expressed their disdain with tweets like: "A joke about R. Kelly assaulting Blue Ivy is not a joke targeting him. It's making light of what he did and punching down at his victims" (Twitter, 2015). This tweet was written by a verified account and received a high number of likes and retweets, with comments that reinforced the opinion given. The character in *Difficult People* faced a similar backlash as the writers, and so the overarching purpose of the fictional storyline appears to have been misunderstood: the purpose of the joke was to cause controversy for the character, and therefore the character had to deal with the repercussions of their actions, ultimately deciding to remove the tweet. The real-world writers faced a similar response and found themselves in the same scenario they had written for their character. However, the events of the show could not be reversed as easily as deleting a tweet, and by persecuting the writers, the real-world digital vigilantes appear to have underscored the social commentary written into the episode by behaving in the same way as their fictional counterparts. The character who was persecuted wrote the tweet to 'punch up' at R Kelly and received a negative response from her followers. This in turn led to the creators of the show receiving the same negative response in real life. The creators of the show not only wrote the tweet but also the fictional backlash which followed, and thus were already aware of the implications of the tweet, having condemned it themselves.

Comedy has been widely researched, though perhaps not as widely as other genres that are considered of a higher cultural capital, such as drama or blockbuster films that are accessible to a wider audience, and as such are under more pressure to be enjoyable for everyone. That being said, due to the discourse around comedy it still remains a relevant subject for discussion. Its relevance stems from the fact that "comedy plays an absolutely pivotal role in the construction of a cultural identity" (Medhurst, 2007, p. 1) and therefore helps to shape society and the people within it. The reason that comedy has not been as widely studied as the other genres is that "comedy has also been perceived as ephemeral or lacking in intellectual weight" (Stott, 2005, p. 18), because it is generally something that must be taken at face value. Here we should recall the perceived responsibility of texts of a higher cultural capital to tackle weightier issues. Based on Bourdieu's analysis, comedy should hold a low intellectual weight. However, with the development of Web 2.0 and social media, comedy can be shared widely, changing both its delivery and reception, which provides audiences an opportunity to express both enjoyment and offence.

The examples featured in this chapter include cases where discourse has strayed from fan response to social commentary, and developed into, or displayed elements of, digital vigilantism. Many of the examples began with audiences engaging in discussion, who were then joined by individuals who had never experienced the source text first hand. These responses then led to tensions between practitioners and their employers, which resulted in the enforcement of the actions and opinions of the digital vigilantes, or of the individuals showcasing vigilante-like behaviour. Though this discourse may not have been intentional, it directly affected the practitioners and as such the scale and implications of the response online developed into acts of digital vigilantism.

The next section of this chapter discusses the methodological approach taken to research this topic, explaining why the cases studies were chosen and how they are relevant to the research. The section 'Subscribe to Digital Vigilantism' examines vigilant audiences of YouTube, with a specific focus on the channel of Felix Kjellberg, known as PewDiePie, which has received both support and condemnation from vigilant audiences. Kjellberg has been accused of being racist and anti-Semitic, and so he lost contracts with big businesses including Disney. Yet he has also received support from audiences when at risk of losing his title as the most subscribed channel on YouTube. This section also discusses the case of Mark Meechan, a YouTuber whose comedy video resulted in him being prosecuted for a hate crime, despite him maintaining that the content of the video was not intended to cause offence. Both cases cover the way in which content, later described as satire, has been condemned by audiences. One of the key issues of both cases was the lack of clarity surrounding the satirical intention of the uploads, and the retrospective definition assigned by their creators. Kjellberg and Meechan, in their roles as YouTube content creators, lacked the credibility that would have been conferred by their having established careers as comedians, and the role of YouTube personality blurs the lines between reality star and fictional character.

The next section, 'Dapper Laughed' focuses on the work of Dapper Laughs, whose real name is Daniel O'Reilly. O'Reilly originally made short videos on the platform Vine, using shock tactics and offensive topics to attract viewers, but later moved from the platform to television. However, his offensive comedy, though originally what attracted his audience, eventually resulted in the cancellation of his series with ITV. The section also examines the comedian Frankie Boyle, who has been accused of producing racist and callous work both on television and on Twitter, but who successfully sued the newspaper, *The Mirror*, for defamation after they published such claims. Unlike Boyle, an established comedian, O'Reilly faced similar issues to Kjellberg and Meechan, in that his character Dapper Laughs was confused with his real self. However, O'Reilly played on this confusion following the response to his television work. The cases examined in this section discuss how vigilant audiences can follow targets from digital spaces into television and the wider community. Certain content appears to be deemed acceptable in digital spaces due to the space having a lower cultural value, but when moving onto television broadcast it is held to a higher level of scrutiny.

The third section is titled 'Your Fey is Problematic' and examines television comedy, and the issues faced when audiences conflate writer with character with actor. This section focuses on the works of Tina Fey and Ricky Gervais, who each have different approaches to dealing with vigilant audiences. It discusses issues of agency, and how individuals with different backgrounds or experiences can discuss and comment on topics that others may be unable to tackle. The concept of agency, or perceived agency (or lack thereof), affects the way in which audiences respond to and interpret a text, and thus whether the audiences may then become vigilant to certain content. The section also touches on how both Fey and Gervais have taken different approaches to responding to vigilant audiences and the affect this has had on their work, and how the cultural capital of their work, being primarily television-based rather than online, has affected reactions to it. Following Gray,

> Debates about what is it permissible to mock tend to be predicated
> upon assumptions about the target; whether an individual or a group is

vulnerable or too powerful, whether a joke serves to change or aggravate a situation. Narrative comedy complicates the mix further: its targets are fictional and in theory, one cannot hurt a fiction; but we are aware that things are not quite so simple. All arguments, however, that explore laughter's relationship to powerful emotions assume clear boundaries between joker, audience and target; the joker acts, the target suffers, the audience laughs (or not) (Gray, 2005, p. 146).

Methodology

The topic of comedy, audiences and digital vigilantism is ever changing, and as such this research was conducted with grounded theory, as its methods "consist of systematic, yet flexible guidelines for collecting and analysing qualitative data" (Charmaz, 2014, p. 2). As social trends and audience reactions develop, the subject of the research was continually developing, especially in the case of Kjellberg in the next section, and therefore the research approach had to be adaptable to new information and events.

This research also had an ethnographic approach, as I observed audiences engaging with texts — and each other — on Twitter and other digital spaces. Ethnography is appropriate as it "is the study of culture and ethnographic descriptions are creative endeavors that allow researchers a window to the world of a particular culture" (Schembri & Boyle, 2013, p. 1252), with digital vigilantes forming the particular culture in this instance. This research examined the way that audiences and businesses have responded to comedy practitioners and their content, as "typically ethnography begins in observation, proceeds analytically to deconstruct culture and social meaning, and then uses words to reconstruct reality as verbal description" (Margolis, 2002, p. 373). Data was collected by following popular events that appeared in the news, and searching for key terms on Twitter, such as #subscribetopewdiepie. I then examined the most popular tweets in terms of likes and retweets, which signified agreement from other users of the site. It was also important to follow the practitioners themselves, to witness the discourse they chose to engage with on the platform. Users of Twitter often engage in digital vigilantism based on the posts of other users, rather than responding to a specific original tweet. This meant that it was important to search for discussion that was validated by other users.

One of the major difficulties faced in this research is that comedy is inherently subjective. Every individual will experience comedy differently and, though this is integral to the efficacy of any joke or comedy piece, it can pose difficulties in terms of researcher bias. For this reason, I have refrained from presenting a judgement as to whether the cases cited are offensive, but rather provided a discussion on the reaction of audiences and digital vigilantes regarding each case. Another issue came from the ever-changing digital space. The discussion of Kjellberg could run on indefinitely due to his continued activity and discourse online.

Across the board, new examples of difficult comedy become apparent almost daily. For the purpose of this chapter, research was focussed primarily on Twitter, and avoided detailed discussions on personal blogs, Instagram and other social media. O'Reilly's videos as Dapper Laughs were made on Vine, a now defunct social media platform, so these videos are accessed today through YouTube.

The majority of cases discussed in this chapter feature white males, based in the United Kingdom. The profile of these individuals puts them in a majority, holding a position of cultural power, and as such they are at much greater risk of punching down rather than the more socially acceptable act of punching up. This makes their work inherently more problematic as they lack the agency to make fun of those in a minority. The first example discussed is Felix Kjellberg's YouTube channel. This was chosen because, at the beginning of this research, it was the most subscribed-to channel on the platform. Though online comedy may possess low cultural capital, Kjellberg's reach is so wide that his work may be regarded as having higher capital than he may have intended or expected. This means that, as a practitioner, he may have a greater responsibility to his audience to make his intentions explicit. This research examines responses to his YouTube videos, and his since deleted Twitter account, as well as discourse on Twitter surrounding the Subscribe to PewDiePie campaign.

The case of Mark Meechan is an appropriate comparison as he works in the same sphere, but with a much lower subscriber count and arguably possesses lower capital and responsibility. Despite his smaller audience, Meechan's joke led to prosecution, and therefore showcases the power of digital vigilantes. Dapper Laughs similarly, had lower responsibility due to the lower cultural capital of Vine, but this responsibility increased when given a television show with higher cultural capital. These three examples were selected as they feature individuals whose work relies on the confusion between character and reality, and all experienced changes in their employment or contracts due to the impact of digital vigilantes.

The Internet is a rapidly changing sphere and YouTube is ever-growing, with more than 2 billion active users as of November 2019. This, combined with the fact that 79% of Internet users claim to have a YouTube account, implies that the cultural capital of digital media, and in this case comedy, is changing faster than content creators can keep up with (Mohsin, 2019). Furthermore, Twitter has 145 million users daily (Lin, 2019), which means that there is massive scope for users to see and be drawn into digital vigilantism targeting content they may not have experienced first-hand, leading to further misinterpretation of what the creators may have originally intended. The scope of digital platforms is incredibly wide-ranging, with the potential to encapsulate target audiences of content creators, which makes YouTube and Twitter personalities excellent examples to show the impact of digital vigilantism.

The other examples discussed in this chapter are all comedians, or comedy writers, with more established careers that are not based primarily on YouTube or social media. These individuals are included as they have generated discourse online, in particular on Twitter. Interestingly, of the four practitioners, Boyle, Fey, Gervais and Poehler, the two female Americans, Fey and Poehler, have refrained from engaging in discussions on Twitter directly, putting them slightly out of the remit of this chapter, though still being subject to elements of digital vigilantism regarding their work. Boyle and Gervais however, continually engage in feedback from audiences via social media, making them more of a target for digital vigilantes. Poehler and Fey are relevant to this chapter however, as they discuss the issues they have faced from vigilant audiences through situational comedies, rather than responding directly to individuals. Boyle and Gervais are relevant examples as they faced similar responses to their work as the aforementioned YouTube and Vine personalities, however, they both were established in their field prior to the instances of vigilantism, leading to different experiences and outcomes.

There are many more individuals who could be examined, but these were chosen as they featured heavily in UK news at the height of their notoriety, and were discussed prominently online, particularly on Twitter where the discussions were trending. The main criteria for selection was cases where actions from vigilant audiences interfered with, or were perceived to interfere, with the career of the practitioner targeted.

Subscribe to Digital Vigilantism: How Have Vigilant Audiences Both Condemned and Supported Content Creators on YouTube?

In no other area of life than comedy would it be socially acceptable to "lie to friends and cause them inconvenience, even pain" (Morreall, 2009, p. 2) and yet in the context of comedy it is totally acceptable, as the pain results — theoretically — in laughter. In the realm of YouTube, viewers engage with content creators as though they were friends, with the ability to communicate directly by commenting on a video, or through other social media sites. This section examines the case of PewDiePie (real name Felix Kjellberg), who is well-known for being the most subscribed-to individual channel on YouTube. Over the past two years, Kjellberg has faced a severe backlash for his comedy videos, leading to real-world consequences for his work. Since then, however, he has regained support from his viewers because another channel, T-Series, came close to surpassing him in subscriber count. Lastly, this section looks at a case where an individual was taken to court due to the viewers' reactions to a comedy video he uploaded online.

Kjellberg began his channel in 2010, originally focussing on game playthroughs. His comedic reactions while playing the games were a significant factor in his growing popularity on the platform. In 2017 Kjellberg shifted from his original style of YouTube content, making more comedy vlogs and fewer video-game playthroughs. As part of these comedy videos, Kjellberg made a since deleted video where he ordered a selection of services from the website *Fiverr*. These services included paying a pair of men to dance while holding up a sign which read "Death to all Jews". Following on from this, other videos included paying a man dressed as Jesus to say 'Hitler did absolutely nothing wrong' (Winkler, Nicas, & Fritz, 2017). As a reaction to this, "in 2017 YouTube removed some advertisers from his channel... and Disney-owned Maker Studios cancelled a contract because some of his content appeared to be anti-Semitic" (Meyers, 2017). Several videos were removed by Kjellberg following the controversy. In defence of his content, Kjellberg also published a blog post on 12 February 2017, stating that "[he] was trying to show how crazy the modern world is, specifically some of the services available online" (Kjellberg, 2017).

If "comedy is the imitation of the ridiculous or unworthy aspects of human nature" (Stott, 2005, p. 19), then viewing Kjellberg's work as problematic is... problematic. The satirical nature of his content was not explicit, and as such Kjellberg failed to emphasise the ridiculousness of the work to audiences, which would have shown them that Kjellberg was not agreeing with the sentiment of the jokes, but rather condemning it. However, confusion has arisen around the difference between PewDiePie the character, and Kjellberg the content creator, much like the tweet in *Difficult People.* The complicated boundary between author and character will be discussed in more detail later in this chapter.

A major issue in this case is that much of the backlash developed following the publication of articles that condemned Kjellberg's content, and vigilant audiences responded directly to the content of the articles, rather than referring back to the original video. In John Cleese's live show *John Cleese Live! !—The Alimony Tour* (Cleese, 2011), Cleese discusses the concept of feeling anxiety as a result of comedy. He explains that when the film *A Fish Called Wanda* (dir. Crichton, 1988) was being viewed during its test screenings, the three most offensive moments of the film were also widely agreed to be the funniest. He then goes on to explain the reasoning behind this, stating that "when you get into taboo areas [...] there's always a little bit of anxiety" (Cleese, 2011). For some, the anxiety Cleese refers to leads to a viewer becoming so tense that they feel that they are offended, but for the majority this is what creates the comedy. Cleese describes this as: "You get the normal laugh, and then you get the extra energy that comes from that little bit of anxiety being liberated" (ibid.). To experience comedy is to willingly put yourself into a position of anxiety. Whether this is anxiety that you are personally subject to, or an anxiety that stems from witnessing another person experience anxiety — thus gaining pleasure from witnessing them be subject to it — is not entirely relevant. Anxiety caused from a comedic set up must not be so overwhelming that it overpowers the comedic relief, but there will always be different levels of anxiety that viewers or readers can cope with.

When Kjellberg's videos were cut and clips taken out of context, the set-up and punchline were separated, leaving the anxiety unliberated, and audiences offended. When discussing the situation in his blog post, Kjellberg stated that although not intentional, he understood that the jokes were "ultimately offensive" (Kjellberg, 2017). This response echoes Chaplin's delayed response to *The Great Dictator* but whether this came from personal reflection or purely to appease digital vigilantes may never be known.

However, recently audiences have rallied around Kjellberg, as another channel came close to surpassing his number of subscribers. T-Series is a channel dedicated to videos advertising and showcasing Bollywood films and music, and is "India's largest Music Label & Movie Studio" (T-Series, 2018). Fans and subscribers of Kjellberg's channel engaged in Twitter campaigns, using a variety of hashtags including #pewdiepievstseries to encourage others to subscribe to the PewDiePie channel. An individual known on Twitter as TheHackerGiraffe also claimed to have hacked thousands of computers to send out a message asking recipients to unsubscribe from T-Series and subscribe to PewDiePie. However, they also claimed that the reasoning behind their actions was actually to raise awareness of the dangers of having poor security, "Spread the word with your friends about printers and printer security! This is actually a scary matter. Will tweet everything about this entire #pewdiepie hack later to explain to everyone exactly what went down" (TheHackerGiraffe, 2018). The user also expressed an understanding of vigilant audiences who responded to their invasive actions by tweeting later "To all those who wanna dox me, you'll never find out where I live!" (TheHackerGiraffe, 2018).

As the 'Subscribe to PewDiePie' meme spread however, it developed consequences outside the remit of the original light-hearted campaign. A self-proclaimed fan vandalised a World War Two memorial with the campaign slogan, causing Kjellberg to condemn the actions on his YouTube channel, telling his viewers "don't do anything illegal because obviously that would look bad on me" and that the vandalism is "obviously disgusting" and that he does not condone such actions (Kjellberg, 2019). A conflict developed between vigilantes acting for, and against, Kjellberg.

On 15 March 2019, there was an even greater shift in the campaign, as a terrorist who attacked a mosque in New Zealand used his online broadcast to record his final words: "Subscribe to PewDiePie". Though this does not directly fit into the subject of digital vigilantism, it occurred as a response to popular media, and is it interesting to note Kjellberg's response to the attack. Initially he only discussed the event on his Twitter account, stating that he was "absolutely sickened having my name uttered by this person" (Kjellberg, 2019), and continued to post videos pertaining to the meme/campaign. However, on 29 April 2019 Kjellberg uploaded a short video to YouTube declaring that he wanted to end the meme, explaining that though he appreciated the support, he "didn't want hateful acts to overpower all these amazing things that people are doing" (Kjellberg, 2019), stating that he should have ended the 'Subscribe to PewDiePie' campaign following the Christchurch shooting. Kjellberg, as a practitioner, lost control of his work as audiences engaged with and changed its meaning. Though Kjellberg attempted to regain control and enjoyed the support of a large group of digital vigilantes engaging in playful behaviour to boost his subscriber count, ultimately his actions were ineffective as the discourse developed by digital vigilantes and news reporters was too great.

DV is "a form of mediated and coordinated action" (Trottier, 2017, p. 57), so although in this case the audience was not necessarily persecuting Kjellberg, they are showcasing similar actions and behaviours as digital vigilantes to maintain their perceived ideal social order. Though there was originally a highly tongue-in-cheek element to the campaign, its coordination and unremitting execution imitates the actions of digital vigilantes, though individuals engaged in actions that opposed Kjellberg's original intention.

In 2016, a YouTuber, Count Dankula, whose real name is Mark Meechan, posted a video in which he had trained his girlfriend's pug to respond to anti-Semitic language and perform the Nazi salute. The video was viewed over 3 million times before it was removed from YouTube

(BBC, 2018). Meechan claimed that the video was made solely to annoy his girlfriend, but as it was uploaded to an open platform, the video was available to the public to view, and subsequently Meechan was taken to court under the Communications Act of 2003, which "makes it an offence to use a public communications network to send certain types of messages including those that are grossly offensive or threatening" ('PF v Mark Meechan — Judgments & Sentences — Judiciary of Scotland', 2018).

Other comedians took to defend Meechan, with Ricky Gervais tweeting "If you don't believe in a person's right to say things that you might find 'grossly offensive', then you don't believe in Freedom of Speech" (Gervais, 2018). Returning to the discussion of cultural capital, different levels of comedy come with a different cultural capital. Digital comedy such as that on YouTube is relatively new, but is comparable to slapstick in that slapstick is often considered to be of the lowest cultural capital. Slapstick is said to be "popular, rather than literary, low physical comedy" (Dale, 2002, p. 1). In addition to this, in a paper originally written in 1987 discussing situational comedy, Paul Attallah states that "in the classic dichotomy between high art and low art, television definitely occupies the region of low art" (Attallah, 2010, p. 14). The paper was written before the advent of YouTube, and as such the platform is excluded from the analysis, but based on the placement of television as lower than film, books and plays, YouTube would arguably be classed as a lower artform than even television. From this we can infer that the more accessible, or popular, comedy is, the more it must be of interest to the lowest level of society, or at least carry the lowest cultural weight. YouTube is an entirely accessible source of entertainment, and therefore arguably on the lowest rung of the ladder of cultural capital. This then raises questions of whether comedy on this platform should be judged on the same level as other means of speech or comedy production, or whether the content creator should be more considerate of the potential reach of their work. Attallah also states that "There is a strong sense in which television and everything connected to it is seen as unworthy [...] of critical evaluation" (ibid., p. 90), and this statement could also be applied to content on YouTube.

Though vigilant audiences highlighted the video and were the reason why Meechan was taken to court, audiences also raised nearly

£200,000 to cover Meechan's legal fees, via a GoFundMe account he set up. Meechan posted several update videos in the year following the upload of the original video, *M8 Yur dug's a Naazi*. In the first video he stated that "the public response to the video was kinda overwhelmingly positive [sic]", however, he described how one of Meechan's neighbours approached him in their street and told him "you Nazi bastard, you're a Nazi bastard [sic]". The neighbour's vigilante actions, which were physical rather than digital, went on to include emptying a bin from the dog park on Meechan's front door. Meechan explains in the video that they reported the neighbour for these actions, expecting a charge for damage to property. However, the neighbour was later arrested for a hate crime — not for their physical actions, but for accusing Meechan of being a Nazi (Meechan, 2016).

Meechan goes on to defend his video by saying "I've had Jewish people messaging me saying that they don't agree with what I did but they say I shouldn't have been arrested for that [sic]", and that "[he] didn't expect it to be on the front page of Reddit [sic]". He also implies that he lost his job due to the high level of media coverage of the video, though his employer refused to provide a reason for the termination of his contract. Meechan also states that, if you watch his videos, he makes it very clear that he does not agree with discrimination of any kind, but that it is clear he is a fan of offensive comedy, such as the work of Frankie Boyle who is discussed later in this chapter. Meechan reiterated that "[he doesn't] think we should bring harm to anyone for any reason", however, Meechan also believed that with the backing of the English or Scottish Defence League, he would have been able engage in similar behaviour without facing any charges, and if he were part of an organisation, Meechan felt that his actions would be "recognised as free speech", even though his actions as an individual were taken to court.

In Meechan's third video, he briefly explains some of the details around his court case. In the video he mentions witnesses speaking at the trial and asks his audience "Do not [...] contact them or harass them [sic]", implying that digital vigilantes may have tried to defend Meechan by turning on those speaking against him in court. It is important to note that Meechan has a much lower subscriber count on YouTube than

Kjellberg and as such his video may have gone unnoticed by the courts had it not been for digital vigilantes sharing the video.

This section shows the ways in which audiences can both condemn and support content creators on YouTube and can carry those vigilante elements into real world spaces, through printer hacking, or court cases. The speed with which content can be uploaded and spread, often further than initially intended, allows audiences to engage with content quickly and form instant opinions and reactions to it. In the case of Felix Kjellberg, the Subscribe to PewDiePie campaign developed in ways apparently outside of his control. There are also plenty of incidents regarding Kjellberg, and other YouTube content creators, that could inform further research, such as a scandal in 2017 when Kjellberg used a racial slur during a live stream, and again in 2018, when Kjellberg promoted a channel that transpired to be pro-Nazi.

Dapper Laughed: How Have Vigilant Audiences Followed Independent Comedians from Online Spaces to the Mainstream?

This section examines how audiences have followed practitioners from online spaces as they moved to work in television and on stage. In particular, this section focuses on Dapper Laughs, also known as Daniel O'Reilly, who originally began creating content on Vine and was picked up by the channel ITV to develop a television series. The character of Dapper Laughs blurs the line between content creator and character, something that other comedy practitioners appear to try to differentiate between rather than actively confuse. O'Reilly's offensive humour was considered relatively acceptable on the Vine platform, but in moving to television, a platform with higher levels of cultural capital, visibility and regulation, this humour was no longer acceptable. This is further discussed when looking at comedian Frankie Boyle, whose offensive humour, both on television and Twitter, led to claims that his comedy style caused him to step down from his role with the BBC.

Dapper Laughs garnered success on the mobile platform Vine for his short sketches discussing dating, sex, inconveniencing strangers and occasionally British politics. O'Reilly faced some backlash against his comedy, especially due to his inclusion of strangers who may not have been aware of or willing to participate in his videos, as well as the sexist nature of some of his content. However, the fact that this backlash was only minor when his work was restricted to a social media platform is something that ties in with theories of cultural capital, as he represented himself as an individual; he did not represent a production company or channel. Due to the success of his Vine channel, Dapper Laughs was offered his own television programme with ITV2; *Dapper Laughs On The Pull*. ITV defended their choice of the controversial comedian, releasing a statement saying "We realise that all humour is subjective and accept that Dapper's humour is more risqué but feel that his unique brand of banter and brash charm is neither sexist or degrading to women" (ITV, via huffingtonpost.co.uk, 2014). However, during a live show, O'Reilly discusses some of the press response to his television series, where it had been described as a "Rapist's Almanac" (Kern, 2014). During the show, O'Reilly, performing as Dapper Laughs, made a comment directed at a female audience member saying that "she's gagging for a rape" (O'Reilly, 2014). A change.org petition, a form of digital vigilantism, was created asking ITV to pull the show from the air and received 67,860 supporters. ITV later released a statement to say that the show would not be continuing for a second series, after they had "given careful thought to the recent criticism of the character Dapper Laughs, which has focused on his activities outside of the ITV2 programme" (ITV, 2014).

Due to the premise of his Vines and his subsequent show, Dapper Laughs was not seen to be an actor playing a character and so audiences felt that everything that was said was a genuine opinion and belief. In interviews following the incident, the man behind Dapper Laughs, Daniel O'Reilly, revealed that the character was nothing more than that; a character. He went on to explain that he has "never said [he condones] rape" (O'Reilly, via Independent.co.uk, 2015) but in the view of the audience this was not enough to undo the outcry at his comments, which was then reflected in the producers' action.

In late 2014, O'Reilly appeared on BBC's *Newsnight* (2014), and declared that Dapper Laughs was a character he had created and that the views of the character were absolutely not views of his own. He stated of the videos, "that's not real, obviously I don't think that", and that in his work he was "taking the mic out of what [he] thought men think".

Part of O'Reilly's defence was that "[he] didn't see it was [him] saying it, [he] was creating this character", and that "[he] didn't realise [he] was causing that much of a problem". During the interview, O'Reilly declared that "[he did not] want to be seen to approve of it" and that "Dapper Laughs is gone". O'Reilly also spoke of how he was going to work towards preventing the work being shared and that he would no longer be continuing with the character.

However, shortly after denouncing the Dapper Laughs character, O'Reilly released the *Res-Erection* show, which had a trailer featuring Dapper Laughs descending from heaven, and switching places with Daniel O'Reilly who was shown wearing the same outfit that he wore in the *Newsnight* interview. This raised concerns about whether the initial apology was genuine. Although O'Reilly never returned to ITV, he continued to profit from the Dapper Laughs character.

In early 2018, O'Reilly appeared on the UK version of *Celebrity Big Brother* (Channel 5, 2018) and in his introductory video he states "my name is Daniel O'Reilly, but unfortunately some of you may know me as Dapper Laughs" (Channel 5, 2018), making it apparent that he is still content to profit by his infamous character. This links back to the aforementioned issue faced by Dapper Laughs: his mistake was that he was not already rooted in people's minds as a likeable person and as such they were only able to see him as the offensive character, meaning that the actor Daniel O'Reilly had no opportunity to truly justify himself, and therefore "he's reinforcing the behaviour rather than knocking it" (Bennett, theindependent.co.uk, 2014). This left O'Reilly open to digital vigilantes who condemned his offensive actions.

A comedian who has seemingly had more success in walking the fine line between comedic, tongue-in-cheek offence, and harsher, more provocative offence, Frankie Boyle has written about the issues of taste, offence and censorship in comedy. One of Boyle's most controversial tweets, which has since been removed, was "Jimmy Savile did an incredible amount of charity work towards the end of his life, just to be sure he could shag Madeleine McCann in heaven" (original Tweet removed from Google search under the Court of Justice of the European Union (CJEU) right to be forgotten). Making light of missing child Madeleine McCann is considered distasteful as the girl has never been found, and her story was heavily covered by the media, in some ways raising the cultural capital of the case. Boyle made the assumption that the girl is dead, and added a reference to the recent discovery that former children's television presenter Jimmy Savile was a paedophile. This may bring so much distress to the reader, that the anxiety — as mentioned by Cleese earlier in this chapter — caused by discussing the topic cannot, for most people, be outweighed by the release. This attracted digital vigilantes who called attention to the poor taste of the joke. To explain his joke would be to remove the comedic elements to it, as most comedy comes from the relief or surprise generated by the punchline. In the case of this joke, the punchline may have been taken out of context, or audiences understood the context and still rejected it as content that offended them, suggesting that the anxiety generated by the joke was too much. This led to digital vigilantes condemning Boyle and his work.

Frankie Boyle has also written about his opinions and experiences of audiences taking offence at something, without ever experiencing the original text. Following the Charlie Hebdo attacks in France in early 2015, he took to his website to write a blog post about his experiences with offence and comedy, which has since been removed. Boyle explains that "we no longer need to hear the actual content of the thing we're told to be offended by" (Boyle, 2015), and this is a very real problem in the interpretation of comedy. His post generally explains his frustrations with the media, stating that "comedians get attacked for making jokes" (ibid.) and as such audiences — or the media itself — seem to be struggling with the fact that offence, if present, is a part of the comedy, and not an insensitive or inadvertent side-effect of the humour. Frankie Boyle discusses the fact that comedy, in general, is a work of fiction, and that "even on a good day I only really half agree with myself" (ibid.) and thus even if he says something distasteful and offensive it does not equate to his actual beliefs. It is simply that if a joke is funny he will say it anyway, and he does not have any interest in the ensuing aftermath: "I don't really give a fuck about [...] someone who might find a group of words in the wrong order too much to bear" (ibid.). Boyle also discusses the idea of moral superiority, in that we now seem to associate being offended with being morally superior, and therefore more intelligent, which again, could be an application of cultural capital; if you are morally superior, then you are culturally superior. As discussed previously, in the past comedy has avoided such interrogation due to its low cultural capital, but by reading comedy and taking offence to it, the audience has raised its cultural capital. This reading, however, may not always follow the intention of the author, as Boyle defended his comedy by stating that "we have given taking offence a social status it doesn't deserve: it's not much more than a way of avoiding difficult conversations" (ibid.). In an article on satirical literacy and social responsibility, Jessie LaFrance Dunbar discusses "the audience's responsibility as consumers of sociopolitical comedy" (2017, p. 79), and the importance of reading comedy appropriately. This, however, depends on the audience's understanding of the nature of the comedy, which is reliant on the comedian, or practitioner, framing it correctly, as either satire, observation, etc.

Vigilant audiences are not restricted to commenting on issues that exist in online spaces. Though the work of Daniel O'Reilly began on an online forum, when he moved to television and physical spaces, his work began to reach wider audiences who were less familiar with his work, attracting vigilant audiences. In the case of Frankie Boyle, though primarily based on television, he also made use of Twitter, and his comments there opened him up to retort from digital vigilantes. However, in contrast to O'Reilly, Boyle has since continued to work online, using his blog to communicate with vigilant audiences and to continue the discourse surrounding the difficulties of working in comedy.

Your Fey is Problematic: How Are Vigilant Audiences Conflating Character with Writer?

This section focuses on the works of comedy writers and performers Tina Fey and Ricky Gervais, by examining the agency, or perceived agency, which they each have. They have both received responses from digital vigilantes based on their work, and have different approaches to responding to such comments. The issue of audiences conflating fictional character with writer has been present throughout this chapter, but with the previous examples, the individuals were working within a frame in which they were playing a version of themselves. Much of the vigilantism directed towards both Fey and Gervais discusses the actions of the characters that they have written, rather than their personal comments or actions. Though some audiences may be taking issue with the content of the writing, others seem to misunderstand the difference between writer and character, especially when the writer and actor are one and the same. When it comes to digital vigilantism, audiences can spread information and opinions faster than the content created by the targets can be released, especially with regards to television broadcast, which takes longer to produce than online content such as Vines or YouTube videos. Television also holds greater cultural capital than online spaces, and this affects the esteem in which audiences hold the content that they view.

Comedians Amy Poehler and Tina Fey have generated discourse in their work as comedians, using their status to promote feminism on many occasions. Being women in an industry primarily dominated by men brings attention to their work, and they were praised for presenting the 2015 Golden Globes, where they used their comedy personalities to draw attention to much of the sexism that exists in Hollywood. One journalist said that the media coverage of the Golden Globes is "the exact spot where feminism all but dies in America" (Freeman, 2015), and she praised Poehler and Fey for their ability to overcome this in the humour as they presented the awards, describing the event as "a feminist awards show" (ibid.). As women, a category that could be considered a minority in Hollywood, they have the power to punch up, due to the repression they face. Freeman goes on to explain that their gender is not the only reason their performance was so successful: "while they are generally lauded as being the most likable people in show business, they aren't always all that nice" (ibid.). Although what they say might be, to an extent, offensive, or distasteful, the fact that Poehler and Fey are so likeable means that they have the agency to say things that would otherwise be considered unlikeable.

Fey manages the issue of 'punching down' in *The Unbreakable Kimmy Schmidt* (dir. Carlock & Fey, 2015–2019), which follows the tale of Kimmy Schmidt as she adjusts to life after having spent fifteen years kidnapped by a religious zealot and imprisoned in a bunker. The character wears bright colours and is always smiling, upbeat despite her past, and it is easy to forget the trauma that she and her fellow cult members went through. Nevertheless, the show manages to acknowledge the horrible situation while remaining funny and without punching down at the victims. This is primarily down to the optimistic protagonist Kimmy, and her resilience in the face of adversity. The shows punches in all directions, as it targets the poor unfortunate characters as well as the rich and successful ones. Even when Kimmy is the butt of the joke, she eventually succeeds, and each character in the show is the butt of a joke at some point or another. As such it provides its viewers with a level of equality: unfortunate things happen to each of the characters in turn, but with no individual character bearing the brunt of the misfortune. The series is successful in generating (potentially) offensive narratives for its characters without incurring a significant backlash, as it is indiscriminate in its assault but fundamentally on the side of its characters.

Fey has also used the series to discuss issues of agency and taste, most notably in the episode *Kimmy Goes To A Play!* (dir. Carlock & Fey, 2016, release date 15 April). A character named Titus performs a play based on his past life as a Geisha, and audiences within the show flock to watch his performance and shame him for cultural appropriation. The fictional audience is outraged at the idea of the play before seeing it, but change their opinion after watching the play and trusting Titus' authenticity. This episode reads as a response to real-life cases when audiences have reacted negatively to a work before they have experienced it themselves, often discovering the work through digital vigilantes.

Fey has faced commentary from vigilant audiences, as an individual, as a writer and as a character. The website *Your Fave is Problematic* (yourfaveisproblematic.tumblr.com) is dedicated to pointing out and sharing problematic behaviour by a variety of popular individuals and celebrities, with the tagline "Problematic shit your favourite celebrities have done" (Tumblr, 2017). Though there is a definite vigilante element to the website, they do make a point of explaining that they are not trying to actively attack those that they deem problematic, instead asking visitors to the site to keep an eye on their favourite celebrities and "If they do something problematic, call them out on it" (ibid.). Rather than attacking celebrities, the site encourages visitors to educate and inform them. The website has generated discussion around Tina Fey and her work, as she was featured on the website, but other Tumblr users submitted rebuttals of the condemnation. One user points out that "Feminist Humour often employs stereotypes, not [as] a way of reinforcing them but as a way of destabilising them [sic]" (Tumblr, 2016). The user goes on to defend the work by explaining that "when the character [...] does something terrible we are supposed to recognise it as terrible [...] If you jump straight to an offensive reaction, you miss out on this tripartite response" (ibid.). This links back to the concept of cultural capital: if audiences consider comedy to be of low capital then they may only want to accept what they are shown at face value, rather than learning to consume and read the text as discussed previously. However, audiences online are discussing a deeper meaning, which changes their response to the text. In her article on satirical literacy, Dunbar states that "students are ill-equipped to discern, let alone communicate, which aspects of the text are meant to be humorous and which are meant to invite thoughtful consideration" (2017, p. 84), and this is likely to be the case for audiences, who have had no training in reading comedy. This lack of understanding in how to read a text can lead to audiences confusing writers with the fictional characters they have created, or missing the text's intended message.

One major difference between Tina Fey and Ricky Gervais is their online presence. Fey tends to steer away from direct online contact with audiences, while Gervais has a Twitter account with over 13 million followers, and as already mentioned, has spoken out about issues of offensive comedy, such as the case of Mark Meechan. Gervais has also presented the Golden Globes, in the years prior to Poehler and Fey, and has said that hosting the show again "would have been the end of [his] career" (Gervais, 2018, via *The Hollywood Reporter*), due to the controversial nature of a lot of Gervais' work.

Gervais uses his Twitter account not only to engage with his fans, but also those who take issue with his work, using the platform to explain his stance on problematic comedy, as exemplified by this tweet:

> Please stop saying 'You can't joke about anything anymore'. You can. You can joke about whatever the fuck you like. And some people won't like it and they will tell you they don't like it. And then it's up to you whether you give a fuck or not. And so on. It's a good system (Gervais, 2018).

By engaging directly with digital vigilantes, Gervais continues the discussion on his own terms.

Generally, once a piece of fiction has been written, the author can have no more say in it. This can apply to screenplays or television, but also to social media, like Vine and Twitter. If a person says something as a fictitious character or personality then it cannot be rescinded as a joke after readers have been offended by it. A writer is, to most audiences, invisible, and therefore needs to be wary that what they put into their work cannot be misconstrued, and that is their responsibility. If a viewer is offended by something that writer has chosen to say then — if the comedy is good — they were probably meant to be offended. Yet if a viewer is offended by something the writer did not mean then that may be attributed to poor writing. "Once an author is removed, the claim to decipher a text becomes quite futile" (Barthes & Heath, 1977, p. 147) and so the writer is powerless. This ties back to ideas of high-culture and low-culture comedy. Audiences misunderstood the joke, so perhaps it was too high-brow, but to explain a joke is to remove the revelation of the punchline, and thus it ceases to be a joke, or piece of comedy. There are allegedly two ways to remove this issue of offence and censorship from comedy, the first being 'to retain the claim that comedy expresses feelings of superiority' but the second is to discard the first in favour of 'one in which laughter and humour are based in something that is not anti-social' (Morreall, 2009, p. 8).

Conclusion

Comedians in digital spaces such as YouTube or Twitter are seen more as peers than celebrities, actors or writers playing characters. This leaves them open to criticism from digital vigilantes who disagree with the content of their work, even if the work was originally intended as satire or parody. This is further complicated by the current issue of fake news, though that is an area of research outside the remit of this chapter. In online spaces, social hierarchy is removed, and audiences can respond to practitioners in the same way as they may respond to a friend or colleague. This means that they may also hold comedy practitioners to the same standard as they would their real-world associates. In digital spaces, a joke can also become removed from author or context and misunderstood, leading to vigilante-like responses that may in fact align with the point of view of the practitioner to whom they are objecting.

Although "traditions [...] have informed the ways in which comedy and entertainment programming have been shot, promoted and understood" (Mills, 2007, p. 180), with development in media, and changes to the way television is viewed and received, these traditions need to move forward. Comedy needs to have an "unexpected turn or dénouement, the punch line" (Kuipers, 2006, p. 5). As we are exposed to more comedy, from different and sometimes unexpected sources, writers and comedians try harder to surprise their audiences. This can lead to viewers being subject to comedy that they find difficult or uncomfortable, and then sharing their feelings online. Sometimes, this can be justified, if the supposed joke causes genuine offense, such as on grounds of homophobia, racism, sexism, etc. But at other times, humour may raise these issues intentionally, to raise awareness, to parody difficult subjects, or to educate viewers on their own behaviour.

Both author and audience have a responsibility to understand whether a joke is a parody or offensive. As stated earlier, comedy, in general, must be taken at face value, and so for both parties to engage in the comedy there must be an agreement between author and audience. If the practitioner does not contextualise the joke, either by defining it as satire, or by offering an explanation, then the agreement has been broken, but likewise if the audience decontextualises the joke then they too have broken the agreement. Both the lack of clarity and decontextualisation can turn audiences or fans into digital vigilantes as they work to reinforce the worldview that they feel has been broken. It is also a way for audiences to distance themselves from a practitioner whom they no longer wish to be affiliated with. "Humour needs to be both understood *and permitted* in order to be a joke" (Lockyer & Pickering, 2005, p. 80, emphasis in original), and it is the responsibility of both the practitioner and audience to make clear, and understand, its intent. Despite the idea that comedy is of low cultural capital, its words are given weight, and if they are to be treated in this way then comedy in general should be considered of higher standing. However, if we begin to take comedy more seriously, we need to understand that this may change its very nature. Despite this consideration, "no single intellectual viewpoint can hope to account for the complexities of comedy" (Medhurst, 2007, p. 2), and as such the discussion may extend indefinitely.

Overall, this research has shown that there are three key circumstances in which audiences take offence to comedy. The first is when audiences engage with comedic elements that are separated from context, which can occur intentionally to discredit a comic, or accidentally, if discussing a component piece of a wider comedy. When the offensive content is removed from its context, audiences miss the 'release' and are therefore left with the anxiety, and none of the humour. The second is when the audience fails to separate the actor or writer from the flawed character they are performing or writing. When this happens, audiences misdirect anger at an offensive comment or action towards the actor or writer, rather than experiencing the intended story of the flawed character engaging in offensive or problematic actions. The third circumstance occurs when the comedy is, or appears to be, incorrectly positioned in the joke/action, either due to the power dynamic of the practitioner in relation to the text, or the setting in which it is told. Audiences, whether actively aware or not, can differentiate between humour that punches up and that which punches down. This relates back to the release of humour, as audiences' anxiety abates when they understand that the subject of the joke is in a position of power, but when they see the comedian laughing at an individual who cannot defend themselves, or who is in a low position socially and economically, they retain the anxiety and cannot find humour in the message. In online spaces, audiences can share their dissatisfaction with ease and find like-minded individuals. This coordination in online spaces can lead to their criticism developing into digital vigilantism, and subsequently creating issues for the comedy practitioners targeted.

References

Attallah, P. (2010). Television discourse and situation comedy. *Canadian Review of American Studies*, 40(1), 1–24, https://doi.org/10.1353/crv.0.0055

Barthes, R., & Heath, S. (1977). *Image, Music, Text*. New York: Hill and Wang.

BBC (2018, 20 March). Man guilty of hate crime over 'Nazi pug'. (2018). BBC. com, https://www.bbc.co.uk/news/uk-scotland-glasgow-west-43478925

BBC Newsnight. (2014, November 11). "Dapper Laughs is gone" WARNING: OFFENSIVE LANGUAGE — Daniel O'Reilly — Newsnight. YouTube, https://www.youtube.com/watch?v=lBt3fr5viAE

Bourdieu, P. (1984). *Distinction: A Social Critique of the Judgement of Taste*. Cambridge, MA: Harvard University Press.

Boyle, F. (2015). Offence and free speech, http://www.frankieboyle.com/frankie/freespeech.html

Burrell, I. (2014, November 10). ITV under fire over Dapper Laughs' 'rape comedy routine'. *The Independent*, https://www.independent.co.uk/arts-entertainment/tv/news/dapper-laughs-itv-under-fire-over-dating-show-vlogger-s-rape-comedy-routine-9852224.html

Celebrity Big Brother series 22. (2018). [TV Series] Channel 5.

Chaplin, C. (1964). *My Autobiography*. New York: Simon and Schuster, https://archive.org/details/myautobiography00chaprich

Chaplin, C. *The Great Dictator*. (1940). [film] United States: United Artists Corp. Ltd.

Charmaz, K. (2014). *Constructing Grounded Theory*. London: Sage.

Chrichton, C. (1998). *A Fish Called Wanda* [Film]. UK: Prominent Features.

Cleese, J. (2011). *John Cleese Live! — The Alimony Tour* [DVD]. UK: ITV Studios Home Entertainment.

Dale, A. (2000). *Comedy is a Man in Trouble*. Minneapolis: University of Minnesota Press.

Dapper Laughs: On The Pull (2014). [Series] ITV2: Daniel O'Reilly.

Difficult People. (2015–2017). [TV series] Hulu: Julie Klausner.

Dunbar, J. L. (2017). Teaching satirical literacy and social responsibility through race comedy. *MELUS: Multi-Ethnic Literature of the U.S.*, 42(4), 79–91, https://doi.org/10.1093/melus/mlx067

Eleftheriou-Smith, L. (2015, July 26). Dapper Laughs says 'gagging for a rape' comments came from a woman. *The Independent*, http://www.independent.co.uk/news/people/dapper-laughs-attempts-to-defendinfamous-gagging-for-a-rape-comment-10416793.html

Fey, Tina & Robert Carlock, *Unbreakable Kimmy Schmidt*. (2015–2019). [Series] Netflix.

Freeman, H. (2015, January 12). How Amy Poehler and Tina Fey made the Golden Globes the first feminist film awards ceremony. *The Guardian*, http://www.theguardian.com/film/filmblog/2015/jan/12/amy-poehler-tina-fey-golden-globes

Gervais, R. (2018). Twitter, https://twitter.com/rickygervais/status/1079784120945967104

Gervais, R. (2018). Twitter, https://twitter.com/rickygervais/status/976115287991910400

Goodyer, L. (2014). Dapper Laughs stand up comedy london scala part 1. YouTube, https://www.youtube.com/watch?v=9bOZ7Vl5Kuc&feature=youtu.be&t=10m47s

Gray, F. (2005). Privacy, embarrassment and social power: British sitcom. In Lockyer, S., & Pickering, M. (eds), *Beyond a Joke* (pp. 146–161). Basingstoke: Palgrave MacMillan, https://doi.org/10.1057/9780230236776_8

ITV. (2014, November 10) ITV announces Dapper Laughs show is axed. *ITV.com*, https://www.itv.com/news/update/2014-11-10/itv-decides-not-to-continue-dapper-laughs-show

Kern, L. (2014, September 12). you've helped create a rapist's almanac: An open letter to those who brought dapper laughs to TV. *Huffington Post*, https://www.huffingtonpost.co.uk/lee-kern/dapper-laughs-sexism_b_5959094.html

Kjellberg, F. (2019). [online] Twitter via web archive, https://web.archive.org/web/20190315050511/https://twitter.com/pewdiepie/status/1106419935390171136

Kjellberg, F. (2019). Ending the subscribe to pewdiepie meme. YouTube, https://www.youtube.com/watch?v=Ah5MYGQBYRo

Kjellberg, F. (2019). Please stop this PEW NEWS. YouTube, https://www.youtube.com/watch?v=nR3pamVhIMk

Kjellberg, F. (2017). Tumblr, http://pewdie.tumblr.com/post/157160889655/just-to-clear-some-things-up

Kuipers, G., & Simms, K. (2016). *Good Humor, Bad Taste*. Berlin: Mouton de Gruyter, https://doi.org/10.1515/9783110898996.1

Lin, Ying/Oberlo. (2019). 10 twitter statistics every marketer should Know in 2020 [Infographic], https://www.oberlo.co.uk/blog/twitter-statistics

Lockyer, S., & Pickering, M. (2009). *Beyond a Joke*. Basingstoke: Palgrave Macmillan, https://doi.org/10.1057/9780230236776

Lodge, D., & Wood, N. (2008). *Modern Criticism and Theory*. Hoboken: Taylor & Francis, https://doi.org/10.4324/9781315835488

MacDonald, S. (2018, August 9). Mark Meechan: No appeal for man who taught dog Nazi salute. The *Times*, https://www.thetimes.co.uk/article/mark-meechan-no-appeal-for-man-who-taught-dog-nazi-salute-m95ghqkf6

Margolis, E. (1990). Visual Ethnography: 'Tools for Mapping the AIDS Epidemic'. *Journal of Contemporary Ethnography* 19(3), 370-91, https://doi.org/10.1177/089124190019003006

Medhurst, A. (2007). *A National Joke*. London: Routledge, https://doi.org/10.4324/9780203022566

Meechan, M. (2016). Nazi Pug: Update #1. YouTube, https://www.youtube.com/watch?v=7zoqqCnEVLQ

Meechan, M. (2016). Nazi Pug: Update #2. YouTube, https://www.youtube.com/watch?v=lBsPreUiWy0

Meechan, M. (2017). Nazi Pug: Update #3. YouTube, https://www.youtube.com/watch?v=Oy64xTwjZMk

Meechan, M. (2018). The price of freedom is £800. YouTube, https://www.youtube.com/watch?v=5VDfcrDHvzE

Meyers, C. (2017). Social media influencers: A lesson plan for teaching digital advertising media literacy. *Advertising & Society Quarterly*, 18(2), http://www.doi.org/10.1353/asr.2017.0018

Mills, B. (2009). *The Sitcom.* Edinburgh: Edinburgh University Press, https://doi.org/10.3366/edinburgh/9780748637515.001.0001

Mohsin, Maryam/Oberlo. (2019). 10 Youtube stats every marketer should know in 2020 [Infographic]. 29th February 2020, https://www.oberlo.co.uk/blog/youtube-statistics

Morreall, J. (2009). *Comic Relief.* Chichester: Wiley-Blackwell, https://doi.org/10.1002/9781444307795

Morris, D. (1993). The culture of pain. *The Clinical Journal of Pain*, 9(1), 61, http://www.doi.org/10.1097/00002508-199303000-00023

O'Reilly, D. (2014). Dapperlaughs. Vine, https://vine.co/u/955854828289077248

Perez, L. (2018, January 18). Ricky Gervais says hosting Golden Globes again "would have been the end of my career". *Hollywood Reporter*, https://www.hollywoodreporter.com/live-feed/ricky-gervais-says-hosting-golden-globes-again-would-have-been-end-my-career-1075569

PF v Mark Meechan — Judgments & Sentences — Judiciary of Scotland. (2018), http://www.scotland-judiciary.org.uk/8/1962/PF-v-Mark-Meechan

Rolfe Winkler, J. (2017, February 14). Disney severs ties With YouTube Star PewDiePie after anti-Semitic posts. *WSJ.com*, https://www.wsj.com/articles/disney-severs-ties-with-youtube-star-pewdiepie-after-anti-semitic-posts-1487034533

Schembri, S., & Boyle, M. (2013). Visual ethnography: Achieving rigorous and authentic interpretations. *Journal of Business Research*, 66(9), 1251–54, https://doi.org/10.1016/j.jbusres.2012.02.021

Stott, A. (2005). *Comedy.* New York: Routledge, https://doi.org/10.4324/9780203312124

TheHackerGiraffe. (2018). Twitter, https://web.archive.org/web/20181201090000, https://twitter.com/HackerGiraffe/status/1068498480174370816

TheHackerGiraffe. (2018). Twitter, https://twitter.com/HackerGiraffe/status/1070192143657000967

T-Series. (2018). YouTube, https://www.youtube.com/user/tseries/about

Trottier, D. (2017). Digital vigilantism as weaponisation of visibility. *Philosophy & Technology*, 30(1), 55–72, https://doi.org/10.1007/s13347-016-0216-4

Tumblr. (2016), https://mindibindi.tumblr.com

Tumblr. (2017), https://your-fave-is-problematic.tumblr.com/post/1574537743 63/tina-fey

Twitter. (2015). jamilah on Twitter, https://twitter.com/JamilahLemieux/status/ 633336510461272064

Wootson Jr., C. (2017, September 13). This video showed a Nazi-saluting dog. Was posting it on YouTube a hate crime? *The Washington Post*, https:// www.washingtonpost.com/news/the-intersect/wp/2017/09/12/this-video- showed-a-nazi-saluting-dog-was-posting-it-on-youtube-a-hate-crime

Zephyr, T. (2014). Cancel "Dapper Laughs: On The Pull" on ITV. *ITV.com*, https:// www.change.org/p/adam-crozier-cancel-dapper-laughs-on-the-pull-on-itv

Criticism of Moral Policing in Russia: Controversies around Lev Protiv in Moscow

Gilles Favarel-Garrigues

Introduction

During the first half of the 2010s, vigilante groups have increasingly appeared in the streets and on the Internet in Russia. Acting in the name of civil society, the 'activists' (*aktivisty*) patrol the streets in order to find badly parked vehicles (StopXam), inspect shops to check whether they sell expired products (Khryushi Protiv), or hunt and trap alleged paedophiles (Occupy Pedophilia), amongst other things. In spite of the diversity of their targets, Russian vigilantes share a common modus operandi, intertwining physical and digital practices. They remind people of the law, fight with alleged offenders and call the police, but they also film everything they do in order to create content, which they then spread on the Internet (Favarel-Garrigues, 2018; Favarel-Garrigues & Shukan, 2020). They therefore expose and shame on social media the offenders they meet face to face (Trottier, 2017). Their digital activity is sometimes hectic: they manage their own YouTube channels and webpages and renew the content they offer at least on a weekly basis (Gabdulhakov, 2018). Many are able to edit their films professionally, and they select the most spectacular moments during raids and patrols in order to attract viewers to their channels. The most famous vigilante groups, including the one studied in this chapter with more than 1.7 million subscribers to its YouTube channel, earn a regular income from

https://doi.org/10.11647/OBP.0200.05

their initiatives. The existence of an audience therefore plays a crucial role in the activity of these groups.

However, studying this audience from a sociological perspective is difficult for two reasons. Firstly, the literature on vigilantism does not address this issue. Scholars focus on the attitudes of vigilantes, of their victims and of law-enforcement agencies, but not on the audience in whose name laws and moral values are enforced. Secondly, in the specific case of online Russian vigilantes, the identities of the audience, mainly anonymous viewers and commentators, are hidden. Nonetheless, even though people often do not use their real names when commenting on the work of self-proclaimed law enforcers, they do judge it, often either agreeing or disagreeing strongly with the vigilantes' activities and points of view.

This chapter focuses on public debates about Russian vigilante groups and the controversial issues surrounding their activity. Who voices the public criticism and what exactly is being criticised? The discussions encompass issues such as the legality and morality of vigilantes' acts, their retributions, their social usefulness and their efficiency. But do vigilantes care about these criticisms? How does criticism affect their activity? The theoretical framework of this chapter is influenced by pragmatic sociology, particularly the analysis of controversies, which emphasises the role of the audience in public disputes (Boltanski et al., 2007). Cyril Lemieux defines controversies as triadic structures involving "situations where a difference between two parties is brought before a public, which is in a third place and therefore in a position to judge"[1] (Lemieux, 2007, p. 195; see also Smadja, 2012). What are the controversial issues that the audience is led to judge concerning Russian vigilantes' activity?

As a case study, this chapter focuses on a particular group named *Lev Protiv* (Leo Against) and embodied by its leader, Mikhail 'Lev' Lazutin, born in 1995. Founded in 2014 and based in Moscow, this vigilante group presents itself as a 'social project', whose mission is to patrol train and metro stations, commercial areas and public gardens, urging smokers, drinkers and partygoers to respect the law. Lazutin gathers a team to conduct these operations, or 'raids': between five and ten people patrol

---

1   "des situations où un différend entre deux parties est mis en scène devant un public, tiers placé dès lors en position de juge."

with him, including sportsmen. They promote a healthy lifestyle and claim to act as role models, showing Russian youth the ravages of alcohol. Most of the time, the raids conclude with a fight. Like all vigilante groups, Lev Protiv justifies its involvement in law enforcement by denouncing the passivity of the police (Abrahams, 1998; Johnston, 1996; Pratten and Sen, 2007; Favarel-Garrigues & Gayer, 2016). Alongside outcasts, homeless people and punks, indifferent and unprofessional policemen constitute one of the main targets of the group, which includes 'civic monitoring' of law enforcement agents in its missions.

From a methodological point of view, I use the data I have gathered on Lev Protiv since 2015, particularly the 150 videos that I have archived (which have often been removed from the activists' channel) and also the commentaries (which have also often been removed). I have created a database of the comments from 59 videos posted until 2018, allowing me to understand which words are used most frequently and which topics are the most controversial. I have also undertaken ethnographic observation of six of the raids by the group in 2017 and 2018, and interviewed people who have relationships with Lev Protiv (as victims, observers, detractors and fans), but I do not use these sources in the present paper, except when the observation helps to understand the group's popularity.

I first focus on the popularity of Lev Protiv and present the information available about the audience of this project. I then turn to the emergence and development of the criticism of the group, and show that the main controversial issues surround the group's focus on economic, legal, social and ethical arguments. While it may not hold true for all groups, in the case of Lev Protiv, the use of the Internet, particularly YouTube, not only allows them to expose their targets but also enables their critics to exert pressure on them to be more accountable to the public they claim to protect.

A Popular Vigilante Show

Lev Protiv offers a regular vigilante show, an impressive spectacle uploaded on YouTube at least once a week. Counting the exact number of videos edited and posted by Lev Protiv since its creation is probably impossible for several reasons. The Moscow branch does not keep all edited videos on its channel. Some of them disappear suddenly for legal or commercial reasons, for instance if an activist commits a punishable act or if the video is not as popular as expected. The main YouTube channel of the group is cleaned on a regular basis, as shown in archives available on the Internet.[2] In 2015 and 2016, the title of each edited video included a number used to classify all the videos on the channel, but this classification system was given up after the 130th episode in October 2016. The opening of a second channel in 2015 has complicated the calculation further.[3] Moreover 'copycat movements' have spread in Russian cities, taking over the brand of Lev Protiv and imitating the style of the Moscow activists (Gabowitsch, 2018). However, in January 2019, 230 videos were accessible on both YouTube channels. It is reasonable to estimate that the Moscow group has produced more than 300 videos since its creation in 2014.

Most of Lev Protiv's videos correspond to a genre, the 'raid show', and generally follow a set scenario. In the beginning, some unproblematic interactions are shown, in which offenders willingly allow Lev Protiv to remind them of the law, and sometimes express support for the group. These sequences prove, according to Lazutin, that a norm is shared by most Russians and that those who do not comply are 'abnormal' and behave 'inadequately'. Then follow interactions in which a discussion takes place without a fight: for example, the activists grab bottles of alcohol and empty them in front of their owners. However, the conflict at this point is limited to a tense and more or less cogent dialogue. Lazutin spends a significant amount of time justifying himself, explaining his motivations and goals in front of the alleged offenders and the audience. Lazutin calls the police when an offender is caught drinking twice or answering with obscene language (*mat*) in public, which is forbidden by the Code of the Russian Federation on Administrative Offenses (article 20.1 on 'petty hooliganism'). The video usually ends with a dispute provoking physical confrontation, with Lev Protiv members getting involved in brawls and sometimes using pepper spray. The need to resort to force is thus shown as a necessary alternative when other forms

---

2   See, for instance, the Internet archive Wayback Machine (first capture of the front page of Lev Protiv's YouTube channel in June 2014): https://web.archive.org/web/* https://www.youtube.com/channel/UCUBoIo2p7GSRMt1YcSswDEw

3   See https://www.youtube.com/channel/UCjkqm5yS4HGjxPFEl1vc4Ew/videos

of interaction have failed. This option is supposed to underline, on the one hand, the uncivilised nature of the offenders who are not willing to comply with the law, and, on the other hand, the consequences of an absent or indifferent police force. Together with images that show the ravages of alcohol, the fight scene is the principal marketing ploy prompting users to click on the video. The offenders are, however, neutralised and handed over to the police when they arrive on the scene. Some raids end up at the police station, where Lazutin finishes performing his duties by writing his deposition.

Although Lazutin's image is intimately tied to these raid shows in the public space, it is important to note that he also posts other content to his YouTube channel, in which he develops a saccharine and compassionate discourse, a far cry from the aggression we see in the raids. Like other vigilante groups,[4] Lev Protiv likes to portray itself in its videos as a group of do-gooders. Disguised as Santa Claus, Lazutin hands out New Year's gifts to children, offers to buy medicine for the elderly at a pharmacy,[5] distributes hot drinks and food to the needy,[6] and speaks out against animal cruelty. One of the most popular videos, seen more than six million times by September 2018, features a wounded cat found in the street and saved by Lazutin.[7] Among the first videos posted in 2019, along with new violent raids, Lazutin shows himself saving dogs and distributing gifts to children living with mental illness. The avenger is also a philanthropist. However, violent images are generally more attractive to viewers than compassionate ones. In January 2019, two videos were released almost at the same time: "We Save Dogs from Death"[8] and "Brutal Raid".[9] After a week, the second one had been viewed twice as many times as the first one (230,000 views for the raid video, 117,000 views for the other one as of 7 February).

Lev Protiv is popular in Russia and Lazutin is a well-known public figure, among young Russians at least. In comparison with other Russian

---

4   Davidych is a good example. As a famous test-driver and street-racer, he began to 'hunt' corrupt traffic police officers while organising charity runs by visiting orphanages. He was arrested in February 2016 and released in 2019.

5   Lev Protiv 64, Helping Pensioners (*Pomosch pensioneram*), 12 November, 2015.

6   Lev Protiv 72, Help the Needy (*Pomogai nuzhdayushimsya*), 19 December, 2015.

7   Lev Protiv, Saving a Kitten from Death (*Spasenie kotenki ot smerti*), 30 September 2015.

8   Lev Protiv, Saving Dogs from Death (*Spasaem sobak ot smerti*), 27 January 2019.

9   Lev Protiv, Brutal Raid (*Zhestkii reid*), 30 January 2019.

vigilante groups (including local initiatives[10] and forbidden groups),[11] Lev Protiv seems to be the most popular project in Russia after Stop-Kham, which was created earlier and is devoted to stopping traffic violations.[12] Both projects have a lot in common: they were initiated by pro-Putin youth organisations and received grants from governmental programs supporting the development of civic initiatives (Hemment, 2012; Rukov & Chesnokov, 2015). In the beginning of Lev Protiv, Lazutin took part in several Stop-Kham raids. Stop-Kham raids in which he participated used to feature on Lev Protiv's main channel.[13]

As shown in Table 5.1, since the creation of the first channel in April 2014, the audience has grown continuously and by 2019 one and a half million people had subscribed to the channel. Yet, the audience of the videos on this main channel is even bigger. In January 2020, the channel had attracted more than 280 million views. Each of the thirteen most popular videos had been watched by more than three million viewers. The most popular video had reached almost 10 million spectators in two months![14] In 2018, a video was typically seen more than 100,000 times after one day, 200,000 times after three days, and about 300,000 times after five to seven days (see Table 5.2). The most appreciated videos are still being viewed two or three years after they were posted on the Internet.

Table 5.1: Progression of the number of subscribers on Lev Protiv's main YouTube channel.

Date	Number of subscribers
July 2015	250,000
July 2016	680,000
July 2017	900,000

---

10   See for instance the Chelyabinsk-based project Trezvye Dvory, which existed from 2014 to 2018.
11   See for instance the Occupy Pedophilia project, which was banned in 2014. For more about this group, see Favarel-Garrigues (2019).
12   See https://www.youtube.com/user/stopxamlive/about; In February 2019, more than 1.5 million people had subscribed to the channel, which is comparable to Lev Protiv's audience, but the total number of views was far greater (390 million for Stop-Kham against 214 million for Lev Protiv).
13   https://web.archive.org/web/20140612084540/http://www.youtube.com/channel/UCUBoIo2p7GSRMt1YcSswDEw
14   Lev Protiv, *Lev protiv skinhedov-natsistov (perepalka)*, 24 November 2018.

September 2018	1,200,000
January 2019	1,500,000
December 2019	1,700,000
June 2020	1,800,000

Source: Lev Protiv's main YouTube channel.

Table 5.2: Progression of views, likes/dislikes and comments for a video posted on July 16, 2018.

Date	Views	Likes	Dislikes	Comments
17.07.2018	127,131	9700	486	273
18.07.2018	193,000	12,000	678	418
19.07.2018	222,000	13,000	828	479
24.07.2018	290,000	14,300	1040	712
31.01.2019	536,000	21,000	1800	1068
15.06.2020	591,000	23,000	1900	1080

Source: Lev Protiv, *Udushayushchii* (Asphyxiating), 16 July, 2018, https://www.youtube.com/watch?v=8WvZ6r-_qAU

Lev Protiv's second channel, opened in 2015, started to become popular in 2016. Called "Lev Protiv Live" until 2018, it is now named "Lev Protiv 2nd Channel" (*Lev Protiv 2 Kanal*).[15] Whereas Lazutin leads the operations in the videos on the main channel, other members of Lev Protiv post videos of raids they conducted by themselves on the second channel. Their videos are successful, even in the cases when Lazutin does not personally take part in the raid. More than 500,000 people had subscribed to the second channel by January 2020. Videos had been watched more than 100 million times, which is more than a third of the total number of views for the main channel. Only four videos had been watched more than three million times, but one of them had reached 10 million views in two years.[16] A third channel, called "Mikhail Lazutin", was begun in 2016: in 2020, 218,000 people have subscribed to it and videos have been viewed more than 22 million times.[17] As we will see further on, these figures are significant enough to generate regular income.

---

15   See https://www.youtube.com/channel/UCjkqm5yS4HGjxPFEl1vc4Ew
16   Lev Protiv, Pathetic Cockerels (*Zhalkie drachuny*), 2 November 2016.
17   https://www.youtube.com/channel/UCjkqm5yS4HGjxPFEl1vc4Ew

As a showman on YouTube, Mikhail Lazutin is a popular public figure. Several interviews with him are available elsewhere on the Internet.[18] Major newspapers have written articles about his project (Sher, 2015). In each raid I have personally observed, I have noticed the presence of fans, asking Lazutin for a selfie, shaking his hand, waving at him or expressing support for his initiative. Such positive opinions are, however, far from being universal. As we will see further on, criticism is widespread on the web and several investigations of Lev Protiv are easily available. The name 'Lev Protiv' also appears in the media each time a brawl gets out of hand and creates severe damage.[19]

In Search of an Audience

All interactions shown in Lev Protiv videos are observed by a third party (the audience), who are supposed to support Lev Protiv's civic stance. The inclusion of this third party is imposed by members of Lev Protiv on the people they confront, evident in the conspicuous presence of a camera, which has at least some relation to the hostility incurred by the group. What is it possible to know about the audience of Lev Protiv? The issue of the audience is a blind spot in the general literature about vigilantism. The comments sections of the group's YouTube channels give little insight: most of the commentators use pseudonyms and almost none of them can be considered as constant contributors to the discussion. This means that there is no core group of identifiable followers. However, the language used in the comments confirms clearly that the audience is young and that male adolescents prevail among the viewers. The audience is at least national (many comments start with "Here in my city...") and seems sometimes to include Russian-speaking people living abroad, notably in other post-Soviet states. It is interesting to note that Lazutin constantly marks himself as an "activist", as distinguished from "those who are indifferent", "passives who do nothing to improve

---

18 See his interview by the blogger Kolhoznik at https://www.youtube.com/watch?v=50RGJSC6C9U

19 In Moscow, Lev Protiv activists beaten during an operation at Kiev Station (*V moskve izbili aktivistov dvizhenia "Lev protiv" vo vremya aktsii na Kievskom vokzale*), Komsomolskaya Pravda, 20 November 2016; Mass Brawl on Bolotnaya Square Started because of a Bottle of Water (*Massovaya draka na Bolotnoi ploschadi nachalas' iz-za butylki vody*), MK, 9 September 2018.

the world in which they live", "couch potatoes surfing the Internet" who constitute probably the biggest part of his audience.

The comments sections also show that Lev Protiv videos are deeply controversial: they are sometimes disliked by a high proportion of viewers and always highly commented upon. The contents provoke discussions and clashes between viewers. Some fans not only support the initiative, but also express their willingness to join the group. In some cases, they provide help by searching and giving the name, or the VKontakte (VK) page,[20] of the smokers or drinkers involved in fights with the Lev Protiv team: "For you, Lev, the links of these bastards",[21] writes one of them in July 2018.[22] But Lazutin also has vocal opponents, both on the spot during encounters and on the Internet.

Reactions to Lev Protiv's raids are sometimes violent. When vigilantes appear in Bolotnaya, a square where revellers gather once a week, they are met with insults. On a few occasions, young people targeted by the group at Bolotnaya have used violence against the activists; in one video they can be seen bearing down on the group menacingly chanting "Healthy lifestyle sucks!" (*Zozh sosyot!*).[23] Sometimes the activists are taught a lesson by adversaries who are greater in number and better organised than expected. In October 2015 at Bolotnaya, one member received an injury to the head during a brawl.[24] Lev Protiv appeared in headlines again in November 2016, when an altercation between youths and the activists degenerated into a brawl in front of a Moscow shopping centre.[25] In September 2018, the Lev Protiv cameraman was doused in pepper spray during a raid. According to Lazutin, all these events reflect the aggression and dangerousness of a population that the police should manage.

The number of available videos *about* Lev Protiv on social networks (especially VK) and on YouTube is also impressive. These videos

---

20 VKontakte (VK) is the most popular Russian online social media and social networking service.

21 They have been recognised because in the video they name the rock band they play in together.

22 Lev Protiv, Filthy Herd on Bolotnaya 1 (*Merzkoe stado na Bolotnoi 1*), 3 July 2018.

23 Lev Protiv, Lev Protiv is Brutally Attacked by a Drunken Crowd (*Zhestokoe napadenie pianoi tolpy na Lev Protiv*), 7 October 2015, 11'08.

24 Lev Protiv, Fight on Bolotnaya Square (*Draka na Bolotnoi ploschadi*), 6 October 2015.

25 Lev Protiv, Assault at Shopping Mall "European" (*Napadenie u TS "Evropeiskii"*), 18 November 2016.

help to identify controversies surrounding Lev Protiv's activity. They voice the criticism of Lev Protiv, which forces Lazutin to answer and to justify himself. Three main groups of authors can be distinguished: individual victims, anonymous collective accusers and well-known YouTubers or bloggers. It should be noted that major Russian human rights organisations have not taken part in this criticism, except Public Verdict, which offers legal assistance to the victims of law enforcement bodies in Russia.[26]

Lev Protiv victims sometimes try individually to raise the awareness of the general public about the danger posed by the group. For example, they create webpages or VKontakte pages in order to inform others about the group and to collect testimonies. However, sometimes these individuals find it difficult to gain support. In June 2018, during a raid that I observed, a man fought against the activists, fell down, could not stand again and was taken by ambulance to a hospital. Two days later, he opened a page on Pikabu[27] called "Lev Protiv Activists Broke My Leg", which gained a huge audience.[28] More than 1,600 comments were published in three weeks; however, most of them were critical towards the self-proclaimed 'victim', suspected to have broken the law and provoked the activists. Victims' threats to sue Lazutin seem to have produced no effect so far.

Anonymous accusers include observers filming Lev Protiv in action in order to prove that they commit offences during their raids. Several videos showing how Lev Protiv members behave during their raids are available on YouTube. These videos show the hidden means used by activists in order to put pressure on alleged offenders: the aggressive use of floodlights, the disciplining of aggressive members in the group by other group members and the occasionally intimidating aspect of some of the members. During one of the raids I observed, a photographer familiar with Lev Protiv activity was following the group in order to publish potential abuses and wrongdoings committed by the group

---

26 See http://vigilant.myverdict.org/
27 Pikabu is a Russian social news aggregation website.
28 How My Leg Was Broken and What To Do Now (*Kak mne slomali nogu i chto teper' s etim delat*), 29 June 2018, https://pikabu.ru/story/kak_mne_slomali_nogu_i_chto_teper_s_yetim_delat_5998252.

on social media. Anonymous accusers sometimes give legal advice to smokers and drinkers stopped by activists.[29]

More structured communities of opponents also exist on Russian social networks. The VK page "Boris For[30]" (*Boris Za*), with around 2,800 subscribers in January 2019, gives "instructions for communicating with activists" and explains the rights of the activists and of their targets.[31] Recommendations include being polite to the activists, obeying their instructions if alcohol is indeed being consumed and filming them in order to prevent aggressive behaviour. Two other pages have been created to criticise and mobilise against Lev Protiv: "The Tiger For" on VK had nearly 2,500 subscribers in January 2019,[32] and "Anti Project (*Proekt*) Lev Protiv", gathered around 600 at the same date.[33] However, as the figures of popularity show, none of these initiatives reach the scale of the audience for the vigilantes themselves.

The most significant impact on Lev Protiv's reputation comes from the videos devoted to the vigilantes posted by famous bloggers and YouTubers. Some bloggers treat this topic in a humorous way,[34] but most of the time the tone is serious, even alarmed. Public figures of the Russian Internet began to worry about this subject in 2016, and have sought to reveal who these vigilantes are, how violent they can be and how their projects are funded. As we will see, they play a significant role in fueling controversies surrounding Lev Protiv.

The first to post videos on the subject, a series of three, was Adam Timaev. Born to a Chechen family, the blogger lives in Moscow. Around 74,000 people had subscribed to his YouTube channel and his videos had been viewed more than 6 million times by April 2019. Timaev shows himself to be an investigator able to reveal the hidden truth about institutions (including Sberbank and the army), as well as popular projects on the web. Lev Protiv is clearly one of his main targets. His first video on this issue appeared at the end of 2016 and had been viewed almost 1 million times two years later. In January 2019, Timaev released

---

29   See, for example, the comments for one of the first articles on this subject: at http://
     seofuck.ru/kak-obojti-zakon-o-kurenii-ili-lev-protiv
30   Boris stands for Boris Yeltsin and his alleged taste for alcohol consumption.
31   See http://vk.com/wall-98572404_766
32   See https://vk.com/tiger_za
33   See https://vk.com/public70622974
34   See https://vk.com/ugarhiki

two videos in which he publicly offended Lazutin and suggested they fight.

The Timaev initiative inspired one of the most popular Russian bloggers, Nikolai Sobolev. Born in 1993, Sobolev started his career on YouTube with pranks and "social experiments" (*Rakamakafo*), then turned to the analysis of trends on YouTube ("YouTube's Life"), before starting a new channel under his own name.[35] His critique has reached a far larger audience. Since 2015, the videos on his YouTube channel have been viewed 467 million times. With 4.6 million subscribers, he is a Russian YouTube star who is fond of youth culture. His videos deal with famous rappers and bloggers, reality shows, extrasensory perception and sects, sports issues and the regulation of the Internet, among other topics. He often posts follow-up videos on particular topics, most of the time because his target has responded publicly to his initial video. Sobolev started to edit videos about Lev Protiv in February 2017. Two years later, they had been watched more than three and a half million times. While this is not a considerable number for Sobolev (this video is not one of his thirty most popular), it does give a large audience to Lazutin's activity. As in the case of Adam Timaev, Sobolev's videos prompted video replies from Lazutin and ended in a tense meeting in the street, where the two YouTubers settled their scores in a non-violent fashion in the presence of a camera and witnesses, including Timaev.[36] This confrontation, which was widely commented upon when a video of it was posted on the web, shows on the one hand that denouncing Lev Protiv has become a noteworthy activity. On the other hand, Lazutin himself interacts with famous bloggers in order to benefit from their popularity.

This was especially the case when the gamer Panda FX, renowned for his videos about football videogames, criticised Lev Protiv on his channel in September 2018. Lazutin reacted by filming a video where he approached Panda FX in the locker room of a football stadium and asked him to dress in order to settle their scores in the street. This video was widely discussed on the Russian web as a fight between two public

---

35 See https://www.youtube.com/channel/UCNb2BkmQu3IfQVcaPExHkvQ
36 https://yandex.ru/video/search?text=%D0%BB%D0%B0%D0%B7%D1%82%D0%B8%D0%BD%20%D1%81%D0%BE%D0%B1%D0%BE%D0%BB%D0%B5%D0%B2&path=wizard&noreask=1&filmId=8659422307530055862

figures. Lazutin was criticised by his own fans for being a hooligan and for adopting a provocative attitude. He finally apologised for having been unable to repress his anger and removed the video from his channel. These repeated public confrontations with famous bloggers and YouTubers may help to explain the rapid increase of Lev Protiv's audience during the second half of 2018. Whereas it took two years for the group to pass from 500,000 subscribers to a million (from April 2016 to April 2018), it took only nine months to attract 500,000 more by February 2019. And whereas it took several years to reach 100 million views by April 2018, it took only seven months to reach 100 million more.

Controversies Surrounding Lev Protiv

Lazutin's popularity has put him under ever-growing scrutiny, and there have been many efforts to reveal the true methods and objectives of the Lev Protiv project. As a "social interaction likely to have an audience" (Lemieux, 2007, p. 195; Smadja, 2012, p. 2), controversy leads the public to judge the relevance of the arguments of the two parties. In the case of Lev Protiv, this judgement depends on the identity of the accusers, on the relevance of the accusations and on the robustness of self-justification by Lazutin. The four main controversial issues regarding the activists deal with their earnings, the legality of their methods, the efficiency of their activity and the strength of their reputation.

Through its connections with other pro-Putin *aktivisty*, Lev Protiv used to have access to a rare resource: funding granted by the Civic Chamber in support of the development of civil society in Russia (Daucé, 2014, p. 15). Lev Protiv is thus peculiar in that it used to be state-sponsored. In 2014, the Lev Protiv project received over five million rubles from the Civic Chamber via "The Nation's Health League". The funds were paid to a non-commercial organisation called "Multinational Country", registered in the town of Lyubertsy.[37] In describing itself, the project insisted upon the legitimacy of the work that these "social *aktivisty*" carry out "conjointly" with the police, in order to implement the ban on smoking in public places. In 2015, the project received 7 million rubles via the "Russian Union of Youth", but the funds were paid to

---

37   See https://grants.oprf.ru/grants2014-2/winners/rec2471/

the organisation "Young Talent", also based in Lyubertsy. The project proposal stated at that time that offenders would be reprimanded and handed over to the police.[38] The grants stopped in 2016. Like Stop-Kham, Lev Protiv are not a group of reservists unconditionally devoted to the powers-that-be; they are young people who negotiate their potential support and who aim to preserve a certain degree of autonomy.

The first controversies that emerged around questions of money date back to 2015 and reveal that a lucrative business is hiding behind the group's charitable acts. Are they zealous activists or mere crooks? One of the most common criticisms of Lev Protiv in 2016 dealt with the allocation of State subsidies in 2014 and 2015; "where are the 12 million?" was at that time an oft-repeated question on the lips of the group's detractors.[39] In response to this criticism, Lazutin often replied that he never even saw the money, and that he was the victim of an orchestrated swindling operation organised by corrupt 'officials'. Be that as it may, the controversy puts emphasis on the question of the oversight of government funds granted to non-commercial organisations, at a time when cracks in this system are being reported (Transparency, 2016). What is more, it is thought that receiving government subsidies gives "ordinary kids who yesterday were still sitting in class" an "illusion of impunity" (Alexandrov, 2015).

The denunciation of the profits realised by Lev Protiv also includes the financial rewards from Lev Protiv's digital activity. Firstly, the group makes money through its YouTube channels. It is unfortunately impossible to know the exact amount, and websites devoted to estimates are hardly reliable, since they show large disparities in their estimates and vary on a daily basis. In January 2019, SocialBlade (a website that tracks statistics and analytics for social media sites) estimated Lev Protiv's earnings from their main channel to be no less than 3,800 euros per month. Estimated earnings from the second channel reached no less than 778 euros per month. A minimum estimate of the profits reached about 4,500 euros per month in January 2019. In June 2020, however, this estimate was far lower (about 600 euros per month).[40] Besides

---

38   See https://grants.oprf.ru/grants2015-1/winners/rec4173/
39   Bloggers Timaev and Sobolev have contributed to the diffusion of this information.
40   This estimate includes three channels: Lev Protiv's first and second channel, and also Mikhail Lazutin's own channel.

earning money from the advertisements on YouTube, Lazutin often promotes a product in the beginning of the videos: for example, for a particular pizza delivery service or sports-betting organisation. These sources of profit help to explain a shift in the terms used by Lazutin to present the group's activity: whereas it used to be a "social project", now it is "work".[41] The commercial dimension of the project fuels the denunciation of the hypocrisy of the alleged do-gooders. This accusation has also been taken up by leaders of provincial copycat movements (Gabowitsch, 2012), disappointed in a leader who is not the slightest bit interested in their work at a local level, and who in their eyes "only cares about his YouTube channel".[42]

Another concern deals with the legal or illegal nature of the methods the group employs. In the videos, as well as during the observations I carried out, speeches about rights prevail in dialogues between activists, smokers, drinkers and onlookers. All parties claim that they are acting to protect their rights. The constant use of a camera is controversial and the focus of many objections on the part of targeted individuals. "You do not have the right to film me": asking not to be filmed is a classic reaction of those who are targeted by the group. The activists respond with an irrefutable argument: according to the Constitution of the Russian Federation, they have the right to film an offence being committed. This is also how they justify using a powerful floodlight at night, blinding their targets and exposing them to harsh light. The legality of the other methods employed by the activists is also constantly questioned. In the beginning of the raids, Lev Protiv used to use a water spray in order to extinguish the cigarettes of those who were refusing to cease smoking in forbidden places. The spray was at that time the signature of the Lev Protiv brand. Facing accusations of spoiling others' property, the group stopped acting in this way. However, seizing the open beer can of an offender raises a similar question. If it is right to remind someone that they are contravening the law against drinking in certain public places, is it right to stop the offence by confiscating alcoholic drinks? I have

---

41 See for instance Lazutin's interview at https://www.youtube.com/watch?v=50RGJSC6C9U

42 For instance, this was the case in Krasnoyarsk. In March 2016, the leader of the local chapter declared that he had decided to stop his activities, disappointed by Lazutin's search for glory and money. See http://www.prima-tv.ru/news/society/41892-dvizhenie_lev_protiv_samoraspuskaetsya

already mentioned the raid I observed in June 2018, during which a man fighting with the activists fell down and claimed to have had his leg broken. After having posted his story on Russian social networks and in front of critical comments, the victim had to justify himself. Not only did he show proof of his broken leg and say that he had offended Lazutin because of his anger, but he also insisted on his right to break the law as long as he is ready to assume the consequences — which in this case, would have been a fine. However, this argument has hardly convinced his video's audience and many commentators have criticised his cynical vision of crime and punishment. Contrary to other complaints publicised by his victims, Lazutin did not even answer to this accusation in order to justify himself.

A third concern over the actions of the vigilante group deals with the use of coercion. As discussed earlier, violence occurs in most of the raids. Do activists have the right to incapacitate offenders? In their videos, the activists take pains to show that they are not responsible for the escalation to violence, but that they use violence in response to aggressive behaviour. During one raid, I heard Lazutin, in front of the camera, warn a man just before the fight started: "according to the legislation on self-defence, I have the right to hit you if you hit me". But the activists' justification of the use of violence with the need to defend themselves does not convince those who argue that the activists frequently provoke drunk people in order to infuriate them, to push them to their limits in order to guarantee bankable images of a fight. As argued in a critical paper about Lev Protiv: should criminal offences committed by people fighting against administrative offences be tolerated (Alexandrov, 2015)?

The efficiency of the activists is also criticised. Many commentators note that Lev Protiv does not prevent people from continuing to meet up at Bolotnaya square or around train stations. According a typical comment, the group would be better advised to fight "against the causes, and not the consequences of the problem". In response, Lazutin asserts that his goal is not to help the drunkards he meets because, according to him, they are already lost. They are "cattle" (*bydlo*), i.e. dehumanised. Therefore, the main objective of constant brawls with 'the cattle' is to show a good example to the youth watching the videos throughout the country. As Lazutin puts it during an exchange with one drunk individual: "You show a bad example, and I show a good one.

There is good and there is evil".[43] This self-presentation as a role model fuels another widespread criticism. By giving free reign to their violent impulses, Lazutin and his band are a far cry from being role models. Is it morally right and socially useful to justify the use of force to fight against tobacco and alcohol consumption? Is this permanent readiness to fight in order to enforce the law a good example for Russian youth? Is it right to provoke a fight in front of those children that the activists pretend to defend? Are they then law enforcers or hooligans? As put straightforwardly by one man taken to task by the youths: "Who are you guys precisely? Are you pigs (cops)? Because honestly the more I look at you the more you look like troublemakers"[44] It is, moreover, surprising that Lazutin's advertisements for gambling, hardly compatible with a role model for young people, are not more criticised.

Another area that receives little criticism is Lev Protiv's vision of political order. Controversies around the group deal more with its hidden financial goals and questionable methods of fighting than with the political meaning of the spontaneous involvement of men, including athletes, in law enforcement. Although rarely mentioned, the argument has nonetheless been made that Lev Protiv would be well able to join, if needed, the army of "Putinist red guards", in reference to the group's early ties to Nashi, and the creation of Anti-Maidan collectives, eager to come to blows to defend the regime against the risk of revolution in all its forms. This is apparent in some of the terminology used to describe the *"aktivisty"*, referred to as the former Communist Party Youth Organisation (*"komsomols"*), *"timurovtsy"*,[45] and even the Chinese Red Guard (*"khunveibini"*). However, this argument is partially refuted by Lazutin's critical stance towards the regime since 2016, i.e. after governmental grants ceased. Lazutin's credo is order, and he judges politicians by this criterion: he always insists on the fact that his raids occur "near the walls of Kremlin" in order to show that ruling elites are

---

43   Lev Protiv, *Udushayushchii* (Asphyxiating), July 16, 2018, https://www.youtube.com/watch?v=8WvZ6r-_qAU

44   Lev Protiv, *Lev Protiv ne na tekh narvalis'* (Lev Protiv did not pick the right ones), YouTube, June 14, 2007, https://www.youtube.com/watch?v=ot6UW68DcZQ

45   *Timurovtsy* refers to early Soviets who undertook charitable acts; the term comes from a book by Arkadii Gaidar, *Timur and His Crew* (*Timur i ego komanda*), published in 1940, in which a group of young adolescents secretly helped the needy and fought petty criminals. In one of its most famous scenes, Timur and his friends prevent a gang from doing harm by exposing their activities to the villagers.

powerless. He used to quote Vladimir Putin when he was financed by governmental funds (from 2014 to 2015), but this is less the case since 2016. In an interview, Lazutin confessed his interest in Navalny's anti-corruption investigations, but disapproved of his calls to take part in unauthorised demonstrations, believing that he was encouraging the youth to wreak havoc.[46]

What, then, is Lazutin's ideology? Some critics describe the activists, not without a certain social disdain, as stupid brutes, and compare them to the ultra-nationalists that participate in the "Russian March" parade (Alexandrov, 2015). It is true that before starting his project against alcohol and tobacco consumption in public places, Lazutin, at that time aged seventeen to eighteen, was a fan of prominent neo-Nazi activist Tesak, organising his own "safaris" against alleged paedophiles and sharing the neo-Nazi beliefs of his idol (Favarel-Garrigues, 2019; see also Kasra, 2017). However, five years later, it would be wrong to associate Lev Protiv with Russian neo-Nazi activists for several reasons. Firstly, in 2019, as a young father, he distances himself from the mistakes he made when he was younger. He develops the image of a responsible Christian, quoting Jesus Christ and calling for love.[47] Secondly, many adversaries mock Lazutin's patronym, Dzhemalovich, which is not ethnically Russian. Indeed, Lazutin's father is half Kurdish, half Georgian.[48] In one video, activists beat a man who had previously called Lazutin a *khach* (darky), an offensive and demeaning term used by ethnic Russians against Caucasus people. This terminology echoes offensive criticism that is regularly formulated on the web: Lazutin has no legitimacy to clean Russian society because he is even not ethnically Russian. In fact, white supremacists feature among the subcultures drinking in Bolotnaya park during Lev Protiv raids. Lazutin and his friends denounce the intolerance and the hatefulness of these nationalists. One of Lev Protiv's most popular videos is named "Leo Against Skinheads and Neo-Nazis".[49] But as Marlène Laruelle has shown, nationalist speech is plural in today's

---

46   Mikhail Lazutin, Answers to questions (*Otvety na voprosy*), 17 April 2019, https:// www.youtube.com/watch?v=8hXTGfBVQXs

47   Ibid.

48   Ibid.

49   Lev Protiv, Leo Against Skinheads-Nazis (Brawl) (*Lev Protiv skinkhedov-natsistov* (*potasovka*)), 24 November 2018, https://www.youtube.com/ watch?v=wJJaD8966Pc&t=65s This video had reached 10 million views after two months.

Russia (Laruelle, 2017). Besides a healthy lifestyle and strict obedience to the law, Lazutin promotes patriotism and a form of nationalism based on belonging to a multi-ethnic and multi-faith country. Such a post-Soviet vision of nationhood, which is for instance celebrated during Second World War commemorations, corresponds to government rhetoric in Russia, valuing all components of the Russian ethnic mosaic.

Conclusion

More than four years after its creation, criticism and controversy have had no detrimental effects on the popularity of Lev Protiv so far, unlike in the case of other vigilante initiatives such as "Occupy Pedophilia" or "Davidich on the hunt" (*Davidych na okhote*). On the contrary, they have fuelled the group's success: Lev Protiv gained further subscribers when popular bloggers started to relay the various criticisms. In fact, as the producer of a vigilante show, Lazutin has included the management of criticism in his work. He spends a significant amount of time answering to his critics and justifying himself. He has perfectly interiorised the idea that accountability is a fundamental feature of the neoliberal grammar of 'projects' in the development of civil society (Daucé, 2014).

This case study suggests the need to examine more generally how vigilante groups gain audiences and how they strive to be accountable, whatever the context. Firstly, in order to appreciate and explain the popularity of a group like Lev Protiv, it would be useful to watch new YouTube content from the group and from their critics, and to do so with the vigilante channel's subscribers, to observe as well as discuss their reactions. Such a method would help to explore the audience's expectations, disappointments and criticisms toward the group, and how these evolve over time. Secondly, we may inquire how vigilante groups build their accountability in reaction to criticisms and controversies. By resorting to violence in order to maintain order and/or to implement the law in the name of a community, vigilante groups are controversial by nature and always have to justify themselves. However, the use of the Internet, especially YouTube, to publicise their activity places contemporary vigilantes in front of a permanent audience that scrutinises them, points out controversial issues and puts pressure on them to react to criticism on time and be more accountable. This constant pressure to keep viewers watching videos might constitute a specific feature of vigilante groups using digital media, compared to those using classic forms of vigilantism.

References

Abrahams, R. (1998). *Vigilant Citizens: Vigilantism and the State*. London: Polity Press.

Alexandrov, G. (2015, October 23), Lev Protiv. Slaboumie i trusost (Lev Protiv: Cretinism and Cowardice), *Vestnik Buri*.

Boltanski, L., Offenstadt, N., Claverie, E., & Van Damme, S. (2007). *Affaires, scandales et grandes causes. De Socrate à Pinochet*. Paris: Stock.

Daucé, F. (2014). The government and human rights groups in Russia: Civilized oppression? *Journal of Civil Society*, 10(3), 239–54, http://doi.org/10.1080/17 448689.2014.941087

Favarel-Garrigues, G. (2018) Justiciers amateurs et croisades morales en Russie contemporaine. *Revue française de science politique*, 68(4), 651–67, http://doi. org/10.3917/rfsp.684.0651

Favarel-Garrigues, G. (2020). Moral crusade and anti-pedophile vigilantes in Russia. *Global Crime*, forthcoming, http://doi.org/10.1080/17440572.2019.16 76738

Favarel-Garrigues, G., & Shukan, I. (2020). Perspectives on post-Soviet vigilantism. Introduction. *Laboratorium: Russian Review of Social Research*, 11(3), 4–15, http://doi.org/10.25285/2078-1938-2019-11-3-4-15

Favarel-Garrigues, G., & Gayer, L. (2016). Violer la loi pour maintenir l'ordre. Le vigilantisme en débat. *Politix*, 115(3), 7–33, http://doi.org/10.3917/ pox.115.0007

Gabdulhakov, R. (2018). Citizen-led justice in post-communist Russia: From comrades' courts to dotcomrade vigilantism. *Surveillance & Society*, 16(3), 314–31, http://doi.org/10.24908/ss.v16i3.6952

Gabowitsch, M. (2018). Are copycats subversive? Strategy-31, the Russian runs, the immortal regiment, and the transformative potential of non-hierarchical movements. *Problems of Post-Communism*, 65 (5), 297–314, http://doi. org/10.1080/10758216.1250604

Hemment, J. (2012). Nashi, youth voluntarism, and Potemkin NGOs: Making sense of civil society in post-Soviet Russia. *Slavic Review*, 71(2), 234–60, http://doi.org/10.5612/slavicreview.71.2.0234

Johnston, L. (1996). What is vigilantism? *The British Journal of Criminology*, 36(2), 220–36, https://doi.org/10.1093/oxfordjournals.bjc.a014083

Kasra, M. (2017). Vigilantism, public shaming, and social media hegemony: The role of digital-networked images in humiliation and sociopolitical control. *The Communication Review*, 20(3), 172–88, http://doi.org/10.1080/10714421 .2017.1343068

Laruelle, M. (2017, March 16). *Putin's Regime and the Ideological Market: A Difficult Balancing Game*. Carnegie Endowment for International Peace, Task Force White Paper.

Lemieux, C. (2007). À quoi sert l'analyse des controverses? *Mil Neuf Cent*, 25, 191–212, http://doi.org/10.3917/mnc.025.0191

Pratten, D., & Sen, A. (eds) (2007). *Global Vigilantes*. London: Hurst.

Rukov, K., & Chesnikov, I. (2015, 20 July). Posle "nashei" ery (After 'our' era), *Iod*.

Sher, M. (2015, September 21). Pravookhranitel'naya samodeyatel'nost' (DIY law-enforcement), *Kommersant*.

Smadja, D. (2012). La boîte noire de la controverse. *Raisons politiques*, 47(3), 5–11, http://doi.org/10.3917/rai.047.0005

Transparency International Russia. (2016). *Prozrachnost' rossiiskikh NKO* (The transparency of Russian non-commercial organizations), Moscow.

Trottier, D. (2017). Digital vigilantism as weaponisation of visibility. *Philosophy & Technology*, 30(1), 55–72, http://doi.org/10.1007/s13347-016-0216-4

Far-Right Digital Vigilantism as Technical Mediation: Anti-Immigration Activism on YouTube

Samuel Tanner, Valentine Crosset and Aurélie Campana

The 'Alps Mission' and Far-Right Activism

How do far-right activists, digital media platforms and audiences interplay in the production and diffusion of discriminatory and harmful speech? Hate speech, identity claims, anti-immigration rhetoric and calls to prevent refugees from entering certain territories are all expressions of a far-right populist discourse that has become increasingly visible in the public domain in Canada, Europe and the United States (Eisler 2016; Marwick & Lewis, 2017; Perry & Scrivens, 2015). For example, the 21st April 2018, Generation Identity (*Génération identitaire* or GI, the youth wing of *Les Identitaires*), a French far-right movement, launched what they called the "Alps Mission" in the Hautes-Alpes, France.[1] A few hundred people, arguing that they needed to protect the white Christian identity of the European people,[2] put up a blockade to prevent

---

1   The mission lasted until 29 June 2018, though only about ten people from GI patrolled the area from 22 April on.
2   Their slogan is "Us before others" (*Les nôtres avant les autres*).

   https://doi.org/10.11647/OBP.0200.06

migrants — mostly from the African continent — from entering French territory from Italy. Holding up gigantic "NO WAY" banners and orange security nets symbolising the physical barriers they created to prevent migrants from entering French territory, militants presented themselves as the defenders of Europe. Interestingly, the militants involved were not just from France but from different European countries as well as the United States and Canada, an ironic blurring of the "us" in their slogan. It was not the first time GI had been active: in June 2017, the group had chartered a vessel to prevent NGOs from rescuing migrants in the Mediterranean Sea between Italy and Libya, the beginning of a "summer of disturbances" (Warren, 2017) targeting NGO rescue missions.

According to its website,[3] GI uses tactics such as demagogic discourse and exploitation of resentments to mobilise the population against traditional and mainstream political parties and elites, who are portrayed as corrupt and uninterested in the population and its immediate troubles, as well as responsible for numerous social and political problems (e.g. illegal immigration, unemployment, the negative impact of globalisation on local areas). It contrasts a hard-working population involved in everyday economic and social struggles with elites presented as profiteers (Laclau, 2005) and can therefore be considered a far-right populist group.

In this chapter, far-right populist activism is understood as a program of actions that promotes an ethnocentric understanding of people and national identity, as well as a rejection of immigration and traditional political adversaries. One of the defining features of populism is the claim by the activists involved that they are taking charge of or responsibility for a cause on behalf of a silent majority or a wider population. Populist societal vigilantism activities are often aimed at attracting a large audience, which provides both support and legitimacy. The audience — defined as that part of the public interested in a cause or a group — must therefore be taken into account when considering how vigilante groups use media. Their activism entails mobilising a wide range of actions in both the physical and the digital sphere. The digital media platforms involved are Web 2.0 Internet-based applications, which make it possible for people to create and exchange

---

3   https://generationidentitaire.org/presentation/

user-generated content, often selected to support their personal or political opinions (Van Dijck, 2013). The presence and anti-immigration actions of such groups have been documented in Bulgaria (France 24, 2016), Canada (Rémillard, 2015; Tanner & Campana 2019), France (Gardenier & Monie, 2018), Germany (El Jabri, 2018), Italy (Segond, 2018) and South Africa (Fourchard, 2016) and the phenomenon seems to be spreading, at least in the Western world. Given GI's objectives of promoting collective security, maintaining an exclusivist version of identity and protecting its territory faced with what is seen as the failure of traditional authorities, as well as its insistence on self-governance (Mudde, 2017), it can be considered to be a vigilante group.

Les Johnston defines vigilantism as involving six elements (Johnston, 1996): 1. *Planning, premeditation and organization* — vigilantes engage in some form of preparatory activity, such as surveillance of an individual or group and/or observation of a particular location; 2. *Private voluntary agency* — vigilantism is undertaken by private agents (as opposed to public actors) who are not approved or endorsed by the state; 3. *Autonomous citizenship* — vigilantism is engaged in voluntarily by private citizens who are not supported by the state and is often used in reference to popular movements engaged in what they see as self-protection; 4. *Use, or threat of use, of force* — violence, or the threat to use violence, is a common trait of vigilantism and a necessary dimension of vigilante actions, whether the violence is symbolic, such as calling for the expulsion of illegal migrants, or physical; 5. *Reaction to crime and social deviance* — vigilantism aimed at crime control is distinct from vigilantism intended to promote societal control or "the maintenance of communal, ethnic or sectarian order and values" (Johnston, 1996, p. 228). Both types are related to a defence of some type of rules or norms, whether institutionalised or not, but the second type is concerned less with deviance and more with values, culture or political ideas. Finally, 6. *personal and collective security* — vigilante action is usually a reaction by individuals who feel that their security is in jeopardy. Johnston's definition supports our contention that GI can be considered a societal vigilante group. Its actions are planned and organised — the barrier and the banner were put up by autonomous, private citizens acting voluntarily, without help or contributions from the state or authorities. Although there is no documented use of force, activists called for the expulsion of illegal migrants, an act of symbolic violence. Finally, taking control of the frontier between France and Italy was presented as necessary to ensure the collective security of the population and maintain its communal (French) and ethnic (white) order and values (Christian).

Moving beyond efforts to define such groups, and following the approach proposed by Favarel-Garrigues and Gayer (2016), as well as Pratten and Sen (2007), in this chapter we focus on the practices and actions of societal vigilantes. More specifically, we analyse not only how far-right populist activists use YouTube to promote and diffuse vigilante discourse, but also how the audience affects this process. What influence does the combination of digital media platforms, vigilante groups and audience have on the diffusion and visibility of far-right populism? Our analysis focuses on the *materiality* of the digital platforms through which digital mediation takes place (Kinsley, 2014). Materiality refers to the principle that a system or object, including digital platforms, should be understood not only in terms of its structure (what it is) but also in terms of its effects (what it does) (Drucker, 2013). Far-right populist discourse and content are the result of interaction between digital platforms (e.g. YouTube) and users (e.g. far-right populist activists). Looking at this process from a Latourian and Actor-Network Theory (ANT) perspective (Akrich, 1992; Latour, 1994; 2005; Law & Hassard, 1999), GI's far-right populist activism as expressed in the Alps Movement can be understood as *technical mediation* between humans (activists), objects (digital media platforms) and the audience.

This study focuses on a specific YouTube channel, run by Lauren Southern, a Canadian far-right populist activist who took part in the April 2018 Alps Mission. After looking at the literature on the relation between activism and digital media, we present an alternative framework — technical mediation and ANT — and show how this perspective provides new insights. We then explain our methodological approach and present a case study of technical mediation between Lauren Southern, YouTube and the audience. Finally, we discuss our main contributions and suggest a tentative path for the prevention and regulation of far-right content and online societal vigilantism.

Far-Right Populist Activism and Digital Platforms

Research on the relation between media and social movements has produced much relevant literature (Foellmer et al., 2018; Gerbaudo, 2012, 2018). Some researchers have focused on how digital media contribute to the visibility of social movements by making it possible to promote a particular cause (Wolfson, 2014). Others, adopting the "connectivity paradigm" or the ability of Web 2.0 — given its platforms are fuelled by user-generated content — to foster online sociability and interactions, have looked at how these new capacities and their interpretation by users allow the mobilisation of social movements (Bennett et al., 2014; Kavada, 2015; Van Dijck, 2013). Platforms — in conjunction with how people use them — not only contribute to shaping a sense of community among their users (Burgess & Green, 2008; Gillespie, 2010) but also supply "validation, momentum and legitimacy in shaping social groups' preferences, thus fostering their mobilisation" (Ellinas, 2018, p. 1). In this sense, such platforms are "important organizational agents" in the structuring and programming of social movements (Bennett et al., 2014, p. 233). Digital platforms provide access to an agenda that encourages far-right populist activists to adopt a particular frame with regard to crucial issues "such as immigration and crime, helping legitimise a political space in which the radical right can thrive" (Ellinas, 2018, p. 1; Mazzeloni et al., 2003) and making it possible for the phenomenon known as the "alt-right" to generate new perspectives.

According to Marwick and Lewis (2017, p. 3), the "alt-right" can more accurately be described as "an amalgam of conspiracy theorists, techno-libertarians, white nationalists, Men's Rights advocates, trolls, anti-feminists, anti-immigration activists and bored young people". Although some individuals within the alt-right, such as Richard Spencer or Milo Yiannopoulos, have become more widely known, their popularity has had a limited shelf-life. Most scholars recognise that the movement has "no real organizational structure" (Wendling, 2018, p. 5) and can "scarcely be called an organized movement" (Hawley, 2017, p. 11). However, its presence and visibility in the public sphere and in debates is large and growing. Its use of digital platforms such as Twitter, Gab, Discord and 4chan, just to name a few, has become a central topic for research. While the aim of alt-right activism is to promote identitarian and white nationalist or white supremacist discourse, its actual output consists largely of trolling, shaping and propagating "fake news", or making use of irony and (dark) humour directed at certain categories or topics in society, such as immigrants and feminism.[4] These strategies are supported by the diffusion of memes or "digital items with common characteristics that are imitated and reiterated around the web" (Nissenbaum & Shifam, 2017, p. 483) and used to "capture lurkers' attention and to win their hearts and minds" (Hawley, 2017, p. 73). The idea of a "Molotov JPEG", coined by Hawley (ibid.), captures this dynamic perfectly: memes can be used to 'set fire' to public opinion.

Alt-right activists look for provocations in the public domain that they can use to attract attention to their message of white nationalism. Contrary to traditional online activity by far-right groups, most of which is confined to confidential Internet sites such as stormfront.org, alt-right digital practices have spread beyond cryptic and confidential platforms to penetrate public discourse. Alt-right discourse that appears on specialised channels such as 4chan or Gab or mainstream social media platforms like Twitter is now picked up by traditional media (Marwick & Lewis, 2017; Wendling, 2018; Philips, 2018) and widely diffused in public spaces. Looking at digital media platforms and their appropriation by alt-right activists reveals that their influence extends far beyond local street demonstrations. However, the degree of impact that online content has on the hearts and minds of the population remains an empirical question. Do social media and digital platforms have any influence beyond the online sphere, and, if so, how much and how is it achieved? Here, the concept of performativity — the possibility that an artefact or a technology produces an effect in the everyday life of those who use it or somehow relate to it — seems relevant.

According to Paolo Gerbaudo, whose work focuses on the role of social media in social movements and collective action, digital platforms produce effects in the real world by generating different configurations of how people perceive and understand their environment and their relation to it, thus bringing novelty or change into being and shaping

---

4   There is some conflict here between activism that is sincere, or goal-oriented, versus less sincere trolling (for example, being an 'edgelord'). Although this issue is important, it is beyond the scope of this chapter to analyse when alt-right activists are goal-oriented and ideologically driven or simply trolling.

social movements such as the Arab Spring or the Occupy movement. Social media facilitate and enable the organisation of collective actions (Gerbaudo, 2012). To capture these performative effects, Gerbaudo coined the concept "choreography of assembly", the process by which activists' use of digital platforms enables "a process of symbolic construction of public space *which facilitates and guides the physical assembling* of a highly dispersed and individualised constituency" (ibid., p. 5, emphasis added). This symbolic construction acts as a crucial vector in shaping a sense of purpose and togetherness among activists and their audience. In line with Bennett et al.'s work (2014), this performativity affects the hearts and minds of those who are part of the assembly or influenced by it. According to Gerbaudo, "what [...] has possibly brought [digital media platforms] so much attention is their *internal or local use*: their use as means of organization of collective action and [...] as a means of mobilization in the crucial task of gathering people on the streets" (Gerbaudo, 2012, p. 3, emphasis added). Finally, he points to the central role of what he refers to as "soft leaders", or "influential Facebook admins and activist tweeps [and YouTubers] who become choreographers, involved in setting the scene and constructing an emotional space within which collective action can unfold" (Gerbaudo, 2012, p. 5). Lauren Southern is illustrative of such "soft leaders". The notion of "influencers" also describes such activists, or "people who shape public opinion and advertise goods and services through the 'conscientious callibration' of their online personae" (Lewis, 2018, p. 4). Lauren Southern is not so much selling goods and services, but as a content creator, she rather "adopts the techniques of influencers to build [an] audience [...] and sell [it] on far-right ideology" (ibid.) and thus be considered as a "political influencer" (ibid.).

Understanding the Relation Between Digital Media Platforms and Activists: Technical Mediation

Considering the performative effect of digital media offers an alternative perspective that falls between a utopian stance, in which such technology provides networks of hope (Castells, 2012), and a dystopian one, according to which social media allows some people to assuage their consciences by taking part in social or political causes online, operating from the comfort of their sofa but without any true commitment, a phenomenon known as slacktivism (Kristofferson et al., 2014; Morozov, 2009a, 2009b ; Gladwell, 2010). Mattoni and Treré (2014) warn that scholars should not fetishise digital media or evaluate them strictly on the basis of what they make possible — they do not mobilise and influence public debate by themselves. Actors, however, use and appropriate them precisely for such purposes. What sort of interactions occur between technology and activists, between soft leaders and among audiences?

We argue that technology and digital media platforms should be considered in their *materiality*, that is as having

> some property [...] that provides users with the capability to perform some action. Calling these properties out with the adjective 'material' seems a ploy to remind the reader that the software-[or digital media platform]-in-use does things that cannot be reduced to human intention or action (Leonardi, 2010, p. 3).

In contrast to the way in which digital media platforms are understood from an instrumentalist perspective, we suggest that they are not neutral tools but have a significant effect on the ends to which they are put (Bourne, 2012; Feenberg, 1999). This materiality should be taken into account in their use by, or interaction with, activists. To better grasp these dynamics, we adopt a conceptual framework based on the Actor Network Theory — ANT (Akrich, 1992; Latour, 1994; 2005; Law & Hassard, 1999). ANT's central notion, *technical mediation*, entails looking at societal vigilantism as a program of action, a series of objectives, decisions and intentions by agents in episodes in which digital media platforms, far-right populist activists and the audience interplay.

Bruno Latour grounds the concept of technical mediation on four elements. The first is *translation*, "which does not mean a shift from one vocabulary to another [...] but the displacement, drift, invention, meditation, the creation of a link that did not exist before and that to some degree modifies two elements or agents" (Latour, 1994, p. 32). The agents involved can be human or nonhuman. However, since it is uncommon to refer to nonhumans as agents, ANT uses the term *actants* for both humans and nonhumans — "a borrowing from semiotics that describes any entity that acts in a plot until the attribution of a figurative or non-figurative role" [e.g. front or back stage], in his example the roles are "'citizen' or 'gun'"(ibid., p. 33). Following Latour, neither far-right populist activists nor digital media platforms can be considered responsible for the meme of the Molotov JPEG. Instead, such symbolic constructs are shaped by interaction, or mediation, between the two types of actants (at least). Human and nonhuman actants exchange properties, characteristics and competences, giving one another new possibilities, new goals, new functions (ibid., p. 35) that need to be accounted for to understand how the technical mediation is unfolding. In this endeavour, one has to account for obstacles that may arise during the unfolding and analyse how actants negotiate them. (For example, many far-right activists turned to an alternative digital media platform, Gab, after Twitter and Facebook strengthened their regulations against hate speech.) Introducing the idea of technical mediation makes it possible to provide a microanalysis of how far-right activists, digital media platforms and audiences interplay in the production and diffusion of discriminatory and harmful speech. What is the sequence of the *mediation* and *translation* processes staging these actants?

The second meaning of technical mediation is *composition*, in which action is understood not as the exclusive property of humans but rather as belonging to an association of entities, or actants. In composition, "actants are in the process of exchanging competences, offering one another new possibilities, new goals, new functions" (ibid, p. 35). The final product of this composition is a *blackbox* "that makes the joint production of actors and artifacts entirely opaque" (ibid., p. 36). This is where the analytical challenge takes place: can we open the blackbox? Can we provide a more fine-grained analysis that makes it possible to better grasp the mediation that occurs between human and nonhuman actants? This process is the third meaning of technical mediation — *"reversible blackboxing"* — and is composed of seven mechanisms: disinterest, interest, composition of a new goal, obligatory passage point, alignment, blackboxing and convergence.

Disinterest refers to the first step, where actants are considered in parallel. At this point in the mediation process, the two actants evolve separately, showing no interest in each other. Enlistment brings a new step — interest — to the technical mediation process and the actants connect. Such connection, or assemblage, is related to an exchange of properties between the entities and provokes a new goal. The process remains highly iterative and dependent on the nature of the interactions between the actants in a network. This step is followed by an obligatory passage point that introduces a qualitative novelty whereby the assemblage identifies "what counts" as decisive or as knowledgeable (Latour, 2005). This translation comes with obstacles and constraints that the actants have to overcome in order to align with each other. The new assemblage that emerges from the successful overcoming of obstacles presents new modes of functioning and capacities. According to this perspective, blackboxing is a process of composition, in which technology and society are co-emergent, which assembles power relations in particular configurations and renders them fixed, invisible and logical. Convergence refers to the final product and is important in understanding technical mediation. For the topic under discussion here, technical mediation in shaping a societal vigilantism program and promoting anti-immigration discourse involves an assemblage composed of at least Lauren Southern, YouTube and the audience. The result is the production of memes as blackboxes — or, in the larger program of promoting anti-immigration and white nationalist societal vigilante discourses, as Molotov JPEGs.

Finally, the fourth meaning of technical mediation is *delegation*, when meaning is "materialized" into or "engraved" on (Latour, 1994, p. 38) matter, which then has the power to influence the actions of individuals.

Methodology

To analyse the societal vigilantism program and the promotion of anti-immigration discourse exemplified by the Alps Mission, we undertook a case study of one activist — Lauren Southern — and her commitment to promoting Génération Identitaire's Defend Europe mission, largely through YouTube. Southern is representative of far-right soft leaders — or political influencers — in her exploitation of the interactive and participatory character of digital media platforms to set the scene and bring "a degree of coherence to people's spontaneous and creative participation in the [online] protest movements" (Gerbaudo, 2012, p. 13). Her leadership consists of proposing "collective images" and "forms of actions [...] or 'scripts'" that participants are invited to perform (ibid., p. 44). YouTube, even more than television, is a particularly unstable object of study, marked by dynamic change (both in terms of videos and organization), a diversity of content (which moves with a different rhythm to television but likewise flows through, and often disappears from, the service), and a similar quotidian frequency, or 'everydayness' (Burgess & Green, 2018, p. 6).

For the sake of the analysis, and in order to understand the technical mediation, or the interplay between Southern, YouTube and audiences, we adopted a sociotechnical approach to the microanalysis of a video available on Southern's YouTube channel and produced while actively taking part in the Alps Mission. We selected the video from among the 136 videos she had uploaded on her channel[5] based on its "raw" character, meaning that it was unedited, in process (rather than edited afterwards) and live streamed. It therefore provided valuable material for the study of the chronology of the technical mediation process, and significant empirical material for the analysis of the blackboxing involved in Southern's societal vigilantism.

We extracted the selected video and converted it into an MP4 file, as this format is more convenient for analysis. We then made a complete transcription of its content, capturing not only the audio but the setting (including the presence of people around the activist, actions unfolding around her, interactions with individuals that the viewer does not see in the video, etc.), context, live comments and also how the message is staged.

The technical mediation to be analysed includes the sender (Southern), the technology (digital media platform YouTube) and the audience (identified only by the pseudonyms they used when posting). These nodes are crucial parts of the choreography of the presentation of the Alps Mission as framed in the video produced on Southern's YouTube channel. The video, as a meme, a Molotov JPEG, is intended to set fire to public opinion, at least as it is exemplified by Southern's audience, and thus provides a frame, or a symbolic space, that "keys" (Goffman, 1974) the public's interpretation of the event. Our objective is to analyse the genealogy of that meme to show how it is the outcome of crossing-overs of properties between the actants involved in the technical mediation.

---

5   https://www.youtube.com/channel/UCla6APLHX6W3FeNLc8PYuvg

Analysis: Societal Vigilantism as Technical Mediation

In this section, we focus on *reversible blackboxing*, Latour's third meaning — or way of understanding — technical mediation, as it seems the most promising to help us better understand how a network of actants contribute to making digital societal vigilantism visible. We analyse each of the seven mechanisms discussed in the earlier exposition of Latour's theory.

Disinterest: To analyse the actants involved in the mediation process, let's start by providing a precise description of each one. First, Lauren Southern. Born in 1995 in Canada, she is a central figure in Canadian far-right populist activism as well as an Internet personality and influencer. At the age of 20, she ran as candidate for the federal Libertarian Party in a district in British Columbia, getting 0.9% of the vote. Until 2017 she worked as a journalist for *Rebel Media* — a copycat version of *Breitbart*[6] — founded in 2015 by Ezra Levant, another important figure in Canadian far-right populism. She was active as a YouTube vlogger until autumn 2018 and is still followed by 685K people.[7] She has produced and posted 115 videos at the time of writing, whose duration varies between two minutes and 90 minutes. Her viewing metrics vary between 38K and 2.9M views. The videos consist mainly of interviews with figures involved to varied extents in far-right populist activism, or reports on events where far-right populism is denounced, or multiculturalism, LGBTQ+, or civic rights are promoted. In the latter cases, Southern, adopting a provocative or trolling style, interviews activists or militants involved with such causes. In a video posted in 2015, she holds a sign saying "There is no rape culture in the West" at a SlutWalk demonstration

---

6   *Breitbart* is a populist ultra-conservative news network created in the United States in 2007. Its stated editorial position is based on opposition to the establishment, or the elites, whether Republicans or Democrats.

7   In one of her last videos, posted on 14 August 2018, Southern announced that she was taking a new direction and has stopped posting on her YouTube channel (at the time of writing). She announced that she was not going to post on YouTube for a while, since the format she was using "did not get the proper depth of analysis [the issues we are dealing with] deserve [...] I want to step away from this media rat-race of ego and narcissism and I just want to tell the truth, that is all that I wanted to do since the beginning of all these crazy shenaningans. So, I am absolutely thrilled to announce that I won't just be disappearing of the Internet after taking a step away from YouTube. I going to be changing my pace and dedicating all of my time and energy to making full-scale and in-depth documentaries [...]".

in Vancouver. In another, shot during a demonstration by LGBTQ+ activists in March 2016, she argues that there are "only two human genders". In response LGBTQ+ demonstrators empty a container of urine on her. On two occasions, Southern was banned from entry into the UK and New Zealand based on the alleged risk she presents by stirring up ethnic and religious tensions. Her views include antifeminism, xenophobia, Islamophobia and anti-multiculturalism (Shaw, 2018). In May 2017, Southern was involved in GI's attempt to stop the NGO ship *Aquarius* from leaving Sicily to search for and rescue migrants off the coast of Northern Africa. She and her colleagues were arrested and detained by the Italian Coast Guard but justified their actions by stating: "If the politicians won't stop the boasts, we'll stop the boats" (Claxton, 2017), referring thus to a vigilante repertoire of actions. In April 2018, Southern took part in the Alps Mission. In giving visibility to far-right populist discourse and content, Southern undertakes what Neveu (2011) refers to as political work in which the human actant designates, nominates, provides a language and orders the world.

The second entity, the non-human actant, is YouTube. Launched in 2005 by Steven Chen, Chad Hurley and Jawed Karim and bought a year later by Google, YouTube is a "software for distributing, accessing and combining (or 'publishing', 'sharing' and 'remixing') media content on the web" (Manovich, 2013, p. 24). Its goal is "to remove the technical barriers to the widespread sharing of video online" (Burgess & Green, 2009, p. 1). One of its primary missions, as stated on its site, is to provide, or supply, a channel through which "everyone can make their voice heard and discover the world" and its stated goal is to promote four fundamental freedoms: freedom of speech, freedom of information, freedom of opportunity and freedom of belonging. YouTube hopes to provide everyone with an equal opportunity to speak and become informed (Gillespie, 2010). According to recent numbers, "over 1.9 billion logged-in users visit YouTube each month, and every day people watch over a billion hours of video and generate billions of views".[8] The platform also hopes to make the world more connected and is available in a total of 80 different languages (covering 95% of the Internet population).[9] YouTube's mission statement fits with rhetoric emphasising

---

8   See YouTube for press: https://www.youtube.com/intl/en-GB/yt/about/press/
9   Ibid.

the Internet's potential for democratisation and enthusiasm for the medium's most popular characteristics, namely its "User Generated Content" (UGC) (Gillespie, 2010) and the "participatory culture" that is generally held to be part of the Internet (Jenkins, 2006). According to Burgess and Green (2018; 2009) YouTube may be thought of as a "patron", enabling — but also constraining — collective creativity by fostering the participation of a large number of actors in the creation and broadcasting of contents, while maintaining control of the conditions under which "creative content is produced, ordered, and re-presented for the interpretation of audiences" (Burgess & Green, 2009, p. 60). The content produced on the platform is thus the result of the interplay between the platform's architecture — its affordances — and user tactics (Cardon, 2008).

YouTube is distinct from other digital media platforms (e.g. Facebook, Instagram, Twitter; Murthy & Sharma, 2019) in that, in contrast to platforms such as Facebook — which is based on public, or semi-public, profiles as well as the accumulation of friends and the expansion of one's network (boyd & Ellison, 2007; Van Dijck, 2013) — its main purpose is providing a platform for broadcasting videos.[10] However, YouTube users, namely broadcasters and the audience, are able to interact and communicate on the platform (Murthy & Sharma, 2019). YouTube is characterised by a series of affordances that make it possible to express a reaction to a video. While an earlier version of YouTube emphasised sharing "self-made amateur videos" rather than "professionally generated content" (Van Dijck, 2013, p. 110), today it stands at a crossroads, making available both amateur videos as well as more familiar forms of mass media executed by professionals (2009, p. 60; Van Dijck, 2013).

YouTube also provides access to the third actant, the *audience*. As Gross argues, "web-based media have made multidirectional, audience-generated communication a reality, giving citizens the opportunity to join the party as producers rather than consumers [...] the top-down tyranny of the media has been effectively challenged" (2009, p. 67). It therefore becomes necessary to take into account not only UGC

---

10   Michael Golebiewski and danah boyd specify that YouTube is both a social media platform (it allows the possibility of building links between users), as well as a search engine, thus indexing content (Golebiewski & boyd, 2019)

but also the audience: "practices of participation [...] the practices of audiencehood — quoting, favouriting, commenting, responding, sharing and viewing — all leave traces, and therefore they all have effects on the common culture of YouTube as it evolves" (Burgess & Green, 2009, p. 57). In contrast to the predominant model in broadcasting, the audience can participate directly in increasing YouTube's popularity and the attention it generates. Through its Most Viewed, Most Responded, Most Favorited and Most Discussed metrics, YouTube makes it possible to create "a simplified and atomised model of audience engagement — based on the raw frequencies of views, comments, response videos, and additions to users' favourites" (ibid., p. 41). Measures of audience involvement then serve as the basis for promotion of what is determined to be the most popular content, fostering a "feedback loop between the perceived uses of and value logics of YouTube and its 'actual' uses and meanings" (ibid.).

While YouTube as a platform depends on a business model, terms of use and legal conditions (such for example as legal restrictions on content), its existence is also strongly linked to a large technical network that enables users to watch and broadcast videos. The physical and immaterial functions of the platform that make it possible to circulate professional and amateur contents depend on a series of interdependent components. For instance, it requires a device such as a smartphone, computer or tablet to watch or broadcast videos. A broadband Internet connection is necessary to make the video available and allow it to circulate. These different devices are part of a large network of material and immaterial processes that not only makes it possible to send and view content, but also modifies the composition or the state of the actants — human and nonhuman — involved in the process.

Interest: Southern is interested in becoming more visible, or promoting and gaining wider visibility for her views. Actant #1 (Southern) turns to actant #2 (YouTube) in order to reach actant #3 (the audience). There is no information available about why Southern chose YouTube as the way to achieve her goals, but it seems reasonable to think that the platform's affordances played a role in her decision and fulfil her requirements. YouTube provides a valuable way to diffuse ideas, since the costs related to both production and diffusion of content (UGC) are low while the opportunity to reach a wide audience is great.

While vlogs are not systematically hosted by YouTube, the platform is widely recognised as a way to encourage social participation and is a crucial tool for those looking for visibility (Burgess & Green, 2009, p. 53).

On the second day of the Alps Mission, using a smartphone equipped with a camera, Southern used the YouTube app to stream live for sixteen minutes and fifteen seconds, providing an update on the situation. From the beginning of the livestream, which was of poor quality due to a bad network connection, Southern appeared in 'selfie mode' and let the audience know that she was broadcasting live. She was seen outdoors, in close proximity to the demonstrators, with the Alps in the background. She varied the shots by moving her mobile phone, showing some of the actants who took part in the demonstration. She also filmed actants who were part of the "anti-program". Anti-program here refers to any action or event that disrupted the societal vigilantism of the Alps Mission or Southern's livestreaming. These included representatives of the mainstream media[11] as well as the police. Her live broadcast also contained interviews — in the form of informal conversations — with other far-right figures. Among these were US activists Brittany Pettibone and Martin Sellner, whom she presented as the "mastermind" of the Alps Mission. Pettibone and Sellner are well-known identitarian activists and YouTubers active in the anti-immigration movement. Pettibone has 115k followers and her channel contains 129 videos. Sellner has 85K followers and his channel has 341 videos.

Just seconds after Southern launched her livestream, the audience reacted via the YouTube "live comments" function, which is described as a "module which lets you engage with the broadcaster and the broader YouTube community" (YouTube, 2010). Livestream comments were numerous and appeared very quickly, revealing interest in the activists' actions. While there were a few comments that were sceptical about the Mission or critical of it, and even insults aimed at Southern, most comments were supportive. It was common to see encouragement of the cause and the particular action. Some comments included right-wing

---

11   It's not clear why these anti-program individuals were included. Perhaps to allow the vigilantes to present themselves as being supported by locals in contrast to local attitudes toward the mainstream media.

symbols. Negative comments largely addressed the bad quality of the broadcast, holding the technical device (the nonhuman actant) responsible.

Fig. 6.1 Lauren Southern's livestream interface while she is interviewing Brittany Pettibone. Screenshot, 24 January 2019, YouTube.

Fig. 6.2 Screenshot of Southern's livestream showing live comments, starting 30 seconds after the beginning of the video. Screenshot, 24 January 2019, YouTube.

Composition of a new goal: At this stage, the interaction of the main actants produces a new actant, actant #4. In technical mediation, a new actant is characterised by a goal that differs from that of previous actants (Latour, 2007). Neither human nor nonhuman goals are set in advance. Instead, a program of actions unfolds as the result of a new mediation — translation — between, in this case, human and nonhuman actants. In her societal vigilantism program, Southern specifies her approach to one event — the Alps Mission — where her goal is to prevent the entrance of illegal migrants and call attention to the wider problems they create for society. The composition of a new goal should, however, be considered in relation to what the interactions of human and nonhuman actants are as a result. For instance, the use of the livestreaming option offered by YouTube enabled the live broadcasting, but also came with constraints — the poor quality of the image was an obstacle. The tailoring of a new goal was also affected by the context — for example, Southern had to consider the actions going on around her in shaping and diffusing her message / content. If she had decided not to livestream but instead to edit the images before uploading them to her YouTube channel, the content would probably have been different.

The translation that occurs between human and nonhuman actants transforms each of the entities through the exchange of properties, or crossovers. Such evolution in its turn produces a new state, or step, in the technical mediation. Southern becomes a visible personality promoting and amplifying an anti-immigrant discourse, while YouTube's algorithms are affected by the presence of actants (influencers or soft leaders) such as Southern, posting similar contents promoting anti-immigrant discourses. The platform's algorithms are impacted by the presence of the video. These algorithms, which are the basis on which videos are recommended, play a central role in the management of the platform, as stated by YouTube: "Your activity on YouTube, Google and Chrome may influence your YouTube search results, recommendations on the Home page, in-app notifications, and suggested videos".[12]

Given recent revelations by Google employees, it seems clear that "YouTube represents one of the largest scale and most sophisticated industrial recommendation systems in existence" (Covington, Adams & Sargin, 2016, p. 1). Diffusion of YouTube's content relies on intermediary recommendation algorithms that filter as well as classify content in order to better align it to users, based on their Internet consumer habits (Van Dijck, 2013). In consequence, YouTube recommends the content

---

12   https://support.google.com/youtube/answer/6342839

that users access according to a code, which governs their experience of the Internet while promoting content selected according to an algorithm. Covington et al. (2016) reveal how YouTube uses "deep learning" to feed its recommendation algorithms. The system is grounded on two neuronal networks: the first deals with "candidate generation" and the second with "ranking". The neuronal networks are fed by diversified criteria, such as i) the user's record of use of the Internet; ii) "collaborative filtering", based on the similarity between users ("expressed in terms of coarse features such as IDs of the video watched, search query tokens and demographics" and iii) "data impressions" accessed via "a desired objective function using a rich set of features describing the video and user" (ibid., p. 2). Once these filters have operated, a list of videos, sorted by score, are promoted to the user. However, to make a final determination of the efficiency of the algorithm, or model, YouTube uses live experiments: "In a live experiment, we can measure subtle changes in click-through rate, watch time, and many other metrics that measure user engagement" (ibid.).

YouTube's algorithms are capable of making selected contents highly visible. However, the recommendation algorithm requires the presence and participation of an audience that leaves traces of its activity and behaviour online. The audience, by clicking, watching, commenting and liking Southern's video, coupled with the record of its past Internet activities, contributes to the choice of the Alps Mission video, as well as other videos with similar contents, by the recommendation algorithm. The algorithm engages and both assembles and reassembles a specific audience by overvaluing and favouring some content over others. In Southern's case, the other channels recommended on her YouTube channel (such as *Breitbart* and Brittany Pettibone's channels) also promote alt-right, far-right or conservative contents. That recommendation process is the outcome of an interplay, that is a property of associated entities between the user and YouTube's algorithm. While the user's track records and habits on the Internet modify the code, it allows for increasingly fine-tuning the recommendations at the same time.

The interplay between actants transforms each of them, largely through the exchange of properties that creates novelty — links or connections that did not exist before — displacement, or drifts. The new actant, #4, can be understood in terms of the following equation:

Southern (actant #1) + (YouTube #2 + audience #3) = livestream update of the second day of GI's Defend Europe program, the Alps Mission (actant #4).

Obligatory passage point: As the livestreaming continues, new actants appear and disappear (and sometimes reappear) in the frame. The audience is active throughout the live broadcast and sometimes requires Southern's attention, as she has to read the comments posted by her followers and viewers. The mediation, translation and composition processes are characterised by friction, resistance and even opposition between the actants, each of which is potentially capable of putting an end to the livestream. For example, Southern struggles with the bad quality of the stream, which makes it difficult for the audience to follow the message and increases audience discontent, which is expressed numerous times, as in the following screenshot taken directly from YouTube.

Fig. 6.3 Audience reacting to the bad streaming of Southern's video. Screenshot, 24 January 2019, YouTube.

At points, Southern also struggles with the use of her mobile phone, as her hand shakes, possibly revealing anxiety. The idea of an *obligatory passage point*, step 4 in reversible blackboxing, captures the need to overcome obstacles and resistances, such as those exemplified by the audience's discontent. Since Southern's objective is to diffuse her anti-immigration message as widely as possible, she has to keep the audience involved. The audience becomes part of the translation process and is an important actant that Southern has to consider and adapt to in the ongoing streaming process, providing a clear example of an exchange of properties between two actants. The audience, through the comments it posts, makes sense of and is responsive to the message, while Southern adjusts her message in response to her audience. YouTube's affordances — and the audience's use of such affordances — clearly impacted Southern's program and how she reported on the situation. At some points, she moved her phone, positioning it differently in physical space while asking if the image was better. At other times she read comments and even responded to some of them, addressing the audience directly. While many comments expressed support for Southern's cause, this was not the case with all those who posted. Some even criticised the lack of interaction with the audience. One user commented: "literally no reason to be live if you're not actually going to talk and just pretend this is a pre-recorded YouTube video".

The outdoor setting in which the livestream occurred presented challenges to all actants, human and non-human. For instance, while broadcasting Southern also had to remain aware of her environment as the situation unfolded and things changed around her, such as the unexpected arrival of the police, whose intentions were unclear. All actants must successfully negotiate a series of such constraints or obstacles — obligatory passage points — that pave the path to the accomplishment of a particular program.

Alignment: If obstacles are overcome, a new assemblage or collective (actant #5), is formed with new modes of functioning and new capacities. Once all actants have successfully negotiated the constraints in the obligatory passage point, *alignment* takes place (Latour, 1994). The collective formed by Southern-enabled-by-her-smartphone-while-livestreaming-on-YouTube-and-overcoming-obstacles is now capable of providing visibility to the goal, which is better control of the borders between France and Italy through the deployment of a barrier. Southern also counts on Pettibone and Sellner to offer more details about the Alps Mission, particularly the support they received from the local population, concrete actions taken to reach the mission's objectives, their experiences of violence from antifascists and the inaction of local authorities, including the failure of the police to protect the territory. *Alignment* involves Southern, Pettibone and Sellner, enabled by nonhuman actants such as YouTube and Southern's smartphone, providing an alternative media frame on the Mission to the one offered by mainstream media (which is perceived as being too lenient toward illegal immigrants) and, according to Pettibone, "will paint [the Alps Mission as] something else". While the message promoted by Southern, Pettibone and Sellner seems to be widely shared by the audience, who are presented from the start as "identitarian activists" and YouTubers, technical problems blur the message for some time. Southern needs to make several attempts (such as moving her phone in an attempt to get a better connection or requesting sympathy from the audience by attributing the bad connection to other actants, such as the altitude) to improve the quality of the livestream and to contain audience frustration to limit the risk of losing audience members. At points, Southern apologises to the audience for the bad quality of the livestream, another way to overcome this problem. Despite the obstacles and the low resolution of the livestream that forms part of the collective (actant #5), the message is delivered, revealing *alignment*. In the end, resistances and obstacles are managed and parameters reach a settled state and stability. This brings the process to a new step: blackboxing (actant #6).

Blackboxing: In the blackboxing step, all actants in the mediation process are integrated. The pieces identified with the previous actants are stitched together and the result is not a collection of struggles or a shaping process but a finished product — a blackbox. In the present case, the product is what the audience sees on Southern's YouTube channel once the livestream becomes a video (a finished product). This video, or meme, is material that contributes to shaping an emotional and symbolic space, an actant that plays a part in shaping the debate, or discourse, about the status of the frontier and illegal immigration. In other words, it becomes a "Molotov JPEG" ready to set fire (and intended to do so) to public opinion (Hawley, 2017). The extent to which such a meme produces *convergence* in the public or influences its decisions is beyond the scope of this chapter. However, once the livestream becomes a video, a blackbox, it is put to the test by the audience, which comments on it and rates it. Within a nine-month period, Southern's video had been watched 134K times and received 7.6K likes and 384 dislikes as well as 1,570 comments. Comments include mere registrations of presence, critiques, insults and trolling as well as approval of Southern and GI's position. The video also develops a 'life' of its own beyond YouTube through its circulation across other platforms (Facebook, Twitter, Google+, etc.) thanks to the share option.

Convergence: To make a difference, heterogeneous actants (most of them the product of assemblages) must come together. In doing so they exchange properties, functions and goals, forming a complex network — a blackbox — that cannot be easily parsed or deconstructed into its constituents (the sum of the actants that compose it). The blackbox described in step six is now available to join the larger realm of the societal vigilante program directed against immigration that includes defence of borders as well as race and identity debates (actant #7). It becomes part of Southern's collection of videos on her YouTube channel, but it also has its own life, as shown by its role in our study and this chapter. In this sense, Southern has succeeded in meeting her primary goal of providing visibility to the Alps Mission.

Technical mediation allows for change in the substance of message and discourse. Southern's program — "to-act-in-order-to-make-the-Alps-Mission-visible" — was articulated around a specific platform, whose use led to production of a message that differs from the one that would have been produced if Southern had used another platform. Southern's objective, as realised through YouTube, undergoes a process of translation: from the securitisation of the border between Italy and France by activists, it becomes the live reporting of the situation by a soft leader or influencer (Cotter, 2018; Gerbaudo, 2012). Southern's program is thus delegated to a smartphone (equipped with camera, microphone and connection to the Internet) and a platform (YouTube). She delegates the action of "seeing" to the cellphone and YouTube, producing an additional *displacement* (Latour, 2007, p. 197). According to Latour, this displacement is spatial and temporal and allows the spectator to watch — and, to some extent, participate through the commenting function — without leaving his or her seat. The displacement is spatial in the sense that the Defend Europe and Alps Mission now include a new actant — Southern's video — broadcast and archived on YouTube. The displacement is temporal in that the Alps Mission can now appear at any time on YouTube as well as on other platforms where it can be shared. A series of objects-institutions perpetuate the visibility of the mission — securing the French-Italian border against immigrants — although the action itself is over and its protagonist now involved in other activities or actions. In this sense, the whole process of technical mediation makes it possible to shape a new meme that serves as a brick in the construction of the societal vigilante program promoted by GI. The analysis framed by Southern and other GI activists (e.g. Pettibone, Sellner), as well as support from the audience and the local population have all been "boxed" in the Defend Europe Alps Mission video.

Discussion and Conclusion

Following Gerbaudo's suggestion that is important to understand how digital platforms "contribute to the symbolic construction of public space, which facilitates and guides the physical assembling of a highly dispersed and individualised constituency" (Gerbaudo, 2012, p. 5), we analysed the role of a soft leader in shaping online social vigilantism. More specifically, we focused on how the far-right populist activist Lauren Southern, YouTube and the audience produce a meme (a video) that contributes to shaping an emotional and symbolic space characterised by anti-immigrant and identitarian discourses and symbols. Using Actor Network Theory (ANT), we showed that the shaping and visibility of such symbolic and emotional space is the result of a series of mechanisms that characterise technical mediation between entities, both human (Southern, the audience) and nonhuman (YouTube, algorithms). ANT appears promising as a way to approach the analysis of technical mediation once it is recognised that technology has to be considered in its materiality — that a technology-in-use 'does things' that cannot be reduced to human intention or action only (Leonardi, 2010). This recognition requires acknowledging that the shaping of the emotional and symbolic space in question cannot be analysed and understood simply as the results of intention or as an exclusively human project. Nonhuman objects also have to be accounted for in the analysis.

Several points should be emphasised with regard to the contributions made by the present chapter. To do this, we turn to Latour's fourth meaning of technical mediation, *delegation*. Latour argues that: "techniques modify the matter of our expression, not only its form.

Techniques have meaning, but they produce meaning via a special type of articulation that crosses the common-sense boundary between signs and things" (1994, p. 38). Meaning is "materialized" or "engraved" in matter (ibid.) and thus has the power to influence action. Latour's classical example is the speed bump that forces the driver to slow down. The speed bump modifies our expression, since the driver's slowing down is now motivated not by a moral rationale (to be careful because there may be pedestrians) but rather by an instrumentalist one (I have to slow down, otherwise I'll damage my car). Following Latour

> The engineers' program, make cars slow down on campus, is now inscribed in concrete and, in considering this shift, we quit the relative comfort of linguistic metaphor and enter unknown territory. [...] [W]e remain in meaning but no longer in discourse: yet we do not reside among mere objects. Where are we? (ibid., p. 39).

This question is crucial not only for the study of speed bumps but also for understanding the emergence of memes central to shaping the emotional and symbolic space and program of societal vigilantism. In Latour's words, the shift is "actorial" (ibid.), which refers to the performative effect of the new entity (composed of human and nonhuman actants). The meme is not composed only of Lauren Southern, its enunciator, nor is it completely Southern's responsibility: "An object stands in for an actor and creates an asymmetry between absent makers and occasional user" (ibid., p. 40). The shift is also spatial: the meme's visibility goes beyond the local space of the Alps Mission. Finally, the shift is temporal: the meme is present all the time on the web although: "the enunciator of this technical act [Lauren Southern in the present case] has disappeared from the scene — while someone, something, reliably acts as lieutenant, holding the enunciator's place" (ibid., pp. 39–40). In this sense, delegation expresses an exchange of properties between the actants, or entities, involved in the technical mediation. The delegation of some roles to nonhumans (digital media platforms) means that humans are not in complete control: the nonhuman actant does more than express the will of the humans — it affects it. That means that while soft leaders play a crucial role in spreading digital societal vigilantism, they are only one piece of the puzzle. Other actants must be involved in the choreography if the program of actions promoted by societal vigilantes is to be sustainable. Translated into a Latourian approach, unless *disinterest* is transformed into *enlistment* and *composition of a new goal*, there is no chance that such choreography will transform into delegation.

In the process of delegation and exchange of properties between human and nonhuman actants, one should not only consider far-right activists, but also YouTube's algorithm, which contributes to the visibility of the societal vigilantism program and discourse in the public domain largely through the associations it makes between similar contents (anti-immigrant, identitarian, etc.) and its role in assembling an audience. This audience is composed mainly of individuals whose practices and track records on the Internet are characterised by consuming and producing videos, discourses and images that share the same anti-immigration and identitarian characteristics and is assembled by 'collaborative filtering' through which, based on the audience's demonstrated preferences, the algorithms recommend additional content. The audience also provides fodder for collaborative filtering and contributes to the viability of individual videos. The audience thus has an effect on both the discourse (e.g. live comments favourable to Southern's action may make her feel supported and lead her to further polarise her discourse) and on YouTube's algorithms. Through its interaction with the video by commenting and liking (or disliking), the audience's actions affect YouTube's recommendation algorithms. If there is no interaction with the video, it will sink into limbo, while positive interactions increase its visibility on other YouTube channels and, eventually, in the public domain. In this sense, developing a relationship between an audience and a particular form or content of discourse is delegated to nonhumans — the YouTube platform and its algorithms.

One should not assume that there is a unidirectionality of delegation from nonhuman to human, but rather that there is a shared governance in the production of memes between human and nonhuman actants. More specifically, neither the human nor the nonhuman actants are in complete control in the technical mediation and the production of a societal vigilantism program and discourse (e.g. in the production of memes). They need to be "actioned" and in this case this is done by collecting humans' Internet consumption and track records. Of course, YouTube relies largely on its algorithms, but also depends on human actants, such as 'soft leaders' and YouTube "influencers" (Cotter, 2018), an audience.

Finally, and provocatively, this chapter shows that the symbolic and emotional space "is a *space-that-results-from-a-technical-mediation-between-human-and-nonhuman-actants-that-are-not-isolated-from-each-other*" (Callon, 1991, p. 143). Such space is the result of a complex series of *inscriptions*, or "the result of the translation of one's interest into material form" (ibid.). This process of inscription is cumulative, and several layers of inscriptions may exist simultaneously. The symbolic and emotional space is thus the result of negotiations and enrolments of a network of actants.

To conclude, the sociotechnical perspective adopted in the present chapter offers insight into how anti-immigration discourse and harmful societal digital vigilantism proliferate and gain traction among audiences. It contrasts with technological determinism expressed by the notion of "radicalization by algorithm" (Tufekci, 2018; Ribeiro et al., 2019) — according to which audiences might be at risk after being exposed to far-right content pushed by YouTube's algorithm designed to maximise the company's profit (Munger & Philips, 2019, p. 7). We agree with Munger and Phillips that YouTube should be apprehended in its "capacity to create radical alternative political canons and interpretative communities *to match*" (ibid., p. 6). YouTube supplies symbolic and emotional content to individuals who reject mainstream media for all sorts of reasons, and whose criterion of assessment rather rests on emotion, beliefs and desires rather than being grounded in a thorough fact-checking process (as traditionally executed by mainstream media). In the current debates about post-truth (McIntyre, 2019), our chapter makes a contribution in showing how truth does not only rest on emotions and beliefs — rather than facts — as documented (ibid.) but also, and more concerningly, on infrastructures. These infrastructures enable a series of human actions, such as sharing, clicking and commenting, but also non-human actants like algorithms and collaborative filtering. The materiality and performativity of these actants affects the economy of information in turning "fake news" and harmful discourse into political canons that are increasingly available, with the risk that they find their match in a growing number of 'interpretative communities'.

References

Akrich, M. (1992). The de-scription of technical objects, in W. Bijker & J. Law (eds), *Shaping Technology / Building Society: Studies in Sociotechnical Change* (pp. 205–24). Cambridge: MIT Press.

Bennett, W. L., Segerberg, A., & Walker, S. (2014). Organization in the crowd: peer production in large-scale networked protests. *Information, Communication & Society,* 17(2), 232–60, https://doi.org/10.1080/1369118x.2013.870379

Bourne, M. (2012). Guns don't kill people, cyborgs do: A Latourian provocation for transformatory arms control and disarmament. *Global Change, Peace and Security,* 24(1), 141–63, https://doi.org/10.1080/14781158.2012.641279

Burgess, J., & Green, J. B. (2008) Agency and controversy in the YouTube community, *IR 9.0: Rethinking Communities, Rethinking Place — Association of Internet Researchers (AoIR) conference,* Copenhagen, Denmark.

Burgess, J., & Green, J. B. (2018). *YouTube: Online Video and Participatory Culture,* 2nd edn. Digital Media and Society Series. Cambridge: Polity Press.

Boyd, d., & Ellison, N. B. (2007). Social network sites: Definition, history, and scholarship. *Journal of Computer-mediated Communication,* 13(1), 210–30, https://doi.org/10.1111/j.1083-6101.2007.00393.x

Callon, M. (1991). Techno-economic networks and irreversibility, in J. Law (ed.), *Sociology of Monsters: Essays on Power, Technology and Domination* (pp. 132–65). London: Routledge.

Cardon, D. (2008). Le design de la visibilité. Un essai de cartographie du web 2.0. *Réseaux,* 6, 93–137, https://doi.org/10.3166/reseaux.152.93-137

Castells, M. (2012). *Networks of Outrage and Hope: Social Movement in the Internet Age.* Cambridge: Wiley-Blackwell, https://doi.org/10.7312/blau17412-091

Claxton, M. (2017, May 17). Former Langley libertarian candidate detained in Italy, *The Abbotsford News,* https://www.abbynews.com/news/former-langley-libertarian-candidate-detained-in-italy

Cotter, K. (2018). Playing the visibility game: How digital influencers and algorithms negotiate influence on Instagram. *New Media & Society,* 21(4), 895–913, https://doi.org/10.1177/1461444818815684

Covington, P., Adams, J., & Sargin, E. (2016). Deep neural networks for YouTube recommendations. *Proceedings of the 10th ACM Conference on Recommender Systems,* Boston, USA, 5–19 Sept.

Drucker, J. (2013). Performative materiality and theoretical approaches to interface. *Digital Humanities Quarterly* 7(1), http://www.digitalhumanities.org/dhq/vol/7/1/000143/000143.html

Eisler, P. (2016, November 7). Hate speech slips into US. mainstream amid bitter campaign. *Reuters,* http://www.reuters.com/article/us-usa-election-hatespeech-insight-idUSKBN13225X

El Jabri, A. (2018, August 30). À Chemnitz, l'extrême-droite maintien la tension. *Le Monde,* http://www.rfi.fr/emission/20181113-allemagne-chemnitz-extreme-droite-maintient-tension

Ellinas, A. (2018). Media and the Radical Right. In J. Rydgren (ed.), *The Oxford Handbook of the Radical Right* (pp. 1–18). New York: Oxford University, https://doi.org/10.1093/oxfordhb/9780190274559.013.14

Favarel-Garrigues, G., & Gayer, L. (2016). Violer la loi pour maintenir l'ordre: le vigilantisme en débat. *Politix,* 115(3), 7–33, https://doi.org/10.3917/pox.115.0007

Feenberg, A. (1999). *Questioning Technology.* New York: Routledge.

Foellmer, S., Lünnenborg, M., & Raetzsch, C. (2018). *Media Practices, Social Movements and Performativity: Transdisciplinary Approaches.* New York: Routledge, https://doi.org/10.4324/9781315455938

Fourchard, L. (2016). Engagements sécuritaires et féminisation du vigilantisme en Afrique du Sud. *Politix,* 115(3), 57–78, https://doi.org/10.3917/pox.115.0057

France 24 (2016, October 26). Cagoules et machettes: la malice fascisante bulgare qui traque les migrants. *France 24,* https://www.youtube.com/watch?v=9XygycjLE28"

Gardernier, M., & Monie, A. (2018). De l'utilisation de Facebook à des fins de mobilisation par le groupe Sauvons Calais. *Communication, Information medias theories pratiques,* 35(1), 1–26, https://doi.org/10.4000/communication.7660

Gerbaudo, P. (2012). *Tweets and the streets: social media and contemporary activism.* London: Pluto Press, https://doi.org/10.2307/j.ctt183pdzs

Gerbaudo, P. (2018). *The Digital Party: Political Organisation and Online Democracy.* London: Pluto Press, https://doi.org/10.2307/j.ctv86dg2g

Gillespie, T. (2010). The politics of 'platforms'. *New Media & Society,* 12(3), 347–64, https://doi.org/10.1177/1461444809342738

Gladwell, M. (2010, 27 September). Small change: Why the revolution will not be tweeted. *The New Yorker,* https://www.newyorker.com/magazine/2010/10/04/small-change-malcolm-gladwell

Goffman, E. (1974). *Frame Analysis: An Essay on the Organization of Experience.* Boston: Northeastern University Press.

Golebiewski, M., & Boyd, D. (2019). Data voids. Where missing data can easily be exploited, *Data & Society,* https://datasociety.net/output/data-voids

Google (2017). The Redirect Method: a blueprint for bypassing violent extremism, 1–17, https://redirectmethod.org

Gross, L. (2009). My media studies: Cultivation to participation, *Television & New Media*, 10(1), 66–8, https://doi.org/10.1177/1527476408325105

Hawley, G. (2017). *Making Sense of the Alt-right*. New York: Oxford University Press, https://doi.org/10.7312/hawl18512

Jenkins, H. (2006). *Convergence Culture: Where Old and New Media Collide*. New York: New York University Press, https://doi.org/10.7551/mitpress/9780262036016.003.0012

Johnston, L. (1996). What is vigilantism. *British Journal of Criminology*, 36(2), 220–36, https://doi.org/10.1093/oxfordjournals.bjc.a014083

Kavada, A. (2015). Creating the collective: Social media, the Occupy movement and its constitution as a collective actor. *Information, Communication and Society*, 18(8), 872–86, https://doi.org/10.1080/1369118x.2015.1043318

Kinsley, S. (2014). The matter of 'virtual' geographies. *Progress in Human Geography*, 38(3), 364–84, https://doi.org/10.1177/0309132513506270

Kristofferson, K., White, K., & Peloza, J. (2014). The nature of slacktivism: How the social observability of and initial act of token supports affects subsequent prosocial action. *Journal of Consumer Research*, 40(6), 1149–66, https://doi.org/10.1086/674137

Laclau, E. (2005). *On Populist Reason*. London: Verso, https://doi.org/10.1111/j.1470-9856.2007.00225_7.x

Latour, B. (1994). On technical mediation: philosophy, sociology, genealogy. *Common Knowledge*, 3(2), 29–64.

Latour, B. (2005). *Reassembling the Social: An Introduction to Actor-Network-Theory*. Oxford: Oxford University Press.

Latour, B. (2007). *L'espoir de Pandore. Pour une vision réaliste de l'activité scientifique*. Paris: La Découverte.

Law, J., & Hassard, J. (1999). *Actor Network Theory and After*. Oxford: Blackwell Publishers / *The Sociological Review*.

Leonardi, M. P. (2010). Digital materiality? how artifacts without matter matter? *First Monday*, 15(6), 1–14, https://doi.org/10.5210/fm.v15i6.3036

Lewis, R. (2018). Alternative influence: Broadcasting the reactionary right on YouTube. *Data & Society*, https://datasociety.net/wp-content/uploads/2018/09/DS_Alternative_Influence.pdf

Manovich, L. (2013). *Software Takes Command*. New York: Bloomsbury, https://doi.org/10.5040/9781472544988

Marwick, A., & Lewis, R. (2017). Media manipulation and disinformation online. *Data & Society*, https://datasociety.net/pubs/oh/DataAndSociety_MediaManipulationAndDisinformationOnline.pdf

Mattoni, A., & Treré, E. (2014). Media practices, mediation processes, and mediatization in the study of social movements. *Communication Theory,* 24(3), 252–71, https://doi.org/10.1111/comt.12038

Mazzeloni, G., Stewart, J., & Horsfield, B. (2003). *The Media and Neo-Populism: A Contemporary Comparative Analysis.* Westport and London: Praeger.

McIntyre, L. (2019). *Post-Truth.* Cambridge: The MIT Press, https://doi.org/10.7551/mitpress/11483.001.0001

Morozov, E. (2009a, 19 May). The brave new world of slacktivism. *Foreign Policy,* https://foreignpolicy.com/2009/05/19/the-brave-new-world-of-slacktivism

Morozov, E. (2009b, 5 September). From slacktivism to activism. *Foreign Policy,* https://foreignpolicy.com/2009/09/05/from-slacktivism-to-activism

Mudde, C. (2017). *The Far Right in America.* New York: Routledge, https://doi.org/10.4324/9781315160764

Munger, K., & Phillips, J. (2019). A supply and demand framework for YouTube politics, working paper, https://osf.io/73jys

Murthy, D., & Sharma, S. (2019). Visualizing YouTube's comment space: online hostility as a networked phenomena. *New Media & Society,* 21(1), 191–213, https://doi.org/10.1177/1461444818792393

Neveu, É. (2011). *Sociologie des mouvements sociaux.* Paris: La Découverte.

Nissenbaum, A., & Shifam, L. (2017). Internet memes as contested cultural capital: the case of 4chan's /b/ board. *New Media & Society,* 19(4), 483–501, https://doi.org/10.1177/1461444815609313

Perry, B., & Scrivens, R. (2015). *Right-Wing Extremism in Canada: An Environmental Scan.* Public Safety Canada, https://www.publicsafety.gc.ca/cnt/ntnl-scrt/cntr-trrrsm/r-nd-flght-182/knshk/ctlg/dtls-en.aspx?i=116

Phillips, W. (2018). The oxygen of amplification. Better practices for reporting on extremists, antagonists, and manipulators online. *Data & Society,* https://datasociety.net/output/oxygen-of-amplification

Pratten, D., & Sen, A. (2007). *Global Vigilantes.* London: Hurst.

Rémillard, D. (2015, December 28). La Meute, un groupe contre "l'invasion de l'islam". *Le Soleil,* https://www.lesoleil.com/actualite/la-meute-un-groupe-contre-linvasion-de-lislam-7b25c4b489d894716291effedb8b78a3

Ribeiro, M. H., Ottoni, R., West, R., Almeida, V. A. F., & Wagner, M (2019). Auditing radicalization pathways on YouTube, arXiv preprint, arXiv:1908.08313

Segond, V. (2018, September 27). En Italie, Matteo Salvini diffuse le racism dans toute la société', *Slate,* https://www.slate.fr/story/167627/racisme-italie-conquete-pouvoir-salvini

Shaw, A. (2018, March 12). Right-wing journalist Lauren Southern denied entry to UK, purportedly over criticism of Islam. *Fox News*, https://www.abbynews.com/news/former-langley-libertarian-candidate-detained-in-italy

Tanner, S., & Campana, A. (2019). 'Watchful citizens' and digital vigilantism: A case study of the far right in Quebec. *Global Crime* (forthcoming), https://doi.org/10.1080/17440572.2019.1609177

Tufekci, Z. (2018). YouTube, the great radicalizer. *The New York Times*, 10 March.

Van Dijck, J. (2013). *The Culture of Connectivity. A Critical History of Social Media*. Oxford: Oxford University Press, https://doi.org/10.1093/acprof:oso/9780199970773.001.0001

Warren, R. (2017, July 28). Europe's far right pirates of the Mediterranean are targeting refuge rescue missions. *The Washington Post*, https://www.washingtonpost.com/news/global-opinions/wp/2017/07/28/europes-far-right-pirates-of-the-mediterranean-are-targeting-refugee-rescue-missions/?noredirect=on&utm_term=.09804d0824e0

Wendling, M. (2018). *Alt Right. From 4chan to the White House*. Halifax & Winnipeg: Fernwood Publishing.

Wolfson, T. (2014). *Digital Rebellion: The Birth of the Cyber Left*. Chicago: University of Illinois Press, https://doi.org/10.5406/illinois/9780252038846.001.0001

YouTube (2010). Testing, testing... YouTube begins trial of new live streaming platform, https://youtube.googleblog.com/2010/09/testing-testingyoutube-begins-trial-of.html

Empowerment, Social Distrust or Co-production of Security: A Case Study of Digital Vigilantism in Morocco

Abderrahim Chalfaouat

Introduction

As a licensed nurse in the United States, William M. posed online as a young woman planning to commit suicide who could explain to others how to do so. Using this deception, he formed misleading bonds with visitors to suicide chat rooms to persuade them to end their lives in front of a webcam (Huey et al., 2012). Pursuing his obsession with suicide, William used various screen names, but overlooked the Internet's potential to reveal his real identity. However, some users recognised his exploitation of their psychological vulnerability and his betrayal of social trust while assisting victims to hang themselves (Anderson, 2010).

Investigations started when a team of women took interest in this suicide support. The team featured people who had direct as well as second-hand exposure to William's attempts. (Anderson, 2010). Using her digital literacy, one woman discovered that William used multiple screen names, and more importantly that social media platforms helped him exacerbate suicidal thoughts. Due to their "security demand" (Mireanu, 2014, p. iii), the woman collected William's location and IP address, and communicated the affair to the police in her own hometown, to the FBI, to the Ottawa Police Service, and then to the

 https://doi.org/10.11647/OBP.0200.07

Minnesota police (Huey et al., 2012). Despite inadequate legal measures against encouraging self-harm online, she continued to participate, as an ordinary person, in promoting security and reducing risk factors in her surroundings. She engaged in online vigilantism using her digital skills, trying to help curb a fatal cybercrime. She revisited police departments persistently to prevent William from causing more deaths. During a chat, she also urged William to turn on his webcam, and took a picture of his face (Porter, 2010; Huey et al., 2012). Her perseverance deterred his digital incitement to suicide and helped illustrate the ability of different parties to produce — i.e. to illustrate the co-production of — safety. She saved the life of a depressed friend of hers by initiating an investigation into William's actions before handing the affair over to the police. Meanwhile, in approaching different police departments, she indirectly questioned their role. That is, when law enforcement agencies fail to act because the law does not empower them to do so, they drive citizens to feel a security void that they bridge with collective or individual initiatives with or without police consent. While this can be a symptom of state failure (Szescilo, 2017), the resultant individual and community empowerment strengthens the constructive participation of citizens in controlling their environment.

Digital vigilantism does not deal solely with cybercrime, however. It also denounces embodied infringements of the law (Wehmhoener, 2010). When bystanders witness an event they deem offensive, criminal or discriminatory, they cascade this feeling through uploadable content. This occurred in a rape attempt in Benguerir, near Marrakech in the middle of Morocco. In late March 2018, a video went viral online, especially on Facebook and YouTube. It featured a boy attempting to rape a teenage girl, who was resisting and yelling sharply "don't you have a sister!? Would you want someone to do this to her??" (Khalaf, 2018). Digital vigilantes doxed — or shared personal information about — the assaulter immediately, which facilitated his identification. The video was originally shot to exhibit the attacker's masculine power and film the rape, but the moral outrage on social media urged the police to react. The video and the shared information online, such as name, age and neighbourhood helped in the manhunt, while the press used the doxing to locate the crime scene, identify the victim and show her family's anguish. Together, these factors led the assailant to receive a ten-year imprisonment term. His friend, who shot the incident, received an eight-year sentence. The third boy, who uploaded the video several months after the incident, received a two-year jail term for hiding the evidence instead of sharing it online or handing it on to the police once he obtained it (Babas, 2018). Ubiquitous devices that people buy mainly for communication thus hold "potential for civic engagement and empowerment through social media" (Chen, 2017, p. 2). The catchphrase "don't you have a sister?" also went viral as a hashtag (Khalaf, 2018) to denounce the sexual assault, and it appeared in the titles of songs and amateur short movies on YouTube to frame public denunciation of sexual harassment, and perhaps to link vigilantism with empowerment. As such, technology enables the transfer of frustration online, or the digitisation of vigilantism against hostility and animosity in society.

Digital vigilantism refers to the active online participation of some self-appointed person or group in promoting the rule of law. It is an organic, constructive contribution to social order, aided by the transforming role of the Internet. Though intentional and programmatic, it is performed by actors who do not necessarily "have high levels of [social, economic or symbolic] capital" (Mireanu, 2014, p. 9). It incorporates bottom-up initiatives, sometimes with the consent or encouragement of the state (Chang et al., 2016), to maintain one's secure environment or to enforce the law by exposing wrongdoing online. Vigilantism, consequently, redefines engagement for the public good, since citizens engage directly with a perceived lack of security, lack of state awareness or inadequate state presence.

Digital vigilantism comprises a number of phases. First, social uproar is caused by the amorality and objectionable nature of some uploaded content. Audiences who feel offended display their attitude via shaming or doxing. They create "a mode of informal regulation" or "cyber social control" within online communities (Wehmhoener, 2010, p. 11). This open trial online often triggers different reactions from the police, the press, commentators, friends, family members or colleagues of bullies and victims. The crowdsourcing of content and reactions makes each group a prosumer[1] audience in its own way. They watch the event and interact according to their abilities and responsibilities, towards

---

1   The term 'prosumer' was coined by the American futurist Alvin Toffler in his *The Third Wave* (1980) to denote simultaneous consumption and production

the common goal of maintaining social order. In addition, digital vigilantism warrants autonomous citizenship. Wehmhoener (2010, p. 10) even describes it as "a form of autonomous citizenship", especially when the state condones its potential repercussions or "downside risks" (Chang et al., 2016, p. 108). With the ubiquity of smart devices and social media, ordinary citizens, including illiterate ones, find ways to engage socially (Khamis & Vaugh, 2011). The traditionally literate and illiterate share online spaces and both can have an impact, due to rampant e-interactivity and participation in particular. They collaborate and cross-fertilise, though the limits of that collaboration require clearer demarcation. Recent scholarship has acknowledged that "literacy now encompasses much more than just reading, writing, speaking and listening" but also "computer, digital, and media literacy as well" (Swan, 2017, p. 10). However, whether basic digital skills transform into real-life reading, writing, language accuracy or media interpretation, for instance, requires more research.

Frequent vigilantism may indicate distrust in the authorities. Since "vigilantism results from unwillingness of the ruling upper class to address security needs of poorer populations" (Szescilo, 2017, p. 149), it occurs less in contexts where the police are trusted, or where they automatically guarantee the rule of law. Hoffman (2012) as cited in Szescilo (2017, p. 154) contends that "vigilantism does not play a significant role in countries where the state provides its security institutions with adequate capacities". When citizens trust the agents of the law, vigilantism is less widespread (Scheffers, 2015, p. 12). When corruption, "indicia of illegality" and impunity abound, vigilantes react with doubt, uncertainty and caution. They may refrain from replacing law institutions, lest attention swerves from the criminal action to the vigilante reaction. Instead, due to their shrinking trust in the security system, vigilantes volunteer individually or collectively for self-defence, with or without state encouragement. They contribute their different capacities to meet the increasing "demand for supplementary policing and security services" (Chang et al., 2016, p. 101).

Vigilantism, though it empowers citizens, may cause repercussions. A key downside online is retaliation. Victims, their relatives or sympathisers may seek revenge, especially when sentences are too lenient for the crimes committed. Citizens may develop a habit of meting out punishment with their own hands, which blurs the meanings of law and chaos. Another problem is the infringement upon one's privacy. Anonymous doxing may result in the sharing of information about family members or private relationships that do not pertain to the affair under scrutiny. Unexpectedly, some remote relatives of perpetrators may become victims of cyber-bullying for reasons they may not understand well.

Against this backdrop, this chapter delves qualitatively into a case of digital vigilantism in Morocco. It explores the social and communicative practices of security-seeking citizens. It tackles the empowering impact of digitisation and the context of the Arab Spring on the location of online vigilantism in the kingdom. The analysis considers a case of informal vigilantism; a one-off event that relates to the educational system and to classroom violence in particular. The incident exemplifies the increasing public awareness of online agency, social justice, the rule of law and constructive citizenship, rather than mob justice, in a public sphere where civil agency is regaining prominence.

Online Empowerment in the Arab Spring Context

The Internet, as an online public sphere, provides a space for the interplay of power dynamics, especially when freedom of speech is suppressed in embodied interactions. Citizens use online applications and platforms to contest political practices and engage in community wellbeing. They exert impact by sharing news and views, uploading content to support or denounce given causes, contacting MPs and orchestrating activism. Thus, the Internet empowers committed citizens when political practices neglect public concerns (Khamis & Vaugh, 2011; Eltantawy & Wiest, 2011).

The concept of empowerment is seminal to understand social movement and change. It refers to both a process and an outcome. It is, first, "a process by which people gain control of their lives, democratic participation in the lives of their community, and a critical understanding of their environment" (Perkins & Zimmerman, 2005, p. 570). Empowering processes lead to empowered individuals, organisations or communities (Zimmerman, 2000). Psychologically, when they are empowered, citizens handle personal problems and opportunities, rather than feeling that circumstances constantly weaken them. Beyond individual concerns, empowerment channels the decisions and solutions of organisations and communities to improve their environment. Citizens collectively crowd-source their perceived control (the belief that one can influence the outcomes of a process they take part in), their critical awareness (knowing when to engage in conflict and when to avoid it) and their effective participation to pressure for social and policy change, and to enhance community living (Zimmerman, 2000). Access to resources, especially the media, is a key empowering factor. With ubiquitous media today, empowerment processes grow more decentralised and, probably, more impactful.

When empowerment fails to affect public policies, trust in public institutions wanes. For the Stanford Encyclopaedia of Philosophy, "[t]rust is an attitude that we have towards people [or institutions] whom we hope will be trustworthy, where trustworthiness is a property, not an attitude" (McLeod, 2015, n.p.). Thus, trust co-exists with, sometimes tiny, doubt. For, if the trusted person or institution will pull through for us doubtlessly, then trust is needless (ibid.). However, trust as an attitude accumulates from reliable acts that culminate in trustworthiness as a property. That is, the state slowly and increasingly becomes trustworthy after citizens rely on its services several times, and after it does not betray their confidence. Institutional trust is important because it demarcates official relations and delimits responsibilities. Civic trust in institutions generates social capital, whilst loss of faith in public institutions constitutes a crisis in democracy (Cook & Gronke, 2005, p. 3). Contrariwise, it is difficult to fathom or accept that public institutions betray public trust (McLeod, 2015), which usually arouses defiant symbolic or material reactions. Therefore, lack of trust, or the open expression of distrust, denotes a failure to assume pre-trust or post-trust responsibilities.

Trusting the state becomes hard when it develops a reputation for corruption. Pre-Arab-Spring regimes, for example, repressed free speech, monopolised public media and disdained representative democracy. Consequently, nonconformist voices felt unwelcome.

During the Arab Spring, social media, or "dense informal networks", structured social activism and harnessed mobilisation online (Pérez-Altable, 2016, p. 19). They have affected social life and the perception of social activism (Khamis & Vaughn, 2011). For Howard and Parks (2012), social media activism consists of three key elements: infrastructure; digital content; and the people who produce and consume that content. People are essential for digital vigilantism, possibly more so than infrastructure, since content dissemination online results from their effort and initiatives to express their individual or collective aspirations, concerns or demands. Consequently, for the public, social networks enhance activism for already-existing causes. They quickly recognise that it is "the flow of attention, not information (which we already have too much of), that matters" (Tufekci, 2018) for dissatisfied citizens. Despite the state's mass surveillance, which involved cutting off Internet and cellular services and gate-keeping public-service media, protesters in different Tahrir — or Freedom — Squares kept challenging one government after another in Arab capitals (ibid.). Social media mainly strengthened the public ability to attract attention to the visibility of social agency and advocacy.

Furthermore, the 2011 uprisings contested the concept of security. Protesters demanded political, economic and social security at large, while regimes viewed social unrest as a threat to state safety as a whole. In that conflict between strategic narratives over public safety, the public has become more outspoken, using the empowerment of social media and learning from developments in other Arab Spring countries (cross-fertilisation).

Meeting the practical needs of the uprisings required three roles to be fulfilled. The majority of activists flooded Freedom Squares, whilst others galvanised marches online and denigrated state interventions (Eltantawy & Wiest, 2011; Chen, 2017). A third group formed neighbourhood watches, especially in remote areas. They prevented burglars from exploiting the chaos, and also state militias from exacerbating it for legitimising state power. Neighbourhood vigilantes, accordingly, spread under failed or "dead states", as the Egyptian minister of justice put it (Middle East Online, 2013). State violence resulted in public distrust and the taking of laws into civilian hands. Sometimes, neighbourhood vigilantism led to mob lynching. Videos of slain wrongdoers in the Egyptian countryside, for instance, went viral to warn potential perpetrators (AsiaNews, 2013). In Tunisia, the idea of 'self-protecting civilians' was short-lived because the regime collapsed without squashing protests.

Due to geopolitical proximity, Moroccan citizens often share advocacy strategies with Arab countries. During street protests in 2011, slogans demanded the ousting of corruption and despotism instead of the ousting of the whole regime. Marchers hoped for a democratic transition. The Moroccan regime, however, resorted to an exceptionalist narrative (Chalfaouat, 2015; Chahir, 2019). It spread the idea that Morocco is unique in North Africa: the Ottoman Empire could not conquer Morocco; France took Morocco for a protectorate, not a colony. Following the same logic, replicating Arab Spring revolts in Morocco was needless since the regime was much less coercive than neighbouring ones. The devil lay in the details, however. Though governments performed their duties, policies kept regressing. Meanwhile, analyses on Facebook articulated frustration with the status quo. The spark of the Arab Spring, promoted by ubiquitous smart phones, indicated dissatisfaction with the state. To recognise public activism, the state amended the constitution in 2011, further empowering citizens with participatory democracy measures such as petitions and memoranda. Therefore, the impact of the Internet on public conscience enabled citizens to reinforce the rule of law. Today, protesters still take to the street with political demands. They require the right to jobs, freedom of speech, better infrastructure, etc. Visual content from those events abounds on social media, as exemplified by the Rif Hirak in 2017 (Lorch & Bukhard, 2017) or teachers' marches in 2018 (Chahir, 2019). Yet, when political demands abate, social demands surge. When sit-ins or street marches crumble, social activism shifts to denouncing violence between the police and citizens, or between teachers and students, for instance. Consequently, ordinary citizens use online platforms as communicative catalysts to mobilise bottom-up aspirations. They share videos that record social deviance, street thievery, harassment, police bribery or the exchange of violence. Their active digital vigilantism stresses security to make bullies accountable for their crimes.

In short, developments after the Arab Spring display inextricable and irreversible ties between the offline and the online. As society rushes to cope with technological changes, connected devices empower citizens to record daily events and share content with audiences in uncontrollable trajectories. This online empowerment boosts common citizens' sense of change-making, and their ability to improve their immediate environment. After the Arab Spring, street activism nationally, regionally or locally has not waned, while the amount of smartphones, social media accounts and circulating data has shot up. Though media empowerment does not guarantee change, activism challenges political, economic or social wrongdoing, which supports communities. Via digital devices, access to information and opinions heightens the questioning the status quo. The following section provides a glimpse of the digital landscape in Morocco.

The Digital Reality in Morocco

Communications in Morocco are among the most vibrant in Africa for several reasons. The first is demography. Today, around 87% of the population are younger than fifty-five. Schoolchildren do not receive an adequate education: around 400,000 pupils drop out annually. This youth drain aggravates illiteracy rates and impedes employment plans. Persistent youth unemployment, soaring corruption levels and aspirations for better living conditions push public anger onto social media.

Secondly, ownership of connectable devices has increased. In 2017, 60% of families (20% of the entire population) owned desktops or tablets, with a six-percent increase from 2016. In addition, according to ANRT[2] annual data (2018), 99.8% of Moroccan urban and rural families use mobile phones. Around four members of every family possess phones, amounting to around 25 million mobile phones, 73% of which are smartphones. Eighty-six per cent of the phones are used to access the Internet. Their owners prosume and circulate huge amounts of information, opinions, attitudes and trends. One aspect of the social impact is the diversity of possibilities for connection this enables. Ninety-four point seven per cent of Internet users can be found on Facebook, Instagram or WhatsApp. Ninety-eight per cent of youngsters aged between 15 and 24 (i.e. around 6.5 million), participate on social platforms on a daily basis, while Facebook users number around 17.5 million (NapoleonCat, 2018). Moroccans currently rank fourth in Africa and second in the Arab world on Facebook.

---

2   National Agency for Regulating Telecommunications.

Moreover, the digital infrastructure is helpful. Morocco postures as a technology hub in Africa, due to its geostrategical location at the crossroads of international fibre cables. It participates in a technological race to lead North Africa, adopting policies that encourage connectivity and ensure surveillance and stability (Chalfaouat, 2015). That is why the kingdom ranks eighty-fifth globally in e-governance readiness, offering broadband since 2004 and leading Africa with more than 400,000 active ADSL lines and a high level of wireless connection (4G). To boost mobile broadband connectivity in rural areas, Long Term Evolution services were set up in 2015, after upgrading fibre optic networks.

In addition, around 3000 e-news websites cover national and local events continuously. In 2015, the Ministry of Communication certified 204 online news outlets, added to rampant national, regional and local uncertified news websites and blogs, which boosts immediate access to news and frequent social media interaction. Therefore, the post-2011 power dynamics capitalise on digital transformations to create a perpetual phenomenon of social activism. Activists favour the digital sphere, which has resulted in increased vigilantism, sometimes fuelled by the equally rising symptoms of social problems.

Digital Vigilantism in Morocco

Co-production (public participation in the production) of security in Morocco is not new. Even official institutions and media outlets directly or indirectly encourage the co-production of security. For instance, the police hang photos of wanted criminals inside police stations and city halls, expecting citizens to help. Public radio stations, too, regularly broadcast news about fugitives to warn of the danger they pose, and seek public help in capturing them.

However, organic vigilantism ensues from citizen initiatives, rather than guided participation. In some rural areas, ordinary people conduct their own investigations and sentence perpetrators, especially robbers, in weekly markets (The Journal, 2015). A crowd might fatally assault a culprit so that no one person in the mob would be accused directly. Thus, when burglars exploit the reduced police presence in isolated or remote areas, the public executes them, acting as an unofficial replacement of the state. Instead of benefiting from the situation, robbers often run the risk of becoming its victims.

Some websites likewise encourage the participation of ordinary citizens in reducing corruption, with mixed success. For example, Ushahidi, an international group that monitors election transparency, launched their Moroccan site in 2011, marsad.ma, but the experiment was short-lived. In 2012, it became mamdawrinch.com ("we will not bribe"), a platform for anonymous reporting. Mamfakinch.com ("no concessions"), a blogging platform for reporting corruption and rejecting despotism, waned along with the February 20 Movement and folded after official harassment. The platform challenged official stories and interpretations of events, and exemplified the interplay between state power and social resistance online. It carried weekly coverage of "February 20th Movement protests simultaneously taking place throughout the country, in addition to international chapter protests in Europe and elsewhere" (Errazzouki, 2017, p. 368). It systematically offered a Twitter-linked "live feed where individuals participating in the demonstrations could include a hashtag in their tweets that would automatically stream their tweets on Mamfakinch" (ibid.). After building visitors' trust, Mamfakinch's work galvanised vigilantism as the tweets "tended to include both photos as well as videos and were filtered through a marked map hosted on Google Maps" (ibid.). Street protesters, who accessed the platform feed directly, benefited from its empowering ability to channel their perceived control, critical awareness and effective participation. However, the platform's "brief prominence dwindled when the Moroccan state countered its impact" with surveillance, malware and accusations of undermining national security (ibid., p. 380). Another example, Manchoufouch.com, is a website and Android application that records the time and location of sexual harassment. Yet, the project's ability to gain public trust, empower harassment victims or galvanise agency remains to be seen.

Online vigilantes prefer anonymity due to their distrust of the legal system. Accordingly, organised digital vigilantism is often played down. When some journalists investigate corruption, fraud or mismanagement, other state-related journalists defame them by framing their efforts as disturbing, contradictory or useless. Sometimes, evidence of mass surveillance is produced in order to contain disturbing voices and keep freedom of speech within prescribed limits (Errazzouki, 2017). Most vigilantism websites have folded, to be replaced with social media activism.

Informal digital vigilantism abounds on social media to denounce different types of wrongdoing. Vigilante individuals, organisations, or communities monitor official corruption or scandal, such as when the police force citizens to give bribes (Sekkouri, 2008), riot police suppress citizen behaviour (Chahir, 2019) or a teacher assaults a student. For example, in Targuist, a cannabis-farming city, four videos exposed police officers collecting bribes from drivers, especially smugglers. These videos, which were not uploaded simultaneously, zoomed in on corrupt law-enforcement agents facilitating crime. Social and traditional media widely covered the scandal, which coincided with a royal visit to the region. Consequently, the police officers were arrested or deported thanks to the Targuist Sniper or "Targuist Commando" (Sekkouri, 2008). Vigilantism was thus perceived as a constructive participation in reducing corruption, while the authors of the footage evaded official tracking and punishment.

Other vigilantes denounce organised public insecurity. A pertinent example is the social uproar against Tcharmil, an urban youth sub-culture whose adherents wear unconventional clothing and hairdos, use their own jargon and carry swords in the streets. They "roll out flamboyant clothing and jewellery and fondness for the violent courtesies of the street" (El Maarouf & Belghazi, 2018, p. 293). For El Maarouf and Belghazi, "Tcharmil captures both an enigmatic and an intricate moment of mélange" (2018, p. 292), incarnating the sense of superiority inherent in taking over a public space and the boastful intention of unsettling local stability. Thinking of themselves as renegades, Mcharmlin[3] transform the violence they feel and experience into social deviance and fury at the unwelcoming, unsatisfactory city.

Vigilantism, in contrast, shaped the public reaction to this violence. Online, anonymous citizens launched a "Zero Grissage" campaign to end Tcharmil hostility. Persistent theft and aggression by Mcharmlin obliged some inhabitants in Casablanca to elect neighbourhood watches against attacks (Lesiteinfo, 2016). Due to frustration with Tcharmil's

---

3   Youngsters who follow Tcharmil as a lifestyle.

chaos, and amid mounting distrust, people took the law in their own hands. They accused the state of inability to maintain public security. However, other citizens refrained from forming neighbourhood militias against Tcharmil militias (Bladi.info, 2016). To curb the lawlessness, "between the 1st of January and the 30th of June, 256 171 persons were arrested […] in reaction to the 'Zero_Grissage' hashtagged protests on social media networks" (El Maarouf & Belghazi, 2018, p. 299).

Individual vigilantes, the most widespread type of vigilantism, highlight one-off incidents. People use phone cameras to record attacks by burglars, sexual assaults or problems in medical facilities. In these cases, generally, street vigilantes develop an empowering pattern of documenting misconduct, sharing the material on social media, creating uproar and bringing the wrongdoers to justice. Even when traditional media cover the mishap, viewers rush to social platforms because they trust them more, since they offer the possibility to access unedited content, interact with trustworthy individuals and avoid official censorship and bias.

Analysis of a Digital Vigilantism Case: Student Assaults Teacher

Fig. 7.1 Safi Addakirapress. (2017). Shocking / Student assaults his teacher in Ouarzazate. YouTube, https://www.youtube.com/watch?v=aC-DjWwDFs8&has_verified=1

In this case study, an instance of individual vigilantism morphs into a community reaction and shows the ways digital visibility galvanises social action. This event consists of violence in a school classroom. Though it is an example of juvenile delinquency, it is neither organised, nor presents a threat to public security. It rather represents an instance of a spontaneous, one-off irregularity in which a student, due to details that pertain to his own circumstances, defies common norms and assaults his teacher inside the classroom. That is why, as a backlash to the original act, the digital uproar brings into focus the ways official irresponsibility and individual irregularity lead to public insecurity, though indirectly, in a complex post-2011 media and activism landscape.

Context: Because it is far from the central region, Ouarzazate rarely attracts public attention. The supposedly calm southern city became agitated in November 2017, a few weeks after the onset of a difficult political and academic period. First, the whole country eagerly witnessed the so-called 'blockage', a six-month political impasse after legislative elections in 2016. Video footage captured over-crowded classrooms due to faltering educational planning and incompatibility between infrastructure, human resources and the number of pupils. Equally, the role of teacher-training centres (aka CPRs) was hotly discussed online. For economic and educational reasons, the government had launched a plan to reduce the great shortage of staff by delegating the recruitment of teachers to regional academies. Teachers, especially in the first year of the plan, would join classrooms before receiving training that was not necessarily provided by CPRs. While CPR graduates protested the plan, university graduates were sent to classrooms without training. Online debates spiked when trained teachers were ignored in street protests, while the untrained teachers started teaching. The hasty solution of sending large numbers of untrained teachers into schools was punctuated by police interventions against teacher marches (Chalfaouat, 2017). Consequently, debates about legal fragility, financial precarity, overcrowded classrooms, lack of pre-service training and frequent police crackdowns on teacher protests played out on social media. This soured public opinion, creating conditions for the denunciation of educational policies and teacher vulnerability in schools.

Content: The short video starts with a chaotic quarrel inside a classroom. Many students are on their feet while one approaches the teacher with hostility. The student and the teacher engage in a short fight, before other students pull them apart. Many of the students go back to their seats. Another group of students keeps watching the violent scene, including the one who is shooting the video. Then, the hostile student leaves his seat again to attack the teacher who stands sheepishly close to his desk near the board. The student mutters that he will not accept insults against his mother. He jumps over a number of tables to reach the teacher and punches him repeatedly. The teacher, who seems unable to defend himself, falls down on the floor in utter humiliation. The punching continues for some time. Towards the end, it is not clear whether the other students are trying to terminate the fight or helping their classmate to assault the teacher.

Social media reaction: Once the video reached Facebook, users were outraged. The video circulated virally on a Sunday night, coinciding with an important football match. Social media users generally condemned the assault, notwithstanding the reasons behind the student's misbehaviour. Blame was levelled immediately at the education authorities for the sordid conditions in which teachers worked, even in areas of the country that were assumed to be peaceful. Others denounced the exposure of teachers to crammed classrooms without the necessary pedagogical tools, and accused education authorities of being responsible for students' inadequate upbringing. Teachers in particular felt empowered to demand more legal protection from unexpected incidents.

Press coverage: The highest levels of engagement with this event were from digital media. Many online outlets identified the high school to uncover the hidden sides of the story. They met the student's classmates, whose standpoint was generally neglected in mainstream discussions. They revealed that the teacher had mental-health issues that, in normal circumstances, would have granted him early retirement. Visitors to e-news websites discovered that violent exchanges were common in that classroom. The teacher customarily insulted students, who retaliated by knocking him down. The only new element was the rampant visibility of video footage online. Other pupils accused local education administrations of a failure to deal with the problematic situation before the incident: they had moved the teacher to a junior high school to curb the problematic outbursts, but brought him back because of a staffing shortage.

Other news items and articles delved into the direct reasons for the fight. They explained that the teacher insulted the student with references to his parents' poverty. For instance, chouftv.ma, an online broadcaster, visited the student's father in his greengrocery store, at which point he revealed that his son had been severely insulted in front of his classmates. Media in different cities collected citizens' opinions on the mishap. They generally condemned the assault despite the potential causes. They also blamed the student's parents for his inadequate upbringing. Other citizens stressed the ministry's responsibility for the abyss into which the educational system had sunk. Yet, when asked about the solution, they generally agreed upon the imperative of receiving a good upbringing and being taught the right values at homes and schools. Citizens, too, felt empowered to further demonstrate the need for security in schools and expressed distrust towards the ministry for educational setbacks.

The story also reached local and international broadcast channels. The popular public channel, 2M, described the video content as causing shock and sorrow. As a manifestation of media convergence, or what Chadwick (2013, p. 2) termed as watching "a video of a video of a video", 2M depended on social media debates to criticie the decadent value system inside classrooms and the awful attack on the teacher. The family of the student, on the contrary, was portrayed as begging for their child to be safe, although he had threatened the safety of the teacher. The mother of the student said that her son had been bitten and punched too, hinting at the absence of a secure environment inside his school, as well as in the prison where he was incarcerated at the time. With the viral spread of the video, security in educational institutions was questioned, with most fingers pointing at state representatives. When the school headmaster or the municipal education director (a government official) featured on public media, they reiterated that they knew about the teacher's problematic classroom management, and they utterly condemned the student's misbehaviour. However, they refrained from admitting responsibility for the circumstances that led to the fight. International news outlets in different languages, including Arabic,

French and English, discussed the event, based on the uploaded video, Facebook tweets and statuses, as well as the opinions of Moroccan education experts and commentators.

Workplace reaction: Though the video was released on a Sunday, both the regional and local educational authorities issued press releases. This unprecedented response appeared to result from the online pressure. The authorities condemned the mishap, stressed the teacher's dignity and required a police probe into the issue. Since the teacher did not complain after the fight, the ministry of education filed a suit against the student. Meanwhile, the teacher and the administration behind his problematic situation managed to avoid responsibility and punishment. The teacher was neither arrested nor moved to another school, at least not before the end of the academic year. In addition, education officials contented themselves with issuing press releases that denounced the irregularity, praised the importance of the teacher's dignity and showed solidarity with his family and colleagues. On the other hand, three teacher unions called for a two-day strike to protest against working conditions inside classrooms (Chalfaouat, 2017). The viral video was an opportunity for them to require an end to the official discourse that had blamed teachers for the woes of the educational system before the incident. They also pinpointed the insufficient pedagogical and legal support for teachers inside high schools in particular. In a sense, the video's organisational empowerment further encouraged unions to defend teachers' rights, especially since the strike was the first after the government had passed a law to punish strikes financially. Due to the horror of the video, teachers and unions nationwide felt emboldened to challenge the law by going on strike regardless of potential salary cuts. They seized the opportunity to mobilise against the distressing situation.

The family's reaction: Though the video blemished their image as parents, the student's family engaged in media interviews to share their own interpretation of the event. The father replied to different online outlets and invited some to his greengrocer's shop. The store, for which the student was ridiculed, was a typical venue from which Moroccans usually buy produce. Neither the father nor his job seemed degrading enough to bring insult or mockery. With that psychological empowerment, he could symbolically shift the quarrel in his son's favour. Despite the excessive shaming online, playing the victim of unjust ridicule empowered the father to provide a parallel interpretation to the official one, which attracted online sympathy. The student's mother talked to different media outlets too. With her appearance and manner of speaking, she was portrayed as worthy of sympathy and as comparable to other mothers nationwide. She symbolically rejected any indictment of her upbringing for her son's aggressiveness. They and their son apologised for the assault before the court's final decision, according to their lawyer. Their online visibility and constant communication with the media caused a considerable change in families' perception of the interaction between social media and law enforcement. Their advocacy helped clarify certain neglected points in the story, while their apology, as reported by the lawyer online, aimed to gain the sympathy of the court jury. Contrariwise, little was heard from the family of the assaulted teacher. It is possible they contented themselves with the individual and organisational impact of the video.

State officials' reactions: Officials, especially those from the educational system, reacted in several ways. For instance, the president of the regional academy issued a press release on Sunday 5 November, and talked to the media. He fully denounced the assault, describing it as "non-educational", expressed solidarity with the teacher, his family and colleagues, and pledged to prevent the recurrence of such incidents. In addition, the municipal education director issued another press release. He insisted on maintaining the rule of law and prioritising the teacher's dignity. The delegation also formed a local taskforce to probe the event, and sued the student. Led by the municipal director, the taskforce also visited the assaulted teacher. When they asked him about the mishap, he surprised them by considering it as normal. They shared their astonishment with the press, possibly paving the way for what turned out to be an unexpectedly lenient sentence against the student. The president of the region council also publicised a press release. He asked the head of the government and the ministers of justice and education to amend the penal code in order to criminalise the assault of teachers. In the press release, he apologised to teachers and parents generally for the "classroom combat", and described the assault as "tragic", "horrendous", "bestial" and "sorrowful" (Tatoo, 2017). He also reproached the student's classmates for their inactivity. Moreover, the police announced that they were detaining the student. The public uproar created considerable pressure to imprison the teenager, despite the teacher's prior mistakes. However, the Public Prosecutor in a press conference considered the student a mere "reckless pupil" and described his detention as an "unfortunate development". Nonetheless, signs abounded from senior officials that the student would be released, since he did not necessarily have criminal motives and since the teacher did not file any documented complaint even after the video had spread.

Outcome and constructive co-production of security: Because of the online and offline debates, the student was brought to court. He was sentenced to seventeen days in custody in Ouarzazate, in addition to spending two months in a juvenile rehabilitation centre in Marrakech. His parents, on the other hand, were fined two symbolic dirhams, one to be given to the teacher and one to the municipal delegation.

Since it was so widely viewed, the video's constructive contribution to public security is multi-faceted. To start with, attacking a teacher inside a classroom was scorned and condemned severely. Though the teacher may have triggered the fight, thousands of comments online focused solely on the denigration of the assault and the resulting threat to the teacher's safety in an increasingly hostile educational atmosphere nationwide. Teachers, students and parents, as individuals and organisations, seized the empowerment of the opportunity to demand that schools be made safe from verbal, physical or financial violence, or even sexual harassment. They also demanded measures to be taken to fight the drug consumption that exacerbates school violence. The moral outrage and mode of cyber-social order compelled the student's family to apologise for the mishap online.

Second, different officials became involved in the issue. The head of the government, MPs, ministers and regional and local administrators commented on its developments online, or in press releases, parliamentary questions, media participations, apologies, etc. They might have reckoned on the impact of social distrust online, and agreed that the attack was unacceptable. Equally significant was the participation of police officers and the Public Prosecutor in the debate. They stressed the importance of the rule of law and promised to intervene adequately to maintain it. However, no laws were passed or amended to make the social debates and advocacy online an instance of community empowerment.

Third, media outlets galvanised the issue in different ways. In the absence of raw proof, incomplete and imprecise stories overwhelm public discourse. With the viral video, however, the press approached different stakeholders, including families, classmates and officials. Outlets not only propelled a local event to a national or international audience, but also enabled almost all voices and standpoints to receive a hearing, which vividly enhances freedom of speech. Nevertheless, as in other digital vigilantism events, the press avoided interviewing the culprit and the victim in order not to affect the ongoing legal process, to protect them against mob justice or potential retaliation and to maintain their right to be forgotten.

Furthermore, the video encouraged different facets of empowerment. The public's power of denunciation, to begin with, was emphasised when all influential stakeholders reacted to condemn the assault and require the detention of the wrongdoer. Moreover, students were empowered to rectify any potential misinformation. They shared the video to uncover a problematic situation that would have otherwise gone unnoticed. They protested in front of the school when their classmate was jailed and they talked to the media to add their own details and interpretation of the whole event. Teachers, as individuals and unions, equally felt empowered to fuel the uproar online and in the streets, since it was an opportunity to inform the public about their terrible working conditions. The assault was neither unprecedented nor surprising, given its distressing context. Public shaming of the recorded attack supported teachers to further criticise educational policies that endangered them. Parents were empowered too. Parents increasingly send their children to private schools despite the financial hardship the decision entails. They silently withdraw from overcrowded public schools, whose bad reputation spreads incessantly. The video boosted parents' psychological empowerment, and offered them an opportunity to voice the double-edged, unfortunate dilemma of whether to send their kids to the problematic public sector or to the costly private one.

Meanwhile, developments around the video highlighted official irresponsibility. In a more democratic context, the violent content would uncover the lacunae of regional and local education mismanagement, and condemn officials who denied the teacher early retirement. In addition, the student's family blamed the teacher's illness for their child's offensive reaction, which reduced the prison term. These circumstances alarmed officials, including those in remote areas, about the possibility for sudden public derision of their malpractice. Without self-regulation and professional conduct being ensured, ubiquitous electronic tools can unexpectedly mobilise public debate. Officials must then talk in front of the cameras tactfully, despite a lack of training or the absence of solid justifications for professional incompetence.

Conclusions

To conclude, this chapter answers the research question: how does digital vigilantism manifest in Morocco, especially in terms of empowering different voices? It discusses the ways common citizens' access to the media as a key resource morphs individual initiatives of sharing footage into social outrage online. Community, organisational and, especially, individual empowerment persists in consequence.

As a case in point, the chapter analyses different stakeholders' reactions amidst the frenzy of an instance of school violence. Due to digital vigilantism, different individuals and organisations challenged or rectified discourses about the incident. From the interactions that erupted, several conclusions can be drawn.

First of all, digital vigilantism enhances change in Moroccan society. Victims and bystanders realise the importance of recording and sharing wrongdoing. Public support online empowers them to endure the humiliation of their ordeal. Instead of shying away, they expose their affairs online, which generates shaming and denunciation of perpetrators, and leads to their arrest. In situations such as the case above, sharing wrongdoing may mitigate vulnerability, though not all stakeholders are accountable for their contribution to the problem. However, the resulting online vibrancy embeds the potential for the rule of law to be reinforced. It helps Moroccan citizens to break their silence, since perpetrators are either brought to justice or apologise publicly. In short, social events, digital connection and vigilantism enable online empowerment, leading citizens to appreciate the importance of vigilantism, denunciation and doxing. The concurrent empowerment encourages social change and helps social media to improve citizens' critical awareness and effective participation in improving their immediate environment.

Moreover, digital vigilantism stops short at revealing crimes. Moroccan citizens do not customarily take revenge after vigilantism. The police do not encourage citizens to take responsibility for themselves, as stability is key in the strategic narrative of exceptionalism (Fadel, 2016). Hence, the police foster a differentiation between vigilantism for a better society, and the ability to execute the rule of law. Consequently, citizens' co-production of security is confined to keeping the public sphere under control. Today, common citizens function as a neighbourhood watch on social media. They report to the public online before the police intervene. If the police have already intervened, public pressure demands — and sometimes leads to — stricter sentences. Otherwise, vigilantism keeps the pressure online, without embodied intervention against wrongdoers.

Furthermore, digital vigilantism requires a responsive government. Even though vigilantism facilitates self-help, public contributions to the rule of law need encouragement. This may require setting up some platform for citizens to co-produce security, and the police to recognise doxing during investigations. For more successful vigilantism, the platform could link the promotion of civic virtue to the public interest and the avoidance of retaliation. Moreover, the police can incorporate the ubiquity of online opportunities for citizens by fostering participative security as a legitimate contribution to their work. As a result, substantial efforts may counter the current increased demands for security, and the visible expression of distrust in state efforts.

Finally, the culture of impunity that stems from the flawed judiciary and corrupt administration hinders a clear transition from vigilantism to changing laws. Vigilantism breaks the silence, enables the co-production of security and warns against recidivism. However, annual reports of transparency and anti-corruption institutions, such as the High Council for Accounts, reveal the ways that impunity hobbles development and democracy. Thus, more responsive legal institutions are necessary to reap the benefits of vigilantism. The current situation is on the threshold of a movement towards more respect for laws. Since vigilantism spotlights inadequacies in law enforcement and the repercussions of impunity, responsibility rests with legal agents to reduce the impact of perceived impunity on the social value of laws and on the seriousness of responses to public demands for a safer environment. Otherwise, when such perceived impunity holds citizens back from smooth participation in democratising the lives of their community, distrust deepens, leading to an irreconcilable crisis in democracy.

References

Anderson, A. (2010, April 25). British women turn detective to bring US 'suicide voyeur' to justice. *The Telegraph*, https://www.telegraph.co.uk/news/worldnews/northamerica/usa/7629372/British-women-turn-detective-to-bring-US-suicide-voyeur-to-justice.html

AsiaNews. (2013, September 5). As people take the law in their own hands, lynching and vigilante murders rise. *AsiaNews*, http://www.asianews.it/news-en/As-people-take-the-law-in-their-own-hands,-lynching-and-vigilante-murders-rise-27879.html

Babas, L. (2018, May 11). A ten-year sentence for the man who sexually assaulted a girl in a viral video. *Yabiladi*, https://en.yabiladi.com/articles/details/64755/ten-year-sentence-sexually-assaulted-girl.html

Bladi.info (2016, April 20). Quand les habitants de quartiers font la loi à casa. *Bladi.info*, https://www.bladi.info/threads/habitants-quartiers-loi-casa.428545

Chadwick, A. (2013). *The Hybrid Media System: Politics and Power*. New York: Oxford University Press, http://doi.org/ 10.1093/acprof:oso/9780199759477.001.0001

Chahir, A. (2019, June 9). The collapse of the "Moroccan exception" myth. *Middle East Eye*, http://www.middleeasteye.net/opinion/collapse-moroccan-exception-myth

Chalfaouat, A. (2015). Media, freedom of expression and democratisation in post-colonial Morocco. In P. Molnar (ed.). *Free Speech and Censorship Around the Globe* (1st edn., pp. 465–80). Budapest: Central European University Press.

Chalfaouat, A. (2017, November 6). Why are teachers' rights marginalised in Morocco?. *Middle East Monitor*, https://www.middleeastmonitor.com/20171106-why-are-teachers-rights-marginalised-in-morocco

Chang, L., Zhong, L., & Grabosky, P. (2016). Citizen co-production of cyber security: Self-help, vigilantes, and cybercrime. *Regulation & Governance*, 12(1), 101-14, https://doi.org/10.1111/rego.12125

Chen, G. M. (2017). Social media: From digital divide to empowerment. In C. P., Campbell (ed.). *The Routledge Companion to Media and Race*. (1st edn., pp. 117–25). New York: Taylor & Francis.

Cook, T. E., & Gronke, P. (2005). The sceptical American: Revisiting the meanings of trust in government and confidence in institutions. *Journal of Politics*, 67(3), 784–803, https://doi.org/10.1111/j.1468-2508.2005.00339.x Bas du formulaire

El Maarouf, M. D., & Belghazi, T. (2018). The urban and virtual rhetoric of Tcharmil: Display, violence and resistance. *The Journal of North African Studies*, 23(1-2), 292-310, https://doi.org/10.1080/13629387.2017.1364630

Eltantawy, N., & Wiest, J. B. (2011). Social media in the Egyptian revolution: Reconsidering resource mobilization theory. *International Journal of Communication*, 5, 1207–24.

Errazzouki, S. (2017). Under watchful eyes: Internet surveillance and citizen media in Morocco, the case of Mamfakinch. *The Journal of North African Studies*, 22(3), 361–85, http://www.doi.org/10.1080/13629387.2017.1307907

Fadel, L. (2016, April 17). Morocco boasts stability, but critics say the price is high. *National Public Radio*, https://www.npr.org/sections/parallels/2016/04/17/474368034/morocco-boasts-stability-but-critics-say-the-price-is-high

Huey, L., Nhan, J., & Broll, R. (2013). 'Uppity civilians' and 'cyber-vigilantes': The role of the general public in policing cyber-crime. *Criminology & Criminal Justice*, 13(1), 81–97, https://doi.org/10.1177/1748895812448086

Hoffman, P. (2012, November, 2019). Vigilantism: The Last Resort of the Unprotected, *World Justice Project*, http://worldjusticeproject.org/blog/vigilantism-last-resort-unprotected

Howard, P. N., & Parks, M. R. (2012). Social Media and Political Change: Capacity, Constraint, and Consequences. *Journal of Communication* 62(2), 359–62, http://dx.doi.org/10.1111/j.1460-2466.2012.01626.x

Khalaf, R. (2018, March 28). A man sexually assaulted a girl in Morocco, and his friend videotaped it. *Stepfeed*, https://stepfeed.com/a-man-sexually-assaulted-a-girl-in-morocco-and-his-friend-videotaped-it-4624

Khamis, S., & Vaugh, K. (2011, May 29). Cyberactivism in the Egyptian revolution: How civic engagement and citizen journalism tilted the balance. *Arab Media & Society*, https://www.arabmediasociety.com/cyberactivism-in-the-egyptian-revolution-how-civic-engagement-and-citizen-journalism-tilted-the-balance

Lesiteinfo. (2016, April 19). Quand les habitants de quartiers font la loi à Casa. *Lesiteinfo*, https://www.lesiteinfo.com/maroc/habitants-de-quartiers-loi-a-casa-2

Lorch, J., & Bukhard, J. (2017, August 22). Online and traditional forms of protest mobilization: Morocco's Rif protests and beyond. *MEI.edu*, https://www.mei.edu/publications/online-and-traditional-forms-protest-mobilization-moroccos-rif-protests-and-beyond

McLeod, C., Trust. In Edward N. Zalta (ed.). *The Stanford Encyclopedia of Philosophy* (Fall 2015 edn.). Stanford: The Metaphysics Research Lab, https://plato.stanford.edu/archives/fall2015/entries/trust

Middle East Online. (2013, March 21). Vigilante violence haunts 'Mother of the World'. *Middle East Online*, https://middle-east-online.com/en/vigilante-violence-haunts-'mother-world'

Mireanu, M. (2014). *Vigilantism and Security: State, Violence and Politics in Italy and Hungary*. PhD dissertation. Vienna and Budapest: Central European University.

NapoleonCat (2018, September). Facebook users in Morocco. *NapoleonCat*, https://napoleoncat.com/stats/facebook-users-in-morocco/2018/09

Pérez-Altable, L. (2016). The Arab Spring before the Arab Spring: A case study of digital activism in Tunisia. *Global Media Journal — Arabian Edition*, 4(1/2), 19–32.

Perkins, D. D., & Zimmerman, M. A. (1995, January 1). Empowerment theory, research, and application. *American Journal of Community Psychology*, 23(5), 569-79, https://doi.org/10.1007/BF02506982

Porter, R. (2010). Amateur sleuth unmasks male nurse 'who encouraged dozens to kill themselves online' so he could watch. *Daily Mail*, https://www.dailymail.co.uk/femail/article-1269639/Amateur-sleuth-unmasks-male-nurse-encouraged-dozens-kill-online-watch.html

Safi Addakirapress. (2017). Shocking/ Student assaults his teacher in Ouarzazate. YouTube, https://www.youtube.com/watch?v=aC-DjWwDFs8&has_verified=1

Scheffers, M. J. (2015). *Framing Digital Vigilantism in the Context of the Kopschop-Incident in Eindhoven*. Master's Thesis, Media Culture & Society, hdl.handle.net/2105/34518

Sekkouri, A. M. (2008). On the Targuist sniper's trail, https://ec.europa.eu/europeaid/targuist-snipers-trail-mehdi-sekkouri-alaoui-and-youssef-zaroui-second-prize-arab-world-and-middle_en

Swan, K. (2017) *Gaining Perspective: Social Media's Impact on Adolescent Literacy Development*. Master's Thesis, Education and Human Development, https://digitalcommons.brockport.edu/ehd_theses/767

Szescilo, D. (2017). Citizen's co-production of public safety as a symptom of state failure: The case of South African vigilantism. *Journal of Comparative Urban Law and Policy*, 1(1), 145-52.

Tatoo, M. A. (2017, November 5). After a student assaults his teacher... Choubani calls the government to amend the penal code. *al3omk.com*, https://al3omk.com/243717.html

The Journal. (2015, July 18). 'Vigilante mob' beat a man to death in a Morocco market after accusing him of stealing. *The Journal*, https://www.thejournal. ie/vigilante-mob-morocco-market-2222970-Jul2015

Toffler, A. (1980) *The Third Wave*. New York: Morrow.

Tufekci, Z. (2018, August 14). How social media took us from Tahrir Square to Donald Trump. www.technologyreview.com, https:// www.technologyreview.com/2018/08/14/240325/how-social-media -took-us-from-tahrir-square-to-donald-trump/

Wehmhoener, K. A. (2010). *Social norm or social harm: An exploratory study of Internet vigilantism*. Master's Thesis, Journalism and Mass Communication, https://doi.org/10.31274/etd-180810-1388

Zimmerman, M. A. (2000). Empowerment theory: Psychological, organizational, and community levels of analysis. In J. Rappaport & E. Seidman (eds), *Handbook of Community Psychology* (pp. 43–63). Kluwer Academic Publishers, https://doi.org/10.1007/978-1-4615-4193-6_2

'This Web Page Should Not Exist': A Case Study of Online Shaming in Slovenia[1]

Mojca M. Plesničar and Pika Šarf

Introduction

In the autumn of 2015, the Balkan migrant[2] route, which led people from Greece to central Europe through the Balkans, redirected through Slovenia because Hungary closed its borders. This led to a large number of migrants entering Slovenia, which spurred heated and often hostile debates in the Slovenian public sphere. Many used social media to voice their fears and hatred towards migrants, with some comments bordering on hate speech and many others crossing that line. (FRA Update #1, 2015; FRA Update #2, 2015; Council of Europe, 2018) Since increased expressions of intolerance and hatred never resulted in any kind of action from the public authorities, several civil-society actors started to raise awareness of hate speech by issuing different appeals to the public for respect in public debates.

---

1   The research underpinning this article was funded by the European Union's Horizon 2020 research and innovation programme, under the Marie-Sklodowska-Curie grant agreement for the "Transmaking" project (no. 734855) and from the Slovenian Research Agency for the research project "Automated Justice: Social, Ethical and Legal Implications' (no. J5–9347).

2   As there is no internationally recognised definition of the term migrant, in the present article we refer to the terminology of the International Organisation for Migration, in which the term is understood as "a person who moves away from his or her place of usual residence, whether within a country or across an international border, temporarily or permanently, and for a variety of reasons" (IOM, 2020).

     https://doi.org/10.11647/OBP.0200.08

In a response to the hatred directed at migrants in public posts on Facebook, one anonymous participant used the platform offered by Tumblr to create a page called "Zlovenija". The title is a play on words that combines the country's name, Slovenia, with the Slovenian word for evil, "zlo", resulting in the portmanteau "Evil-venia". Individual Facebook posts expressing hate towards migrants were exposed, and the names and enlarged (profile) pictures of the posts' authors were published on the page. This all followed the page's "manifesto" urging people to consider the norms of civil communication. Not much attention was given to the page by the general public, until some of the posts, with their enlarged photos, were printed and posted in random public spaces throughout Ljubljana, the capital of Slovenia. While they remained in digital form, the comments exposed by Zlovenija did not have a wider reach due to the so-called Facebook filter bubble effects (Bechmann & Nielbo, 2018; Seargeant & Tagg, 2019), especially as they were being published in Facebook groups connecting similar minded individuals. The same effect was observed with groups promoting opposite stances, such as the since-banned group 'Slovenia protect your borders' (*Slovenija zavaruj meje*). The change of platform, however, meant that the same comments and their authors suddenly became subject to public judgment and condemnation for their unacceptable, immoral or even illegal nature. This, in turn, stimulated public interest and discussion, which took place both on the digital platform of Zlovenija as well as in traditional media. The daily newspaper *Delo* was the first to report about the phenomenon in a short opinion piece, which triggered false rumours about the reporting journalist actually being the author of Zlovenija (as seen below) (Krajčinović, 2015).

Consequently, the initiative that started as a spontaneous response to the hatred infecting the country became a powerful tool in the hands of civil society in a matter of just two weeks (Interview with Zlovenija, 2018). What was at first just an obscure Tumblr page became a pillory with a mission to initiate a discussion on the issue of hate speech, remind people that the Internet is a public space and that their words have meaning and consequences, and hold the mirror up to the society and condemn all intolerance and violence (Zlovenija, 2015). The people exposed on Zlovenija were, to our knowledge, not subject to repercussions in the workspace or family context (such as for example in the Charlottesville case, cf. Milbrandt, this volume). They were, however subject to public scrutiny and served as the public face of hatred and intolerance.

Although Zlovenija succeeded in inciting significant conversations about the issue of hate speech, with which Slovenia has an uneasy relationship as we will discuss later, the method it used was nevertheless extreme, and it immediately raised questions about both its legality and its legitimacy. The author(s) of the page[3] acknowledged this concern when they pointed out that:

> this page should not exist because it is extreme as it was created as a response to the silence of those who should be speaking, those who were elected to speak solemnly at a time when the majority loses their minds. But they did not. This page should not exist because it bears witness to the fact that all other ways of maintaining the basic standards of civilisation failed, and we are left with barely holding up the mirror. Here, look at (your own) evil (Zlovenija, 2015).[4]

In this chapter we will examine Zlovenija's approach and the surrounding events by considering different focal points. First, we will analyse the original posts that were published on Zlovenija and look for patterns and commonalities, as well as the criteria used to select them. We aim to provide a close reading of the content that was used and the source of further developments. Second, we analyse the debates on Zlovenija that followed the original posts and include explanations posted by the authors of the original Facebook posts, as well as responses from the general public that were published on the page. Third, we take a broader look at the response of the wider public online, mainly searching through popular online platforms and fora, as well as the reaction of the general media, looking through commentaries and news concerning Zlovenija. We also consider the question of the (il)legality of Zlovenija's approach, focusing on the (il)legality of 1) the original posts, 2) the

---

3   In order to maintain the privacy of the author(s) we refer to them as author(s) throughout the chapter, not indicating their gender or how many of them there were.

4   "Ta stran ne bi smela obstajati, ker je skrajna, ker je nastala kot odgovor na molk tistih, ki bi morali govoriti, tistih, ki so bili izvoljeni za to, da bodo trezno spregovorili v času, ko bo večini odpovedal razum. Pa niso. Ta stran ne bi smela obstajati, ker priča o tem, da so odpovedali vsi drugi načini ohranjanja osnovnih civilizacijskih standardov in nam je preostalo le še nastavljanje zrcala. Izvolite, zazrite se v (lastno) zlo".

reposting of the posts and 3) the publicising of the posts in a physical form by displaying printed versions throughout the streets of Ljubljana. Another focal point of public debates was the question of whether Zlovenija became just another online 'shamer', no better than the original wrongdoers it was trying to expose. We supplemented the literature and textual analysis with additional information we gathered from the author(s) of Zlovenija in an interview we conducted in December 2018. We were able to contact the author(s) through the web page and various other means and we were able to confirm their authenticity, hence their answers give important insights into the operation of the page. Finally, we will attempt to understand and critically assess the ideas and the methods used by Zlovenija, and the repercussions of its activities.

Zlovenija's Outline

Zlovenija started in October 2015 as a spontaneous intervention, almost as a joke, at a time when Slovenia was facing a wave of hatred directed towards migrants, and all formal mechanisms to address the issue of hate speech were failing. The author(s) explained that:

> [Slovenian philosopher and media analyst] Boris Vezjak published one photograph, in which the quotations were exposed. Then I started to post it in a private group and discuss with friends, that we could do something like this. I set up the Tumblr page quite quickly and tried to make a few posts and I thought that it works and then it was launched. [...] We did not think too much about what would happen and what we would do with it (Interview with Zlovenija, 2018).[5]

The idea was simple: the author(s) copied the most brutal, outrageous and vile comments they could find and accompanied them with the name and picture of the person making these hateful comments, as well as a link to the original Facebook post. Tumblr, a visual microblogging website, provided a perfect platform to display the faces of hatred to the

---

5   "Boris Vezjak je objavil eno sliko, kjer so bili ti citati izpostavljani, potem pa [smo začeli to mi] v eni zasebni skupini objavljati in se pogovarjat s prijatelji, da bi lahko nekaj takega naredili oziroma smo dost hitro kar naredili Tumblr in sem probal par sličic in se mi je zdelo, da zelo funkcionira in potem je to zalaufalo. [...] Ni bilo kakšnega hudega razmisleka zadaj, kaj se bo zdaj zgodilo, pa kaj se bo s tem naredilo".

widest audience possible, notably due to the ease with which it enables users to crowdsource new content (Oblak Črnič, 2017).

Even though Zlovenija was actively posting for less than two weeks, its concept evolved over that time. The initial idea of posting hateful Facebook posts with their author's name and picture was supplemented with the section containing the readers' letters. The practice of adding the link to the original post ceased at some point, which remains one of the biggest regrets of the page's author(s), since Zlovenija started to face accusations that the comments were fake and it became impossible to prove their authenticity if the original Facebook comment was already deleted (Interview with Zlovenija, 2018). Moreover, just a few days before Zlovenija was shut down, it provided a new option to the Facebook posters to request the removal of a post in case they deleted the original Facebook comment and apologised. Like the page itself, the invitation to apologise was not very specific or premeditated; it was introduced after initial spontaneous apologies to the Tumblr page from the authors of some of the posts. The apology had to be submitted via the Tumblr page and then it substituted the reposted Facebook post on Zlovenija (ibid.).

Just as the creation and maintenance of Zlovenija was a spontaneous reaction, so too was the decision to shut it down. There are several reasons why it stopped actively posting after less than two weeks, but the main cause was the sudden emergence of posters depicting the Facebook posts exposed on Zlovenija throughout Ljubljana. This was an action that was neither anticipated nor performed by the author(s) of Zlovenija, but according to the author(s) it was also:

> the most interesting insight of the whole project. As long as Zlovenija stayed online, everything was okay, but as soon as the stickers [printed versions of Facebook posts] appeared, it escalated to another level and it became a better story for the media, as it was a real-life shaming pillar (ibid.).[6]

This unexpected turn of events meant that, on the one hand, the impact of Zlovenija went beyond the initial framework, and the real-world platform acted as a reminder to the page's author(s) of how powerful

---

6   "To je bil najbolj zanimiv uvid celega projekta. Dokler je bilo to online, je bilo vse OK, takoj, ko so se pa te nalepke pojavile, je pa to preskočilo na neko drugo stopnjo in postala je veliko boljša medijska zgodba, da je to sedaj sramotilni steber v resničnem življenju".

and potentially dangerous their actions were; it therefore caused them to have a different level of appreciation of their own work (ibid.). On the other hand, the pressure on Zlovenija's author(s) intensified to a much greater degree.

The Facebook posters and their supporters were suddenly more motivated to identify the person(s) responsible for both the online and the offline campaigns, and calls for collective (legal) action against Zlovenija started to emerge. Although the author(s) began the project with a certain level of apprehension or caution, this turned to outright fear after Zlovenija's author(s) discovered that people were starting to seek help to uncover them on one of the boards on 4chan, an image board website known for its anonymity and the lack of rules for posting content. If uncovering the author(s) of Zlovenija had previously seemed impossible, the author(s) feared that with the help of the international community of hackers this became a foreseeable possibility (ibid.).

Both reasons convinced the author(s) to stop their activities — the page on Tumblr is still accessible, but only the manifesto and the apologies remain, while the original Facebook posts have been removed.[7,8]

The Facebook Posts

We analysed the 222 posts, which were originally publicly posted on Facebook and re-posted by the Tumblr page Zlovenija. We did a thematic analysis adhering to Braun & Clarke (2019) concepts of reflexive thematic analysis, leaning towards a deductive, latent and constructionist approach. Subsequently, we combined the findings from our thematic analysis with the insights we gained from the interview with the author(s) of Zlovenija.

---

7   We are indebted to our colleague, Aleš Završnik, who showed great foresight in downloading the contents of the page before it was taken down, and was kind enough to share all that information, which in turn became the basis of our analysis.

8   We were, however, able to identify at least one page that imitated the original Zlovenija's idea for much longer. A page entitled 'Hate Speech' (*Sovraznigovor*) used Zlovenija's framework after the hibernation of the page, but took it to Wordpress and to this day keeps about 90 posts publicly available. We were unable to identify the authors of this page, but given its openly credits Zlovenija for the idea and the smaller scale, we believe we can include these posts in the following analysis. Moreover, we found at least one artist, Tibor Bolha, who publishes on Tumblr as penguindinosaurwar, who took Zlovenija as inspiration and drew the posts by hand — we are using some of those depictions to illustrate this chapter and are grateful for his permission to do so.

Fig. 8.1 A bunch of racist ignorant jerks from my country. Illustration by Tibor Bolha (2015). All rights reserved. Tumblr, https://penguindinosaurwar.tumblr. com/post/132146266303/a-bunch-of-racist-ignorant-jerks-from-my-country

This Facebook profile picture depicts the author of the post targeted by Zlovenija gently petting a puppy, while the post itself said: "The refugees need to be [force] fed just rat poison or closed into a gas chamber.... death to refugees liberty to Slovenians [sic]". The quote is an example of the merging of two of our content categories explained below: calls for violence and implicitly referring to authoritarian regimes. The Nazi regime is invoked by the reference to gas chambers, and the Soviet Communist regime by paraphrasing one of its mottos (death to Fascism, liberty to the people).

Fig. 8.2 A bunch of racist ignorant jerks from my country. Illustration by Tibor Bolha (2015). All rights reserved. Tumblr, https://penguindinosaurwar.tumblr. com/post/132146266303/a-bunch-of-racist-ignorant-jerks-from-my-country

This Facebook profile picture depicts a couple kissing. The post, however, reveals anger and contempt towards the refugees by saying: "Fuck, the refugees have it better than Slovenians [sic] in Slovenia... Now the refugees are all poor and stuff... Go the fuck back... And there they give guns to children while guys nicely fuck away fucking shitheads".

Fig. 8.3 A bunch of racist ignorant jerks from my country. Illustration by Tibor Bolha (2015). All rights reserved. Tumblr, https://penguindinosaurwar.tumblr. com/post/132146266303/a-bunch-of-racist-ignorant-jerks-from-my-country

The Facebook profile picture depicts a dad carrying his smiling child on his shoulders. The post itself combines calls for violence with clear undertones of alarm and insecurity about the future with regard to the refugees: "Military and gas over these terrorists... there is no other solution... or we offer them to peacefully return home... or else... in 2024 there will be more of them than locals in every country..."

The author(s) of Zlovenija deliberately tried to capture a variety of different profiles, young and old, men and women, to show that hatred does not have a uniform face (Interview with Zlovenija, 2018). Most of the hateful Facebook posts were published either as comments on news articles covering the topic of the migrant crisis, which were shared on Facebook or in public Facebook groups known for supporting anti-migrant rhetoric (e.g. "Slovenia protect your borders", "STOP Migrants to Slovenia", "Slovenia our country") that had over 31,000 members at the peak of the migrant crisis (Bajt, 2015).

The posts were carefully chosen to show the immense contrast between the loving grandparents, newlyweds, proud parents or carefree teenagers portrayed in the pictures on the one hand, and the hateful, vile and even brutal comments they were posting online. This is also the reason the profile picture was not always chosen to accompany the comment, but rather the picture that offered the biggest contrast to the hate emanating from the comments (Interview with Zlovenija, 2018). The typical "Zlovenijan" according to the author(s) of the Tumblr page, lives in a rural part of the country, sympathises with right-wing political opinions and may be slightly more religious. The hate and fear expressed in the original Facebook posts fit well with a typical narrative in which members of the lower-middle class fear that their modest way of living will be disturbed by the influx of migrants, and project their own insecurities and dissatisfaction with their social status to attack this perceived threat (Oblak Črnič, 2017).

A great majority of the hateful comments Zlovenija exposed were posted by men (78%) and the author(s) claim a similar if not stronger prevalence was noticeable among the comments they chose from (Interview with Zlovenija, 2018). This is in line with recent studies on how gender determines the content published on social networking sites (SNS) such as Facebook, Twitter and Instagram. Although women were found to be predominant SNS users during the past decade, today men and women are using SNS at very similar rates. However, the divide between the topics they discuss and the language they use is still indisputable. A study that examined a million random Facebook status updates revealed that, while women are more prone to discuss personal subjects with individuals they know, men more often concentrate on sports, business, politics and religion (Wang et al., 2013). Moreover, the language women use while engaging on Facebook is generally warmer, friendlier, more polite and focused on other people, while men are usually socially distant and are more likely to use colder, hostile and authoritative language (Schwartz et al., 2013; Park et al., 2016).

Post content: Through our analysis, we identified four main themes in the Facebook posts: calls for violence, invocations of authoritarian regimes and leaders, expressions of fear and the desire for the protection of the border, slurs and name-calling of the migrants. Some posts exemplify one category, but mostly we can identify multiple themes in any given post. Nearly all of the analysed posts share various expressions proposing different methods of 'dealing' with the migrants crossing the Slovenian border, the majority of which involve great violence and would result in their death. Shooting or the use of any other type of weapon or domestic tool seems to be the most prevalent method, followed by using fire or letting migrants freeze to death. "Bullet in the forehead", "put cyanide in their meals", "let them freeze", "Kalashnikov the only solution", "burn them with napalm", "activate a bomb", are a just a few instances of such calls for the execution of the migrants. In less than 5% of all comments, calls for the elimination of migrants were accompanied by threats to politicians, reporters and humanitarian workers who took part in dealing with the migrant crisis. In approximately 10% of the analysed Facebook posts, we found an invocation of authoritarian regimes, either calling for the return of authoritarian leaders or promoting the idea of re-introducing gas chambers and concentration camps as a solution for the migrant crisis. "Hitler Stalin Tito our only salvation!", "One-way ticket to Auschwitz!", "Gas chambers are a solution", "Where is Hitler when you need him?" are just some of the most illustrative examples. Posts expressing fear of migrants were also quite frequent and usually included the need for the protection of "our" country and defending the border from "them", either by using (para)military force and police or building a fence or a wall.

The majority of the analysed Facebook posts also used various expressions with negative connotation to label migrants, for example the words "animals", "parasites", "beasts", "murderers", "rapists", "trash", "Muslim pigs", "rats", "fuckers", "Neanderthals", "shit", appear continuously throughout the page. This is in line with the psychological mechanisms of feelings of hate, in which the object of hate is reduced to non-human forms, which in turn allows for others to treat them inhumanely (either figuratively or in real life) (Milivojević, 2008).

The authors of the Facebook posts could request removal of their name and profile picture from the Tumblr page Zlovenija,[9] as soon as they deleted the original post from Facebook and briefly explained why they had changed their mind. The explanations, which were in most cases also apologies for unacceptable behaviour, were published on the Tumblr page, where they substituted the original posts and remain available online.

The mechanism of removal was not planned in the initial stages of the project, but rather developed as a spontaneous reaction to some self-initiated expressions of regret and atonement received through the Tumblr page (Interview with Zlovenija, 2018). Although the author(s) claimed that a large share of individuals apologised and sought removal from the page, in fact only 18 individuals pursued this mechanism (13% of all posts), out of which only one individual refused to apologise, even

---

9   However, the removal of posts was not enabled for the posts that were re-posted on the Wordpress page *Sovražnigovor*, which shows that although the authors of the page copied the format of Zlovenija, they did not follow all the aspects of the idea as a whole.

though he deleted the original Facebook post. One of the reasons why the removal of the posts was not pursued more widely might be because the page was mostly unknown to the wider public at the time, and was closed down within days of gaining widespread attention. Nevertheless, the explanations and apologies were a clear sign of Zlovenija's success and an immense reward for the author(s) of the page (ibid.).

The authors of the hateful Facebook comments who interacted with the page provided different arguments to explain their posts. (1) The predominant claim was that their posts were a consequence of fear. They said that they had posted hateful comments because they were afraid for their families, their children and their way of life, which could all be disrupted when the migrants entered Slovenia. Moreover, (2) many of the commentators argued that they posted their comments in the heat of the moment as a result of an instantaneous, reckless decision or wrong information provided by the media or, finally, (3) that they only realised that their posts crossed the line of hate speech when they were exposed by Zlovenija. One comment, for example, included all of the above:

> Please delete my picture from the blacklist, since I kind of responded hastily with hate speech. There are a lot of posts, some of which are true and some are false, which literally make you lose your nerves and you say a lot in the heat of the moment. I have 5 children and I am very scared for them. Please accept my request [to remove the FB post from Zlovenija].[10]

The latter argument (not realising hate speech) is not legally convincing. One of the main legal principles (lat. *"Ignorantia iuris non excusat"* or *"Ignorantia iuris nocet"*) stipulates that not knowing the law does not exclude the liability of the ignorant individual who violates it. Similarly, a rational person is expected to understand that calling for the re-introduction of concentration camps, inciting murder, as well as using racist and xenophobic language is at least immoral if not illegal in a democratic society. However, this argument may be understood through the prism of a wide freedom of expression generally enjoyed in Slovenia, on the one hand, and a lack of public discussion on the topic of hate speech on the other. Both were strengthened by fear and

---

10   "Prosim, da izbrišete mojo sliko iz črne top liste, saj sem nekako iz hitrega odziva komentirala z sovražnim govorom. Veliko je objav, enih resničnih in enih lažnih, ki te dobesedno spravi ob živce in rečeš v efektu marsikaj. Imam 5 otrok in me je zelo strah za njih. Prosim, da moji prošnji ugodite".

misunderstandings surrounding the migrant crisis, which may have given some individuals the courage to post inappropriate content online.

After Zlovenija put the topic of hate speech at the centre of public debates in Slovenia, even Facebook groups that used to incite hatred towards migrants started to warn their users not to use language that could be recognised as hate speech in order not to be publicly shamed on the page (ibid.). Here, it is clear that the intention of the administrators of such groups was not to curb the spreading of hate speech online, but to protect its users and redirect them to use subtler (but still offensive) language. As such, the impact of Zlovenija in mitigating online hate speech is evident.

Some of the apologies expressed deep remorse and genuine concern as a result of being exposed by Zlovenija. However, reasonable ambiguity surrounds the true intent behind the majority of them. The tone of some of the apologies leaves no doubt that the only reason for atoning is the promise of deleting their post from Zlovenija. Regardless, the rationale for introducing the mechanism was to give every exposed individual a chance to correct their wrongdoing, and the author(s) of Zlovenija never felt moral authority to judge on the sincerity of the apologies and substituted the post with an apology whenever someone decided to pursue the mechanism of removal (ibid.).

Media Coverage and the Response of the Wider Public

In the first days after Zlovenija became operational, news about it mostly spread through social media sites such as Twitter, but it remained largely unnoticed until the posts taken from the Tumblr page appeared as posters on random public spaces throughout Ljubljana (ibid.). This was not the work of the same author(s) as the online campaign and the people responsible remain unidentified to this day. The author(s) of Zlovenija find it curious that people did not react while the shaming was only happening online, but acknowledged the shaming campaign the moment the posts appeared offline: "Although this is ironic, because a real-life post will not be seen by 10,000 people, but only by as many people as walk by, while a larger group of people will see it online".[11]

---

11   "Čeprav je to ironično, ker tistega stebra tam ne bo videlo 10.000 ljudi, ampak samo toliko, kot jih bo šlo mimo, medtem ko je to na spletu videla večja množica ljudi".

(ibid.). However, they seem to have been struck by the publicity brought by the posters across Ljubljana and were not prepared to deal with it, which ultimately led to the page being shut down.

It was at this point that the media started reporting about the phenomenon, as well as addressing the issue of hate speech surrounding the migrant crisis. All five analysed articles refrained from either condemning or praising the work of Zlovenija, but raised the question of whether or not it was appropriate to put individuals who spread hateful comments in an online pillory, in order to highlight the problem of hate speech (cf. Milbrandt, this volume). Even the author(s) of the page admitted that the method used was drastic, yet also emphasised that it should not be evaluated in isolation, but in a broader social context (Zlovenija, 2015). The proliferation of online hate speech at the peak of the migrant crisis, coupled with the lack of response from the authorities, led to what they believed was an intolerable situation. In the view of Zlovenija's author(s), the reaction, therefore, pursued a legitimate aim of preventing further escalation of hate directed towards the migrants (Interview with Zlovenija, 2018).

As to the wider public, we gather that Zlovenija was met with a mixed response. Many members of the public agreed with, and even admired the objectives Zlovenija was trying to achieve. On the other hand, it was often condemned for being too extreme, and no better than the people it was trying to expose. In order to determine the attitude of the general public towards the idea of Zlovenija, we first searched through popular online platforms and fora, as well as through online comments concerning Zlovenija published on Slovenian news websites; secondly, we analysed the response published on the page itself ("Readers' letters").

Throughout the migrant crisis, the online media in Slovenia faced an immense increase in the number of published comments. The National Radio Television Web Portal MMC reported that the number of comments published for one news article related to migration exceeded the number of comments they usually receive daily for all news (FRA Update #2, 2015). Due to the unmanageable number of comments that needed to be deleted because they either qualified as, or bordered on hate speech, the working process of the most frequently visited news websites in Slovenia (www.24ur.com) was seriously impaired. This led to them initially limiting online commenting to only one migration-related news article per day, and later disabling commenting altogether (Oštir, 2015). The majority of news websites followed this example and limited or disabled online comments on the news relating to migrants, including all articles related to Zlovenija.

Comments referring to Zlovenija can be nevertheless found on a variety of news websites, as well as online platforms and fora; they are usually hidden among thousands of posts relating to the migrant crisis in general (some examples include "Zlovenija — careful with your opinions", "Now I am really afraid", "Refugee crisis in Slovenia 2015", "Refugee crisis in Slovenia in 2016"). Even the topics that were originally created to comment on the phenomenon of Zlovenija in most cases quickly became preoccupied with other issues, and provided another platform to express negative and hateful comments.

The analysis of the comments addressing Zlovenija revealed three prevailing themes that can be found in almost any debate surrounding it. Firstly, the fear that repeatedly appeared in the apologies posted on Zlovenija was also one of the main topics discussed in the online fora. However, as well as expressions of the fear of the migrants and the Islamisation of Slovenia and Europe as a whole, many users expressed concern about a society in which certain individuals freely express their wish to use gas chambers and burn people alive, and yearn for the return of Hitler or Stalin.

Second, since the author(s) of Zlovenija remain anonymous to this day, almost every discussion about Zlovenija eventually turned into accusations, speculation and a guessing game over who created the Tumblr page. Journalists and bloggers who reported about the phenomenon before it gained widespread attention were frequently accused of being Zlovenija's authors. The rumours led to the public exposure of a journalist working for the Slovenian newspaper *Delo*, even though she expressed her doubts about the methods Zlovenija used. Some users of social media even went a step further and encouraged the "Zlovenijans" to take action and sue the journalist. An eye-catching Facebook post, which was reposted numerous times and includes a picture of the journalist accused of being the author of Zlovenija, reads:

> Nina Kranjčinović, a journalist of *Delo* and the leader of the page Zlovenija. She executed an actual attack on patriotic Slovenians, who

care what is happening with Slovenia. I advise anyone that has been used to incite hatred by the owners and establishers of this web page and whose pictures were published on this extremist web page without their permission to join and file a collective action.[12]

The last theme, hinted at in the quote above as well, was the discussion about Zlovenija's legal repercussions. However, even the discourse on the topic of legality was extremely polarised: on the one hand the question of the legality of the original posts was raised and often accompanied by discussions about the (in)ability of the Slovenian criminal justice system to deal with hate speech. On the other hand, many voiced their concern that the page violated the Facebook authors' rights to privacy, data protection laws and copyright protection. Moreover, as some examples of shaming have shown, being put to the pillory may have devastating consequences for the exposed individuals in their everyday lives, and could result in losing their jobs and family disintegration, coupled with severe emotional distress due to social isolation (Ronson, 2015; Scheff & Schorr, 2017).

The analysis of the 88 letters that were published on Zlovenija reveals a similar divide between the supporters and opponents of Zlovenija's method of holding the mirror up to society: 52% of the readers support the idea behind it (46 letters), while 44% of the letters express a negative opinion about Zlovenija (39 letters); among them 15% (12 letters) think that Zlovenija is no better than the original shamers it was trying to expose. Extreme polarisation is, in general, a key component of hateful comments on Slovenian online news sites, as shown by the study of the characteristics and strategies of online hate speech conducted by Erjavec & Poler Kovačič (2012). However, not all of the readers' letters were suitable to be published on the Tumblr page due to their inappropriate content, which seems to have been a continuation of the same hateful rhetoric that surrounded the original Facebook posts, but directed instead towards the author(s) of Zlovenija (Interview with Zlovenija, 2018).

---

12   "Nina Krajčinović, novinarka Dela in voditeljica strani ZLOvenija. Izvršila je dejanski napad na domoljubne Slovence katerim ni vseeno kaj se dogaja s Slovenijo. Svetujem vsem, ki so jih lastniki in snovalci te spletne strani uporabili za podpihovanje sovraštva in njihove slike brez dovoljenja objavili na svoji ekstremistični spletni strani, da se zberejo in vložijo skupinsko tožbo".

Legal Repercussions

One of the most prevalent themes of the comments referring to Zlovenija was its legality, in particular, whether reposting personal information along with profile pictures violated the authors' right to privacy as well as infringed intellectual property law. Moreover, questions of legality surrounded the very existence of Zlovenija, i.e. the original Facebook posts, mostly focusing on the issue of whether they constitute hate speech worthy of formal criminal prosecution or not. In the following section, we first examine the legality of Zlovenija, and then turn to the question of the lawfulness of the hateful Facebook posts and the (lack of) prosecution of hate speech in Slovenian courts.

Right to privacy: When assessing the violation of the right to privacy, we need to highlight that all posts published by Zlovenija were taken from publicly available ("open") profiles on Facebook. Facebook provides different privacy settings, ranging from completely public profiles with all content opened to everybody, including people without a Facebook profile, to completely closed ("private") profiles where content can only be seen by friends or an even more restricted group, with a variety of options in between. Under Facebook's Statement of Rights and Responsibilities, when publishing content or information using the Public setting *"you are allowing everyone, including people off of Facebook, to access and use that information, and to associate it with you (i.e., your name and profile picture)"*. (Facebook Statement of Rights and Responsibilities, 2018, emphasis added.) The courts in the US have continuously held that one cannot reasonably expect privacy with respect to the information revealed on public social media profiles.[13] (Ping Chang, 2019) In *Romano v. Steelcase* the court noted that:

> when plaintiff created her Facebook and MySpace accounts, she consented to the fact that her personal information would be shared with others, notwithstanding her privacy settings. Indeed, that is the very nature and purpose of these social networking sites, else they would cease to exist. Since plaintiff knew that her information may become publicly available, she cannot now claim that she had a reasonable expectation

---

13   See for example People v. Harris, 945 N.Y.S.2d 505(Crim. Ct. 2012); Moreno v. Hanford Sentinel, Inc. (Cal. App. 2009).

of privacy. As recently set forth by commentators regarding privacy and social networking sites: given the millions of users, "in this environment, privacy is no longer grounded in reasonable expectations, but rather in some theoretical protocol better known as wishful thinking" (Romano v. Steelcase Inc., 2010).

The European Court of Human Rights, on the other hand, has repeatedly acknowledged the importance of online anonymity, which is a significant factor when assessing whether an individual enjoyed a reasonable expectation of privacy, due to the specific nature of online activity in which users may choose to remain unidentifiable (Delfi AS v. Estonia, 2015). In a case concerning the disclosure of personal data from the Internet Service Provider based on a dynamic IP address, the Court rejected the (American) reasoning that by knowingly exposing his online activity to the public, the applicant waived his expectation of privacy. On the contrary, when arguments in favour of finding a violation of Article 8 of the European Convention of Human Rights, the Court reiterated the importance of the aforementioned online anonymity and continued:

> that the fact that he did not hide his dynamic IP address, assuming that it is possible to do so, cannot be decisive in the assessment of whether his expectation of privacy was reasonable from an objective standpoint (Benedik v. Slovenia, 2018).

It is questionable whether the Court would take the same standpoint when assessing a reasonable expectation of the privacy of the publicly available SNS profiles, since choosing to reveal content to the public clearly shows that the individual did not want to remain anonymous online.

A recent case (Egill Einarsson v. Iceland, 2018) sheds light on how the Court might weigh the right to privacy in cases when individuals publish content on open SNS profiles in the future. When assessing whether the national courts struck the right balance between the right to privacy and freedom of expression, the Court attached some importance to the fact that the content was published on an open Instagram profile and was therefore accessible not only to the plaintiff's followers but to more than 100,000,000 Instagram users. Referring to its case law, the Court stated that:

in the light of its accessibility and its capacity to store and communicate vast amounts of information, the Internet plays an important role in enhancing the public's access to news and facilitating the dissemination of information in general. At the same time, the risk of harm posed by content and communications on the Internet to the exercise and enjoyment of human rights and freedoms, particularly the right to respect for private life, is certainly higher than that posed by the press (ibid.)

Based on this reasoning, it is highly plausible that the Court would not find a violation of the right to private life protected in Article 8 of the ECHR if the content was published on an open SNS profile.

IP infringement: Facebook's Terms of Service stipulate that every individual is the owner of the content he or she creates and shares on Facebook (Facebook Terms of Service, 2018). Firstly, an individual is only a holder of the copyright of the content that he himself created. Only appearing on a photo or a video does not grant you copyright in that photo or video, since the owner of copyright is the author who created the work (Copyright and Related Rights Act, 1995). Secondly, not all of the content posted on Facebook could be protected by intellectual property rights. Certain work is only recognised as copyright work, i.e. work protected by copyright, if it meets certain conditions: copyright work is (1) an individual intellectual creation, (2) in the domain of literature, science and art, (3) which is expressed in any mode (ibid.). In order for a work to be protected by copyright, it must involve at least a minimum amount of creativity. Names, titles, phrases or slogans are usually not protected under copyright, therefore a personal name used on Facebook does not enjoy copyright protection.

On the other hand, photos and videos posted on Facebook could, in general, be subject to copyright. However, amateur photographs, including a great majority of Facebook pictures, do not reach a required level of creativity to be considered a personal intellectual creation and are therefore not protected by copyright (Trampuž, Oman & Zupančič, 1997). In any event, the assessment of whether a photograph is copyright work or not has to be made on a case-by-case basis, and the possibility that some of the profile pictures reposted on Zlovenija infringed copyright cannot be excluded.

Prosecution of hate speech under Slovenian law: Hate speech lacks a universal definition and is not recognised as a uniform legal construct, neither in international law, nor in the majority of domestic legal systems (McGonagle, 2013). Nevertheless, the Constitution of the Republic of Slovenia prohibits any incitement to national, racial, religious or other discrimination, and the inflaming of national, racial, religious or other hatred and intolerance, as well as incitement of violence and war (Constitution of Republic of Slovenia, 1991). Particularly serious forms of hate speech, although *per se* not a criminal offence, are also prohibited under criminal law as a criminal offence of Public Incitement to Hatred, Violence or Intolerance under Article 297 of the Slovenian Criminal Code (Criminal Code, 2008). However, the case law of Slovenian criminal courts on the issue of hate speech is very limited. The conditions that need to be fulfilled for an act to be considered criminal pursuant to Article 297 of the Criminal Code are very narrowly defined. The prosecution of hate speech is further complicated by a legal opinion issued by the Public Prosecutor's Office of the Republic of Slovenia, in which an interpretation of Article 297 was adopted that is not only substantially different than the plain text of that provision, but also factually and legally incorrect (Završnik & Zrimšek, 2017).

It seems that, in a conflict between equality, which includes the right to be protected from discrimination and eliminating hateful, racist, xenophobic speech on the one hand, and protecting the freedom of speech and expression on the other, legislature and practice in Slovenia opt for the latter. This might be explained by the experience of the ex-Yugoslavian regime in which criminal law was often (ab)used as a powerful censorship tool. Pursuant to Article 133 of the Criminal Code of the Socialist Federal Republic of Yugoslavia, which prohibited hostile propaganda, individuals could be prosecuted for verbal offences against the state, resulting in limited or even entirely thwarted freedom of speech (Bajt, 2017). As a consequence, freedom of speech has enjoyed almost unlimited protection since the independence of Slovenia, sometimes to the detriment of other human rights. These include equality and protection from discrimination, as well as a very narrow understanding of hate speech in Slovenian criminal legislation and practice.

Conclusion: Zlovenija — the Good, the Bad or the Necessary?

There is little dispute as to whether Zlovenija's methods were troublesome. The author(s) of Zlovenija themselves claim that it "should not exist", acknowledging the issues with the page's methods, as well as the problematic nature of engaging its targets in one big sweep.

On the one hand, the reflections of Zlovenija's author(s) on how events unfolded indicate spontaneity, as well as the resentment that spurred their actions — this can be observed with regard to how the page was created, how its content developed and changed in response to the public response and in the way it went dormant. On the other hand, the author(s)' answers indicate nuanced considerations and self-reflection, especially with regard to the page's imagined and actual impact. While we easily associate the first two characteristics, i.e. spontaneity and resentment, with vigilantism, the other half is harder to reconcile with the common understanding of the concept.[14]

In particular, Zlovenija's attitude towards their "victims" seems more considerate than expected. Shaming typically entails the perceived transgressor becoming the "transgressor-victim" (Cheung, 2014), which may or may not be an intended consequence of the shamers (Trottier, 2018). In the case of Zlovenija this aspect was given a considerable amount of thought by the author(s). This emerges from our interview with the author(s) and is corroborated by Zlovenija's conduct in 2015.

The author(s) expressed some initial concerns about using people's names and faces and the potential consequences their exposure could bear, but ultimately decided the cause was worth the risk. Moreover, once apologies started to come in, the author(s) were moved and immediately proceeded to delete the posts. But most importantly, two aspects of the interview with the author(s) stood out: 1) how Zlovenija may negatively affect the life of exposed individuals, who may be reckless and inappropriate, but are nevertheless ordinary human beings, and 2) (self-)questioning about who should have the authority and power to change people's lives. The author(s) stated, that:

---

14   It bears noting that scholarly interpretations have no qualms in interpreting it as such (Johnston, 1996).

at some point you start to think about it and you realize — these are people with jobs, families, friends. All of them will be harassed. In a way, this is cyber bullying. [...] If he loses his job at least he will learn something, but on the other hand why am I as a person entitled to make this call?[15]

The author(s) further contemplated both the legitimacy and the legality of their actions. All these considerations played an important role when deciding to end Zlovenija's activities and ultimately led to its hibernation (Interview with Zlovenija, 2018).

In this regard, Zlovenija deviates from other examples of naming and shaming that aimed to hold individuals accountable for their illegal or immoral actions. Public shaming, and especially online shaming, may have unpredictable, uncontrollable and disproportionate consequences, which can have a lifelong impact on the target. In one of the most extreme cases, for example, a woman's life was turned into wreckage after her tweet saying: "Going to Africa. Hope I don't get AIDS. Just kidding. I'm white!" went viral and spurred heated responses online. Numerous similar cases of minor online transgressions led to unintended and often disproportionate outcomes by destroying lives and reputation in the name of righteousness (Ronson, 2015). It seems, however, that none of those 'vigilantes' shared the concerns voiced by Zlovenija's author(s), or even felt them. Such was the case after the white supremacist rally in Charlottesville in 2017, when several Twitter accounts shared the pictures of its participants calling out their followers to identify them (Milbrandt, this volume; Penza, 2018). Several individuals were recognised and, as a consequence, lost their jobs, were disavowed by their families, and even received death threats. The main difference, however, is that these consequences were sought by the authors of the account. However, the participants of the rally were not the only ones facing negative consequences, as numerous unfounded accusations based on false identification have previously been made by Internet vigilantes (Milbrandt, this volume; Phillips & Yi, 2018). One such notorious example was in the aftermath of the Boston

---

15　"Na neki točki začneš razmišljat, to so vsi ljudje, ki imajo družine, prijatelje, službe, vsi bodo zdaj šikanirani, na nek način je to kibernetsko nadlegovanje. [...] Če sedaj izgubi službo, se bo vsaj nekaj naučil, ampak po drugi strani, zakaj sem jaz kot (civilna) oseba zdaj to povzročil?"

Marathon bombing, when Reddit and Twitter users immediately started to crowdsource information to identify the suspected bomber whose picture was released by the FBI and shared on social media sites. The action ended in falsely attributing responsibility for the bombing to a missing university student (Starbird et al., 2014).

On the contrary, the intention of Zlovenija's author(s) was not to expose individuals in order to help the authorities with their identification or prosecution, nor to ensure that they experienced any other negative consequence, albeit some were inherent in the practice. Their stated goal was to encourage a discussion on hate speech and to point out unacceptable forms of communication. Any consequences for these individuals were seen as merely negative side effects, while apologies or rationalisations from these individuals were welcomed and fostered. In the distinction between exclusionary and reintegrative shaming (Braithwaite, 1989), Zlovenija's approach leans towards the latter. Depending on how we define victims of intolerance and hate speech, what Zlovenija did may be interpreted as bringing together the perpetrators (FB posters) and the community in which they have committed their offences — against individual victims (migrants) and against the community itself. Moreover, it seems that in some instances when seemingly sincere apologies were issued by the perpetrators, the page might have been successful in achieving some sort of reintegration.

Another important step in the development of the campaign was the decision to end it. As explained earlier, this was largely due to a realisation that the author(s) of Zlovenija seem to have had after the posts on their Tumblr page were printed and posted around the city of Ljubljana. This was, according to the author(s) of Zlovenija, an unwanted and unexpected outcome of the online shaming. Although it put Zlovenija and hate speech in the centre of the public debate, and therefore played an important role in achieving Zlovenija's goals, this course of events was never planned or expected by the author(s) of the online campaign. In fact, while admitting that online campaigns may have a wider outreach and tangible consequences, the author(s) seem to only have realised the full extent of what they were doing when seeing posters in a non-digital environment (Interview with Zlovenija, 2018).[16]

---

16   A Brazilian campaign, "Virtual Racism, Real Consequences", used a similar strategy as Zlovenija as it copied racist Facebook and Twitter comments from public profiles.

These actions by Zlovenija's author(s) seem to distinguish their campaign from similar campaigns or actions, described in this volume. The somewhat reintegrative nature of Zlovenija, discussed above, and the consideration of potential unwanted consequences give the action a slightly different flavour.

It seems clear that the initiators of social interventions should show reasonable diligence when planning a campaign that will have a social impact. This means they should consider and weigh the negative consequences of their actions. However, what happens after that is a value judgment: should they be held accountable if they fail to prevent predictable harm, as manufacturers are similarly liable for the safety of their product, or owners are responsible for the damage caused by a dangerous object? Accountability in these cases arises from the danger such product or activity presents to the individuals or a society. If you play with fire, should you be prepared to get burned?

Zlovenija held up a mirror to society in order to highlight the issue of hate speech in the public sphere. When it started to attract the attention of the press and incited a debate about hate speech, it fulfilled the main aim of its author(s), who felt it would be the best for Zlovenija's legacy to end the project while it was still at its peak. (Interview with Zlovenija, 2018). With every passing day, the debate surrounding Zlovenija moved away from the topics it was trying to highlight, shifting from the discussion about the limits of free speech in a democratic society towards questioning the method Zlovenija used to pursue its goal and often claiming that Zlovenija was no better than those it was trying to expose.

Yet even legal frameworks take into consideration, to some extent, the intent that guides an individual's actions in both criminal and civil areas. If we evaluate Zlovenija as a social phenomenon through the same prism by analyzing only the purpose and goals it was trying to achieve, the difference between Zlovenija and hate speech becomes more obvious. The stated aim of the campaign, that is, to warn against and demonstrate the extent of hate speech, can hardly be deemed unjustifiable.

However, the comments were not gathered and exposed online, but published on billboards near the homes of the racist commentators with the specific aim of alarming the perpetrators (Chang, 2015; Weber 2015).

However, the goal may not be completely isolated from the method, since the two are inherently intertwined, and it was the method that Zlovenija used to pursue its goals that made the whole project so extreme and therefore problematic. It boils down to the fundamental question of means and ends: should society tolerate any approach in the fight against hate speech, or any other illegal or socially undesirable behaviour, as long as it is legally permissible, or can we imagine circumstances in which the ends can no longer justify the means? Would we also sanction an online wall of shame that would expose obese people in order to promote a healthy lifestyle? While the aim may still be laudable, the method feels even more troubling in such a setting.

Zlovenija as a virtual wall of shame was an exceptional reaction to exceptional online behaviour provoked by exceptional circumstances. It was the result of an extraordinary set of circumstances, and is distinctive in how it illustrated social tensions that culminated in citizen-to-citizen exchanges in pursuit of justice. However, in a functional democratic society in which the government is fulfilling its basic duties, there should be no need for it to occur in the first place.

References

Bajt, V. (2015). Anti-immigration hate speech in Slovenia. In: *RAZOR WIRED. Reflections on Migration Movements through Slovenia in 2015* (pp. 51–61). *Ljubljana: Peace Institute*, https://www.doi.org/10.13140/RG.2.1.3372.7122

Bajt, V. (2017). Sovražni govor kot spodbuda kritičnega delovanja. In S. Splichal (ed.). *Zagovor javnosti: Med svobodo izražanja in sovražnim govorom* (pp. 70–77). Ljubljana: Slovenska akademija znanosti in umetnosti.

Bechmann, A., & Nielbo, K. L. (2018). Are we exposed to the same "news" in the news feed? *Digital Journalism, 6*(8), 990–1002, https://doi.org/10.1080/2 1670811.2018.1510741

Benedik v. Slovenia. (2018). ECtHR 62357/14.

Braithwaite, J. (1989). *Crime, Shame, and Reintegration.* Cambridge: Cambridge University Press.

Braun, V., & Clarke, V. (2019). Reflecting on reflexive thematic analysis, *Qualitative Research in Sport, Exercise and Health, 11*(4), 589–97, https://doi. org/10.1080/2159676X.2019.1628806

Chang, L. (2015, December 1). write a racist post in Brazil, and you may find it on a billboard. Digitaltrends.com, https://www.digitaltrends.com/social-media/ nasty-facebook-comments-posted-billboards-anti-racism-campaign/

Cheung, A. S. Y. (2014). Revisiting privacy and dignity: Online shaming in the global e-village. *Laws*, 3(2), 301–26, https://doi.org/10.3390/laws3020301

Constitution of the Republic of Slovenia. (1991). Ustava Republike Slovenije, Uradni list RS, št. 33/91-I, 42/97 – UZS68, 66/00 – UZ80, 24/03 – UZ3a, 47, 68, 69/04 – UZ14, 69/04 – UZ43, 69/04 – UZ50, 68/06 – UZ121,140,143, 47/13 – UZ148, 47/13 – UZ90,97,99 in 75/16 – UZ70a.

Copyright and Related Rights Act. (1995). Zakon o avtorski in sorodnih pravicah, Uradni list RS, št. 16/07 – uradno prečiščeno besedilo, 68/08, 110/13, 56/15, 63/16 – ZKUASP in 59/19.

Council of Europe (2018) Fourth Opinion on Slovenia (21 June 2017) of the Advisory Committee on the Framework Convention for the Protection of National Minorities, https://rm.coe.int/fourth-opinion -on-slovenia-adopted-on-21-june-2017/16807843c7

Criminal Code. (2008). Kazenski zakonik, Uradni list RS, št. 50/12 – uradno prečiščeno besedilo, 6/16 – popr., 54/15, 38/16, 27/17, 23/20 in 91/20.

Delfi AS v. Estonia. (2015). ECtHR 64669/09.

Egill Einarsson v. Iceland. (2018). ECtHR 24703/15.

Erjavec K., Poler Kovačič M. (2012). "You don't understand, this is a new war!" Analysis of hate speech in news web sites' comments. *Mass Communication and Society*, 15(6), 899–920.

Facebook statement of rights and responsibilities. (2018, January 31), https://www.facebook.com/legal/terms/previous?ref=new_policy

Facebook terms of service. (2018, April 19), https://www.facebook.com/legal/terms/update?ref=old_policy

FRA Update #1 (2015). Weekly data collection on the situation of persons in need of international protection, Update #1, 28 September–2 October 2015. European Union Agency for Fundamental Rights, https://fra.europa.eu/sites/default/files/ fra_uploads/fra-2015-weekly-compilation-1_en.pdf

FRA Update # 2 (2015). Weekly data collection on the situation of persons in need of international protection, Update #2, 5 October–9 October 2015. European Union Agency for Fundamental Rights, https://fra.europa.eu/sites/default/files/ fra_uploads/fra-2015-weekly-compilation-2_en.pdf

Interview with Zlovenija. (2018, December). Authors' archive.

IOM. (2020). Who is a migrant? International Organisation for Migration, https://www.iom.int/who-is-a-migrant

Johnston, L. (1996). What is vigilantism? *The British Journal of Criminology*, 36(2), 220–36, https://doi.org/10.1093/oxfordjournals.bjc.a014083

Krajčinović, N. (2015, October 28). Levo mnenje: Sramotilni stebri sončne strani Alp. *Delo*, https://www.delo.si/mnenja/kolumne/levo-mnenje-sramotilni-stebri-soncne-strani-alp.html

McGonagle, T. (2013). The Council of Europe against online hate speech: conundrums and challenges, Expert Paper, doc.no. MCM 2013(005), the Council of Europe Conference of Ministers responsible for Media and Information Society. 'Freedom of Expression and Democracy in the Digital Age: Opportunities, Rights, Responsibilities'. Belgrade, 7–8 November 2013.

Milivojević, Z. (2008). *Emocije — razumevanje čustev v psihoterapiji*. Novi Sad, Psihopolis.

Muscanell, N., Guadagno, R. (2012). Make new friends or keep the old: Gender and personality differences in social networking use. *Computers in Human Behavior,* 28(1), 107–12, https://doi.org/10.1016/j.chb.2011.08.016

Oblak Črnič, T. (2017). Fenomen ZLOvenija. Časopis za kritiko znanosti 45(268), 181-198.

Oštir, D. (2015, September 18). Pojasnilo: Zakaj je komentiranje pri člankih o beguncih onemogočeno, https://www.24ur.com/novice/slovenija/pojasnilo-zakaj-je-komentiranje-pri-bengunskih-clankih-onemogoceno.html

Park, G., Yaden, D. B., Schwartz, H. A., Kern, M. L., Eichstaedt, J. C., Kosinski, M., Stillwell D., Ungar L. H., Seligman M. E. P. (2016). Women are warmer but no less assertive than men: Gender and language on Facebook. *PLoS ONE,* 11(5), https://doi.org/10.1371/journal.pone.0155885

Penza, D. E. (2018). The unstoppable intrusion: The unique effect of online harassment and what the united states can ascertain from other countries' attempts to prevent it. *Cornell International Law Journal,* 51(1), 297–318.

Phillips, J., & Yi, J. (2018). Charlottesville paradox: The 'liberalizing' alt-right, 'authoritarian' left, and politics of dialogue. *Society,* 55(3), 221–28, https://doi.org/10.1007/s12115-018-0243-0

Ping Chang, C. (2019). Searching on Facebook Through the Lens of the Concept of Privacy. In Alhajj, R., Bakshi, S., & Özyer, T. (eds). *Social Networks and Surveillance for Society.* Springer International Publishing, https://doi.org/10.1007/978-3-319-78256-0_8

Romano v. Steelcase Inc. 907 N.Y.S.2d 650. (Sup. Ct. Suffolk Co. 2010).

Ronson, J. (2015). *So You've Been Publicly Shamed*. New York: Riverhead.

Seargeant, P., & Tagg, C. (2019). Social media and the future of open debate: A user-oriented approach to Facebook's filter bubble conundrum. *Discourse, Context & Media,* 27, 41–48, https://doi.org/10.1016/j.dcm.2018.03.005

Scheff, S., & Schorr, M. (2017). *Shame Nation: The Global Epidemic of Online Hate.* Naperville, Illinois: Sourcebooks.

Schwartz, H., Eichstaedt, J., Kern, M., Dziurzynski, L., Ramones, S., Agrawal, M., Shah, A., Kosinski, M., Stillwell, D., Seligman, M., & Ungar, L. (2013). Personality, gender, and age in the language of social media: The open-vocabulary approach. *PLoS ONE,* 8(9), https://www.doi.org/10.1371/journal.pone.0073791

Starbird, K., Maddock, J., Orand, M., Achterman, P., & Mason, R. M. (2014). Rumors, false flags, and digital vigilantes: Misinformation on twitter after the 2013 Boston marathon bombing. *IConference 2014 Proceedings*, 654–62, https://www.doi.org/10.9776/14308

Trampuž, M., Oman, B. & Zupančič, A. (1997). Zakon o avtorskih in sorodnih pravicah (ZASP): s komentarjem. Ljubljana, Gospodarski vestnik.

Trottier, D. (2018). Coming to terms with shame: Exploring mediated visibility against transgressions. *Surveillance and Society*, 16(2), 170–82, https://doi.org/10.24908/ss.v16i2.6811

Wang Y. C., Burke M., & Kraut R. (2013). Gender, Topic, and Audience Response. *Proceedings of the SIGCHI Conference on Human Factors in Computing Systems*, 31–34, https://doi.org/10.1145/2470654.2470659

Weber, G. (2015, December 1). This Brazilian campaign is putting racist Facebook comments on billboards. *Slate*, https://slate.com/technology/2015/12/this-brazilian-campaign-is-putting-racist-comments-on-billboards.html

Završnik, A., Zrimšek, V. (2017). Sovražni govor po slovenski kaznovalni zakonodaji in sodni praksi. Časopis za kritiko znanosti 45(268), 59–73.

Zlovenija. (2015, October), http://zlovenija.tumblr.com/

'Make them famous': Digital Vigilantism and Virtuous Denunciation after Charlottesville

Tara Milbrandt[1]

Introduction

"If you recognize any of the Nazis marching...send me their names/ profiles and I'll make them famous" (@YesYoureRacist). These words helped to propel an effective — if somewhat controversial — social media campaign in August 2017, when members of the public were sought to help identify participants who were filmed and photographed during a widely publicised and violent white supremacist rally that transpired in the streets of Charlottesville, USA. Following their identification, otherwise anonymous rally participants were broadly exposed ('outed') within their broader communities and across their social networks. This opened them up to adverse effects that extended beyond the symbolic realm of the digital-media-sphere. Operating as both informal punishment and public pedagogy, this grassroots campaign of "digital vigilantism" (Trottier, 2017) carried a tacit warning to possible future participants at similar public events: *appear at your peril.*

This chapter explores the socio-moral complexities of digital vigilantism (DV) through an interpretive and visual sociological case study of this campaign. Broadly, DV may be defined as "a process where

---

1   I would like to thank Daniel Trottier for all that he has done to make this timely collection possible. I would also like to thank Doug Harper for offering his visual sociological eye to earlier iterations of this chapter. Much appreciated!

https://doi.org/10.11647/OBP.0200.09

citizens are collectively offended by other citizen activity, and coordinate retaliation on mobile devices and social platforms" (Trottier, 2017, p. 55). While they are not equivalent, one possible and often prominent component of DV is "doxing", which involves the excavation and online circulation of otherwise personal information about subjects, released non-consensually by a third party. This tactic is generally deployed to publicly shame or otherwise harm identified subjects by virtue of such intractable exposure.[2] In the case at hand, DV work was primarily focused upon a type of "deanonymizing doxing" (Douglas, 2016). Doxing practices are morally controversial due to the disproportionate harms they can open people up to (e.g. harassment, threats, violence), their privacy-violating dimensions and the affront they may represent to the "sacredness" of the modern person (Joas, 2013). However, the public nature of the events that materialised in Charlottesville in August 2017, and their perceived significance — as marking a dangerous moment in contemporary US history — created fertile conditions for what one commentator called a "shame pass" (Teitel, 2017, para. 4) to apply. In the prolific public discourse these events generated, some commentators questioned whether or not it was reasonable for a participant in such a high-profile event to expect to remain anonymous afterwards, anyway, and so, could "outing" rally-goers even be considered a violation?

This chapter begins with some contextualising of the original event — the Charlottesville rally — to highlight the broader constellation of circumstances that empowered the social media call and response to identify and expose participants, far and wide. Following this, I formulate the creative, rhetorical and moral dimensions of this social media campaign, focusing on the nature of its call to action, and analyzing specific demonstrations of its putative success. Approaching DV as a complex "member's method" for creating and maintaining a sense of order from below (cf Garfinkel, 1967), I analyze the complex interplay of images and words found in prominent social media postings, foregrounding the tacitly shared understandings that energised this campaign, and which rendered its call to action meaningful.

---

2   Doxing, or as it is sometimes spelled "doxxing", originated in hacking culture and was made globally famous by the Internet group "Anonymous" (see Coleman, 2015). For an in-depth conceptual elaboration on doxing, and its variants, see Douglas, 2016; this volume).

Throughout, I attend to the imagined audience of strangers that was given presence through the Twitter account "YesYoureRacist": dispersed allies united by a shared definition of urgency, and willing to suspend moral reservations over its DV tactics by participating in, or otherwise supporting, a campaign to make Charlottesville rally-goers 'famous'. Finally, I formulate what this social media campaign arguably achieved and what, specifically, it contributed to the collective conversation and aftermath of Charlottesville 2017. Drawing inferences from a doomed anniversary rally that occurred one year later, I speculate on its broader societal implications.

Above all, I argue that it helped to crystallise a broadly felt and unified refusal of the terrain that was being sought by organisers, participants and supporters of the Charlottesville rallies, namely, to legitimate the articulation of violent white supremacy in contemporary American public life as but one kind of 'expression' amongst others. Utilising the tools of digital media, it worked to deny the possibility that participants — present *and future* — could attend a rally associated with such sought-after legitimation anonymously, and thus without risk or consequence to their future selves. This went beyond the condemnation of a disturbing event. By getting personal, this DV campaign introduced a dangerous type of "fatefulness" into rally participation, by creating conditions in which later exposure amounted to a loss of control for the pictured participant (Goffman, 1967). This included reputational harm and exclusion from full social participation. In doing so, it helped to constitute opposition to what the rally represented on deeply socio-moral grounds, irreducible to legalistic definitions of protected forms of speech and assembly. Positive participation in the rally could not be represented as one's mere alignment with one controversial 'side' or position amongst others, within a pluralistic social landscape. Rather, it amounted to becoming morally tainted through one's association with a deplorable and destructive force against a pluralistic social world.

Throughout the study, I highlight the mixed nature of visibility (cf. Brighenti, 2007). I emphasise what this case reveals about its simultaneously emboldening and dis-empowering possibilities in a digital-media-infused public culture, where expressive conduct undertaken in one setting and time may come back to haunt actors later and elsewhere, especially when representations are placed before different and unanticipated audiences. As a heuristic strategy to understand the significance of DV within today's digital-media-infused landscape, I ask the reader to consider this question: *what would have been different about Charlottesville 2017 without the social media campaign aimed at identifying and outing participants before a broader public?*

The materials I draw from are widely available in the public sphere: social media postings, news media reports, public comments, audio-video materials found on the Internet in the form of posted footage, and a short news documentary. In keeping with my primary analytic interests, and out of an ethical commitment to not reproducing the phenomenon under investigation — whether in the form of unwanted or sought-after notoriety on the part of participants previously unheard of — I have opted to anonymise these materials in my re-presentation of them.[3]

A Potent Constellation of Circumstances: Contextualising a Social Media Campaign

To understand the social media campaign aimed at 'outing' Charlottesville rally participants, specifically how it worked, what it did, and what it reveals about DV and the complexities of public visibility in contemporary society, it is important to understand the exceptional circumstances in which it took shape, gained traction and became — for the most part — defined as morally acceptable, and even virtuous citizen activity.

A Contentious Rally: Charlottesville, 2017

On 12 August 2017 a "Unite the Right" rally was held in Charlottesville, USA in the city's recently re-named *Emancipation Park*.[4] Hundreds of

---

3   This does not include individuals who were already high-profile and/or recognisable public figures prior to the events being considered.

4   The park's name has been a source of significant recent controversy. In under two years it moved from being called "Robert E. Lee Park" after Confederate general Robert E. Lee (until May 2017), to "Emancipation Park", standing for a social ideal (June 2017-July 2018). In July 2018 it was re-named again, this time with the conspicuously politically neutral name of "Market Street Park", which is its current name (at the time of writing).

participants converged at a pre-rally march the night before on the University of Virginia grounds. This was catalyzed by a controversial municipal decision (3:2) to remove Confederate monuments from two city parks, and in particular a statue of Robert E. Lee, who was a Confederate States Army soldier and commander (between 1862–1865) during the American Civil War. This statue, like Lee's legacy, is a site of significant ongoing controversy.[5] Its immanent removal was the stated impetus for the rally in Charlottesville, whose organisers equated the removal to a problematic rewriting of history.

While the social issue of how to address historical monuments is complex, it is important to be clear that the version of American history being defended here was tied indisputably to groups and sentiments associated with violent white supremacy, including anti-Semitism, and advocates for a white ethnostate.[6] The August events followed smaller rallies held that same summer. One in May was organised by a high-profile white supremacist speaker in the US, who offered a Nazi-style salute and shout of "Hail Trump, hail our people, hail our victory" during a speech following the US election result announcement of Donald Trump's presidency in 2016 (Global News, 2016). The second, in July, was organised by a branch of the Ku Klux Klan called the called the Loyal White Knights.

Not coincidentally, a poster promoting the August rally (Fig. 9.1) contained symbolism reminiscent of fascist propaganda films such as Leni Riefenstahl's *Triumph of the Will* (1935), along with a listing of the names of several known (in the US) and "proud white nationalists" (MSNBC News, 2017b). A mythical and militaristically ordered image

---

5   After the violence in Charlottesville in August 2017, the family descendants of Robert E. Lee, as well as Jefferson Davis and Stonewall Jackson, called for the Confederate statues to be removed from the park, suggesting that they would be more appropriately exhibited in a museum. For further background and detail on the controversy over Confederate monuments in Charlottesville, see "Blue Ribbon Commission on Race, Memorials, and Public Spaces Report to Charlottesville City Council", December 19, 2016. This committee was formed in 2016 and was tasked with addressing recent controversies pertaining to historic monuments in Charlottesville, Virginia.

6   Regardless of the complex factors (economic, cultural, biographical) that might have 'motivated' different people to attend and participate in such an event, there is an indisputable violation of modern social justice ideals at work. Such groups and sentiments are premised on a racist hierarchy that presumes essential differences in value and 'rightful' social position amongst different categories of people.

of a victorious future is implied, with soldiers standing guard, ready to sacrifice themselves for a glorious cause; there is a "hailing" (Althusser, 1970) of the imagined participant who is willing to play a part in such an endeavor, who may be emotionally stirred by an idea of restoring 'greatness'. In light of the above, the presence of overtly racist and anti-Semitic symbolism during the rally would have come as no surprise to attendees in August, thereby invalidating the possibility for anyone to later claim ignorance or innocence.

Fig. 9.1 Unknown creator, "Unite the Right" Charlottesville rally poster, August 2017, published under fair use.

An Inter-Tribal Assembly of the "Far-Right"

The stated intention of the August 2017 rally was "to unify the white nationalist movement" across the US, according to one prominent organiser.[7] Also dubbed an event in support of "freedom of speech", it

7   This organiser, Damigo, is founder of "Identity Evropa", which is an American neo-Nazi and white-supremacist organisation founded in March 2016, which was

drew together approximately five hundred supporters, many of whom were affiliated with different groups and organisations, including members of various white-nationalist and white-supremacist groups — including chapters of the Ku Klux Klan (KKK), neo-Confederates, neo-Nazis and members of organised militia groups.[8] Participants came together as a single 'we' in shared physical spaces, marching and moving through these spaces, shouting and chanting slogans in unison.

Fig. 9.2 CNN Screengrab, Charlottesville "torch" march, August 12, 2017, CNN News, https://www.cnn.com/2017/08/12/us/white-nationalists-tiki-torch-march-trnd/index.html

The sights and sounds of participants openly and enthusiastically engaging with globally condemned symbols associated with some of modern humanity's most deplorable events circulated widely in the streets of Charlottesville, as seen in the prolific mainstream news reports and videos posted online by media workers, photographers, spectators and participants. Many attendees were seen giving Nazi salutes, and heard chanting phrases such as "white lives matter", "white power", "you will not replace us", "Jews will not replace us" and Nazi-associated slogans, such as "blood and soil" (CNN, 11 August 2017). Several participants held KKK paraphernalia, Confederate flags and objects featuring potent symbols of global injustice such as swastikas (see Olesen, 2016). Many carried torches, producing visually dramatic effects in global media representations of the gathering (Fig. 9.2). Joined with such slogans and signage, the use of flaming

---

rebranded three years later as "American Identity Movement".

8   See "Unite the Right Rally", on Wikipedia.org for a useful, descriptive overview of the rally. See also "2017: The Year in Hate and Extremism", by Heidi Beirich and Susy Buchanan, *Southern Poverty Law Center,* Spring 2018 Issue, https://www.splcenter.org/fighting-hate/intelligence-report/2018/2017-year-hate-and-extremism

torches was visually potent, as it is a well-known symbol of anti-black intimidation used by the KKK in the US post-Civil war period, and of anti-Semitic intimidation in Nazi Germany in the 1930s and 1940s (Bond, 2017). While positive engagement with such sights and signs may violate global ideals associated with a diverse and viable modern society — including human dignity, equality and inclusion — their public display and articulation in the US are constitutionally protected as "expressive" activity.

"Extreme" and "violent" manifestations of "white nationalism" have become a significant and "growing concern around the world" in recent years, not just in the US (Carranco & Milton, 2019, para. 8). Supporters of far-right, anti-Muslim and anti-immigrant groups, and those advocating for a white ethno-state, have been self-consciously working to move away from the cultural and political margins, infiltrating mainstream institutions in parts of Europe, as well as within the US and Canada. A key finding by a Swedish researcher who infiltrated the alt-right movement in Europe for a year, and marched with white supremacists in Charlottesville in 2017, is that participants in such groups are seeking ultimately to "change the culture" by "making their ideas mainstream". Working to shift the limits of acceptable speech further and further to the political right, this includes a sought-after ability to freely give expression to "their racist ideas in the public square" (Hermansson, quoted in Illing, 2017, para. 9).

In the language of French sociologist Emile Durkheim (1995[1912]), the Charlottesville rally can be considered an inter-tribal assembly of the far-right in America. It was symbolically connected with similar collective formations across the broader Western world at this time, especially in parts of Europe.[9] In his classic study of religion, Durkheim emphasised the significance of "reunions, assemblies and meetings" for members of groups to "uphold and reaffirm... the collective sentiments and the collective ideas which makes [their] unity and personality". Such concentrated events can be potent occasions of

---

9   These include Europe's *Generation Identity*, Scandanavia's *Nordic Resistance Movement*, Canada's *Aryan Guard*, and the UK-based neo-Nazi group *Combat 18*, as well as the increasingly influential far-right, anti-immigrant and populist political parties such as Greece's *Golden Dawn*, Hungary's *Jobbik*, Germany's *AfD* and Italy's *Lega Norda* (now called *Lega*), to name but a selection.

moral remaking; through being "closely united to one another", group members "reaffirm in common their common sentiments" (Durkheim, 1995[1912], pp. 474–5). Qualitatively unlike online spaces, events involving physical co-presence are uniquely powerful as they provide concrete occasions for participants to shore up shared beliefs and sentiments through enacted social practices, such as marching, cheering and chanting together (Rawls, 2001). Icons and symbols that express group sentiments are thereby "evoked and revitalized" (Inglis, 2017, p. 308). If this is what made the Charlottesville events exciting for the organisers, attendees and supporters of "uniting the right", for the concerned moral majority, it was what made them frightening.

Counter-Rally

The events in Charlottesville drew forth a broad range of groups and individuals from civil society who passionately opposed virtually everything that the "Unite the Right" assemblages represented. In audio-visual footage, anti-racist counter-protestors can be heard shouting down the voices of "Unite the Righters" with slogans such as, "...No Nazis, no KKK, no fascist USA...". The significant counter-rally that the Charlottesville assembly inspired was composed of members of diverse groups from local residents and businesses; students and faculty; members of faith-based, labour and socialist groups; civil rights organisations; and members of anti-racist and anti-fascist social movements, some of whom support the use of direct action, most notably under the banners of Black Lives Matter (BLM) and Antifa.

This counter-rally represented a different vision of society, associated with modern social justice ideals and animated by a shared need to gather, demonstrate, struggle for, and in diverse ways, *enact* shared opposition to what "Unite the Right" represented here. It was in general alignment with these ideals, the belief that what was on display should be afforded no legitimate place in contemporary society, and the perception that this occurrence signified a moment of real and present danger in the US, that the social media call to "make [rally participants] famous" took shape and gained traction.

State of Emergency: Danger and Violence

Following several physically violent exchanges and incidents involving white-supremacy-affiliated rallygoers and anti-racist counter-protesters, on the morning of 12 August a state of emergency was declared. The assembly was defined as unlawful, and the State Governor announced that without additional powers, public safety could not be safeguarded. Most tragically, four hours after the social media call to "make them famous" was issued, a man associated with one of the white supremacist groups drove his car into a crowd of counter-protestors, killing civil-rights activist Heather Heyer and seriously injuring several others. In addition to the violence on the streets, numerous accounts and documentary representations from that day suggested that law enforcement was not effectively protecting people, especially members of targeted groups, from threat and violence. This included a disturbing video that circulated online showing an African American man being savagely beaten by six white men, as well as urgent calls for police protection, left unaddressed, by Jewish members inside a synagogue threatened with violence outside.[10] Reflecting the tumultuous nature of the entire event, two state police officers also died in a helicopter crash while monitoring the streets below. There was much fear, violence and carnage, as early opponents to the rally had predicted.

VICE News Documentary: Potent Symbolism, Public Visibility, Dangerous Legitimacy

Dramatic images from the rally, publicised extensively around the digital-media-connected world, circulated on the 24/7 news cycle. A particularly influential representation took the form of a twenty-minute documentary called *Charlottesville: Race and Terror*, made on the scene by VICE News. It aired the next night, generating over 50 million views across multiple viewing platforms. The film was itself treated as a news story within international media, "lay[ing] bare [the] horror of neo-Nazis in America" (Gabbatt, 2017). Three prominent themes can be distilled from this documentary, which form an important cultural

---

10   The man was charged with assaulting a white supremacist, but was later acquitted (Shapira, 2018).

backdrop for understanding the significance of the events and most importantly, for present purposes, to understand the nature of the social media response and DV campaign they elicited.

By VICE News

Aug 21 2017, 1:30am Share Tweet Snap

"CHARLOTTESVILLE: RACE AND TERROR"

'Jews will not replace us': Vice film lays bare horror of neo-Nazis in America

A Vice News film crew embedded with a far-right speaker in Charlottesville last weekend seeks to highlight the motivations of white supremacists

White nationalist demonstrators clash with counter demonstrators at the entrance to Emancipation Park in Charlottesville, Virginia on Saturday 12 August. Photograph: Steve Helber/AP

Fig. 9.3 VICE News screengrab, August 21, 2017, https://www.vice.com/en_ca/article/qvzn8p/vice-news-tonight-full-episode-charlottesville-race-and-terror and The Guardian News screengrab, August 16, 2017, https://www.theguardian.com/us-news/2017/aug/16/charlottesville-neo-nazis-vice-news-hbo

One striking feature was how brazenly participants and organisers interviewed by Elle Reeve of VICE News expressed racist and specifically white supremacist sentiments that are normally prohibited — at least informally — from public expression in American public life. Anti-black and anti-Semitic statements were made repeatedly, with confidence, and without shame. For example, one participant explained, "We're showing this class of anti-white vermin that this is our country" (VICE News, 2017). Some of the participants spoke openly about their willingness to use violence, if deemed "necessary", particularly the high-profile alt-right activist Christopher Cantwell, who revealed a cache of guns to the reporter.

A second striking theme was the emphasis on being public; showing America that they were not an "Internet meme" but were, rather, "a big real presence that can organise in physical space" (Reeve, in VICE News, 2017). Vocal participants articulated the belief that these rallies marked a turning point for the far right, making reference to anticipated future events and guided by a hierarchical vision that this is "our" country (and so, not "theirs").

A third theme was participants' focus on being law-abiding citizens whose expressive activities were protected by the US First Amendment. Speakers noted their proper use of bureaucratic procedures, e.g. in obtaining a legal march permit in advance. Participants framed the rally as formally legitimate, i.e. compliant within the current legal-rational order (Weber, 1978). A couple of participants from Quebec, who were later "outed" as recruiters on an anti-racist website based in Canada, mocked the Canadian legal-moral context, stating that in Canada you can "get arrested for hurting somebody's feelings" (VICE News, 2017).[11]

As condensed in this news documentary, the rally was performatively announcing, to America and beyond, that what can be seen and heard on the streets of Charlottesville has a legitimate and growing place in contemporary society.[12] It sought to constitute the cultural legitimacy of such expression, by giving it manifestation in the camera-filled public realm of co-present persons and to the gaze of local, national and global

---

11   See Curtis et al. (2018). "Alt-right in Montreal: How Charlottesville exposed the key players in the local white nationalist movement", in *Montreal Gazette*, 14 May 2018, https://montrealgazette.com/news/local-news/alt-right-in-montreal-how-charlottesville-exposed-the-key-players-in-the-local-white-nationalist-movement

12   The Canadian contingent implied that what took place was part of a trans-national social movement, not something only relevant or meaningful to residents of Charlottesville, Virginians or Americans who feel that they have something to lose by the removal of Lee's statue from the park.

news media. It was performative, in that it sought to "realize" what it was claiming already existed (Butler, 2015, pp. 28–29); its "successful" enactment implied the possibility of future re-enactment (Blitefield, 2006).

The perceived significance of the rally was effectively summed up in an article written by Matt Thompson and published in *The Atlantic* on day two of the Charlottesville events. Drawing attention to the conspicuous absence of participant concealment, the journalist likened the rally to a "pride march" for violent white supremacy:

> [T]he images we saw in Charlottesville today and yesterday [...] draw their menace not from what *is* there — mostly, young white men in polos and T-shirts goofily brandishing tiki torches — but from what *isn't*: the masks, the hoods, the secrecy that could at least imply a sort of shame [...] *We used to whisper these thoughts,* the new white supremacists suggest. *But now we can say them out loud.* The 'Unite the Right' rally wasn't intended to be a Klan rally at all. It was a pride march [...] The shameless return of white supremacy into America's public spaces seems to be happening by degrees, and quickly... (Thompson, 2017, para. 4–5, emphasis in original).

Highlighting the strikingly blatant nature of what could be seen, the concerned reader is left with the frighteningly unanswerable question: what is next...? The ensuing DV campaign can be understood in response to this concern, as a concerted attempt to deny the participants the cover of remaining anonymous in the days that followed.

Moral Equivalence as Implied Affinity: A Presidential Response

Now infamously, US President Trump did not initially denounce white supremacists by name. In his first public statements on 13 August, Trump condemned what he called "this egregious display of hatred, bigotry and violence on many sides; [brief pause], on many sides" (CNN, 2017). He also noted on 15 August that "you had people, that were very fine people, *on both sides.*"(CNBC News, 2017, emphasis added). Critics — including members of the Republican Party — widely condemned Trump for implying moral equivalence, which was widely taken to imply his ideological affinity with white supremacy. Prominent members of the 'alt-right', including former KKK leader David Duke, certainly interpreted it that way, identifying Trump as an heroic ally in a much-reported-upon Tweet: "Thank you President Trump for your honesty & courage to tell the truth about #Charlottesville & condemn the leftist terrorists in BLM/Antifa" (Duke, cited in Price, 2017).

The ominous spectacle of violent white nationalism and white supremacy in twenty-first-century public culture was given an additional layer of urgency by a populist President's refusal to name or condemn it as such. Offering a stark contrast, in a country grappling with similar formations including the rise of the far-right AfD political party, and speaking to the global significance of the events in Charlottesville, German Chancellor Angela Merkel offered this comment, "It is racist, far-right violence, and clear, forceful action must be taken against it, regardless of where in the world it happens" (Merkel, quoted in Wildman, 2017, para. 1).

"Make Them Famous": Understanding a Campaign of Digital Vigilantism

As and after the events transpired in Charlottesville, multiple online sites and feeds were created and/or used to identify and subsequently expose otherwise anonymous rally participants as such, to people within their home communities and institutional affiliations. The popular Twitter account "@YesYoureRacist" (YYR), which I primarily focus on, was the highest profile and most coordinated example of this. Its creator called upon others — online allies, far and wide, members of the public who shared concern and outrage for what was occurring in Charlottesville's public realm — to help him "make them [rally participants] famous". Some celebrities used their status to supplement and amplify such efforts, including American actress Jennifer Lawrence, who posted this note on her Facebook profile, addressed to her sixteen-million-plus Facebook followers, above four images from the rally: "These are the faces of hate. Look closely and post anyone you find. You can't hide with the Internet you pathetic cowards!" (Lawrence, quoted in Wiest, 2017, para. 4). As this comment implies, the Internet creates new conditions for otherwise anonymous individuals to become "unmasked" when they participate in socially maligned events in the public sphere, as long as there are willing and able collaborators, and platforms accessible for such work.

YYR was created in 2012 by a young anti-racist activist from North Carolina. Essentially, it is an online space in which participants 'call out' instances of everyday racism, mostly occurring within the United States, including offensive statements made by President Trump and his supporters, by celebrities and public figures, as well as ordinary people who claim to be 'not racist, but...'. Screenshots of later deleted social media posts are often re-posted, along with brief ripostes. Rooted in a type of digital accountability, where people's fleeting words and deeds "live on" in ways that cannot be un-said or un-done, such a space creates a type of "mediated solidarity" (Dant, 2012, p. 50–1) within a structurally unequal and highly fractured society. Here, manifestations of racism and white supremacy — whether obvious or subtle — are identified, reproduced and denounced by a vigilant association of like-minded others who are similarly keeping watch, however geographically dispersed they may be.

Fig. 9.4 Logan Smith, YesYoureRacist Twitter screengrab, August 12, 2017, https://twitter.com/YesYoureRacist?ref_src=twsrc%5Egoogle%7Ctwca mp%5Eserp%7Ctwgr%5Eauthor

Building on this existing feed, and in response to its founder's call-to-action, YYR gained over 300,000 followers the weekend after the

Charlottesville rally, reaching close to 350,000 by 15 August 2017. Throughout the summer and into late autumn of 2017 YYR garnered 392,000 followers, morphing for a concentrated period of time into a space primarily focused on DV activities related specifically to identifying and exposing Charlottesville rally-goers.

Although neither the activist behind this campaign nor YYR supporters utilise such terminology, conceptually, this social media campaign fits several criteria for "digital vigilantism", as developed by media scholar and sociologist Daniel Trottier. Galvanising members of the digitally connected public to participate in the denunciation of rally participants, it worked as a form of "weaponized visibility" by creating — or threatening to create — forms of visibility through the posting of digital materials. Its public manifestations and effects were "unwanted", "intense" and "enduring" (Trottier, 2017, p. 55) for subjects. In response to deeply felt offence over what was occurring in Charlottesville, and using the threat of infamy, digital media activists disrupted any expectation of anonymity or temporal boundedness that may have been presumed by rally-goers. Physical and digital spaces were creatively connected through these efforts to identify and expose the rally's attendees, and presumed temporal boundaries were broken. The social consequences of past activities during a tumultuous weekend spilled into the future for correctly identified participants. New kinds of risks and possibilities were thereby introduced into their lives, outside of the temporal, spatial and social boundaries of the original events. While the use of such tactics may appear exceptional at first glance, they mirror practices of online communication that have become commonplace amongst social media users around the world. As Trottier puts it, "an increase in online sharing of personal information — as evidenced from the growth of services like Facebook, Twitter and Instagram — contributes to DV, as they provide both a platform and a set of practices that render DV meaningful and practical" (ibid., p. 61). Such practices contribute to a blurring of the border between private and public domains, and also between spectating audience member and citizen-activist.

Let us next explore this campaign and its consequences in more empirical detail. How was it put forth and taken up? What were the members of its intended audience, recipients who were sympathetic to the call to "make [rally-goers] famous", presumed to know and assume about the social world (cf. Schutz, 1953), as applied to the example at hand? How was subject identification given moral justification, and how was "success" being tacitly defined through this DV campaign? What was actually accomplished and what, overall, has this DV campaign contributed to the Charlottesville story and beyond? While it has become common to skim over posted content in our speedy and reactive digital-media-saturated culture, in order to generate critical insight into the subtle workings of contemporary culture, it is important to slow down in our interpretive work of socially impactful texts and images, to understand *how* things mean (Rose, 2016).

A Digital Call to Action and its Anticipated Audience

Fig. 9.5 Logan Smith, YesYoureRacist Twitter screengrab, "Social media call to action", August 12, 2017 and MSNBC News screengrab, "naming and shaming", August 15, 2017, https://www.nbcnews.com/news/us-news/logan-smith-activist-behind-yesyoureracist-outs-charlottesville-white-nationalists-twitter-n792936

"If you recognize any of the Nazis marching in #Charlottesville, send me their names/profiles and I'll make them famous #GoodNightAltRight 9:43 AM–Aug 12, 2017" (@YesYoureRacist). This digital media call to action was made on day two of the "Unite the Right" rallies in Charlottesville, which indicated an emergent — not pre-planned — understanding that the marchers 'should' be publicly identified. Four photos were assembled beneath these words, which depicted mostly clean-cut young white men — framed as "Nazis marching" — carrying bamboo torches while congregating during a night-time demonstration against the backdrop of a prominent university building. A socially complex argument is made through this compilation of words and images, which we shall consider in some detail.

Words: The textual call is addressed to a general "you". "If you recognize any of the Nazis marching in #Charlottesville..." (Fig. 9.5). Members of its intended audience are presumed to understand that "Nazis marching" refers to persons associated with violent racism, extreme, and potentially fascistic beliefs and practices, including but not limited to anti-Semitism. They are also assumed to be social-media literate, for instance, to know that images from the rally can be found that other people have posted online, which depict still-anonymous participants (#Charlottesville and #GoodNightAltRight). This open call invites any connected reader to take (digital) action by engaging in such identification work, to move from a passively concerned member of the public to one who is actively engaged in "Internet sleuthing".[13]

A digital division of labour is established, with the curator at the other end, promising to utilise the platform and his cultural resources to make once-identified subjects "famous". The receptive audience member (the "you") is presumed to know and assume that such infamy will be consequential for the pictured rally-goer in a negative way and that *this is a good thing.* The question of what it will mean to subject rally participants to negative infamy within an expansive social sphere, unable to conceal such participation after the dust settles in Charlottesville, and what could be "good" about such public visibility, is left implicit. Whereas in countries such as Germany, where the display of Nazi symbolism is legally prohibited as hate speech, and such exposure can lead to formal charges, in the current American context the consequences of such DV tactics lie primarily within the socio-moral sphere.

Images: The four assembled images reinforce the textual message at the same time as the words help to explain the significance of what can be seen there. The words and the images are thus mutually reinforcing.

---

13   For two recent studies that explore facets of "Internet sleuthing" see Myles et al. (2017) and Yardley et al. (2016).

Appearing as otherwise ordinary college students, the pictured participants depart from stereotypical images of a neo-Nazi, such as the armed men interviewed for the VICE news documentary, at the same time as they are described as "Nazis marching". Their conventional, clean-cut and more or less middle-class appearance is reinforced against the backdrop of a socially respectable institution — the University of Virginia. Participants appear casually oblivious to being photographed; nobody is masking his face or appears reticent about his visibility here. In the prominent image, the torch-bearing men appear as if they are moving towards their social media audience, whose receptive members are being explicitly called upon to take action.

Responding to a Social Media Call to 'Name and Shame'

Dozens of images of primarily white male participants were posted onto YYR, with words implying that the pictured subjects needed to be identified, that doing so was morally justified and that readers should re-tweet (RT) such images (Fig. 9.6). Images typically focused on individual participants. This had the effect of stripping each of the anonymising cover of the crowd. If, in the crowded streets and parks, like-minded others offered kinship and strength in numbers, this protective cover was dissolved in the individualising spaces that were created online. Organisationally, these compilations resembled police 'wanted' posters. Often appearing in mid-chant, evidence of the social 'crime' was contained in the image: the pictured subjects could be seen as self-incriminating, as willing and enthusiastic agents, through their visible participation in a maligned event and implied association with symbolic expressions of violence, hatred and racism.[14]

What happens between the posted image and the positive identification is left opaque. The invisible work of doing Internet sleuthing — here, of connecting faces in pictures with names of verifiable people — creates an asymmetrical relation of visibility. Such work, revealed by its effects, seems both magical and inevitable. Once a picture is posted, it seems as if it is an omniscient Internet that is doing

---

14 Such visualising tactics are comparable to how Michel Foucault (1977) described and formulated the "art of punishing" in modern schools, factories and prisons through disciplinary processes of individuation.

such work, and that it is merely a matter of time before anonymous faces are rendered identifiable.

Next let us formulate what 'success' meant in this context by exploring some prominent examples of positive identification. Success in this DV context involved two dimensions: correct identification and evidence of offline effects, i.e. practical intervention into the lives of others.

Fig. 9.6 YesYoureRacist Twitter screengrab, "RT to identify", August 12, 2017.

The Meanings of Successful Identification

A former employee: The first posted instance of successful identification involved a young man from California, who reportedly lost his job as a result of being correctly identified as a Charlottesville rally participant. Framed for its audience as an update, and demonstrating the efficacy of the social media campaign and Internet sleuthing work that was invisibly taking place, the post noted that the now exposed individual "no longer has a job" (Fig. 9.7).

Fig. 9.7 YesYoureRacist Twitter screengrab, "Update", August 13, 2017.

Sociologically, it is important to consider what is presumed to be self-evidently positive about such a development. A clue can be found in the former employer's note that was included in the social media post, next to a photograph from the rally with an identifiable man — presumably the former employee — holding a torch and positioned in the center. After expressing its thanks for "bringing this to our attention", an apology is offered for a "delayed response". By noting it was "inundated with inquiries" regarding its (now former) employee's attendance at the rally, the business makes known to the reader that this "incident" is considered significant by a multitude of unseen members of the public. It is stated that, "We feel it is imperative to let you know that [he] is no longer employed [here]" (Fig. 7).

A sense of perceived urgency and civic duty is suggested in this communication; the business is hereby publicising to the wider world that they no longer have a formal association with the man seen in the picture. The note is more than factual information; it carries moral overtones that imply responsibility on the part of this organisation (a local business) to a broader public, to announce that its contractual relationship with the man who attended the rally has been terminated. Signs also appeared in the shop window, and inserts were placed in menus at all three of its Berkeley, California locations. "Effective Saturday 12th August [name of man] no longer works [here]. The actions of those in Charlottesville are not supported by [name of business]" (Pershan, 2017). In making such announcements, the former employer helps to amplify the public shaming effects for the now exposed individual by naming him and creating further exposure of the perceived significance of his rally participation.

As this example demonstrates, the type of visibility that is produced by DV carries with it the capacity to intervene into a subject's life in materially consequential ways. In this case, correct identification and exposure within the subject's local environment affects his social status and "life chances" (Weber 1978; Giddens 1973, pp. 130–1), namely the ability to maintain employment following the significant publicity received by his (now former) employer concerning his off-work activities, which led to his obligatory resignation.

Unicorn Riot @UR_Ninja
When we asked other #UniteTheRight attendees about their 'white genocide' claims, some of them responded violently

♡ 14.4K   12:01 PM - Aug 12, 2017   ⓘ

💬 16.9K people are talking about this   ›

Fig. 9.8 Unicorn Riot, posted to YesYoureRacist Twitter screengrab, "Some of them responded violently", August 13, 2017.

A son is publicly "disowned": Different versions of public dis-association can be found in other examples, including the case of a young man who was publicly "disowned" by his family of origin after having been correctly identified on YYR as a vocal rally participant. He appears in a short video that was taken during the rally, and embedded into a YYR post, where he is sarcastically named as a "charming Nazi" (Fig. 9.8). In this video he can be heard making statements about so-called "white genocide" while looking into a stranger's camera. While he appears naively indifferent to being captured on film in this moment, an unseen person knocks the camera out the photographer's grasp, suggesting hostility between the presence of some participants wishing not to be "caught" on film and those who are digitally documenting what is taking place in the streets.

Letter: Family denounces Tefft's racist rhetoric and actions

By Pearce Tefft on Aug 14, 2017 at 8:21 a.m.

1 / 2   Peter Tefft, center, was among the 'pro-white' demonstrators who marched at the University of Virginia on Friday. His father wrote a letter to his hometown newspaper dishowsling his son's views. Credit: Photo by Evelyn Hockstein for The Washington Post.

My name is Pearce Tefft, and I am writing to all, with regards to my youngest son, Peter Tefft, an avowed white nationalist who has been featured in a number of local news stories over the last several months.

We have been silent up until now, but now we see that this was a mistake. It was the silence of good people that allowed the Nazis to flourish the first time around, and it is the silence of good people that is allowing them to flourish now.

Peter Tefft, my son, is not welcome at our family gatherings any longer. I pray my prodigal son will renounce his hateful beliefs and return home. Then and only then will I lay out the feast.

Other relatives of Pete Tefft are also publicly disavowing him.

Fig. 9.9 Inforum, "Public letter", August 14, 2017, https://www.inforum.com/opinion/letters/4311880-letter-family-denounces-teffts-racist-rhetoric-and-actions

Two days after this identification, his father published a "heartbreaking" letter to the editor, addressed both to his son and to a wider audience, in a local community newspaper (Suerth, 2017, para. 1). The father disavows his son, until he "renounce[s] his hateful beliefs", and states his wish to "loudly repudiate my son's vile, hateful and racist rhetoric and actions"([name of father], quoted in *Twin Cities Pioneer Press*, 2017).

In this letter, the father identifies his son as "an avowed white nationalist", and connects what is happening ("now") with the "silence of good people that allowed the Nazis to flourish the first time around"(Fig. 9.9). As in the case of the former employer, the articulation of moral responsibility within the context of a broader socio-political world is made evident. It may be surmised that the man's father, and family at large, experienced — or feared experiencing — blame (possibly threats) for conduct and statements made by the young man bearing their (family) name, as they made a point of articulating in public statements that he "didn't grow up with [hateful beliefs]". "Why must we be guilty by association?", the father asks (rhetorically) in this letter.[15] This public letter was widely reported upon as part of the story of Charlottesville, offering an emotionally poignant side of its digital shaming aftermath. It is not merely that the young man was symbolically disowned by his family but that this was done so publicly.

"Angry torch guy": The most prominent example of successful identification was of so-called "angry torch guy", a young man whose image appeared in the first call to action and has since become iconic of the rally and its digital-shaming aftermath. Mouth agape, the man in the center appears to be in mid-shout. He looks intoxicated by the scene around him, a night-time gathering filled with other white men holding flaming torches. Such an image connotes fascist rallies and dangerous mob behavior, where fanatical and naive followers stand ready to act as parts of a larger group, stirred by a charismatic speaker (Fig. 10).[16]

---

15   In news media interviews, members of the young man's extended family have said that some of them have been "targeted by death threats" over the actions of their identified family member (Suerth, 2017, para. 15).

16   The photographer behind this now famous image shared this view. In an interview about it, Samuel Corum, of Anadula Agency in Turkey, described the "energy in his face", surmising that when we saw the man yelling, his interpretation was that "He had a purpose and his face showed it". (McAndrew, 2017b).

Yes, You're Racist @YesYoureRacist · 12 Aug 2017
Replying to @YesYoureRacist
This angry young man is Peter Cvjetanovic, a student at @unevadareno

Peter Cvjetanovic

○ 1.8K   ⟲ 33K   ♡ 31K

Fig. 9.10 YesYoureRacist Twitter screengrab, "This angry young man", August 12, 2017.

Following the man's correct identification and public exposure as the person behind the picture, calls were made for Nevada University, where he is a student, to expel him. Over ten thousand people signed an online petition (through Change.org), and calls were made to "flood" the university student office with phone calls demanding the student's expulsion. In addition to the worldwide circulation of this image, his identification elicited significant controversy and debate on his home campus. The image, paired with his name, was widely circulated across social media by fellow students, including a note drawing attention to his membership in a campus fraternity, and the statement "DO NOT LET HIM GO UNSHAMED" (Toppo, 2018, para. 8). His campus fraternity revoked his membership, stating that the Charlottesville rally was "disturbing, disheartening and contrary to our values" (ibid.). He subsequently quit his part-time job, explaining during a radio interview that he did not wish to "pick at the scab of Charlottesville". The potency of association and implication of "moral taint" (Rosati, 2008) was made visible in other ways. For example, images found online from his social media posts appeared to connect him to a US Republican Senator Dean Heller; this created an additional linkage between the current US government and sentiments that were given expression during the Charlottesville rally. The cycle of attempted dis-association continued; in a Twitter response the Senator attempted to distance himself from this, stating "I don't know this person & condemn the outrageous racism, hatred and violence. It's unacceptable & shameful. No room for it in this country" (Heller, on Twitter, 12 August 2017).

The President of the public university responded in a statement "denouncing all forms of bigotry and racism" stating that these "have no place in a free and equal society". It was also emphasised that, "peaceful assembly and exchange of ideas is part of the bedrock of any free society" (Johnson, in Toppo, 2018). The man behind the picture was not expelled, as doing so would have infringed upon his First Amendment right to expression, since "...you can't discipline someone for looking angry..." (para. 17).[17] While he was not formally punished, the attention and public scrutiny that ensued from the DV campaign certainly gave him unwanted notoriety ("fame"). In public interviews he has stated that his life, as a result of being correctly identified as the person behind the picture, is now "spiraling out of control" (McAndrew, 2017a, para. 1).

Talking to media in interviews, he has expressed concern that he may be unable to secure employment upon graduation, in light of his unexpected global infamy. He also defended his participation at Charlottesville, describing himself as proud of his white European heritage, and referring to his trip to Virginia as a moment in which he "dabbled in alt.right ideology" (Toppo, 2018). Regarding the iconic photo he explains that, "I got caught in the heat of the moment", but insists he is "not the angry young man" seen in the photo, i.e. that he is not reducible to the image of this moment.

As is typical in cases of online shaming (cf. Ronson, 2015), attempts at visibility management backfired and drew significant ridicule and consternation on social media. This example highlights how, once identified, the participant lives with a type of public scrutiny. Following an attempt to explain and defend his presence at Charlottesville, on a subsequent YYR post a comparison was drawn between the image of "Angry Torch Guy" and the iconic photo showing Hazel Bryan, who became a poster-girl for anti-black racism during a delicate moment

---

17   Minimally, the university president's statement symbolised a perceived responsibility to denounce "all forms of bigotry and racism" in light of the revelation that one of its students had attended the Charlottesville rally; this opened its administration up to significant criticism regarding the implications of the continued membership of a "white supremacist" at this educational institution.

during the US Civil Rights era, after being seen and photographed shouting down African American student Elizabeth Eckford.[18] Like the image captured with Bryan shouting at Eckford — a split second in time — the now fateful photo of "Angry Torch Guy" has come to function as both an artifact of collective memory and site for public-sphere engagement (Lucaites & Hariman, 2001). While both subjects — Bryan in 1957 and the rally participant of 2017 — have become subject to infamy and negative iconicity due to a single, captured photo in which they come to represent a larger social issue and historical moment, the digital difference is that in addition to being "unwanted" and "enduring" (Trottier 2017, p. 55), there is a scrutinising *intensity* for the identified subject today. This difference illustrates the potency of a 24/7 news cycle, paired with the pervasiveness of social media in public culture today.

Moral Taint and the Power of Association

As these examples dramatise, and the social media campaign of identifying and outing rally participants in Charlottesville helped to establish, to participate in such an event at this time was to endanger one's reputation, existing social ties, institutional affiliations and life chances. An important — if under-recognised — dimension here is that others become (potentially) tainted through their connection with the participating individual by virtue of an implicit vicarious responsibility (Rosati, 2008). It is against this subtle backdrop that the campaign to make participants "famous" worked. Even the Tiki brand, whose bamboo torches were prominent during the rally, sought to distance itself symbolically from further association with the Charlottesville events. Using the platform Facebook, the company issued the following statement: "We do not support their message or the use of our products in this way [...] Our products are designed to enhance backyard gatherings and to help family and friends connect with each other..." ("Tiki" brand public statement, in Ortutay, 2017). Along similar lines,

---

18 Eckford was one of nine African American girls arriving for her first day of school at Central High in Arkansas, and was shouted at by an angry white mob of segregationists, which included young Bryan, and was ultimately prevented entry into the school by the National Guard. For further background see "Little Rock Nine", https://www.history.com/topics/black-history/central-high-school-integration

and as but one of many examples of online platforms banning the participation of white supremacist groups and individuals, the popular online dating app OkCupid permanently banned Christopher Cantwell — the committed participant who appeared prominently in the Vice video, stating that "There is no room for hate in a place where you're looking for love" (OkCupid posting, cited in Bonos, 2017).

Such expressions of "moral taint" and formal dis-association challenge the image of society as a mere aggregate of rights-bearing individuals. While on the surface, this DV campaign may appear individualistic in its orientation and politics, its efficacy clearly depended on the collaboration of others — individuals and organisations — who shared the basic judgment that animated the campaign, namely, that violent white supremacy must be unequivocally denounced and afforded no legitimate place in contemporary society. To participants, present and future, and to the broader social world, its moral lesson is that while a person might be 'free' as an individual to attend what they wish, to say what they like and to associate with whom they please within the formal bounds of law, no one is free from being held to account for this in terms of its broader social meaning and significance. A high-profile DV campaign, such as the case under consideration, contributes to a general re-thinking of what it means to openly participate in any socially controversial public event.

A Case of Mis-identification

There was at least one high profile case of outright mis-identification causing harm. A University of Arkansas professor was mistakenly identified as having been one of the rally participants, based on his physical resemblance to one of the rally participants who was seen and photographed wearing an Arkansas Engineering t-shirt. As was widely reported, the man wrongfully identified "was flooded with vulgar messages on social media and accused of racism, and his home address was posted on social networks" (Victor, 2017). Offering insight into the effects of doxing in relation to the Charlottesville events, on *National*

Public Radio (NPR) he reported that he and his family contacted police and left their home for the weekend out of fear of misplaced aggression.

Additionally, a de-contextualised photo of an American YouTube personality wearing a swastika on his armband, that came from a "prank" video he had made during a Trump rally which he had posted months prior to the Charlottesville events, was given circulation on the same Twitter thread. While it was removed, with apology for the "confusion" its posting generated, it had negative consequences for the person it featured, who was pressured to respond to backlash over the error.

Such incidents were used as the basis for many media commentators and members of the public to question or criticise the DV campaign altogether, and highlight its *intrinsic* risks and dangers. While the activist who first issued the call to make rally participants "famous" sought to rectify instances of mistaken identification, some drew upon such incidents to argue that such campaigns are indefensible forms of "mistake-prone mob vigilantism" (Gass, 2017), inhabit a "swampy low ground" on the Internet (Ellis, 2017) and contribute in socially negative ways to a surveillance society. In effect such criticisms render distinctions of intention irrelevant. According to such criticism, the end cannot justify this means. Following the incident with the University of Arkansas professor, and taking a stand against doxing, irrespective of political motivation, the crowdfunding platform Patreon suspended the activist's account (YYR) on the grounds that it was in violation of "Patreon Community Guidelines". Patreon's decision serves as an important reminder that DV activism *always and necessarily* depends upon the continued accessibility of public or social media platforms, and that use can be revoked at any time. This raises important questions about how platform decisions about content moderation are made, and how such curation shapes public discourse (see Gillespie 2018).[19]

---

19   While this subject exceeds the scope of this study, I will note that into 2019, social media platforms such as Facebook and Instagram have begun publicly to ban the accounts of known white supremacist groups and speakers, defined in its community guidelines as dangerous individuals, even if their speech does not formally break a law.

Virtuous Denunciation

Arguing that their denunciation was virtuous, and demonstrating the ongoing negotiation and interpretive work involved in legitimating their methods, media activists occasionally posted notes on the feed, indicating that people should "keep up the good work" in the ongoing effort to identify and expose participants to their broader communities. In response to occasional criticism that was expressed in some of the posted comments concerning the ethics of naming names, it was periodically pointed out that rally participants could not reasonably have expected to remain anonymous, and that the significance of the events demanded such a response.

The unlikely voices of some prominent writers and activists who had previously and influentially cautioned against "online shaming" and "call out culture" were given a voice in different news media articles, following posted comments about the events. Two such examples are British journalist Jon Ronson, author of *So You've Been Publicly Shamed* (2015) and Toronto community organiser and poet Asam Ahmad, whose influential article published in *Briarpatch* in 2015 criticised "callout" culture among progressive activists, pointing to what he called its "mild totalitarian undercurrents" (Ahmad, 2015, para. 4).[20] As Ronson posted, in Twitter comments that were further circulated in various news media articles, "[The Charlottesville white supremacists] were undisguised in a massively contentious rally surrounded by the media... There's a big difference between being a white power activist [or] white supremacist and being, say, [name redacted]" (Ronson, cited in Blum, 2017; Chappell, 2017; Pringle, 2017).[21] Along similar lines, Ahmad asserted that "Every single white supremacist deserves to be publicly

---

20   Also addressed to left-leaning readers, in late August of 2017, Ahmed published a follow up piece in *Briarpatch* titled "When Calling Out Makes Sense", https://briarpatchmagazine.com/articles/view/when-calling-out-makes-sense

21   The case referenced here is often cited as an iconic example of the excesses of social media shaming and 'trial by Twitter.' The target became a trending social media story after sending an offensive, racist comment ('tweet') on Twitter prior to boarding a plane. As she slept on the flight, her comment was reposted tens of thousands of times, where it generated significant denunciation around the digitally connected world, including a hashtag asking if she had landed. By the time she exited the plane, she had become the recipient of significant online vitriol, including threats of violence. She was fired from her job as a communication director the next day.

shamed and face the consequences of their actions" (Ahmad, cited in Gass, 2017). In light of the exceptional nature of the events to which they were responding, readers familiar with, and sympathetic to such criticisms about the excesses of online shaming were hereby offered a tacit pass to "shame away".

Yes, You're Racist @YesYoureRacist · 12 Aug 2017

Nazis are marching without fear. Counterprotesters are getting mowed down in the street.

Whether you like or not, it's time to pick a side.

197   5.0K   7.7K

Fig. 9.11 YesYoureRacist Twitter screengrab, "Whether you like it or not, it's time to pick a side", August 12, 2017.

Additionally, postings often reinforced a sense of the present as an urgent time for moral clarity and judgment, sometimes quite self-consciously, especially following the death of the counter-protestor, and injuries to others, when they were violently struck by a car driven by a rally-goer. "Nazis are marching without fear. Counter-protestors are getting mowed down in the street" (Fig. 9.11). Addressed to an audience presumed to be concerned by what can be seen in the two images — marchers holding flags bearing swastikas and the moment a car "mows down" counter-protesters — the reader is called upon to pass judgement on what is occurring. Here the symbol of violence (a flag bearing a swastika) and the actualisation of violence (a car driving through bodies of people) are joined together in meaning. "Whether you like it or not, it's time to pick a side" (ibid.). Later referred to as "the photo from Charlottesville that will define this moment in American history" (Rosenberg, 2017), the second image subsequently won a Pulitzer Prize for "Breaking News Photography".[22] Haunted by symbols of what should be in the past, the present was interpreted as a potentially defining moment of American history-in-the-making, and characterised as a time in which there is no spectator position. The audience member who was presumed to be both ambivalent about DV tactics, and morally attuned to political dangers on the horizon, is asked the implicit question: which side are you on?

News Media as Reportage and Collaboration

From the beginning, news media articles and interviews with the activist behind the original call to action helped to amplify and widen the audience scope of the DV campaign, by reporting on it as newsworthy and recirculating images and examples from it. While my primary focus has been on digital media audience activism in this case, and the co-ordinating work of ordinary citizens in response to this call, it is important to emphasise that by reporting on this campaign as part of the story of Charlottesville 2017, news media reportage and popular commentary — on air, in print and online — very actively, if inadvertently, contributed to both its publicity and efficacy, even when it was expressly critical of the methods of doxing and shaming (for an example of this, see Ellis, 2017). Regardless of the discursive context in which they were placed, by recirculating images and names of 'outed' rally participants from social media postings, with very few exceptions, and by reporting on this campaign as something interesting and controversial, news media contributed to the infamy of the pictured and identified participants. While not unique to this case, news media actors functioned as important co-collaborators in the creation of digital naming and shaming effects (see Hess & Waller, 2014, pp. 103–4).

In most of the prolific news stories found online, on television and in print, different opinions from various experts and commentators who were asked to 'weigh in' on the DV campaign were included, from media scholars and civil libertarians, to anti-violence educators and public

---

22   Ryan Kelly of *The Daily Progress* was the photographer behind this image, called 'Charlottesville Car Attack', which later won a Pulitzer Prize for "Breaking News Photography".

intellectuals. Serving as proxy for the ambivalence that was present within the wider public concerning the 'outing' of rally participants, on-air news commentators occasionally voiced their own reservations concerning DV tactics. For example, following an interview with the activist behind the prominent social media call, in which he was asked to explain what he was "trying to accomplish", two MSNBC newscasters are heard briefly struggling over its ethical implications. One mused on what she considered the absurdity of anybody expecting "privacy" after having participated in such a public event:

> to those who participated in the rally over the weekend who've been complaining for the last twenty-four hours that they don't deserve to have their names and faces out there, I say, you've got to be kidding me, you were a part of this.

In the next moment she adds, "But it is dangerous business, right? People have families, and extended families. Now that we live in this world of social media [shakes her head], I don't know. This is a very complicated issue". "It is", reiterated her on-air co-worker (MSNBC News, 2017a). Moral ambivalence over the use of such tactics was often made part and parcel to the story. By framing it in this way, and not merely reporting upon its factual elements, news media thus contributed to making the DV campaign topical, inviting the audience to weigh in on it as a complicated socio-moral issue of the times.

Those who argued that the DV campaign was morally justified, in spite of its risks and limitations, typically drew attention to the exceptional nature of the events to which the 'call' to name and shame were addressed, exacerbated by the inadequacy of the US President's response. A columnist for the *Toronto Star* summed this position up as follows, "In light of the horrific events in Charlottesville, VA., this weekend, I firmly believe that a shame-pass is in order....It's nothing but necessary in a nation whose leader refuses to condemn voices of hate..." Speaking to its relevance beyond the borders of the US, she went on to urge her audience of newspaper readers to "shame away", arguing that to have participated in the Charlottesville rallies could not be dismissed as a "lapse in judgment" as it is to participate in something that is "a direct threat to the way of life of every decent person on this earth" (Teital, 2017, para. 4-5). As this example reveals, the line between commentating on the campaign and actively contributing to it was exceedingly thin.

Clearly, the effectiveness of 'naming and shaming' becomes intensified through the news media reportage and the commentary it elicits, whether the emphasis is more critical, supportive or mixed. Beyond the specificities of the case at hand, this highlights the importance of reflexivity in all manner of reportage and commentary; since public shaming and other related dimensions of DV initiatives depend upon significant collaboration to be effective, it becomes increasingly difficult, if not impossible, not to be implicated in some manner and thus it is important to take this into account in any such re-presentation.[23]

Aftermath, One Year Later

One year later, under heavy police presence, a coalition of individuals associated with the far-right in America organised a rally in Washington after being denied a permit for such an event in Charlottesville. Framed by its organisers as a second "Unite the Right" event, this would-be anniversary event — doomed before it began — brought together a couple of dozen supporters. In addition to the heavy police presence in Washington, a state of emergency was declared in Virginia by the state Governor *in advance* of the Charlottesville anniversary. In notable contrast with the five hundred or so persons who had congregated the previous August, formally permitted to do so, and buoyed by the belief that this moment represented a positive "turning point" in their movement, the sparse assembly of participants was massively outnumbered by thousands of counter-demonstrators. In a country with a population exceeding 327 million people, from the vantage point

---

23 Of course, this also includes scholarly writing. In the case of this study, and in keeping with the ethical protocols put forth by the editors of this collection and agreed upon by contributors, I have sought to maintain the anonymity of rally participants who were not public figures prior to the Charlottesville events. At the same time, I must recognise the limitations of this approach, since the ample news stories that have circulated about previously unknown, and subsequently identified individuals have typically included their names alongside their images. Minimally, by not embedding names of such participants into the writing of this chapter, Internet searches of such names will not pull up this particular text.

of uniting the right, this event was nothing short of a spectacular and demoralising failure.

Mirroring the tactics used during the previous year, local activists engaged in pre-emptive naming and shaming tactics, aimed at discouraging participation, by publicising names of known organisers in advance. As reported in the *New York Times*

> activists posted personal information of organizers online, and encouraged people to alert employers of their affiliations, put up fliers outing them in their neighbourhoods, and uncovered their "ties to more 'respectable' right-wing organizations that help them hide their true intentions (Fausset et al., 2018).

Connections were made in news reports between this conspicuously sparse turnout and the previous year's outing "by both online activists and mainstream media outlets" (Fausset et al., 2018, para. 3). Organiser Jason Kessler attributed the small numbers to an "atmosphere of intimidation" (ibid., para. 4). In a sense, as both the organiser's remarks and the news reports implied, the social media activists had taken the enjoyment out of the event for participants. Specifically, the consequences of the 'outing' tactics the previous year seemed to have successfully diminished participants' capacity to feel powerful and effervescent one year later, while physically surrounded by like-minded others in the public realm.

It would be unwise to infer from this conspicuously meagre anniversary rally that the white supremacist movement is withering in the US, that the 2017 social media campaign was alone responsible for what happened the next year, or that any complex social formation can be diminished through such means alone. As critical race scholars and anti-racist educators importantly highlight, it is relatively easy to condemn overt manifestations of racism, while its invisible institutional structures remain intact (see Paradkar, 2017). Since this time, there has been much concerned discussion about the overall rise of the alt-right, and violent manifestations of explicitly racist, white supremacist, anti-immigrant, anti-Black, anti-Semitic and anti-Islamic sentiments in numerous countries around the world, at the cultural and formal political level. At the cultural level, the successful failure of the 2018 "Charlottesville anniversary" rally, however, suggests some efficacy on the part of the vigilant social media campaign, in dissuading all but the fully committed participant from taking the gamble of marching in the streets, facing the cameras, and living with the kind of infamy that was generated following Charlottesville 2017. In so doing, it helped to accentuate the urgency of the moment, a time in which actors and groups bearing symbols and expressions of violent white nationalism and white supremacy are seeking legitimate presence in the mainstream. The hope is that this will also contribute to making a difference at the formal political level, in delegitimating political actors who seek or draw support from groups or individuals associated with such manifestations.

Discussion and Conclusion: Solidifying Meaning, Refusing Moral Equivalency, Getting Personal

Let us revisit the question posed at the outset: what would have been different about Charlottesville 2017 without the social media campaign aimed at outing participants as such? In other words, what did this campaign produce and achieve, and what are some of its significant social implications?

The DV campaign helped to crystallise the meaning of what kind of event the "Unite the Right" rally was within the broader public culture: an ominously exceptional, socially dangerous and potentially historically significant moment within contemporary US society.

It contributed to a united refusal within civil society to normalise and thereby legitimate the expression of violent white nationalism and white supremacy, legitimation that was being sought by rally organisers, vocal participants and event supporters who assembled in Charlottesville in August 2017 under the banner "Unite the Right". Thus, it can be understood as an attempt to socially refuse the public manifestation of violent white supremacy in twenty-first-century public life as but one controversial orientation amongst others, a refusal maintained even when symbolising this expression through signage and space is granted constitutional protection. "Nazis marching", argued YYR, can be afforded no socially comfortable place within the contemporary public landscape. The current laws in the US may permit such manifestations in the name of the First Amendment — freedom of expression — as well as the right to assemble, if done lawfully; however, this campaign performatively argued that the violation such manifestations represent to individuals, groups and the society at large, demands their immediate and targeted denunciation.[24]

If we understand DV as rooted in conduct that some consider 'offensive', it must be noted that the kind of offense at stake in this case goes beyond interactional conflict or norm violation. Affective support for this social media campaign, even if it was tinged with some reservation concerning tactics, revealed a shared sense that what was seen and heard in Charlottesville was socially criminal even if it was formally permitted. It violated strongly held sentiments "deeply written" into the collective consciousness, to use the language of Durkheim; its manifestations threaten and harm individuals — especially those who are members of particular minority groups, fomenting destructive forces within society. In this sense they threaten everybody's well-being.

The DV campaign, including the ambivalence it evoked, helped to create conditions to articulate a clear rejection of the trappings of moral equivalency, on the grounds that it is a moral outrage to consider violent manifestations of racism and anti-racist responses to such manifestations as mere differences in content. As suggested earlier, the first response by President Trump, in which he referred to "violence on many sides" and "very fine people" on both sides, could have only intensified the felt necessity of such a refusal for the moral majority of concerned and outraged spectators to the events that transpired in Charlottesville. In this respect, the DV campaign also posed a challenge to those who were critical of its method, as this, too, might inadvertently reproduce such a political ('neutral') position.

The refusal to legitimate the terrain of violent white nationalism and white supremacy was largely achieved by making participation in such events particular, personal, risky and potentially *fateful* for the previously unknown and presumed anonymous participant. This was the unique aspect that the DV campaign added to Charlottesville 2017, and as I have argued here, its power lay primarily in the socio-moral domain. Whereas the vigorous public opposition, including the counter-rallies, was largely articulated in relation to social justice principles, the targeting

---

24   Indeed, it can also be said that one of those same principles, namely 'freedom of expression', is also in part what empowered the DV campaign to engage in its tactics of naming and outing participants as it did.

of individuals and the naming of names, encouraged and coordinated through contemporary tools of social media, created the conditions for a type of accountability and consequence for the otherwise unremarkable individual rally participant. The DV campaign took things beyond the level of general condemnation of a disturbing and reprehensible event, by making anyone's positive association with and during such an event live on in ways that were socially consequential.

The prolific circulation of particular instances of correct identification and exposure, we can surmise, constituted a public pedagogy of sorts, whose primary lesson to anyone who participates in such an event, now and into the foreseeable future, is to expect significant visibility and not to imagine that it will be possible to remain anonymous after the dust has settled. Participation at any level — organiser, speaker, marcher, bearer of sign, holder of torch, chanter of slogan — was thereby constituted as socially risky and even dangerous for the individual, in that it promised to make such participation matter afterwards and outside of the original event. In Goffman's sense, "fatefulness" refers to "the mark of the threshold between retaining some control over the consequences of one's actions and their going out of control" (Goffman, 1967, p. 27). This is precisely what the "angry torch man" alluded to when he referred to his post-identification life as now "spiralling out of control". This is the unique, potent and indeed morally controversial aspect that the DV campaign, led by YYR, 'added' to the Charlottesville events and their aftermath.

For the individual, says this campaign, there can be nothing casual about participation in a rally tainted by the threat or actuality of violent white supremacy. The possibility of dabbling or casually playing at being a 'weekend white supremacist', without facing worldly consequences in the days after, was powerfully challenged. We can speculate that such a lesson would be most effective for the participant for whom attendance was likened to a type of thrill-seeking or weekend adventure, and less so for the ideologically "true believer" (cf. Hoffer, 1951), since the former — if not the latter — is more likely to have affiliations with those to whom such participation would be considered repugnant, and which his (or her) subsequently exposed participation may jeopardise. The most powerful, if also invisible, force that enabled this DV campaign to have the effects that it did was the unspoken moral force of a shared vision of a world in which racially motivated hatred and violence must be *made* to have no legitimate place.

Campaigns of digital vigilantism can, of course, be inspired and undertaken from a variety of possible interests — political, socio-cultural, personal and otherwise. Making a case for the importance of detailed and socially contextualised scholarly investigation into such manifestations and their consequences within a complex and pluralistic social world, the example we have explored here offers insight into how such methods can be mobilised on behalf of social-justice interests.

References (scholarly texts)

Althusser, L. (1970). Ideology and ideological state apparatuses. In *Lenin and Philosophy, and Other Essays*. Trans. B. Brewster (pp. 127–88.) London: New Left Books.

Blitefield, J. (2006). It's showtime!: Staging public demonstrations, Alinsky-style. In L. Prelli (ed.). *Rhetorics of Display* (pp. 255–72.) Columbia: University of South Caroline Press.

Brighenti, A. (2007). Visibility: A category for the social sciences. *Current Sociology*, 55(3), 323–42, http://doi.org/10.1177/0011392107076079

Butler, J. (2015). *Notes Toward a Performative Theory of Assembly.* London and Cambridge: Harvard University Press, http://doi.org/10.4159/9780674495548

Coleman, G. (2015). *Hacker, Hoaxer, Whistleblower, Spy: The Many Faces of Anonymous.* London and New York: Verso.

Dant, T. (2012). *Television and the Moral Imaginary: Society Through the Small Screen.* London: Palgrave Macmillan, http://doi.org/10.1057/9781137035554

Douglas, D. (2016). Doxing: A conceptual analysis. *Ethics and Information Technology*, 18 (6), 199–210, http://doi.org/10.1007/s10676-016-9406-0

Durkheim, E. (1995 [1912]). *The Elementary Forms of Religious Life.* Trans. K. Fields. New York: The Free Press.

Durkheim, E. (1993 [1984]). *The Division of Labor in Society.* Trans. W. D. Halls New York: The Free Press.

Foucault, M. (1977). *Discipline & punish: The Birth of the prison.* Trans. A. Sheridan. New York: Vintage Books.

Garfinkel, H. (1967). *Studies in Ethnomethodology.* Englewood Cliffs, N. J.: Prentice-Hall.

Giddens, A. (1973). *The Class Structure of the Advanced Societies.* London: Hutchinson.

Gillespie, T. (2018). *Custodians of the Internet: Platforms, Content Moderation, and the Hidden Decisions that Shape Social Media.* New Haven: Yale University Press.

Goffman, E. (1967). Where the action is. In *Interaction Ritual* (pp. 149–270). Garden City: Anchor Books.

Hess, K., & Waller., L. (2014). "The digital pillory: media shaming of 'ordinary' people for minor crimes". *Continuum: Journal of Media & Cultural Studies,* 28(1), 101–11, http://doi.org/10.1080/10304312.2013.85486

Hoffer, E. (1951). *The True Believer: Thoughts on the Nature of Mass Movements.* New York: Harper & Brothers.

Inglis, D. (2017). Creating global moral iconicity: The Nobel Prizes and the constitution of world moral culture. *European Journal of Social Theory,* 21(3), 304–21, http://doi.org/10.1177/1368431017703642

Joas, H. (2013). *The Sacredness of the Person: A New Genealogy of Human Rights.* Trans. A. Skinner. Washington: Georgetown University Press.

Lucaites, J. L., & Hariman. R. (2001). Visual rhetoric, photojournalism, and democratic public culture. *Rhetoric Review,* 20(1–2), 37–42.

Myles, D., Benoit-Barné, C., & Millerand, F. (2018). 'Not your personal army!' Investigating the organizing property of retributive vigilantism in a Reddit collective of websleuths. *Information, Communication & Society,* 21, 1–20, http://doi.org/10.1080/1369118X.2018.1502336

Olesen, T. (2016). Politicizing cultural sociology: The power of/in global injustice symbols. *International Sociology,* 31(3), 324–40, http://doi.org/10.1177/0268580916629613

Rawls, A. W. (2001). Durkheim's treatment of practice: Concrete practice vs representations as the foundation of reason. *Journal of Classical Sociology,* 1(1), 33–68, http://doi.org/10.1177/1468795X0100100102

Rosati, M. (2008). Evil and collective responsibility: The Durkheimian legacy and contemporary debates. In W. S. F. Pickering and M. Rosati (eds). *Suffering and Evil: The Durkheimian Legacy.* (pp. 136–47). New York and Oxford: Durkheim Press/Berghahn Books.

Rose, G. (2016). *Visual methodologies: An introduction to researching with visual materials,* 4th *Edition.* London and Thousand Oaks: Sage.

Schutz, A. (1953). Common-sense and scientific interpretation of human action. *Philosophy and Phenomenological Research* 14(1), 1–38.

Trottier, D. (2017). Digital vigilantism as weaponization of visibility. *Philosophy & Technology,* 30, 55–72, http://doi.org/ 10.1007/s13347-016-0216-4

Weber, M. (1978). *Economy and Society (2 vols).* G. Roth and C. Wittich (eds). Berkeley: University of California Press.

Yardley, E., Lynes, A., Wilson, D., & Kelly, E. 2016. What's the deal with 'websleuthing'? News media representations of amateur detectives in networked spaces. *Crime, Media, Culture*, 14(1), 81–109, http://doi.org/10.1177/1741659016674045

References (media sources)

Ahmad, A. (2015, March 2). A note on call-out culture. *Briarpatch*, https://briarpatchmagazine.com/articles/view/a-note-on-call-out-culture

Blue Ribbon Commission on Race, Memorials, and Public Spaces. (2016, December 19). Report to Charlottesville City Council.

Bond, S. (2017, August 15). A short history of torches and intimidation. *Forbes*, https://www.forbes.com/sites/drsarahbond/2017/08/15/a-short-history-of-torches-and-intimidation/#6323fe166762

Bonos, L. (2017, August 17). OkCupid kicks out white supremacist Chris Cantwell: 'There is no room for hate'. *Washington Post*, https://www.washingtonpost.com/news/soloish/wp/2017/08/17/okcupid-kicks-out-white-supremacist-chris-cantwell-there-is-no-room-for-hate/

Blum, S. (2017, August 15). Doxxing white supremacists is making them terrified. *Vice Media*, https://broadly.vice.com/en_us/article/7xxbez/doxxing-white-supremacists-is-making-them-terrified

Carranco, S., & Milton., J. (2019, April 27). Canada's new far right: A trove of private chat room messages reveals an extremist subculture. *Globe and Mail*, https://www.theglobeandmail.com/canada/article-canadas-new-far-right-a-trove-of-private-chat-room-messages-reveals/

Chappell, B. (2017, August 15). After son is ID'd at supremacist rally, his father responds publicly. *National Public Radio*, https://www.npr.org/sections/thetwo-way/2017/08/15/543619397/after-son-is-idd-at-supremacist-rally-his-father-responds-publicly

CNBC News. (2017, August 15). President Donald Trump on Charlottesville: You had very fine people, on both sides. *CNBC News*, https://www.youtube.com/watch?v=JmaZR8E12bs

CNN. (2017, August 12). Trump condemns 'hatred, bigotry and violence on many sides' in Charlottesville, https://www.cnn.com/2017/08/12/politics/trump-statement-alt-right-protests/index.html

Curtis, C., Carranco, S., & Milton, J. (2018, May 14). Alt-right in Montreal: How Charlottesville exposed the key players in the local white nationalist movement. *Montreal Gazette*, https://montrealgazette.com/news/local-news/alt-right-in-montreal-how-charlottesville-exposed-the-key-players-in-the-local-white-nationalist-movement

Dejean, A. (2017, August 17). The case for naming and shaming white supremacists. *Mother Jones*, https://www.motherjones.com/politics/2017/08/the-case-for-naming-and-shaming-white-supremacists

Domonoske, C. (2017, August 14). On the internet, everyone knows 'you're racist': Twitter account ID's marchers. *NPR*, https://www.npr.org/sections/thetwo-way/2017/08/14/543418271/on-the-internet-everyone-knows-you-re-a-racist-twitter-account-ids-marchers.

Ellis, E. G. (2017 August 17). Whatever your side, doxing is a perilous form of justice. *Wired*, https://www.wired.com/story/doxing-charlottesville

Fausset, R. (2018, August 12). Rally by White Nationalists Was Over Almost Before It Began, *New York Times*, https://www.nytimes.com/2018/08/12/us/politics/charlottesville-va-protest-unite-the-right.html

Fausset, R., Kovaleski, S. F., & Feuer, A. (2018, August 13). A year after Charlottesville, disarray in the White Supremacist Movement. *New York Times*, https://www.nytimes.com/2018/08/13/us/charlottesville-unite-the-right-white-supremacists.html

Gabbatt, A. (2017, August 16). 'Jews will not replace us': Vice film lays bare horror of neo-Nazis in America. *The Guardian*, https://www.theguardian.com/us-news/2017/aug/16/charlottesville-neo-nazis-vice-news-hbo

Gass, H. (2017, August 17). Fallout from modern protests: naming and shaming online. *The Christian Science Monitor*, https://www.csmonitor.com/USA/2017/0817/Fallout-from-modern-protests-naming-and-shaming-online

Global News. (2016, November 22). White nationalists praise president-elect with Nazi salute. *Global News*, https://globalnews.ca/tag/national-policy-institute

Guynn, J. (2017, August 15). Top Dog worker in Berkeley loses job after he's outed as Charlottesville protester. *USA Today*, https://www.usatoday.com/story/tech/2017/08/15/top-dog-worker-loses-job-after-being-outed-charlottesville-protester/569487001

Heller, D. (2017, August 12). Twitter post @SenDeanHeller, *Twitter*, https://twitter.com/sendeanheller/status/896547850573819904

Illing, S. (2017, November 29). A grad student spent 12 months undercover in Europe's alt-right movement. *Vox*, https://www.vox.com/policy-and-politics/2017/10/11/16424576/europe-alt-right-nationalism-racism-trump-brexit

McAndrew, S. (2017a, August 13). UNR pictured at Charlottesville rally: things 'spiraling out of control. *Reno Gazette Journal*, https://www.rgj.com/story/news/education/2017/08/13/unr-heller-make-comments-after-student-linked-white-nationalist-charlottesville-rally/563064001

McAndrew, S. (2017b, August 16). UNR student and photographer share details behind photo at nationalist rally. *Reno Gazette Journal*, https://www.rgj.com/story/news/education/2017/08/16/

story-behind-viral-photo-unr-student-yelling-white-nationalist-rally/573805001

Merica, D. (2017, August 13). Trump condemns 'hatred, bigotry and violence on many sides' in Charlottesville. *CNN*, https://www.cnn.com/2017/08/12/politics/trump-statement-alt-right-protests/index.html

MSNBC News 1. (2017a, August 15). Activist Logan Smith on why he outs white supremacists on Twitter. MSNBC.com, https://www.msnbc.com/msnbc-news/watch/activist-logan-smith-on-why-he-outs-white-supremacists-on-twitter-1025128515652

MSNBC News 2 (2017b, August 19). White nationalists: Rebranding under 'free speech' flag? MSNBC.com, http://www.msnbc.com/am-joy/watch/white-nationalists-rebranding-under-free-speech-flag-1028274243758

Ortutay, B. (2017, August 14). Social media helps expose white nationalists at Charlottesville Rally. *The Toronto Star*, https://www.thestar.com/news/world/2017/08/14/social-media-helps-expose-white-nationalists-at-charlottesville-rally.html

Paradkar, S. (2017, August 18). What white supremacy looks like, minus the paraphernalia: Paradkar. *Toronto Star*, https://www.thestar.com/news/gta/2017/08/18/what-white-supremacy-looks-like-minus-the-charlottesville-paraphernalia-paradkar.html

Pershan, C. (2017, August 17). Former Top Dog employee says he isn't a white supremacist, despite marching in Charlottesville rally. *Eater San Francisco*, https://sf.eater.com/2017/8/17/16163874/berkeley-top-dog-employee-resigns-denies-white-supremacist-charlottesville

Perry, D.M. (2017, August 17). Why it's important to name the Nazis. *Pacific Standard*, https://psmag.com/social-justice/naming-and-shaming-american-nazis

Price, G. (2017, August 15). White supremacist David Duke thanks Donald Trump for slamming Antifa and leftists at press conference. *Newsweek*, https://www.newsweek.com/duke-trump-thanks-antifa-651184

Pringle, R. (2017, August 18). Digital vigilantism after Charlottesville: get ready for more naming and shaming. *CBC News*, https://www.cbc.ca/news/technology/charlottesville-racism-twitter-doxxing-1.4251566

Ronson, J. (2015). *So You've Been Publicly Shamed*. New York, Riverhead.

Rosenberg, A. (2017, August 13). The Photo from Charlottesville that will define this moment in American history. *The Washington Post*, https://www.washingtonpost.com/news/act-four/wp/2017/08/13/the-photo-from-charlottesville-that-will-define-this-moment-in-american-history/?utm_term=.de52eef173e6

Selk, A. (2017, August 14). Twitter campaign is outing people who marched with white nationalists in Charlottesville. *The Washington Post*, https://www.washingtonpost.com/news/the-intersect/

wp/2017/08/14/a-twitter-campaign-is-outing-people-who-marched-with-white-nationalists-in-charlottesville/?utm_term=.4aa1ea7eff65

Shapira, I. (2018, March 16). Black man beaten in Charlottesville found not guilty of assaulting white supremacist. *Washington Post*, https://www. washingtonpost. com/local/black-man-beaten-in-charlottesville-found-not-guilty-of-assaulting-   white-supremacist/2018/03/16/92160a88-288f-11e8-b79d-f3d931db7f68_story. html?utm_term=.5823b4300d91

Suerth, J. (2017, August 15). The white nationalist whose father disowned him says family was doing the 'safest thing'. *CNN*, https://www.cnn. com/2017/08/15/us/dad-charlottesville-rally-letter-trnd/index.html

Sydell, L. (2017, August 15). Some are troubled by online shaming of Charlottesville rally participant. *National Public Radio*, https:// www.npr.org/sections/alltechconsidered/2017/08/15/543566757/ twitter-account-names-and-shames-far-right-activists-at-charlottesville

Teitel, E. (2017, August 16). Shame the Charlottesville white supremacists on social media. *Toronto Star*, https://www.thestar.com/news/canada/2017/08/16/ shame-the-charlottesville-white-supremacists-on-social-media-teitel.html

Thompson, M. (2017, August 12). The hoods are off. *The Atlantic*, https://www. theatlantic.com/national/archive/2017/08/the-hoods-are-off/536694

Toppo, G. (2018, September 27). Education for All... Even a 'Nazi'? *Inside Higher Ed*, https://www.insidehighered.com/news/2018/09/27/university-tests-free-speech-mettle-ensuring-graduation-charlottesville-marcher

Twin Cities Pioneer Press. (2017, August 14). Fargo father writes letter disavowing son who marched in Charlottesville. *Twincities.com*, https:// www.twincities.com/2017/08/14/fargo-father-writes-letter-disavowing-son-who-marched-in-charlottesville

Van Boom, D. (2017, August 14). Yes, you're racists: Twitter user names Virginia protestors. *CNet*, https://www.cnet.com/news/yes-youre-racist -twitter-user-names-charlottesville-unite-the-right

VICE News Documentary. (2017, August 14). *Charlottesville: Race and Terror*. VICE.com, https://news.vice.com/en_us/article/qvzn8p/vice-news-tonight -full-episode-charlottesville-race-and-terror

Victor, D. (2017, August 14). Amateur sleuths aim to identify Charlottesville marchers, but sometimes misfire. *New York Times*, https://www.nytimes. com/2017/08/14/us/charlottesville-doxxing.html

Wiest, B. (2017, August 15). Jennifer Lawrence asks the internet to help identify Charlottesville white supremacists. *Teen Vogue*, https://www.teenvogue.com/ story/jennifer-lawrence-help-identify-charlottesville-white-supremacists

Wildman, S. (2017, August 16). Why you see swastikas in America but not in Germany. *Vox*, https://www.vox.com/world/2017/8/16/16152088/ nazi-swastikas-germany-charlottesville

Doxing as Audience Vigilantism against Hate Speech

David M. Douglas

Doxing, the public release of personally identifiable information, is both a means of harassment and intimidation, and a tool for activism. Releasing personal information about individuals whose actions or stated beliefs harm others, or undermine social cohesion, removes the anonymity or obscurity that may foster these forms of antisocial behaviour. However, doxing may also be used to target those whose actions or beliefs pose no risk to others, or who merely do not follow social norms. In societies that value individualism (such as Western liberal democracies), anonymity and obscurity are important means of protecting individuality from the pressures of conformity and popular opinion, and allow us to develop ourselves and experiment with ways of living. Depriving someone of the protections anonymity and obscurity grant them should not be taken lightly. For doxing to effectively support activist goals, it must expose wrongdoing that the broader population (the activist's *audience*) will accept as a legitimate concern. Otherwise, activists risk creating sympathy for their target and ostracising themselves from the audience they wish to persuade.

Other chapters in this volume by Mojca M. Plesničar and Pika Šarf, and Tara Milbrandt analyse specific instances in which doxing was used by activists to shame those who use hate speech on social media, or who were present at a white supremacist rally, respectively. This chapter supplements these discussions by presenting a moral justification for doxing as audience vigilantism in response to hate speech. It draws on Daniel Trottier's (2017) account of digital vigilantism and Emma

 https://doi.org/10.11647/OBP.0200.10

Jane's (2017) analysis of feminist "digilantism" in response to Internet harassment and sexist hate speech. I argue that doxing that deanonymises a proponent of hate speech is an appropriate means of combating hate speech if it is intended to begin a process of deradicalisation.

Identifying sources and promoters of hate speech via doxing serves several purposes. Firstly, it increases the risk of engaging in hate speech by removing the speaker's anonymity and increasing their vulnerability to legal sanctions and social ostracism. Secondly, it draws attention to threatening behaviour that might otherwise be ignored. Finally, it may serve as a response by the vilified group, or their supporters, that they do not trust the authorities to adequately respond to acts of hate speech against them. Doxing may also be employed to delegitimise public officials who are either themselves anonymous sources of hate speech, or who support it, since promoting hate speech is incompatible with the duty of service to all citizens that public service requires.

This defence of doxing has a number of limitations. As it is a response to the tension between tolerance and freedom of speech, it is intended to apply to liberal democracies that value both. It also does not justify releasing any sort of personally identifiable information (that is, information about someone that can uniquely distinguish them from other people) about practitioners of hate speech. It uses an earlier analysis of doxing (Douglas, 2016) that distinguishes between doxing that is intended to remove someone from obscurity or anonymity (deanonymising doxing), doxing that make it easier to physically locate someone (targeting doxing) and doxing that reveals personal information that undermines the identified person's credibility (delegitimising doxing). Targeted doxing should also be avoided as the response risks going beyond what Kelly D. Hine calls "socially tolerable bounds" (1998, p. 1253) in her defence of vigilantism. In this case, targeted doxing creates the opportunity for vigilantes to physically intimidate or harm the identified individual. Outside of the potential harm caused to the targeted individual, this may undermine broader support for acts against hate speech.

I also acknowledge that unlike the cases of sexist hate speech Jane describes (in which the audience responds to specific messages by named individuals who do not disguise their identity), there is a significant risk of false positives, in which innocent individuals are erroneously identified as sources or promoters of hate speech. The negative consequences of mistaken identification mean that those who have erroneously identified an innocent person must take responsibility for correcting this error if this form of deanonymisation is to be permissible.

I will support this argument with short descriptions and discussions of two examples where doxing has been used to either identify proponents of hate speech, or where it is used by hate speech proponents to intimidate activists working against them. I also use the examples of sharing racist speech found on Facebook on the Zlovenija Tumblr page and identifying the participants of the "Unite the Right" rally that are described in other chapters by Plesničar and Šarf, and Milbrandt, respectively. Given the important of hate speech to my defence of this form of audience vigilantism, that is where I will begin my discussion.

Hate Speech

Raphael Cohen-Almagor (2015, p. 148) defines hate speech as "bias-motivated, hostile, malicious speech aimed at a person or a group of people because of some of their actual or perceived innate characteristics". It may also be described as group libel or group defamation (Waldron, 2012, p. 39). More generally, Jeremy Waldron (ibid., p. 4) describes hate speech as something undermining the public good that individuals in a society, from diverse backgrounds and belonging to different groups, will be able to live their lives without facing "hostility, violence, discrimination, or exclusion by others". It undermines the dignity of those singled out by hate speech by attacking their status as equal members of the community (ibid., p. 5). On a more visceral level, it provokes memories of historical oppression that continue to resonate with those whose identities have been marked as inferior in the past, and who still face discrimination today. In Charles R. Lawrence III's powerful words:

> There is a great difference between the offensiveness of words that you would rather not hear — because they are labeled dirty, impolite, or personally demeaning — and the *injury* inflicted by words that remind the world that you are fair game for physical attack, evoke in you all of the millions of cultural lessons regarding your inferiority that you have so

painstakingly repressed, and imprint upon you a badge of servitude and subservience for all the world to see. (1990, p. 461, emphasis in original)[1]

The continued existence of implicit and explicit biases against minorities (including hate speech itself) suggests that even well-intentioned states fail to practically reflect their stated commitments to political and social equality. Waldron (2012, p. 31) is right in saying that "the position of minority groups as equal members of a multi-racial, multi-ethnic, or religiously pluralistic society is not something that anyone can take for granted". The targets of hate speech may also believe that the state (or those implementing and enforcing the state's laws) will not take their concerns seriously (Schwencke, 2017).

The legal tolerance for hate speech differs between societies, even among those recognising the importance of freedom of expression (Sumner, 2003, pp. 144–45). The United States places a strong emphasis on the importance of freedom of expression, and so permits hate speech that would be illegal in other liberal democracies (Cohen-Almagor, 2015, p. 205; Mill, 2018). Even in liberal democracies that criminalise hate speech (such as Australia and the UK), the extent of the limitations they impose on freedom of expression is contested (Mill, 2018).

The targets of hate speech and those who regard it as a serious threat to social cohesion often resort to private measures (including vigilantism) to counter the expressions of hate they face. Such actions are self-defence by the targeted group, and serve two purposes: silencing the hate speech itself (the retributive purpose), and signalling to the broader community that such speech is unacceptable (the expressive purpose). Popular support for the vigilante's actions depends on the vigilante's justifications for why suppressing this instance of hate speech is more important than tolerating the speaker's right to express it.

Digital Vigilantism (DV) and 'Digilantism'

Trottier describes digital vigilantism (DV) as a response to a transgression that "seek[s] to render a targeted individual (or category of individual) visible through information sharing practices such as assembling and

---

1   I originally came across this quote in *Hate Crimes in Cyberspace* by Danielle Keats Citron (2014, p. 17).

publishing their personal details" (2017, p. 57). It is made possible by computer-mediated communication systems that facilitate informal groups in coordinating actions in response to transgressions, and dispersing once satisfied that their goal is achieved (ibid.).

Jane's concept of "digilantism" overlaps with Trottier's account of DV, and further shows how these activities differ from traditional vigilantism. Jane defines digilantism as "politically motivated (or punitively politically motivated) practices outside of the state that are designed to punish or bring others to account, in response to a perceived or actual dearth of institutional remedies" (2017, p. 3). This description goes beyond the traditional account of vigilantism described by Les Johnston (1996) by incorporating responses that might otherwise be classified as "activism" (Jane, 2017, pp. 3–4). Violence or threatened physical violence usually appear to be a necessary part of vigilantism (Dumsday, 2009; Hine, 1998, pp. 1248–9). Without physical violence (or the threat of it), vigilantism may appear to be just particularly robust activism. Nonetheless, the connection between vigilantism and violence may be maintained by broadening the concept of violence as "avoidable insults to basic human needs" (Gatlung 1990, p. 292). While Johan Gatlung uses this definition to underpin his conceptions of structural and cultural violence (which describe the processes of exploitation and the symbols and language that justify both direct physical violence and exploitation, respectively), this definition may be used to describe vigilantism as violence (either direct, physical violence, or the structural or cultural violence traditionally thought of as "non-violent") in response to direct, structural or cultural violence by the targets of such violence. Hine (1998, p. 1222) mentions citizens confronting and harassing drug dealers to force them to leave their community, and residents threatening to launch civil law suits against property owners to compel them to evict criminals, as examples of non-violent vigilantism. Such "non-violent" vigilantism should not be criminalised, Hine (ibid., p. 1252) argues, as the tendency to over-punish transgressors using physical violence makes vigilantism costly to society, rather than vigilantism itself. This allows Hine's concept of vigilantism without physical violence to fall within the scope of DV and digilantism.

A major form of DV is "weaponising" visibility through "naming and shaming" transgressive individuals or groups (Trottier, 2017, p.

56). Those targeted by DV are removed from obscurity by the public exposure of a transgression (or alleged transgression).[2] The power of such shaming comes from both the audience witnessing it, and the identified individual's knowledge that there is such an audience, who may themselves participate in further shaming them. In DV and digilantism, these are *mediated* audiences: they witness transgressions through computer-mediated communication systems, such as social media platforms. Furthermore, the audience can increase the visibility of the transgression by sharing and commenting on it on social media. As such, the vigilante audience need not be limited to the same geographical area or country as the targeted transgressor. Transgressions visible and provocative enough to provoke widespread disgust may face a global vigilante audience. Controversial, poor-taste or merely misunderstood social media posts are examples of such transgressions.

Doxing

Doxing is the deliberate release of personally identifiable information in a form that is easily accessible to others, usually with the aim of intimidating the identified person (Hawley, 2019, p. 201; Douglas, 2016, p. 199). Joan Donovan (2017) rightly notes that doxing offers "a powerful leveller for those who seek social justice when they know criminal justice is far out of reach". Using doxing to draw attention to wrongdoers is a form of private justice that comes under the umbrella of DV (Trottier, 2017, p. 56).

The information released by doxing are forms of identity knowledge about specific individuals. Elsewhere I distinguish between three types of doxing: deanonymising, targeting and delegitimising (Douglas, 2016, pp. 203–6). These types differ in what information is revealed about someone and the motive for doing so. Deanonymisation reveals information that connects an individual's anonymous or pseudonymous identity to their regular identity. Targeting reveals information about an individual that allows them to be physically located, such as their home address or workplace. Delegitimising reveals potentially embarrassing or

---

2   Daniel Solove vividly calls this the "digital scarlet letter" (2007, p. 76).

humiliating information about an individual. Each kind of doxing takes something from the identified person: anonymity (deanonymisation), obscurity (targeting) or credibility (delegitimisation) (ibid., p. 204). Recognising the different types of doxing is important to determine whether there is a plausible moral argument for releasing personal information.

Seeking anonymity is not necessarily a sign of wrongdoing. Gary T. Marx (1999) lists fifteen common rationales for anonymity (or pseudonymity) that are socially desirable. The purpose of seeking anonymity must be considered if deanonymisation is to be justifiable. There are clear cases for justifying deanonymisation when anonymity is adopted to avoid accountability for wrongdoing, and when a pseudonym is used to mislead others (for example, by using an alias to associate themselves with a particular group for some benefit). In these cases, doxing is a form of whistleblowing.

Deanonymisation only requires revealing information that establishes a connection between a pseudonym or actions performed anonymously, and some form of identity knowledge of an individual. One form of identity knowledge is an individual's *locatability*, which includes both their physical location and the means through which they can be contacted (ibid., p. 100). Revealing locatability information about an individual increases their vulnerability to harassment (if contact information is disclosed) and physical harm (if location information is disclosed).

If deanonymising and targeting doxing answer the 'who' and 'where' questions about an identity (ibid., p. 101), delegitimising doxing reveals 'why' this particular individual is of interest. It purports to reveal a transgression by the identified individual for which they deserve (in the view of those doxing them) to be publicly shamed. These transgressions may be breaches of social norms, immoral activities, deceptive or harmful behaviour, or anything else that may undermine the individual's reputation or publicly humiliate them. The transgression is from the perspective of those performing the doxing: the identified individual or the wider community may not recognise it as particularly troubling, threatening, controversial or transgressive at all.

Doxing in Response to Hate Speech

I consider four examples where doxing is used to either identify members of groups that promote hate speech, or members of groups that protest hate speech. These examples are: Anonymous' #OpKKK campaign to reveal the identities of Ku Klux Klan members; the display of racist speech found on Facebook, posted with the author's identity on the Zlovenija Tumblr page; the identification of individuals pictured taking part in the 2017 "Unite the Right" rally at Charlottesville, Virginia in the US; and attempts by right-wing groups to identify participants in Antifa protests. In each case, individuals or groups attempt to uncover and disclose identity knowledge (such as the common or legal names) of individuals. In the case of #OpKKK, the hacktivist collective Anonymous sought to reveal the membership of the Ku Klux Klan so that they could not conceal their racist beliefs and activities. In the Zlovenija example, the anonymous activists were naming individuals who expressed hate speech on social media. In the case of identifying participants in the "Unite the Right" rally, individuals sought to remove the obscurity of those who promoted hate speech in a public space. The final case, attempts by right-wing groups to identify members of Antifa groups, differs from the others in that doxing is being used against those who protest against hate speech. It serves as a contrast with the other cases in order to establish that the context within which doxing is used is significant for whether a group may use it to defend itself.

Anonymous and #OpKKK

The Ku Klux Klan (KKK) are an American white supremacist group that has existed in various forms since around 1866 (Law, 2009, p. 128). While its activity and membership has waxed and waned since the group's emergence, its long history of violence and the distinctive costumes that conceal its members' identities have made the KKK particularly notorious in the United States. It currently exists as a collection of localised groups that share the name, rituals and the white supremacist ideology of the original group (Southern Poverty Law Center, n.d.).

The impetus for #OpKKK was the distribution of leaflets by a KKK chapter threatening to use "deadly force" against those protesting the police shooting of Mike Brown in Ferguson, Missouri, on August 9, 2014 (Gilbert, 2014). Activists identifying themselves with Anonymous hacked two Twitter accounts connected to the KKK, and claimed to have gathered information about their members through their access to these accounts (Woolf & Stafford, 2015). Around this time, news reports from left-wing web sites stated that several US senators and mayors were on Anonymous' list of KKK members (Anonymous OpKKK, 2015). A Twitter account associated with Anonymous distanced itself from these reports (ibid.). A list of around 350 names was eventually released by those involved in #OpKKK (Anonymous, 2015). Some of those listed had already publicly stated their membership of the KKK (Woolf, 2015). The document listing the names of alleged KKK members contains a preface describing the activists' methods of data collection and a thoughtful account of their reasons for releasing this data (Anonymous, 2015).

Zlovenija

As Plesničar and Šarf describe in their chapter, Zlovenija was a Tumblr page where the anonymous author(s) posted screen captures of racist speech that related to migration to Slovenia. Examples of hate speech were removed if the speaker apologised. The anonymous authors of Zlovenija removed the examples of racist speech after posters displaying the posts featured on the site began to appear on the streets in Ljubljana and due to concerns about organised attempts to deanonymise the author(s).

Identifying "Unite the Right" Rally Participants

The August 2017 "Unite the Right" white-nationalist rally in Charlottesville, Virginia and the digital vigilantism that occurred in response are described in detail by Tara Milbrandt in another chapter of this book. For the purpose of this chapter, I will focus on two aspects of the doxing that happened to rally participants: whether the response was motivated by an acceptable goal, and the instances of mistaken identification that occurred.

This example differs from #OpKKK as the targets are limited to a particular group: those present at the Charlottesville rally in support of white nationalism. The identified individuals also made no attempt to conceal their identities at the rally. The @YesYoureRacist Twitter account also only listed the names of the identified individuals, making it deanonymising doxing (as they were removed from obscurity). It was also delegitimising doxing as it portrayed the identified individuals as white nationalists. It was not targeting doxing, as no locatability knowledge was revealed by the account.

Identifying Antifa Protesters

Anti-fascists (or Antifa) seek to disrupt the ability of fascist and far-right groups to organise and communicate their views to the public (Bray, 2017, pp. xiv–xv). Doxing perpetrators of hate speech (those creating or spreading hostile, biased and malicious works targeted at specific groups of people) is a controversial method of combating the support and propagation of such speech. For example, doxing is one tactic adopted by Antifa groups to silence members of fascist and far-right groups (ibid., pp. 86–87), although not all Antifa groups accept it as a legitimate tactic (Bartlett, 2015, p. 67). Similarly, fascist and far-right groups themselves use doxing to intimidate critics (such as journalists) (Wilson, 2018) and to expose Antifa members (Bartlett, 2015, p. 68).

Unlike the previous examples, this case covers instances where doxing is used against those who vigorously oppose hate speech and the right-wing groups who are at least sympathetic to it. This example is important for establishing that the activist's cause in doxing others is important for determining whether it can be defended as socially useful vigilantism. In other words, whether doxing opponents is self-defence for the activists themselves, or self-defence for both the activists themselves and the broader community.

Doxing as Audience Vigilantism

Doxing as a tool for audience vigilantism has three stages: uncovering personally identifiable information, releasing and announcing that information, and the audience acting on that information. For simplicity, I will call these the *discovery*, *release* and *response* stages of doxing as audience vigilantism. The discovery stage may be performed in secret by activists, while the release and response stages require audiences who serve as the potential vigilantes who will act against the identified individual. How the information is disseminated and presented in the release stage affects the potential audience, the likelihood that the audience will respond and how that audience will harass or shame the identified individual.

The discovery stage is performed by the activist, who has identified a transgressor (or potential transgressor). The activist uses whatever information is available to them to search for further identity knowledge about the transgressor. The activist may seek assistance in identifying an individual by releasing whatever information they have and asking others for further information. In this case, the discovery stage merges with the release and response stages.

The release stage has two components: the publication of identity knowledge about the targeted individual(s), and publicising the release of this information. Gaining publicity for the information release is necessary to create an audience who may act on it. Social media can serve a role, as it does for the discovery stage: in addition to providing evidence of the target's transgressions, it also offers an avenue for publicising the release of identity knowledge. In the #OpKKK example, the release stage was Anonymous' posting of information onto Pastebin (Anonymous, 2012) and announcing this on Twitter. In the Zlovenija example, the release stage was the posting of the racist speech and the identity of the speaker on the Zlovenija page. In the "Unite the Right" example, this stage was the posting of pictures of rally participants on the @YesYoureRacist Twitter account, which served as both publishing and publicising the release of this identity knowledge.

The response stage is the actual vigilante action the audience performs. It is the activist's goal in discovering and releasing information about the target. The audience may respond by further publicising the transgression and the transgressor's identity, or by using the identity knowledge to contact the transgressor. The first response seeks to shame the identified individual, while the second harasses or threatens them (or worse). The second type of response is traditional vigilantism, as it includes the threat of violence (Johnston, 1996). DV and digilantism only necessarily involves increasing the target's visibility, and so may include acts where only the first response occurs, or where both the first and the second occur. Ethical evaluations of vigilantism (such as Dumsday (2009)) may therefore be applied to cases that involve both the first and second response. As the literature on traditional vigilantism may be directly applied to the second type of response, my discussion will focus on the first type, where shame is used to punish the transgressor.

In both types of response, the audience's active involvement takes the response beyond the activist's control. The appearance of posters around Ljubljana containing posts from the Zlovenija page is an example of how the audience's response can differ from what the activist anticipates. As Jane (2017, pp. 5–6) rightly notes, digilantism (and social media activity generally) are characterised by "[c]haos, speed, unpredictability, strong affect, and spur-of-the-moment decisions". This unpredictability and lack of control makes audience vigilantism risky to initiate, and serves as a *prima facie* moral objection against it as the response is likely to be disproportionate to the transgression.

The #OpKKK example demonstrates the care necessary in performing the discovery and releases stages of doxing as DV, and the external factors that can compromise its effectiveness. The legitimate #OpKKK list described in broad terms how they collected the listed data. The decentralised and anarchic nature of Anonymous creates difficulties for the audience in clearly distinguishing between the 'legitimate' Anonymous #OpKKK list and the independent list. The apparent source of the first list did not claim to belong to Anonymous or to be connected with #OpKKK (Woolf & Stafford, 2015). This nuance and the confusion caused by the false initial reports of politicians appearing on the list reduced the impact that the release might otherwise have had. While Anonymous' unique character made it particularly difficult for the audience to identify 'official' Anonymous information releases from others, this problem exists for any activist group. An effective and responsible DV campaign therefore needs to present a clear identity to avoid confusion within the audience it seeks to inform and motivate.

Jane (2017) notes that Hine's account offers two criteria for vigilantism that should not carry criminal liability. These criteria also suggest how we might begin to morally evaluate DV. These criteria are that the vigilante's actions are based "on an accurate perception of social need", and that the act is within "socially tolerable bounds" (Hine, 1998, p. 1952). These criteria suggest some constraints on the possible motives and actions that might be defended as morally permissible DV. The first, an accurately perceived social need, limits the permissible causes that may motivate DV. These causes must be reasonable in the sense that they can be justified to those with other perspectives within their community (Stanley, 2015, p. 108). This rules out conspiracy theories and extremist political, racial or religious causes, as they cannot be described and defended using premises and evidence that are in principle justifiable to all. Following Hine, I will call this the *legitimate social need* criterion. This restriction on extremes also carries over to the second criterion, which is that the digital vigilante acts must not cause physical harm to persons, and the disruption caused must be temporary and limited to those responsible for the concern identified in the first criterion. Permissible DV cannot be indiscriminate, and must respond to injustices that are, in principle, recognisable to those unaffected by it. Again following Hine, I will call this the *socially tolerable bounds* criterion for DV.

The emphasis these criteria place on DV to be understandable and, in principle, acceptable to the broader community highlights how DV (and doxing as DV in particular) is *audience* vigilantism. DV's effectiveness in addressing the social concerns that motivate it depends on how well it presents its cause to the audience. Without audience support, this form of vigilantism cannot achieve its intended purpose. Extreme methods and political causes risk alienating audiences and creating sympathy and community support for the targets of DV. Activists who utilise audience vigilantism therefore have an interest in keeping their actions within limits to encourage and maintain popular support for their goals.

Shaming as Audience Vigilantism

Audience vigilantism replaces the physical violence of traditional vigilantism with the shaming of individual(s) who have transgressed against the community. Jacob Rowbottom (2013, p. 1) lists three goals for "naming and shaming" individuals: informal punishment, informing the public about their conduct and expressing disapproval for that conduct.

The use of shame as a legal punishment for wrongdoing offers a useful starting point for considering it as a vigilante punishment.

Shame punishments express that the punished is a certain sort of person (Nussbaum, 2004, p. 230). Shame punishments for hate speech, for example, express that the punished individual is a bigot with a hatred of a certain group of people. The person is made visible as someone of poor character, and so shame punishments risk permanently staining the identity of those they punish (ibid., p. 231). In contrast, guilt punishments express only that the punished has performed a wrongful act (ibid., p. 230). Nussbaum (ibid., p. 207) describes guilt as "a type of self-punishing anger, reacting to the perception that one has done a wrong or a harm". Guilt punishments condemn the act, while shame punishments condemn the person.[3]

This connection between shame and guilt suggests how shame punishments might be employed without necessarily alienating the transgressor from respectable society. Brooks (2008, p. 330) argues that shame punishments can be justified if used to inspire guilt within the wrongdoer. This moves the purpose of shaming from humiliation to *reintegration*: the individual's stigmatisation is temporary until they themselves recognise the wrongness of their actions. Reintegrative shaming follows the transgressor's shaming with efforts to return them to respectable society through limiting the time they are shamed, offering forgiveness for their actions and recognising that the transgression should not define the person's identity (Braithwaite, 1989, pp. 100–1). The purpose is to move from condemning transgressors *themselves* (they are being shamed by others for wrongdoing) to condemning their *actions* (they themselves feel guilt for wrongdoing, and this guilt can motivate them to change their behaviour). It should encourage them to change their behaviour and attitudes, and encourage their community to forgive their transgression, rather than permanently alienate them from it.

While these discussions of shame punishments within a legal system suggest that shaming may be justified as a punishment, its use by vigilantes introduces problems that make it more difficult to justify. Solove (2007, pp. 94–98) lists several concerns about Internet shaming: its permanence, its disproportionality, the lack of due process and its

---

3   Zlovenija is an example of this distinction. As the authors removed the post if the person who made the racist comment apologised, they inspired guilt in the speaker without permanently shaming them.

abuse for bullying and personal disputes. The permanence of Internet shaming (due to the accessibility of the shaming material via search engines, and the possibility that others have copied and redistributed it even if the original poster removes it) makes returning to obscurity (effectively reintegrating into society) difficult after being shamed. This is one of the motivations of the "right to be forgotten" (Jones, 2016, pp. 9–15).

The widespread accessibility of the humiliating material also makes Internet shaming particularly harmful. It lacks the definite end of reintegrative shaming, and the transgression may continue to define that person in their interactions with others. The widespread integration of the Internet into daily life makes it difficult to distance oneself from it to avoid encountering harassment (Franks, 2012, p. 682).

The risks associated with shame punishments imposed by vigilantes make them difficult to defend without considering their context. For those unable to seek legal action against legitimate threats to themselves and their communities, and who lack other effective alternatives to defend themselves against aggression, shaming punishments may be justified provided that they are used carefully. The shaming of hate-speech proponents should be directed towards encouraging them to reconsider their views and reintegrate into the broader community. Excessive shaming and public humiliation risk being counter-productive, as social support (and the loss of it) is an important factor in holding and rejecting radical beliefs (Koehler, 2017, p. 17). The concept of reintegrative shaming also suggests how shaming by a vigilante audience might be kept within "socially tolerable bounds". Defending themselves against hate speech also serves as an 'accurately perceived social need' for minority groups.

#OpKKK certainly fulfils the legitimate social need criterion for DV: the KKK exists, it has a history of violence and the fact that some members are comfortable enough to publicly claim to be members suggests that legal responses to the hate speech it promotes are insufficient. Publicising the membership of the KKK draws attention to the threat the organisation poses to others within US society. What of the socially tolerable bounds criterion? Ideally, those identified as KKK members would go through a process of reintegrative shaming, which may involve publicly renouncing their membership and assisting law enforcement agencies with information about criminal activity performed by the organisation. This, of course, carries personal risk for such individuals, but it serves as a clear public signal of guilt about their former harmful transgressions. The community would also be obliged to protect those who have renounced their transgressions from reprisals. The former transgressor and the community are then reconciled through their newfound mutual assistance: the community through reforming someone whose views and actions were harmful to others and obtaining useful information to prevent further hate crimes and hate speech, and the transgressor through protection against reprisals and gaining a more balanced and nuanced perspective on the society in which they live.

The Zlovenija page was motivated by a concern about the racism within public discussions of migrants arriving in Slovenia. It had a legitimate social need as a formal attempt to combat the hate speech found on social media. It also arguably meets the tolerable social bounds criterion. While an argument can be made that including a direct link to the speaker's Facebook post increased the risk of targeting doxing occurring (since it increased the ease with which location information about the individual could be found if it is included in the person's profile), the Zlovenija authors acted responsibly by removing the identity information they posted once they became concerned that they were losing control over how this information was being used. Their removal of posts after the speaker apologised also demonstrates the authors' responsibility in seeking to limit the shaming of those they identified.

The violence and hate speech at the "Unite the Right" rally provide clear evidence that there is a legitimate social need to defend the community against white nationalism. The apparent reluctance of law enforcement to intervene and keep protesters and counter-protesters apart (Thompson, 2017), and the presence of citizen militias whose sympathies were unclear (Gunter & Hughes, 2018) might also be used to argue that the legal means of protecting the community are insufficient and that audience vigilantism is necessary.

These limitations assist in meeting the tolerable social bounds criterion. However, revealing any form of identity knowledge makes it easier to find locatability information about an individual, so the fact that @YesYoureRacist did not itself reveal locatability information does not mean that those identified could not be targeted (Ellis, 2017). The relative anonymity of participating in a large public protest might also encourage individuals to express views they might otherwise conceal. Presence in a crowd creates the possibility of *deindividuation* occurring, which might drive individuals to extreme acts that they would otherwise avoid (Douglas, 2010).

These objections may be addressed by emphasising the importance that the shaming of audience vigilantism must be reintegrative. As in the previous example of named-and-shamed KKK members, those identified as white nationalists should be assisted in coming to recognise the prejudices that drive their views and to renounce their earlier racist beliefs. As with reintegrating former KKK members, it will be difficult for many to readmit those who previously supported racist views back into their community. Nonetheless, such acceptance, after those who have been shamed feel genuine guilt for their actions, is necessary to reduce the risk of ostracism, which would further alienate and radicalise those with racist and prejudicial views.

The example of doxing Antifa activists is crucial to establish the importance of the legitimate social need criterion. If the activist's cause is irrelevant to this evaluation, any moral permissibility granted to the doxing of far-right activists would also hold for doxing Antifa and other social justice activists. Both Antifa and far-right groups attempt to suppress opposing political speech, and both perceive themselves as defending their communities. However, the legitimacy of their perceptions of their community and the threats they are reacting against differ significantly.

Far-right or 'alt-right' groups that attempt to suppress subversive expression believe they are defending their community against cultural, moral and/or social corruption. However, their flawed or self-serving understandings of culture and race undermine their conception of 'community'. The concept of 'whiteness' motivating many far-right and alt-right activists incorporates (at least elements of) white supremacy, the ideology that 'white people' are in some way intrinsically superior to other peoples, and this superiority justifies these people having unearned privileges and power in society (Beirich & Potok, 2011). The doxing of anti-fascist and other social justice activists by far-right and alt-right activists is the use of audience vigilantism to silence challenges to white privilege. To meet the legitimate social need criterion, far-right and alt-right activists would need other groups in society to accept the legitimacy of white privilege (and that others must therefore accept their intrinsic inferiority). Any society that claims to accept political and social equality (such as liberal democracies) must reject such claims. Fascists and far-right extremists therefore lack the legitimate social need criterion for audience vigilantism.

Conclusion

Vigilantism of any form will always be morally controversial. Nonetheless, for those who have legitimate concerns about the ability of law enforcement to protect themselves and their communities from harm, vigilantism may be a defensible option. Digital vigilantism, in the form of doxing those who threaten harm to communities, is a viable option if it incorporates reintegrative shaming. Without the possibility that those who are exposed by digital vigilantism can be reintegrated into their communities, DV risks further alienating them and reinforcing their extreme views.

Not all justifications for doxing transgressors are equally legitimate. Hate speech, however, certainly is a legitimate concern. Where the law prohibits hate speech, its victims should seek legal avenues against it. If the law is silent about serious expressions of hate, those who face them may have a legitimate reason to turn to the use of audience vigilantism (including doxing) to defend themselves, provided that this serves as the start of an effort to reintegrate proponents of hate speech into a tolerant society that respects others.

References

Anonymous. (2015). Official OpKKK HoodsOff 2015 Data Release. *Pastebin.com.* Paste Site, https://pastebin.com/wbvP95wg

Anonymous OpKKK. (2015). *Snopes.com,* https://www.snopes.com/fact-check/anonymous-opkkk

Bartlett, J. (2015). *The Dark Net.* London: Windmill Books.

Beirich, H., & Potok, M. (2011). White supremacy. In S. M. Caliendo & C. D. McIlwain (eds), *The Routledge Companion to Race and Ethnicity* (pp. 232–34). London; New York: Routledge.

Braithwaite, J. (1989). *Crime, Shame and Reintegration*. Cambridge: Cambridge University Press.

Bray, M. (2017). *Antifa: The Anti-Fascist Handbook*. Melbourne: Melbourne University Press.

Brooks, T. (2008). Shame on you, shame on me? Nussbaum on shame punishment. *Journal of Applied Philosophy*, 25(4), 322–44, https://doi.org/10.1111/j.1468-5930.2008.00403.x

Citron, D. K. (2014). *Hate Crimes in Cyberspace*. Cambridge, Mass.: Harvard University Press.

Cohen-Almagor, R. (2015). *Confronting the Internet's Dark Side: Moral and Social Responsibility on the Free Highway*. New York: Cambridge University Press.

Donovan, J. (2017). Refuse and resist! *Limn*, https://limn.it/articles/refuse-and-resist

Douglas, D. M. (2016). Doxing: A conceptual analysis. *Ethics and Information Technology* 18(3), 199–210, https://doi.org/10.1007/s10676-016-9406-0

Douglas, K. M. (2010). Deindividuation. In Jackson, I. I. R. L. & Hogg, M. A. (eds), *Encyclopedia of Identity* (pp. 199–202). Thousand Oaks: SAGE Publications.

Dumsday, T. (2009). On cheering Charles Bronson: The ethics of vigilantism. *The Southern Journal of Philosophy*, 47(1), 49–67, https://doi.org/10.1111/j.2041-6962.2009.tb00131.x

Ellis, E. G. (2017, August 17). Doxing is a perilous form of justice — even when it's outing Nazis. *WIRED*, https://www.wired.com/story/doxing-charlottesville

Franks, M. A. (2012). Sexual harassment 2.0. *Maryland Law Review*, 71(3), 655–704.

Gatlung, J. (1990). Cultural violence. *Journal of Peace Research*, 27(3), 291–305, https://doi.org/10.1177%2F0022343390027003005

Gilbert, D. (2014, November 21). Anonymous hacks Ku Klux Klan Twitter accounts and websites following Ferguson threats. *International Business Times UK*, https://www.ibtimes.co.uk/anonymous-hacks-ku-klux-klan-twitter-accounts-websites-following-ferguson-threats-1475127

Gunter, J., & Hughes, R. (2018, August 9). Charlottesville remembered: 'A battle for the soul of America'. *BBC News*, https://www.bbc.com/news/world-us-canada-44619374

Hawley, G. (2019). *The Alt-Right: What Everyone Needs to Know*. New York, NY: Oxford University Press.

Hine, K. D. (1998). Vigilantism revisited: An economic analysis of the law of extra-judicial self-help or why can't Dick shoot Henry for stealing Jane's truck? *The American University Law Review, 47*, 1221–54.

Jane, E. A. (2017). Feminist digilante responses to a slut-shaming on Facebook. *Social Media + Society*, 3(2), 1–10, https://doi.org/10.1177%2F2056305117705996

Johnston, L. (1996). What is vigilantism? *The British Journal of Criminology*, 36(2), 220–36, https://doi.org/10.1093/oxfordjournals.bjc.a014083

Jones, M. L. (2016). *Ctrl + Z: The Right to Be Forgotten*. New York: NYU Press.

Koehler, D. (2017). *Understanding Deradicalization: Methods, Tools and Programs for Countering Violent Extremism*. London and New York: Routledge.

Law, R. D. (2009). *Terrorism: A History*. Cambridge: Polity Press.

Lawrence III, C. R. (1990). If he hollers let him go: Regulating racist speech on campus. *Duke Law Journal*, 1990(3), 431–83.

Marx, G. T. (1999). What's in a name? Some reflections on the sociology of anonymity. *The Information Society*, 15(2), 99–112, https://doi.org/10.1080/019722499128565

Mill, D. van. (2018). Freedom of speech. In E. N. Zalta (ed.), *The Stanford Encyclopedia of Philosophy* (Summer 2018). Metaphysics Research Lab, Stanford University, https://plato.stanford.edu/archives/sum2018/entries/freedom-speech

Nussbaum, M. C. (2004). *Hiding from Humanity: Disgust, Shame, and the Law*. Princeton, New Jersey: Princeton University Press.

Rowbottom, J. (2013). To Punish, inform, and criticise: The goals of naming and shaming. In J. Petley (ed.), *Media and Public Shaming: Drawing the Boundaries of Disclosure* (pp. 1–18). London: I. B. Tauris & Co.

Schwencke, K. (2017, July 31). Confusion, fear, cynicism: Why people don't report hate. *ProPublica*. text/html, https://www.propublica.org/article/confusion-fear-cynicism-why-people-dont-report-hate-incidents

Solove, D. J. (2007). *The Future of Reputation: Gossip, Rumor, and Privacy on the Internet*. New Haven: Yale University Press.

Southern Poverty Law Center. (n.d.). Ku Klux Klan. *Southern Poverty Law Center*, https://www.splcenter.org/fighting-hate/extremist-files/ideology/ku-klux-klan

Stanley, J. (2015). *How Propaganda Works*. Princeton, New Jersey: Princeton University Press.

Sumner, L. W. (2003). Hate crimes, literature, and speech. In R. G. Frey & C. H. Wellman (eds), *A Companion to Applied Ethics* (pp. 142–53). Malden, MA: Blackwell Publishing.

Thompson, A. C. (2017, August 12). Police stood by as mayhem mounted in Charlottesville. *ProPublica*. text/html, https://www.propublica.org/article/police-stood-by-as-mayhem-mounted-in-charlottesville

Trottier, D. (2017). Digital vigilantism as weaponisation of visibility. *Philosophy & Technology*, 30(1), 55–72, https://doi.org/10.1007/s13347-016-0216-4

Waldron, J. (2012). *The Harm in Hate Speech*. Cambridge, Mass.: Harvard University Press.

Wilson, J. (2018, June 14). Doxxing, assault, death threats: The new dangers facing US journalists covering extremism. *The Guardian*, http://www.theguardian.com/world/2018/jun/14/doxxing-assault-death-threats-the-new-dangers-facing-us-journalists-covering-extremism

Woolf, N. (2015, November 6). Anonymous leaks identities of 350 alleged Ku Klux Klan members. *The Guardian*, https://www.theguardian.com/technology/2015/nov/06/anonymous-ku-klux-klan-name-leak

Woolf, N., & Stafford, Z. (2015, November 3). Anonymous denies releasing incorrect Ku Klux Klan member information. *The Guardian*, https://www.theguardian.com/technology/2015/nov/03/anonymous-denies-involvement-ku-klux-klan-data

ZLOvenija. (2015), https://zlovenija.tumblr.com/

Citizens as Aides or Adversaries? Police Responses to Digital Vigilantism

Rianne Dekker and Albert Meijer

Introduction[1]

On social media, citizens are engaging in tasks that traditionally fall within the authority of law enforcement agencies (LEAs). Examples include web-sleuthing collectives solving criminal cases or searching for missing persons (Yardley et al., 2016), specialised networks of paedophile-hunters (Campbell, 2016; Nhan et al., 2017), hacktivist groups revealing cybersecurity breaches or hacking back (E Silva, 2018; Schmidle, 2018) and online neighbourhood-watch schemes (Lub, 2018). Social media has opened up new sources of information about crime to citizens, and it facilitates participation in crime fighting. This includes public denunciation of unwanted behaviour, digital forensics, open source intelligence and crowdsourcing. Cultural norms on social media incite such new forms of civic engagement with public security: social media is non-hierarchical and users have traditionally approached it as a communitarian space governed by libertarian values (Nhan et al., 2017, p. 345).

Online acts of criminal investigation, crime prevention and the denunciation of crime and deviance by citizens, have been gathered

1   The research leading to this chapter has received funding from the European Union's Horizon 2020 Research and Innovation Program, under Grant Agreement no 700281.

under the labels 'do-it-yourself (DIY) policing' and 'digital vigilantism' (or 'digilantism'). Both concepts refer to citizens performing activities that fall within the discretion of LEAs. At the same time, there is a notable difference between these concepts: DIY policing or digital civilian policing emphasises that it is motivated by a desire to assist law enforcement, for example by analysing available information to identify evidence and suspects (Nhan et al., 2017, p. 347). Usually, DIY police participants collect information on actual or potential crimes and relay this information to law enforcement (Huey et al., 2012, p. 85). In some cases, this is volunteered and in others it occurs in response to official calls for assistance with police work. In contrast, the concept of digital vigilantism stresses the active bypassing of law enforcement and using the public nature of social media for retaliation (Trottier, 2017). Digital vigilantism also includes pursuit and denunciation of a broader set of offences that are immoral rather than illegal. It is characterised by a general perception that law enforcement and the criminal justice system are falling short and different methods of criminal investigation and justice are required (Johnston, 1996; Schuberth, 2013). One could say that the concept of DIY policing highlights the desirable side of participative practices (citizens wanting to contribute to law enforcement efforts), whereas digital vigilantism highlights its negative side (citizens taking public security matters into their own hands).

The concepts of DIY policing and digital vigilantism reflect a normative discussion about the role of citizens in policing, as well as different perceptions the police may hold towards this relatively new type of co-production of public security (cf. Brandsen & Pestoff, 2006). Public security is traditionally governed by the state holding the monopoly on the legitimate use of physical force in a central and hierarchical way, making co-production in this domain disputed. Police responses to different acts of online engagement with public security highlight where normative boundaries between DIY policing and digital vigilantism are drawn. The law enforcement perspective, however, is often missing in research into online engagement with public security. In what cases do the police consider citizens engaged in policing with the support of Web 2.0 as aides or as adversaries? Based on qualitative analysis of round-table discussions among representatives of European law enforcement agencies (LEAs) and other public organisations active in the domain of public security — including local governments, ministries and national and supranational networks and agencies — this chapter addresses the research question: How do law enforcement authorities decide whether digital contributions of citizens to public security are acceptable?

It is relevant to study law enforcement's stance on the issue because we have seen examples of DIY policing and digital vigilantism in many different countries and even across borders. This study focuses on the perspectives of European law enforcement agencies and reflects upon the generalisability of their views to other police forces worldwide. Furthermore, public debate on the desirability of online citizen engagement with public security is growing. As authorities in the domain of public security, LEAs are in a position to informally and formally encourage or discourage various acts of online engagement with public security. According to Huey et al. (2012, p. 95) "continued efforts should be made to understand further police attitudes towards these groups and how more fruitful co-operative relations could be developed".

By studying the perceptions of LEAs we also contribute to a theoretical understanding of which new patterns of co-production between law enforcement agencies and (collectives of) citizens are developing in an information age. Public administration literature claims that social media is strengthening co-production (Linders, 2012; Meijer, 2012). This chapter develops a typology to come to a more fine-grained understanding of the manifold forms of online co-production of public security, and discusses several ways to guide desirable and undesirable practices.

Online Co-Production of Public Security

Over the past decades, governments have moved from providing public services themselves to increasingly involving civil-society actors and citizens in the provision of public services. Public administration studies of co-production describe examples in healthcare, social welfare, community services and other public domains (Brandsen & Pestoff, 2006; Voorberg et al., 2015). Co-production has also made its way into the domain of public security, with strategies of plural policing and community policing. The concept of plural policing relates to how responsibilities for policing and security services extend from sovereign states to private companies, transnational arrangements and citizens (Loader, 2000; O'Neill & Fyfe, 2017). Community policing has emerged as a police operating paradigm of close collaboration with citizens to maintain public security. Community policing entails informing and engaging citizens as experts within their local context, and being responsive to their information and requests (Mastrofski et al., 1995; Skogan & Williamson, 2008). In these policing strategies, non-state actors and citizens are not only 'clients' of the police, but also active contributors to the production of public security (Percy, 1978). Consequently, modern sovereign states no longer have a monopoly on the use of legitimate force within given spatial boundaries.

The platforms of Web 2.0 are strengthening collaboration with citizens in various public domains, including public security (Linders, 2012). They facilitate sharing and discussion of user-generated content within communities of interest (Haythornthwaite, 2005, p. 140) and enables a direct connection with government (Frissen et al., 2008). Meijer (2012, p. 1158) outlines how new media are an important facilitator for new forms of co-production, because the costs of connecting to citizens have been reduced drastically and the new technologies create opportunities to interact 24/7. The Citizen's Net (*Burgernet*) application (app) — one of the cases in this study — enables the Dutch police to send out a digital message to call upon the help of citizens within a specific geographical area. It enables citizens to participate in solving local crime or missing-persons cases in the 'golden hour' directly after the incident. Citizens can respond with their information and receive a message when the situation is solved and their information is no longer requested. Such instantaneous, rich and synchronous forms of interaction between citizens and government can hardly be created without the networked infrastructure provided by social media.

Linders (2012) proposes a typology of co-production supported by social media in which collaboration between government and citizens can take different forms. He distinguishes "government as a platform", "citizen sourcing" and "do-it-yourself government" (ibid., p. 447). In government as a platform, the initiative for co-production lies with government, reaching out to citizens for specific forms of input. The "Citizen's Net" (*Burgernet*) app from the Dutch police would be an example of this (cf. Meijer, 2012; 2015). In citizen sourcing, the initiative for co-production lies with citizens. The public helps government to be more responsive and effective, for example, by reporting local disturbances to the police. Government holds the primary responsibility for action, but citizens influence the direction and outcomes, improve the government's situational awareness, and may even help to execute government services on a day-to-day basis. Already, in these government-led types of digitally supported co-production, we see the risk of citizens infringing upon each other's privacy, and the risk of citizens taking vigilante actions. Participation is sometimes motivated by entertainment and a notion of gaming, besides or instead of a motive of civic responsibility (Meijer, 2012, p. 1168): "Intervening in police work turns into a real life game in which everybody can participate. Get a text message, look out of your window, and catch the thief". Excitement about participation in police work can become problematic when it turns into a competition between citizens, and this might encourage unethical or even illegal behaviour in order to solve crime.

These risks become even greater when online co-production is not initiated by, or does not occur in close collaboration with government. Do-it-yourself policing and digital vigilantism would fall into the category of 'do-it-yourself government'. Social media has opened up opportunities for this type of citizen-to-citizen co-production of public security. This poses larger risks to government than online forms of co-production that are initiated and closely coordinated by government (Linders, 2012). While possibly being very effective and low-cost for government, communities of interest engaged with this form of co-production may step out of line. How is this 'line' defined by government actors in the domain of public security? And how does this distinction generate different police responses that are intended to fit online co-production within their standards of fruitful cooperation? These questions, which are still unanswered in public administration literature, will be addressed in this chapter.

Method

Data on attitudes and responses towards online co-production of public security were collected in round-table discussions amongst public security practitioners. Six European practitioner workshops on various topics related to DIY policing and digital vigilantism were organised over the course of 2017 and 2018 in the context of the Horizon 2020 project Medi@4Sec (www.media4sec.eu). The topics of these workshops were: DIY Policing, Riots & Mass Gatherings; the Dark Web; Everyday Policing; Trolling; and Innovative Market Solutions. A variety of practitioners from European LEAs and other organisations active in the domain of public security were invited, based on their experience with the workshop themes. This included representatives of local and national police forces, police colleges and police networks, but also representatives from local, regional and national governments, NGOs, private companies and research institutes (Table 11.1). Practitioners came from various Northern, Southern, Central and Eastern European countries, but representatives from countries that were more actively engaging with social media — such as the UK and the Netherlands — were overrepresented (Figure 11.1). The numbers of workshop participants ranged between 30–40 for each workshop, creating a total of 215 workshop participants. This total includes approximately 30 participants who attended multiple workshops, so the total of unique participants is around 150.

The round-table discussions were led according to the World Café format. This format entails collaborative group dialogues wherein knowledge is gathered and shared amongst practitioners. It stimulates thinking about *current* and *ideal* practices by creating an informal sphere of discussion (Stewart, 2005; Fouché & Light, 2011). The goal of the round-table discussions in the World Café format was to formulate recommendations and action points for public security actors. Discussions at each table included between four and six practitioners and took 30 to 45 minutes per round table, before participants moved on to a second round table with a different composition of practitioners. Each practitioner participated in two round-table discussions per workshop. Two 'table hosts' from the project consortium moderated the discussions and took notes. After a short round of introduction, the main questions leading the debate in each of the workshops were: In what ways have you/has your organisation encountered this phenomenon? What are current practices? How could these be improved into ideal practices? The round-table discussions took place under Chatham House rules, creating an open discussion. Table hosts summarised the discussion on paper and publicly presented the main outcomes to the workshop participants to collect final questions and feedback.

Table 11.1: Sectors represented by workshop participants

Sector	N
Police	109
Research	28
Private sector	24
Local government	18
Regional/national government	21
NGO	13
Other	2
Total	215

Fig. 11.1   Countries represented by workshop participants (Total N=215)
*Three private-sector delegates represented organisations from the
United States.

For the research aims of this chapter, anonymised summaries of the
round-table discussions were qualitatively coded. This entailed a
process of open coding in dialogue with the focus of the research
question. We coded (1) various forms of online citizen co-production
of public security that are distinguished by law enforcement authorities;
(2) the response they received; and (3) whether they are deemed
acceptable or unacceptable and why. This explorative analysis provides
an image of which acts of online co-production of public security are
considered to be helpful or disruptive by law enforcement authorities

in Europe, and how they are therefore met with different responses. It reveals how police professionals discursively construct citizens as aides or adversaries.

A limitation of our method is that the workshops and round tables each focused on a distinctive topic, such as 'DIY Policing' and 'Everyday policing' (with a more positive connotation) or 'trolling' (with a negative connotation). This influenced the tone of the discussion, but still left space for different interpretations and opinions — as the data show. Because the round-table discussions took place under Chatham House rules, our analysis was based on anonymised summaries of the discussions and we were unable to link statements to specific actors, nor could we distinguish whether statements were broadly supported by different actors. The summaries represent the majority views and the data are presented as general opinions. This means that we refrain from making statements on the prevalence of views and only use direct quotes when these were very strongly voiced and stressed in the summary reports.

Results

Online co-production of public security is responded to in various ways by practitioners, highlighting different attitudes towards different forms of engagement. The sections below outline which acts of online engagement are considered helpful and which are considered disruptive by LEAs and other public security actors. Based on analysis of practitioner dialogues, we interpret where these discursive boundaries are drawn by focusing on specific policing tasks and images of the citizens involved.

Accepted Forms of Online Co-Production of Public Security

Online acts of denouncing crime are generally evaluated positively by public security practitioners. Sometimes denunciation happens implicitly when criminal acts are shamed or mocked, and sometimes this is done directly when citizens discipline the behaviour of others on social media. This type of online engagement is generally considered as a helpful form of crime prevention. Public security actors expect it to create enhanced awareness of the rule of law and to reinforce societal norms of accepted behaviour and deviance. Discussions during the trolling and DIY policing workshops highlighted that this form of engagement in crime prevention is seen as a positive contribution to police efforts.

More institutionalised forms of participation in crime prevention are also welcomed. For example, when citizens are sharing police warnings through social media — as discussed in the Everyday Policing workshop. This is expected to raise citizens' overall awareness of public security risks and to enable them to deal with minor issues amongst themselves before they escalate to a level requiring police intervention. This more formal and government-led form of engagement and collaboration in crime prevention is expected to enhance citizens' trust in the police as a modern, professional and open organisation, and to reinforce good relations between police and the public. The Innovative Market Solutions workshop indicates that several European police forces are using, acquiring or developing online tools or apps to encourage participation in crime prevention.

Other acts of online policing, besides engagement with crime prevention, are seen as more risky, but are generally valued when they resemble offline forms of collaboration with police. Two aspects mentioned during the DIY policing workshop are key in distinguishing these types of acts as helpful: first, collaborating with the police by, for example, bringing tips on cases, evidence or suspects to the police. Citizens doing this are seen as aides when they share the objectives of public security actors and are collaborating within their professional standards. A second aspect based on which practitioners distinguish this behaviour as acceptable is when online co-production focuses on cases directly affecting citizens' own neighbourhoods or communities. When citizens are former or potential victims and have a legitimate concern for their personal safety, public security practitioners are understanding of their engagement and involvement. Both aspects reflect the ideal of community policing.

Online co-production in activities that go beyond this operating philosophy of community policing are approached more reluctantly. Online open source investigations by the Bellingcat collective and by citizens after the Boston Marathon bombings were referenced during the DIY policing workshop as prominent examples of this. Their actions were considered as risky, since they led to premature accusations and interference with ongoing operations. However, several practitioners in the DIY Policing, Riots and Mass Gatherings and Everyday Policing workshops noted that citizens engaging in these types of online co-production of safety were also sometimes aiding police work. They can act as additional 'eyes and ears' of the police when they are investigating large amounts of evidence using their own expertise and professionalism (cf. Nhan et al., 2017). Collectives engaged in investigating crimes and public disorder are seen as having a broad range of skills, which can provide interesting new leads. Also, citizens policing the social spaces of Web 2.0 — for example in tracing illegal activity on the Dark Web — are considered helpful. Many public security practitioners see their organisations as under-resourced, which prevents them from having a meaningful presence online (Dark web workshop; cf. Huey et al., 2012). Online engagement with crime and deviance beyond citizens' own locality is approached with caution, but some practitioners note that it is only logical that social media are pushing the boundaries of the locally-based model of community policing towards matters outside of citizens' own communities and towards the online space (DIY Policing workshop).

Unacceptable Forms of Online Co-Production of Public Security

Forms of online co-production that go beyond collaboration with LEAs within the citizens' local context are generally deemed disruptive. Public security actors in the DIY Trolling workshops expressed two main concerns: these forms of online co-production can be harmful to other citizens and society and they can be harmful to the efforts of law enforcement.

Harm to Citizens and Society

Three arguments were presented about why online co-production can be harmful to citizens and society: Firstly, online co-production is seen as harmful to other citizens and society when *premature accusations that other citizens are criminal offenders are voiced online.* Online collaboration can give way to rampant speculation, including the mislabelling of innocent actions as suspicious activities and the misidentification of innocent individuals as legitimate suspects (cf. Nhan et al., 2017, p. 353). This may happen, for example, in online neighbourhood-watch groups (DIY Policing workshop). Online manhunts are most harmful when they concern innocent suspects, but even when speculations in the end turn out to be correct, some public security practitioners see this as harmful to the suspect and prosecution of the case. Using online naming and shaming as a means of reprisal brings unnecessary harm to the suspect, and it is not usually possible for the suspect to be forgotten by having all online material deleted after sentencing is completed (cf. Kohm, 2009; Mayer-Schönberger, 2009). DIY Policing and Trolling workshop participants noted that the public shaming of suspects can lower the sentencing in court. Here, practitioners distinguish acts of naming and shaming as a way of crime prevention and retaliation. It is only accepted when its main purpose is warning others not to engage in or not to become a victim of this kind of behaviour.

Secondly, it was argued that online engagement with public security may *focus only on effectiveness and not on process values.* It was mentioned in the DIY Policing workshop that individuals and collectives who are engaged with public security mainly strive for effectiveness, and that this is the only measure on which they grade their success. They aim for quick and high numbers of apprehensions. However, they do not adhere to other public values that enable due process in criminal investigations (cf. Jørgensen & Bozeman, 2007; De Graaf & Meijer, 2019). The values that were mentioned as lacking include the protection of data and privacy, necessity and proportionality, non-discrimination and accountability for one's actions. Decisions about who to punish and how to do this are not transparent, accountable or democratically legitimate in such cases. In this respect, the authority of online crime fighters is highly questionable, even when their targets are quite obviously engaged in criminal behaviour (cf. Rizza et al., 2012). Also, citizens' measurement of effectiveness was critically discussed in the DIY Policing workshop. It was stated that digital vigilante groups often target 'low-hanging fruits' that are easily caught but are also causing relatively little harm. Apprehending more professional offenders requires more elaborate investigation, which takes time, and apprehension rates might thus be lower. However, when measured in years of sentencing instead of numbers of apprehensions, police cases can be seen as more successful.

Another related concern of public security practitioners is when individuals or groups engage in *unprofessional practices of criminal investigation and punishment* (DIY Policing workshop; cf. Huey et al. 2012). Acts that are clearly labelled in the DIY Policing and Trolling workshops as 'vigilante' include entrapment, for example by acting as a decoy to uncover paedophiles, infiltrating websites and organisations, illegitimate ways of collecting evidence (for example the use of drone images) and doxing (Trolling workshop). The latter entails acts of harvesting and publishing private information about a particular individual online (cf. Trottier, 2017). This is seen as not only harmful to suspects, but possibly also to the digital vigilantes themselves when they are dealing with dangerous suspects. They can become a victim of criminals who feel threatened by digital vigilantes.

Harm to Police Operations

Practitioners also identified several dangers to police work of online co-production of public security. Again, three arguments were provided. First, practitioners on a local and national level voiced a very practical concern that an abundance of online engagement can *overburden police with information and demands for intervention* (Everyday Policing workshop). These demands might not always be met in case of petty incidents, because the police have to prioritise due to limited resources (cf. Nhan et al., 2017). When the police become more easily approachable through its social media presence or specialised apps, practitioners expect that the threshold to seek the help of law enforcement will become lower (DIY Policing workshop). Particularly, practitioners fear a growing number of requests related to offenses in cyberspace such as trolling, cyber-bullying and online shaming. However, much of this is not illegal and is dealt with most easily by moderation implemented by social media platforms, or solved by citizens amongst themselves (Trolling workshop). The presence on social media of police and police apps raises the expectation that all notifications will be dealt with. If this expectation is unfulfilled, that might undermine trust in police and encourage vigilante acts.

Practitioners are also concerned that online engagement with crime may *jeopardise ongoing police investigations and criminal prosecution of cases.* Citizens can, for example, resort to unlawful acts to collect evidence, tamper with evidence or publish information online that is kept classified in a police investigation (DIY Policing workshop). Public anti-authoritarianism — which is typical to some online platforms — coupled with a personal sense of right and wrong, often conflicts with legal standards and complicates police efforts. In response, we learned during the Innovative Market Solutions workshop that LEAs are using data mining and analysis tools to keep track of online engagement with ongoing police investigations (cf. Žitnik et al., 2018). This helps identify information that might distort the investigation, such as incorrect information that causes panic or leads to harmful actions. Information from online sources may also bring new leads for the investigation. Some practitioners, however, note that online publics only rarely bring new information to the table and often cause more harm than benefit (DIY Policing workshop; cf. Huey et al., 2012). According to these practitioners, the expertise and successes of digital vigilante groups are exaggerated by the groups themselves and in news reports of their activities.

Relatedly, there is a concern that online co-production of public security *undermines police authority.* When stories of successful apprehensions are uncritically shared and picked up by news media, and when there is no accountability or transparency about the actions that did not lead to success, public security practitioners are concerned that this may undermine trust in the police and eventually police authority and legitimacy (DIY Policing workshop). An example that was discussed during the DIY workshop was that of online paedophile-hunter groups. In an increasing number of grooming trials, evidence from these groups is used. The groups are actively listing successful apprehensions and convictions on their websites.[2] When the police are seen as ineffective and inefficient, citizens may increasingly resort to taking matters into their own hands — with the risk that their

---

2   See for example www.darkjustice.co.uk.

unprofessionalism has negative consequences, as well as the lack of due process to other citizens and society outline above.

Discussion: Online Citizens as Aides and Adversaries

Our analysis of discussions amongst European practitioners about online co-production in public security reveals that discursive boundaries of helpful and harmful acts of are not only drawn based on involvement in specific police tasks, such as crime prevention vs. investigation and prosecution. Discursive boundaries are primarily drawn based on the resemblance with the existing operating paradigm of community policing (Mastrofski et al., 1995; Skogan & Williamson, 2008). While there are many differences between countries in adopting this policing paradigm, among Northern and Western European countries it has become relatively popular. Countries that are more democratically consolidated tend to have stronger relative preferences towards community-oriented policing over zero-tolerance styles (Lum, 2009). Distinctions between DIY policing and digital vigilantism by public security practitioners in these countries are based on this model.

Citizens are considered as aides to police efforts when they engage with cases relating to their local context and when they closely collaborate with law enforcement. When online engagement goes beyond this familiar model of co-production, citizens are more likely to be considered adversaries. This concerns involvement in cases outside of citizens' own local contexts and when they do not collaborate with law enforcement, or when they do so only at a later stage in order to be able to claim their own successes. These groups are seeking a broader audience in order to publicly denounce and retaliate against crime, instead of wanting to solve issues locally within the criminal justice system. From the perspective of public security actors, this is what distinguishes harmful digital vigilantism from helpful DIY policing.

Based on these two distinguishing features of DIY policing and digital vigilantism, we can develop a more fine-grained typology of online co-production in the domain of public security, including examples of behaviours that were brought up in the discussions (Table 11.2).

Table 11.2: Typology of online civic engagement in public security

	Cases within citizen's local context	Cases outside of citizen's local context
Close collaboration with law enforcement	Discussing tips on suspects or missing persons based on evidence posted by police on social media	Investigating evidence from social media sources on rioters, hooligans or terrorists and bringing this to the police
Late or no collaboration with law enforcement	Neighbourhood watch groups working independently from local police, bringing offenders to justice themselves	Online entrapment of offenders and bringing these cases to the police only afterwards, hacking or phishing and doxing suspects without bringing these cases to the police

Public security organisations in various European countries are at different stages of maturity in responding to these various types of online co-production. This depends on the technological resources of the police force, the political context of the country and the local police culture. Presumably, the differences with countries beyond the EU are even larger. Police forces with less financial and technological resources, within authoritarian political systems and with a repressive police culture will engage less in co-production of public security with online citizens. Representatives from European LEAs who participated in our workshop share a similar ideal of better engaging with DIY policing and more strongly denouncing digital vigilantism.

Two ideal typical forms of DIY policing and digital vigilantism are highlighted in the upper-left and lower-right boxes of Table 11.2. There is consensus that local, collaborative forms of engagement with public security, such as sharing and discussing tips on suspects or missing persons based on evidence posted by police on social media, should be better facilitated and encouraged. Some police forces are already doing so by hosting various social media channels on which calls to action are posted, or having specialised apps to ask for collaboration in local cases. Examples are Amber Alert and the Dutch 'Citizen's Net' app (cf. Meijer, 2012; 2015). More common are police forces that only host one centralised social media account, which is used to disseminate information to the public and not to interact with the public. This type of social media adoption reinforces a traditional and hierarchical model of the police as knowledge broker (Nhan et al., 2017, p. 344).

There is also relative consensus that ideal typical forms of digital vigilantism — as highlighted in the lower-right box of Table 11.2 — should be more strongly denounced by LEAs. Even though, in some cases, the specific expertise and resources of online publics are valued, the police consider the independence with which these groups are working and claiming successes as harmful to society and to police authority. Public security actors fear that only the positive successes of these individuals and collectives are celebrated, while the many compromises that are made with regard to public values other than effectiveness, such as the privacy of suspects, are too easily ignored. While harmful acts towards others, such as trolling and doxing, may be unethical but not illegal, some public security actors wish to pursue current regulations more strictly, or to expand them. Other public security actors wish to publicly counter the successes of digital vigilantes by providing information on negative side-effects and offering a counter-narrative.

Literature on digital vigilantism suggests that these forms of guidance would have limited effects. Since social media spaces are governed by libertarian and sometimes anti-authoritarian values, online publics will not always self-identify as vigilante or be willing to follow the procedures of law enforcement. Also, because social media spans national borders, citizens engaging in DIY policing will belong to multiple jurisdictions that may have different guidelines. As stated earlier, countries with more authoritarian governance systems are not likely to have a tradition of community policing or to employ a positive stance towards the online engagement of citizens in police work. In these cases, police attitudes towards citizens prevent them from taking online co-production seriously. There is a police subculture of distrust, in which citizens are stereotyped either as "know nothings", "suspicious persons" or "assholes" (Manning & Van Maanen, 1978, pp. 223–4). This mutual distrust might be reinforced by the anonymity of social media (Walker et al., 2006) and will complicate attempted collaboration in online spaces.

The two forms of online civic engagement that were debated more intensively are found in the upper-right and lower-left boxes of Table 11.2. Public security actors see some merit in both, but are also concerned with their negative effects. When collaborative engagement occurs outside citizens' local contexts, their level of expertise was debated. Are they able to bring new leads to the table that the police investigation would not have uncovered? Some practitioners pointed towards strained police resources and the "wisdom of the crowds" (cf. Surowiecki, 2004) that online citizens can contribute to the investigation. Besides this crowdsourcing of intelligence, others value the specific expertise of some citizens in more specialised investigations, such as cybercrime. The motives of citizens to help in cases outside of their own communities are questioned, however. Why would citizens offer their time and skills to collaborate with law enforcement when they have no direct fear for their own safety, or for that of others within their community? Some practitioners fear that the desire to match or outsmart law enforcement will lead these citizens to take bold measures, and to lose sight of public values that are equally as important as effectiveness.

Meijer (2012) describes how online co-production in the domain of public security can indeed be motivated by entertainment, or even have an element of 'gaming' to it. However, in this digital age, engagement with criminal cases outside of one's local context can also be motivated by local concerns and a sense of civic responsibility. In her seminal book *The Death of Distance* (1997) Cairncross claims that the revolution in telecommunications technologies makes geographical distance less significant. Studies on the effects of Web 2.0 also note how social media makes geographical borders less relevant. However, other borders remain present: for example, language barriers preventing people from communicating with each other, and social borders distinguishing cases which *feel* familiar enough to engage with. Due to the media-rich and personal nature of social media communication, citizens can feel closely engaged with cases from which they are geographically far removed. This may motivate them to contribute digitally to policing efforts.

In the case of online engagement with local cases without collaboration with the police, citizens' own methods of seeking justice are problematised most. Engagement with local issues of public security is valued. However, it is exactly because matters are close to home, that public security actors fear it is tempting for citizens to take matters into their own hands. For example, neighbourhood watch groups may use their online platforms to encourage people to bring suspects to justice themselves. When collaboration with the police is not sought, or is sought only at a late stage, practitioners fear that methods of investigation and punishment are unlawful, unprofessional and cause harm to suspects, to other citizens, and to social cohesion in local communities. European police forces are developing apps to facilitate engagement in prevention and investigation, according to law enforcement standards. For example, the police in Nice (France) piloted the app C-Now (previously Reporty) in which citizens can take videos of incidents and crime and live-share this information, including geolocation, with emergency operators. The Dutch police is developing apps to engage citizens in finding missing persons (*Samen zoeken*) and securing evidence after a crime (Sherlock).

Conclusions

Online forms of co-production of public security are here to stay, but the rules of this 'game' have yet to be established. DIY policing and digital vigilantism can be considered as examples of "do-it-yourself government" (cf. Linders, 2012). These forms of online co-production are initiated by citizens, take place relatively independently of government law enforcement, and are therefore most ambiguous. As authoritative actors within the domain of public security, law enforcement agencies and other public organisations involved with public security play an important role in establishing the boundaries between acceptable and unacceptable forms of online engagement. In their responses to different forms of online civic engagement, they discursively set these boundaries. This chapter has therefore addressed the question of how law enforcement authorities define the boundaries of which digital contributions of citizens to public security are acceptable, and which unacceptable.

An analysis of round-table discussions between European public security practitioners, during six workshops, highlights that discursive boundaries of accepted forms of online co-production are drawn based on the existing philosophy of 'community policing'. In this policing-operation paradigm, engagement is characterised by close collaboration with law enforcement and involvement in cases concerning citizens' local communities. Acts of online engagement with matters of public security that fall outside of this definition — either on one or on both conditions — are met with more skepticism and reluctance. They are considered to bring risks of harm to others in society, as well as to police work and police authority.

Broad definitions of DIY policing and digital vigilantism generate only limited understanding of the different responses of LEAs towards online civic engagement. Developing a more fine-grained distinction and typology based on these two key features of community policing is helpful to understanding normative boundaries drawn by authorities, and probably also by less authoritative actors towards this phenomenon. As authorities in the domain of public security, LEAs and local, national and international public security organisations are in a position to formally and informally define the boundaries of accepted acts of DIY policing, which will probably also permeate to less authoritative actors and citizens (cf. Schneider, 2014).

Our research details shared perceptions of LEAs in Europe regarding online engagement of citizens in security practices. It provides important insights in what is seen as acceptable and unacceptable behaviour on the Internet. Unfortunately, based on the anonymous character of the round-table discussions and reporting, we were not able to distinguish differences in opinion between LEAs in different European countries or between actors working for different types of public security organisations. This raises a set of new questions. Further research should focus on investigating the similarities and differences between countries with different political contexts and police cultures. Comparative research enables us to understand how national security cultures translate into police engagement with online co-production of public security. In addition, we need to investigate the actual responses of the police to find out whether their actions indeed fit the matrix that we developed based on their statements. Are they indeed more supportive of local practices and practices in close collaboration with law enforcement?

The research maps current views but also raises questions about the future. Police notions of what is a 'local context' and 'close collaboration' — the two key dimensions in our model — may start to shift and change. Local context used to be defined in a geographical sense, but this is shifting with the death of distance and it may require a new meaning in the "space of flows" (Castells, 1999, p. 294). Citizens might feel close affinity with others in different localities, which motivates them to engage with their public security issues. Furthermore, close collaboration was previously defined as following police orders: government-as-a-platform forms of co-production. Now, this may become a more horizontal collaboration. These shifts will define what LEAs see as acceptable and unacceptable forms of online citizen engagement and what they label as DIY policing and digital vigilantism.

For some European law-enforcement authorities, it has been difficult to diverge from their traditional authoritative role as knowledge brokers, and instead to actively engage with social media to guide the online activities of citizens. They generally feel that there is little that they can do to stop new forms of online engagement with public security and it is also not in their best interest to do so. Therefore, we observed a shared desire amongst the group of public security practitioners to provide more guidance in online civic engagement with policing. By stonewalling or denouncing all types of online citizen engagement, LEAs would miss out on an opportunity to acknowledge legitimate concerns for public security, with the risk that citizens might lose trust in the police, causing the erosion of police legitimacy (cf. Crump 2011; Meijer & Thaens 2013; Warren et al. 2014; Grimmelikhuijsen & Meijer 2015). They feel that judgements on these co-production initiatives should not be left only to online collectives themselves, or to the public courts of news media and public opinion.

Several options to provide more guidance, including regulations, training, moderation and apps were proposed. They are mostly proposed within the traditional domains of community policing such as crime prevention, tracing missing persons and addressing local nuisance, disorder and petty crimes. In more specialised disciplines and larger cases such as white-collar crime, sexual assault and murder cases, online civic engagement is generally deemed less suitable and guidance was not proposed in order not to inadvertently encourage involvement. Public security actors wish to direct online publics to key areas of investigation and help focus their efforts. Furthermore, police guidance would help to ensure transparency in evidence collection and study, and it is expected to steer citizens towards more professional norms.

Many acts of digital vigilantism cannot be forbidden as being unlawful, but are simply unethical. In the case of unlawful acts, it is doubtful whether public security actors will achieve the desired goal of guiding digital vigilantes towards DIY policing characterised by close collaboration with law enforcement and involvement in only local matters. Digital vigilantes might not self-identify as such, and even if they do, their vigilante acts might be an active choice based on anti-authoritarianism and distrust in government law enforcement. At the same time, providing more guidance to those engaged in DIY policing may come at a price. It can create an implicit incentive for citizens to get (more) involved in matters of public security, although this has not been the primary goal: public security actors only wished to guide existing involvement, as an overabundance of tips and requests is already a concern. Coordinating DIY policing activities may also create new liabilities for the police when acts by citizens that have been coordinated by the police cause harm after all (cf. Huey et al., 2012). Lastly, facilitating online involvement in public security can stimulate an atmosphere of social control and mutual distrust amongst citizens (cf. Schreurs et al., 2018). Existing social, cultural and political divides in society might become more prominent. These matters should be taken into account by public security actors when providing more guidance to DIY policing.

References

Bekkers, V. J. J. M., & Meijer, A. J. (2010). *Co-creatie in de publieke sector; Een verkennend onderzoek naar nieuwe digitale verbindingen tussen overheid en burger.* Den Haag: Boom Juridische Uitgevers.

Brandsen, T., & Pestoff, V. (2006). Co-production, the third sector and the delivery of public services: An introduction. *Public Management Review,* 8(4), 493–501, https://doi.org/10.1080/14719030601022874

Cairncross, F. (1997). *The Death of Distance: How the Communications Revolution Will Change our Lives.* Brighton: Harvard Business School Press.

Campbell, E. (2016). Policing paedophilia: Assembling bodies, spaces and things. *Crime, Media, Culture,* 12(3), 345–65, https://doi.org/10.1177/1741659015623598

Castells, M. (1999). Grassrooting the space of flows. *Urban Geography*, 20(4), 294–302, https://doi.org/10.2747/0272-3638.20.4.294

Crump, J. (2011). What are the police doing on Twitter? Social media, the police and the public. *Policy & Internet*, 3(4), 1–27, https://doi.org/10.2202/1944-2866.1130

De Graaf, G., & Meijer, A. (2019). Social media and value conflicts: An explorative study of the Dutch police. *Public Administration Review*, 79(1), 82–92, https://doi.org/10.1111/puar.12914

E Silva, K. K. (2018). Vigilantism and cooperative criminal justice: is there a place for cybersecurity vigilantes in cybercrime fighting? *International Review of Law, Computers & Technology*, 32(1), 21–36, https://doi.org/10.1080/13600869.2018.1418142

Fouché, C., & Light, G. (2011). An invitation to dialogue: The World Café in social work. *Qualitative Social Work*, 10(1), 28–48, https://doi.org/10.1177/1473325010376016

Frissen, V., Van Staden, M., Huijboom, N., Kotterink, B., Huveneers, S., Kuipers, M., & Bodea, G. (2008). *Naar een 'User Generated State'? De impact van nieuwe media voor overheid en openbaar bestuur*. Report for the Dutch Department for the Interior, The Hague.

Grimmelikhuijsen, S. G., & Meijer, A. J. (2015). Does Twitter increase perceived police legitimacy? *Public Administration Review*, 75(4), 598–607, https://doi.org/10.1111/puar.12378

Haythornthwaite, C. (2005). Social networks and internet connectivity effects. *Information, Communication & Society*, 8(2), 125–47, https://doi.org/10.1080/13691180500146185

Huey, L., Nhan, J., & Broll, R. (2012). 'Uppity civilians' and 'cyber-vigilantes': The role of the general public in policing cyber-crime. *Criminology and Criminal Justice*, 13(1), 81–97, https://doi.org/10.1177/1748895812448086

Johnston, L. (1996). What is Vigilantism? *British Journal of Criminology*, 36(2): 220–36, https://doi.org/10.1093/oxfordjournals.bjc.a014083

Jørgensen, T. B., & Bozeman, B. (2007). Public values: An inventory. *Administration & Society*, 39(3), 354–81, https://doi.org/10.1177/0095399707300703

Kohm, S. A. (2009). Naming, shaming, and criminal justice: Mass-mediated humiliation as entertainment and punishment. *Crime, Media, Culture*, 5(2), 188–205, https://doi.org/10.1177/1741659009335724

Leach, P. (2003). Citizen Policing as Civic Activism: An International Inquiry. *International Journal of the Sociology of Law*, 31(3), 267–94, https://doi.org/10.1016/j.ijsl.2003.09.006

Linders, D. (2012). From e-government to we-government: Defining a typology for citizen coproduction in the age of social media. *Government Information Quarterly*, 29(4), 446–54, https://doi.org/10.1016/j.giq.2012.06.003

Loader, I. (2000). Plural Policing and Democratic Governance. *Social and Legal Studies*, 9(3), 323–45, https://doi.org/10.1177/096466390000900301

Loveluck, B. (2016). Digital vigilantism, between denunciation and punitive action. *Politix*, 115(3), 127–53, https://doi.org/10.3917/pox.115.0127

Lub, V. (2018). *Neighbourhood Watch in a Digital Age. Between Crime Control and Culture of Control*. Cham: Palgrave McMillan, https://doi.org/10.1007/978-3-319-67747-7

Lum, C. (2009). Community policing or zero tolerance? Preferences of police officers from 22 countries in transition. *The British Journal of Criminology*, 49(6), 788–809, https://doi.org/10.1093/bjc/azp039

Manning, P., & Van Maanen, J. (1978). *Policing: A View from the Street*. Santa Monica, CA: Goodyear.

Mastrofski, S. D., Worden, R. E., & Snipes, J. B. (1995). Law enforcement in a time of community policing. *Criminology*, 33(4), 539–63, https://doi.org/10.1111/j.1745-9125.1995.tb01189.x

Mayer-Schönberger, V. (2009). *Delete: The Virtue of Forgetting in the Digital Age*. Princeton University Press, https://doi.org/10.1515/9781400838455

Meijer, A. J. (2012). Co-production in an information age: Individual and community engagement supported by new media. *VOLUNTAS: International Journal of Voluntary and Nonprofit Organizations*, 23(4), 1156–72, https://doi.org/10.1007/s11266-012-9311-z

Meijer, A. J. (2015). E-governance innovation: Barriers and strategies. *Government Information Quarterly*, 32(2), 198–206, https://doi.org/10.1016/j.giq.2015.01.001

Meijer, A. J., & Thaens, M. (2013). Social media strategies: Understanding the differences between North American police departments. *Government Information Quarterly*, 30(4), 343–50, https://doi.org/10.1016/j.giq.2013.05.023

Nhan, J., Huey, L., & Broll, R. (2017). Digilantism: An analysis of crowdsourcing and the Boston marathon bombings. *The British Journal of Criminology*, 57(2), 341–61, https://doi.org/10.1093/bjc/azv118

O'Neill, M., & Fyfe, N. R. (2017). Plural policing in Europe: relationships and governance in contemporary security systems. *Policing and Society*, 27(1), 1–5, https://doi.org/10.1080/10439463.2016.1220554

Percy, S. L. (1978). Conceptualizing and Measuring Citizen Co-Production of Community Safety. *Policy Studies Journal*, 7, 486–93, https://doi.org/10.1111/j.1541-0072.1978.tb01797.x

Rizza, C., Pereira, Â. G., & Curvelo, P. (2014). "Do-it-yourself justice": Considerations of social media use in a crisis situation: The case of the 2011 Vancouver riots. *International Journal of Information Systems for Crisis Response and Management (IJISCRAM)*, 6(4), 411–15, https://doi.org/10.4018/ijiscram.2014100104

Schmidle, N. (2018, May 7). The digital vigilantes who hack back. *The New Yorker Magazine*, https://www.newyorker.com/magazine/2018/05/07/the-digital-vigilantes-who-hack-back

Schneider, C. J. (2014). Police 'image work' in an era of social media: YouTube and the 2007 Montebello summit protest. In Trottier, D. & Fuchs, C. (eds). *Social Media, Politics and the State: Protests, Revolutions, Riots, Crime and Policing in the Age of Facebook, Twitter and Youtube* (pp. 227–46). New York: Routledge, https://doi.org/10.4324/9781315764832

Schreurs, W., Kerstholt, J. H., de Vries, P. W., & Giebels, E. (2018). Citizen participation in the police domain: The role of citizens' attitude and morality. *Journal of Community Psychology*, 46(6), 775–89, https://doi.org/10.1002/jcop.21972

Schuberth, M. (2013). Challenging the weak states hypothesis: vigilantism in South Africa and Brazil. *Journal of Peace, Conflict & Development*, 20, 38–51.

Skogan, W. G., & Williamson, T. (2008). An overview of community policing: origins, concepts and implementation. In: Williamson, T. (ed.) *The Handbook of Knowledge-Based Policing: Current Conceptions and Future Directions* (pp. 43–58) Chichester: John Wiley & Soons, https://doi.org/10.1002/9780470773215.ch1

Smit, P. H. (2017, October 10). Dankzij deze apps kan iedereen straks meespeuren met de politie. *de Volkskrant*, https://www.volkskrant.nl/binnenland/dankzij-deze-apps-kan-iedereen-straks-meespeuren-met-de-politie~a4520905

Stewart, A. (2005). On conversation and collective questioning: theory and practice of the World Café. *System Thinker*, 16(5), 9–10.

Surowiecki, J. (2004). *The Wisdom of Crowds: Why the Many Are Smarter Than the Few and How Collective Wisdom Shapes Business, Economies, Societies and Nations*. New York: Doubleday.

Trottier, D. (2017). Digital vigilantism as weaponisation of visibility. *Philosophy & Technology*, 30(1), 55–72, https://doi.org/10.1007/s13347-016-0216-4

Voorberg, W. H., Bekkers, V. J. J. M., & Tummers, L. G. (2015). A systematic review of co-creation and co-production: Embarking on the social innovation journey. *Public Management Review*, 17(9), 1333–57, https://doi.org/10.1080/14719037.2014.930505

Walker, D., Brock, D., & Stuart, T. R. (2006). Faceless-oriented policing: traditional policing theories are not adequate in a cyber world. *The Police Journal*, 79(2), 169–76, https://doi.org/10.1350/pojo.2006.79.2.169

Warren, A. M., Sulaiman, A., & Jaafar, N. I. (2014). Social media effects on fostering online civic engagement and building citizen trust and trust in institutions. *Government Information Quarterly*, 31(2), 291–301, https://doi.org/10.1016/j.giq.2013.11.007

Yardley, E., Lynes, A. G. T., Wilson, D., & Kelly, E. (2016). What's the deal with 'websleuthing'? News media representations of amateur detectives in networked spaces. *Crime, Media, Culture,* 14(1), 81–109, https://doi.org/10.1177/1741659016674045

Žitnik, A., De Vries, A., Reuge, E., Tani, K., Kermitsis, M., Rijken, M., Van Staalduinen, M., Denef, S., & Oggero, S. (2018). Catalogue of Existing Technologies and Solutions. Deliverable 2.2. Medi@4Sec Project deliverable 2.2, http://media4sec.eu/downloads/d2-2.pdf

More Eyes on Crime?: The Rhetoric of Mediated Mugshots

Sarah Young

In September 2017, a man in North Carolina, USA was arrested for a probation violation. While the arrest was standard, the man's booking photo was not — his mugshot featured him, arm raised with a smile on his face, eating a bologna sandwich, prompting the photo to go 'viral' (Elsesser, 2017).

Introduction

While it may not be typical for an arrestee to be photographed eating a sandwich, the booking photo described above illustrates a growing trend in the United States — the participatory online mugshot. While the publication of online mugshots may be more popular in America than elsewhere (Collier, 2014), these photos have been known to go viral and trend world-wide. Combining traditional uses of the mugshot for information management and classification purposes (Finn, 2009) with participatory digital technologies, online mugshots provide a space where the public can elevate the exposure of arrestees by making the images viral, as in the example of the North Carolina man above, who now and forever has the dubious association of having the bologna-sandwich mugshot. Proponents argue that increased mugshot visibility aids department transparency and provides more information for the community (Murray, 2015), but is justice and "more eyes on crime" the rhetoric that is extolled in online galleries? I argue no, especially in one prominent example of Maricopa County Sheriff's Office's former Mugshot of the Day (MotD) program from Arizona, USA.

  https://doi.org/10.11647/OBP.0200.12

In 2011, controversial Joe "Sheriff Joe" Arpaio, the self-proclaimed "America's toughest sheriff" (BBC News, 2017), launched the MotD program through the MCSO's webpage. While Sheriff Joe's base supporters and audience may predominately be in the desert southwest of the United States, where voters kept Arpaio in power as County Sheriff from 1993 to 2016 and whose "brand of politics made him the most popular politician in Arizona" (Kiefer, 2016), Arpaio and his policies have received world-wide notoriety. In the heyday of his popularity, Arpaio boasted of having two hundred TV interviews per month and thousands of articles written about him from all over the world (Santos, 2012) in places like England (BBC News, 2017) or Australia (Duffy, 2018). Some of his more famous American supporters and advocates of his justice policies range from actor Steven Seagal (Ohlheiser, 2014) to President Donald Trump (Hirschfeld Davis & Haberman, 2017).

Run from 2011 to 2016, the Mugshot of the Day! site allowed the public, under the guise of a voting game, to view all the jail bookings for the last three days to elevate the visibility of their mugshot of choice to the leaderboard. The top eight mugshots were featured daily on the site's main page, and the most popular shot of the day was featured at the top of the homepage and labelled, "Mugshot of the Day!" This program was justified by Sheriff Joe reportedly saying, "More eyes on arrestees may result in more leads to criminal investigators" (Hermann, 2011).

While Arpaio had also used other extreme measures for attention and publicity to show his 'tough' stance on crime, such as when he created the US' first female chain gang (Santos, 2012), required inmates to wear striped outfits issued with pink underwear, housed inmates in tents in the desert heat and fed inmates mouldy bologna (Kiefer, 2016), what is specific about this program is that MCSO was not just asking the public to be vigilante viewers of crime infotainment, and to watch the inmates from a distance, as in a quirky news report on Arpaio's Tent City. Instead, he changed the participatory nature of the audience and created a space where the public could stay distant while also becoming up close and personal with those arrested.

By looking at the MCSO's MotD program, I argue that through the exigency of entertainment on participatory platforms, online mugshots temporarily coalesced a group of digital vigilantes into being, in order to weaponise visibility. This claim is not only an argument that the initial intention of the MotD (entertainment) does not disqualify it as a DV activity (due to the unwanted, intense and enduring visibility it produces), but it also contributes to evolving definitions of how one participates in vigilantism in a digital world, and who can do so. To support this argument, I will use the MSCO site in four ways: 1) argue that online mugshot consumers can be digital vigilantes, 2) argue that entertainment provides this link, 3) discuss the implications of these conclusions and 4) discuss what this means for other online mugshot platforms in a larger context.

The MCSO's MotD Program Creates Digital Vigilantes

Firstly, I will explain how those who interact with online mugshots, especially in the case of MCSO can be considered digital vigilantes. I argue they can be considered this because 1) online mugshots on the MCSO site call into being a group of people that temporarily coalesces 2) through participatory platforms to 3) shame and weaponise visibility against a target.

Individuals temporarily coalesce: According to Charland, one becomes a member of a collective through interaction with its discourse. Identification then is a rhetorical move. One is not always born into associations with others — one can choose to heed the call. There is not necessarily a subject that "would exist prior to and apart from the speech to be judged", instead the discourse can call a subject into being (1987, p. 133). This is true for digital vigilantes as well. Digital vigilantes heed a call for participation and find themselves in the call for action. As Trottier discusses, these individuals do not have to have prior association and are often "unaffiliated with a formal organisation" (2017, p. 57).

Particularly for MCSO, one became a member of the voting collective because they found themselves in the call to vote for the mugshot. To vote on one's favourite mugshot of the day, the user did not have to register or otherwise be involved with the Sheriff's Office or affiliated with any other organisation. One was able to look at the photos, click on their favourite image and tap the "vote" button next to the photo. Once they had voted and their selection was logged by the site, though, they became a member of the collective in that their vote joined with the other votes to work together to elevate the visibility of the photo.

Online mugshots utilise digital platforms to name and shame: Second, in digital vigilantism, the ability both to join the group and to carry out the actions of a digital vigilante are granted through digital, participatory platforms. Jenkins et al. describe participatory culture as a "mix of top-down and bottom-up forces" that alter the traditional roles of producer and consumer (2013, p. 11), and a participatory platform utilises the mix of top-down and bottom-up affordances that allow those at the "top" to provide the space for interaction, but engage the public to produce their own conversation. This follows Trottier's comment that "DV is a product of digital media platforms and user-generated cultural practices" (2017, p. 57).

In the case of MCSO, the members of the voting collective were only able to coalesce, and these members only able to vote, because they could heed the call for membership online on a participatory platform. Voters did not meet in a public square or in a physical location to target particular individuals; voters could just turn on their computers, navigate to the MCSO's site and select their favourite mugshot with a click of the mouse.

Mugshot consumers weaponise visibility: One can coalesce for membership and use participatory platforms without being a digital vigilante though, so an important piece of the argument is that digital vigilantes can inflict some type of punishment on their targets. As Trottier (2017) describes, DV is a process where the coalesced groups "respond through coordinated retaliation" (2017, p. 56), implying that some type of harm results in the process.

One punishment is shame. Shame works by showing others how someone has violated an accepted social norm (Karp, 1998), and while a person might feel fear when they are physically threatened, they might "feel shame when the social self is threatened" (ibid., p. 279). Shame causes feelings of embarrassment because a person believes someone has a low opinion of them, and this can range from close friends even to strangers (ibid., p. 280). As Rosedale concludes, the mugshot creates "a shame-filled expression captured by the photograph" (2014, p. 791). So, when someone's mugshot is visible to the public, this can result in shame even if the person photographed does not even know who will be looking at the photo.

One way that groups can use shame to harm targets is through weaponised visibility. According to Trottier, weaponised visibility makes "explicit use of targets' personal information by rendering them visible to public scrutiny" (2017, p. 65). The more visible a target is, the more others can find out about their actions. This visibility can range from the name-and-shame tactic in which a target's personal information is revealed, to drawing out child predators through shows like *To Catch A Predator*, in which volunteers pose as underage children to bait potential sex offenders (Smallridge et al., 2016), to, as I argue, voting on online mugshots. Even though in the case of MCSO these mugshots were uploaded first by a state entity, the public can turn these photos into weapons of visibility by drawing even more scrutiny to the images.

Trottier (2017) outlines that there are three characteristics of weaponised visibility. It is unwanted, intense and enduring. Each of these facets creates a type of visibility that can bring shame and harm to a target. MCSO's mugshots present the opportunity for a group's members to capitalise on all three of these characteristics to weaponise visibility when voting on their favourite image.

First, when visibility is weaponised, it is *unwanted* and "the target is typically not soliciting publicity" (ibid., p. 55). For the voting public on the MCSO site, the group could use visibility to harm their target because mugshots inherently represent an *unwanted* condition. Typically, a mugshot is a negative reminder of something bad, and the photos dehumanise the photographed (Lashmar, 2013). Rosedale also adds that the mugshot "includes an individual's expression at an embarrassing moment. At the time the photograph is taken, the individual has been 'deprived of most liberties'" (2014, p. 791). So, when interacting with any type of mugshot, the public was already engaging in making more visible an unwanted artefact.

The unwanted nature of MCSO's MotD program is especially apparent looking at one of the major cases testing the legalities of online mugshots. In this suit, the plaintiff unsuccessfully[1] sued the county because he argued MCSO took his property, or more specifically,

---

[1]   It is interesting to note that in dismissing the case, the courts referenced the 1904 case of Shaffer v. United States, which concluded that mugshots can be used as law

his "image, name, and fingerprints" without his permission and posted both his image, arrest details and personal information on their site, thus violating his Fourth Amendment right to be free from unreasonable seizures, Fifth Amendment right to private property, Eighth Amendment right to be free from cruel and unusual punishment and Ninth Amendment right to life, liberty and happiness (Campbell, 2013). One of the main complaints in the suit was that the mugshot was featured publicly, and that users could interact with it and re-publish it on other sites. As listed in the suit regarding MCSO and other entities reposting his photo, "many of these websites, including the County's, permitted site visitors to vote on a 'mugshot of the day', and some even permitted viewers to make comments about images posted on the sites". Clearly, for the plaintiff, visibility was unwanted.

Second, visibility, when weaponised, is *intense*: "content like text, photos and videos can circulate to millions of users within a few days" (Trottier, 2017, p. 55). When voters engaged with the mugshots on the MotD site and elevated photos to the main page, they could increase the intensity of the photo's circulation. No longer relegated to interior pages, once the photos had received enough votes, the images would move and be prominently featured on the site's main page. Then, whenever a visitor clicked on the homepage, the user was greeted with one of eight photos. The magnitude of the intensity of the exposure is illustrated by the number of visitors to the MSCO site, and during the time period when the MotD program was running, then-Sheriff Arpaio boasted that this controversial program had a million hits a day and was "one of the most visible law enforcement sites on the Internet" (Maricopa County Sheriff's Office, 2015a).

Third, weaponised visibility is *enduring* because it can be a top search result or it can morph into its own cultural reference (Trottier, 2017, p. 55). For groups of voters on the MCSO site, voting on a particular photo could make the image more enduring. Once the photo had been elevated to the main page, it remained there for the rest of the day and, as mentioned, it would be the first images seen by site visitors. Although in the case of MCSO the images were removed after three days, thereby limiting the lasting characteristic of endurance for

---

enforcement sees fit because "it would be [a] matter of regret to have its use unduly restricted upon any fanciful theory or constitutional privilege" (Campbell, 2013).

voters on the MCSO's page, voters could still affect the endurance of the images. The most visible mugshots were often downloaded or screenshotted, and featured as content on other news or blogging sites (Stern, 2016) such as the *Phoenix New Times*, who weekly reviewed their own "Mugshots of the Week" based on MCSO's photos (Hendley, 2015) and whose content is still online today. These images were also reposted in places such as tabloid news outlets, who picked up celebrities such as WNBA star Brittney Griner (TMZ, 2015) and private blogs like *Maricopa County Mugshots* (Maricopa County Mugshots, n.d.) which showcased screenshots of offenders.

Overall, then, voters on the MotD program were able to join together to further shame particular targets, thereby weaponising visibility and acting as digital vigilantes. Before continuing, though, it is of note that, by nature of posting the mugshots online for a contest, MCSO was in a way participating in their own weaponisation of visibility against those who had been arrested, thereby strengthening the connection between the state, the public and digital vigilantism. Without these images have being posted, there would not be the chance to vote for the photos in the first place. Even further, MCSO was releasing booking date, full name, booking number, gender, birthdate, height, weight, hair and eye colour, race and arrest reason (Maricopa County Sheriff's Office, 2015b), which further doxed the arrestees and created the possibility of new justice initiatives such as the silencing of protest and dissent (this point will be discussed later in the chapter.)

The Exigency of Entertainment

The previous section detailed how the MCSO's MotD program illustrated the similarities between the digital vigilantes and voters on the site. The following section will detail one significant difference: the exigency of the audience participation. I argue that both the call for participation on the "Mugshot of the Day!" page, together with a sample of the site's 'winners', supports that entertainment, rather than detection of criminals or retribution, evoked participation on the site. This not only challenges Sheriff Joe's supposed reason for creating the program but also adds complexity to the idea of the 'vigilant audience' who is traditionally conceptualised to coalesce for justice-seeking reasons.

Objects and Views Analysis

To make this argument, it is important to understand how the page looked when users would land on the Office's page. Were users greeted with rhetoric for identifying criminals for the sake of keeping the streets safer? Were they greeted with calls for retaliation to harm those photographed? I argue neither, users were greeted with the exigency of entertainment.

Methods: To analyse the page, I used a *content and views analysis* as described by Hart-Davidson et al. (2007), which builds on the work of Rockley & Kostur (2003) and their ideas of content auditing. For the analysis, the "content" portion "is a straightforward list of the content types available on the site" (ibid., 17). The "views" portion "is a different view of content that complements what can be a rather static, product-focused inventory of text types" (ibid.), and instead, views are "a collection of content objects presented to the user in a coherent visual format" (ibid.). In a content and views analysis, a researcher examines a website to see how web content is managed and how content serves strategic goals. This was an effective strategy for this analysis because it offered a way to see what content MCSO allowed, how they let users navigate the space and if the content of the MotD page matched the supposed strategic goals of the office, which was to have more eyes on arrestees. Only the MotD page was used for the analysis because this was the relevant page that facilitated the interaction. For this analysis, while Hart-Davidson et al. stuck to genres in their study with content types like "news and announcements" and "policy statements", this was smaller and focused on one page rather than the site, so I included more specific details of content like "photo of Sheriff Joe".

Results: For content, there were several standard items on the page that ran across the whole site, such as the header element with the photo of Sheriff Joe, department name and image of Sheriff's badge, and there was also the footer element, with the contact information, privacy statement and copyright information. The bulk of the content unique to the page was the photos of the mugshots and the different ways to search for the photo of your choice. The punctuation of the exclamation mark on the phrase "Mugshot of the Day!" was a particularly enthusiastic addition to the site.

To view content on and off the page, there was little variation available. Users could use a menu to navigate around the site to other locations like "About MCSO" or "Victim Services". Users could also use links to peruse specific offenses, and users could search the mugshots by first name, last name or booking number. Users could also click on "Contact Us" and "Privacy Statement". It is of note that below these photos was the disclaimer, "Mugshots reflect the bookings within the last 3 days. Individuals booked prior to that time will not be displayed. **PRE-TRIAL INMATES ARE INNOCENT UNTIL PROVEN GUILTY!**" (Maricopa County Sheriff's Office, Mugshots, 2015, emphasis in original). Table 12.1 provides a snapshot of the results.

Table 12.1: Results of the Content and Views Analysis for the MotD Page

Content	Views
• Photo of Sheriff Joe	• Menus
• Name of Department and tagline	• Links
• Image of Sheriff's badge	• Search
• Name of other website pages	
• Mugshot of the Day! image	
• Categories of crimes	
• Seven "Mugshot Leader Board" images	
• Names and arrest dates of arrestees	
• Disclaimer	
• Contact Us	
• Privacy Statement	
• Copyright	

Discussion: Although Sheriff Arpaio had claimed his mugshot program was about how "[m]ore eyes on arrestees may result in more leads to criminal investigators" (Hermann, 2011), this was not necessarily what was being communicated or displayed on the webpage. Offense-taking and punishment were not presented as the reason to vote. Instead, participants were greeted by the exigency of entertainment. According to a visual analysis of this page, the site was designed to facilitate the easy process of scanning, searching and voting for one's favorite mugshot. Nowhere on this page was there a call to elevate the image of those you recognise from other crimes or details directing onlooker to report tips to the agency. There was a "Contact Us" link, but it was listed in the footer of the page and was an element that ran across the bottom of every page rather than an appeal for the public to identify particular individuals.

Overall, then, the page was focused more on entertainment and letting the audience easily navigate the site to vote, rather than to enable them to assist with law enforcement duties. Thus, I argue that entertainment was the impetus for voter's participation. To further back up this claim, I also looked at a sample of the mugshots that were being selected as the mugshot of the day.

Qualitative Content Analysis

A look at the photos presents an opportunity to see who the voters picked to name and shame. This would help identify the outward manifestations of the rhetoric of the site. With a call for entertainment, who were voters selecting?

Methods: To do this, I selected a random selection of images, and I chose a selection of 285 photos from the summer of 2015. To look at these photos, I conducted a visual, qualitative content analysis. According to Rose, content analysis for images involves "counting the frequency of certain visual elements in a clearly defined sample of images" (2007, p. 61), and then looking at these frequencies to make meaning. Each image was also categorised into only one category. By looking at these mugshots, a pattern emerged that participants were doing more than just keeping an eye out for criminals — I argue they were, for the most part, specifically targeting individuals for their appearance.

Elo and Kyngas outline that the general goal of content analysis is to get a "condensed and broad description of the phenomenon, and the outcome of the analysis is concepts or categories describing the phenomenon" (2007, p. 108). For a greater level of confidence in the data, I also worked with a second coder to achieve intercoder reliability, as recommended by Geisler and Swarts (2019). Multiple coders were essential because as Krippendorff (1980), Geisler and Swarts (2019), and Rose (2007) underscore, qualitative content analysis is useful when it is both replicable and reliable. To be replicable and thus more reliable, more than one person should be able to conduct the same study and get similar results. According to Rose, similar results can be achieved with good coding description with codes "defined as fully as possible" (2007, p. 68). With well-defined categories, each coder could match their code to the description of the classification.

With a second coder, I was able to achieve 270 agreements, which is approximately 95% of simple intercoder agreement, or in other words, the "measure of the extent to which coders assign the same codes to the same set of data" (Geisler & Swarts, 2019, p. 155). In this study, the 5% discrepancy arose most times when an image had more than one category trait, for example a subject had both an out-of-the-ordinary facial expression, but also body tattoos, and coders debated as to which code was more prominent. I was also able to get a 0.920 Kappa agreement as calculated by GraphPad (2014) which was rated as a "very good" strength of agreement.

Results: According to Schreier, "With qualitative content analysis, the coding frame itself can be the main result" (2014, p. 180), and after following the steps of analysis, Table 12.2 details the eleven categories emerged.

Table 12.2: Category Results for MotD Leaderboard

Element/Coder	Coder 1	Coder 2
Attractive Female	182	184
Disheveled Female	8	8
Disheveled Male	6	4
Facial Expression	13	12
Hairstyle	11	12
Injury	9	6

Name	4	4
Other visual	21	23
Pose	8	5
Prominent Tattoo	10	11
Unknown	13	16
Total	**285**	**285**

As shown in Table 12.2, nearly all the mugshots in this period fit into ten identifiable categories with only one "unknown" category that does not appear to correlate to visual characteristics. Looking at the data, the most frequently occurring category was images labelled "attractive female" by both coders. The remaining images were split between the ten other categories. To describe the other categories in alphabetical order: firstly, there were "dishevelled" female and male categories that featured individuals whose appearance might suggest a transient lifestyle. The "facial expression" category featured images where the arrestee wore an unusual expression, such as a wide smile or someone visibly crying. Those in the "hairstyle" category had hair that stood out as the main identifying feature, such as bright purple hair or hair styled straight up in the air, and the "injury" category featured individuals who had identifiably fresh injuries or bandages covering their face. The "name" category was an exception for the results in that the voting tended to be aimed at the arrestee's name rather than their image; for instance, a male arrestee had a name that sounded like a sexual euphemism and a man with the same first, middle and last name appeared in this group. The "other" category featured those with something identifiable about the image that would make the photo stand out, such as an eye patch or face mask, but the difference was more of a one-off than an emerging pattern. Although this was the second-highest-scoring category, it was still significantly less frequent than the top category. The "pose" category featured individuals whose bodies were doing something out of the ordinary, such as a woman whose hands were placed under her chin reminiscent of a 1990's-era professional glamour portrait, and the "prominent tattoo" category featured individuals who had visible face and upper-body tattoos (ones that could be seen in a mugshot profile). Finally, there was an "unknown" category that featured those individuals who were voted onto the leader board, but nothing stood out visually. These could have been individuals who had been featured in the news for exceptional crimes, but as this study looked only at the visual elements, nothing stood out in their appearance.

Discussion: While the exact reason someone voted cannot be determined, due to the anonymous nature of the voting process, the information above can at least provide evidence of a visual pattern. In conjunction with the content and views analysis of the site, and by looking at the results on the leader board, the emergent cluster of visual characteristics provides evidence that voters were not just elevating the criminals that post the greatest threats to the community. For instance, several of the "leading" offenders were arrested for lower-level issues like failure to pay fines or fees. Instead, the majority of those featured were attractive females, followed by the dishevelled, injured, tattooed, and unusually hairstyled. As local Phoenix reporter Ray Stern (2016, n.p.) anecdotally noted about the site, "Typically, the winners were the jail's best-looking female inmates, though occasionally a man would win if he had the right facial tattoos or bizarre appearance".

This overwhelming majority of "winning" attractive females is also another important exploration unto itself in matters of gender, race and class, but for this chapter's argument, these results fit in with work done on engaging in voyeurism as entertainment. The mugshots exist as screen bodies, and in a patriarchal world, as Wise comments, "[w]omen on screen are then the object of the voyeuristic gaze — they are seen as objects of pleasure, often as objects of desire" (2016, p. 16). Voters have singled out younger, attractive females to target with visibility in the name of entertainment, with the voters in control and those featured in the photos forced to sit passively by as others elevate and manipulate their digital exposure.

Oddly enough though, too, this is not the first time Sheriff Joe has facilitated the increased visibility of arrested females. In July 2000, Arpaio started "Jail Cam" that streamed footage from inside the jail "where interested viewers world-wide could watch around the clock coverage of arrestees entering the jail in handcuffs, the booking process and life within the holding cells" (Lynch, 2004, p. 255). This became especially problematic in 2001 when as Lynch reports, "the camera inside the women's holding cell became 'misaligned' and began broadcasting a view of the women's toilet area" and claims were that "these images ended up being linked to several Internet pornography sites" (ibid., p. 258).

Implications of the Claims

After reviewing the literature about vigilantism and comparing this to the MCSO's MotD program, as well as examining the leader board, my main conclusion emerges: through the exigency of entertainment on participatory platforms, online mugshots can temporarily coalesce a group of digital vigilantes that weaponise visibility.

With this conclusion, two main implications also emerge that need to be discussed. Firstly, entertainment can serve as the exigency for individuals to engage in digital vigilantism, and secondly, there can be a relationship between the state and the public when engaging in digital vigilantism.

Entertainment as exigency for acts of digital vigilantism: To begin this discussion, I argue that entertainment can serve as exigency for digital vigilantism. This has implications for 1) mugshots as well as 2) digital vigilantism and the audience.

Firstly, this claim has implications for mugshots, because those who view mugshots have not typically been considered vigilantes. Starting in the 1800s, as the use of mugshots grew in popularity, they began to serve more constructed, supplementary spaces of entrainment. In order to build support for emerging law enforcement groups, some departments, such as the New York City police, began to post mugshots in their offices. Called "rogue's galleries" where spectators could visit the lobby of the department and view displays of the photos, the spaces allowed onlookers to return the gaze of the images (Hall, 2009). They were "understood as a popular form of amusement and as an invitation to practice the art of detection as a personal safety strategy" (ibid., p. 65), and tourists flocked to these galleries (Gunning, 1995). Images of outlaws spread in time to wanted posters, bulletins, most-wanted lists published by the media such as the FBI's ten-most-wanted list, then to television programs such as *America's Most Wanted*. Audiences could consume the images as a pastime, whether seeking to identify criminals or enjoy a voyeuristic look into another's life. In their leisure time, a viewer could inspect, consume, judge, speculate and mingle with the images, all while keeping distance.

The early mugshot viewer was theorised, then, as more of a spectator rather than a participant in interaction with the photo. Interaction was limited to more passive defiance. Hall (2009, p. 8) uses Caldwell's (1995) work and calls the historical mugshot consumer a "vigilante viewer" or one that stands up to the images and the fear they can produce, in order to return the gaze and gain satisfaction that their life is more productive than the photographed. As Hall notes, they did not want "a live encounter with the outlaw" and instead were more interested to "see 'what a real outlaw looks like'" (2009, p. 7). They would also rather have relinquished control of catching and punishing the outlaw to the authorities, often cheerleading law enforcement to do so.

In a change of paradigm, though, the participatory platform transforms what was called the 'vigilante viewer' into a more active participant: the 'digital vigilante'. Whereas vigilante viewers were relegated to being passive participants, viewing the photos at a distance, those who interact with mugshots online can actually harm the individual featured by elevating the images and weaponising visibility. Although the mugshot-consuming digital vigilante might still not want the live encounter, they can now at least engage with the platform and punish the target, whether they know it or even view the target as a 'target'.

Secondly, this conclusion also has implications for digital vigilantism and what it means to be an audience. As discussed, DV's "point of departure is moral outrage or a general sense of offence taking" (Trottier, 2017, p. 57), but in another paradigm shift, entertainment does not fit that description. DV as entertainment doesn't fully fit with the motivations of outrage or offense. Instead of seeking retaliation or punishment, participation is invited by MCSO seemingly for entertainment purposes (even if the pleasure derived from participation comes from schadenfreude or the voyeuristic ability to objectify the accused.) This interpretation also emphasises the power structure of mugshots and the one-sidedness of the entertainment. Although Makinen and Koskela comment that surveillance as entertainment "is increasingly understood in terms of hedonism, pleasure and amusement" (2014, p. 189), especially in the context of mugshots, this pleasure is most likely absent from those featured in the mugshots, and instead experienced by those among the audience who are 'punching down', a term Linton discusses in her chapter in this volume. Overall, though, even though entertainment may seem more light-hearted than more aggressive forms of doxing or 'naming and shaming', it still produces similar results — a watching but participatory audience and a group of those being watched, with the latter assemblage being filled with shame resulting from the weaponisation of visibility.

It may be easier to argue, then, that those who participate in the MCSO's MotD program are just not digital vigilantes, because the call to unite them is more about entertainment and less about retaliation for perceived wrongs. However, I also argue that just because the group might not be called into existence by the allure of retribution, this does not mean that the consequences are different. Those voting on the mugshots are still able to weaponise visibility, even if it is under the guise of entertainment rather than an attempt to right perceived wrongs. Even if entertainment, not retribution, motivated the call for engagement, the fact that users elevated the visibility of individuals still resulted in consequences for the individual being elevated.

While it may be controversial to make this claim, the idea of intention in digital vigilantism at least warrants debate, which hopefully spurs discussions about the types and degrees of digital vigilantism, or stimulates a debate about terminology that would cover the phenomenology of using entertainment as the exigence of the weaponisation of visibility. It also effectually causes one to be alert for other cases in which entertainment provides the exigency for digital vigilantism, such as the work of Driessen and Linton in other chapters of this book.

The state/public/private partnership: My second implication is that if MCSO created groups of digital vigilantes through their participatory platforms under the guise of entertainment, then this means the state and the public do have some connections with digital vigilantism. This claim also has implications because vigilantism has traditionally separated the state and public. As Johnston has argued, vigilantism is carried out by "autonomous citizens" (1996, p. 232) expressly without state authority or support.[2] However, my conclusion supports Trottier's comments that "[w]hile states may not willingly support vigilantism, recent trends in policing are indicative of nodal governance between government, law enforcement, private industry and the general public" (2017, p. 64). This point also calls for more research and debate as to the degree that these entities could and should be connected.

It is also important to add that for the MCSO and other mugshot-posting agencies, not only does the state provide the space and participatory platform for the public to engage with mugshots, but it also contributes to a triangular relationship between the state, the public and private industry that results in unwanted, intense and enduring visibility.

While some municipalities require open access to their public records, and other jurisdictions allow for the release of information only through Freedom of Information Act (FOIA) requests (Birchall, 2016; Martin, 2014; Rosedale, 2014; Shephard, 2014), when state agencies like MCSO post the photos onto their official sites, anyone can screen-scrape mugshots. Unless posting agencies write their own software to stop screen-scraping, as the Charleston, SC sheriff's office has done (Duffin & Fountain, 2018), others can use these photos for their own ends (Rostron, 2013).

A search of online mugshots reveals how *unwanted* this is because, in addition to the aforementioned lawsuit discussed above, outside of the MCSO illustration, there are many other examples of lawsuits where those featured on these mugshots pages sued the publisher (Hartzog & Selinger, 2015; Martin, 2014; Rosedale, 2014; Rostron, 2013) or where those photographed attend "expungement clinics" to learn how to get mugshots and associated arrest information taken offline (Lageson, 2016, p. 26). As stated previously, mugshots are inherently an unwanted reminder of a past indiscretion.

The *intensity* of this relationship is also increased by the triangular relationship. The number of reposts can be in the thousands, and as

---

2   I would argue that Johnston himself could revisit his own argument to see how the resistance or skepticism against law enforcement is, in itself, a motivating factor in vigilante actions, thus establishing at least some rhetorical exigency and relationship between the state and the public.

Kravets (2011, n.p.) reports, one website owner hosting four million mugshots "'screen-scrapes' mugshots at a rate of 1500 per day". These images can travel to other sites, too, and for any given site, mugshots are often just downloaded from one site to another (Vasigh, 2013).

These corporate sites also increase the intensity of online mugshots by allowing for easier searching. Because commercial site providers want to promote their sites, so that they can appear among the top results in any number of locations and searches, they use search-engine optimisation, tag photos in certain ways or pay to appear among the top results of a Google search (Lageson, 2014; Rostron, 2013; Vasigh, 2013). Also, as Vasigh (2013) brings out, there is a difference between mugshots that are available through routine Google searches versus those that take more targeted effort to uncover through specific departmental jurisdictions. One may not know the arresting agency and specific details of an offense to give to law enforcement agencies, but someone "may find an arrestee's mug shot accidently when he or she is not seeking to obtain it but is merely searching online" (ibid., p. 289). Summing up this intensity, Lageson notes:

> [Y]our coworker, first date, or the parents of your kid's new friend at school can all stumble on this information, as a simple arrest — one that might not even lead to charges — appears online, accompanied by a booking photo. This photo and arrest record might be re-posted to a Facebook page, a community blog, on a newspaper police blotter. These data are also purchased in bulk by private companies, whose sites are often paid top results in a Google search (2014, p. 24).

The state / public / private relationship is also *enduring*. Because online mugshots can be posted by any number of hosts, the photos can seemingly multiply on many sites with few ways to stop the reproduction. This is another notable difference to law enforcement sites. As Vasigh (2013, p. 286) notes, "Most sheriff's offices usually delete mug shots of individuals who are not convicted", but this is not necessarily true of other web publishers. Some commercial websites place the burden on the individual and require the mugshotted person to notify them that they were not convicted, before the photo will be removed. Often the sites also charge for removing the photos, and fees could be any amount — for instance, the site Blabbermouth.kc.com tried to charge $199.99 to remove a mugshot (Rostron, 2013) and the site Unpublisharrest.

com was charging $399 (incidentally, both came under the scrutiny of law enforcement themselves for these practices, but this is not always the case.) This is especially problematic because, as one individual interviewed at an expungement clinic stated, "We are here today to try to clear our record. Let's just imagine that I am successful. There is like 3,000 services out there" (2016, p. 26). So even if one could afford a $400 fee once, there could be seemingly no end to the number of fees one would have to pay. While some states ban charging fees for removal (Vasigh, 2013), other states do not, and the practice still proliferates.

Overall, then, not only do the state and the public have a relationship in relation to online mugshots, there is a third connection with private industries who also use these photos to name and shame in their own ways (which also warrants more examination).

Conclusion

Throughout this chapter, I've argued that through the exigency of entertainment on participatory platforms, online mugshots temporarily coalesce a group of digital vigilantes to weaponise visibility. While I used the example of MCSO's MotD program to illustrate this, the conclusions also reveal the need for more research in three areas.

Firstly, while other sites are not necessarily built on "Mugshot of the Day!" voting platforms, being able to post reactions such as Facebook's like, love, haha, wow, sad and angry emojis allows mugshot consumers the ability to increase the visibility of the photographs on other platforms. Visibility has also allowed mugshots on platforms like Facebook to go culturally viral too, with a significant amount of exposure. More recently, there was "Neck Guy", who became a meme due to the circulation on Facebook of his unusually thick neck in his mugshot (Caldwell, 2018), and one of the most notable, visible mugshots was the example of 2014's "hot mugshot guy" or "hot felon", Jeremy Meeks, who was singled out for his model-like appearance. Meeks' mugshot posted by the Stockton Police Department on their Facebook page had over 56,000 likes and 16,400 comments in the first 48 hours of posting, with a repost of the photo by a news station garnering 301,000 likes and 65,000 comments in another twenty hours (Caldwell, 2017). User interaction was so strong that the photo also became a meme, spurring the hashtag #FelonCrushFriday, and Google identified "Jeremy Meeks" as the top trending search on 20 June 2014.

Secondly, the conclusions also indicate the need for additional research about who is targeted when dealing with images and the justice system. For MCSO, the department developed a contest around images in which the public could participate, and at least in half the cases, the public chose to highlight attractive female bodies. The other votes also targeted those who looked out of the ordinary. This is a point worthy of future attention for studies of gender, justice and culture.

Finally, this also invites more discussion of who can be doxed, who can do the doxing and what motivates the doxing. It might seem more acceptable for the state to share mugshots for safety reasons, but when the same information is shared by state or private entities for purposes of entertainment, the rhetorical situation and justifications seemingly change, too. These photos can even become larger tools for public suppression, as is particularly evident in recent examples involving hate groups. Caroline Sinders and Joan Donovan (2018) note that in August 2018, the Berkeley, CA police department tweeted mugshots of counter-protestors at a far-right gathering. This, in essence, served as a silencing device for protests because it added an additional layer of consequence for those arrested, as "[b]y placing the arrested in public view, these far-right groups are able to target and harass those awaiting trial" (ibid., n.p.) and intimidate future protesters. With power in the hands of the state to place the personal information of others onto participatory platforms, it is increasingly important to interrogate the power structures and power diffusions that call for and allow citizens both to carry out and to be a victim of naming and shaming.

While it may be difficult to pinpoint exactly why someone chose to vote for a particular person, it was helpful to analyze both the calls for voting as well as the images that received the most votes, in order at least to provide a snapshot of how the call for participation was framed and what the resulting participation looked like. Overall, the research into these photos ultimately leads me to conclude that through the exigency of entertainment on participatory platforms, online mugshots temporarily coalesce a group of digital vigilantes to weaponise visibility. Thus, the state can play a part in digital vigilantism, ultimately contributing to ever-evolving definitions of vigilantism in a digital world.

References

BBC News. (2017, August 26). Joe Arpaio: Life as 'America's toughest sheriff'. BBC News, https://www.bbc.com/news/world-us-canada-41015549

Birchall, C. (2016). Shareveillance: Subjectivity between open and closed data. *Big Data & Society*, 3(2), https://doi.org/10.1177/2053951716663965

Caldwell, J. T. (1995). *Televisuality: Style, Crisis, and Authority in American Television*. New Brunswick: Rutgers University Press.

Caldwell, D. (2017, April 26). Jeremy Meeks' mugshot, http://knowyourmeme.com/memes/jeremy-meeks-mugshot

Caldwell, D. (2018, December). Charles McDowell's Wide Neck Mugshot, https://knowyourmeme.com/memes/charles-mcdowells-wide-neck-mugshot

Campbell, D. G. (2013, October 18). Jamali v. Maricopa Cnty, https://casetext.com/case/jamali-v-maricopa-cnty

Charland, M. (1987). Constitutive rhetoric: The case of the "peuple québécois". *Quarterly Journal of Speech*, 73(2), 133.

Collier, K. (2014, December). Why the online mugshot industry will never die, https://kernelmag.dailydot.com/issue-sections/features-issue-sections/11068/online-mugshot-extortion-industry

Duffin, K., & Fountain, N. (2018, November 23). Episode 878: Mugshots. *Planet Money, NPR*. https://www.npr.org/sections/money/2018/11/23/670149449/episode-878-mugshots-for-sale

Duffy, C. (2018, January 16). Meet Sheriff Joe Arpaio, the only person pardoned by US President Donald Trump, https://www.abc.net.au/news/2018-01-16/sheriff-joe-arpaio-the-only-person-pardoned-by-donald-trump/9325224

Elo, S., & Kyngas, H. (2008) The qualitative content analysis process. *Journal of Advanced Nursing*, 62(1), 107–15, https://doi.org/10.1111/j.1365-2648.2007.04569.x

Elsesser, S. (2017, September 27). LOOK: Inmate's mugshot of him snacking on sandwich goes viral. *Palm Beach Post*, https://www.palmbeachpost.com/news/crime--law/look-inmate-mugshot-him-snacking-sandwich-goes-viral/85f1TI3NEw4xT8UrwetD7L

Finn, J. (2009). *Capturing the criminal image: From mug shot to surveillance society*. University of Minnesota Press.

Geisler, C., & Swarts, J. (2019). Coding Streams of Language: Techniques for the Systematic Coding of Text, Talk, and other Verbal Data. Fort Collins, CO: The WAC Clearinghouse; University Press of Colorado, https://wac.colostate.edu/books/practice/codingstreams/

GraphPad. (2014, July). QuickCalcs, https://www.graphpad.com/quickcalcs/kappa2

Gunning, T. (1995). Tracing the individual body: Photography, detectives, and early Cinema. In L. Charney & V. R. Schwartz's *Cinema and the Invention of Modern Life* (pp. 15–41). Berkeley: University of California Press.

Hall, R. (2009). *Wanted: The Outlaw in American Visual Culture*. Charlottesville: University of Virginia Press.

Hart-Davidson, W., Bernhardt, G., Mcleod, M., Rife, M., & Grabill, J. (2007). Coming to Content Management: Inventing Infrastructure for Organizational Knowledge Work. *Technical Communication Quarterly*, 17(1), 10–34, https://doi.org/10.1080/10572250701588608

Hartzog, W., & Selinger, E. (2015). Surveillance as loss of obscurity. *Washington and Lee Law Review*, 72, 1343–1989, https://scholarlycommons.law.wlu.edu/wlulr/vol72/iss3/10

Hendley, M. (2015, May 8). Maricopa County Mugshots of the Week: Symbols, https://www.phoenixnewtimes.com/news/maricopa-county-mugshots-of-the-week-symbols-7324760

Hermann, W. (2011, April 19). Arpaio is using county jail's website for a 'Mug Shot of the Day' contest, http://archive.azcentral.com/community/phoenix/articles/20110419sheriff-joe-arpaio-using-county-jails-website-mug-shot-day-contest.html

Hirschfeld Davis, J., & Haberman, M. (2017, August 25). Trump Pardons Joe Arpaio, who became face of crackdown on illegal immigration. *The New York Times*, https://www.nytimes.com/2017/08/25/us/politics/joe-arpaio-trump-pardon-sheriff-arizona.html

Jenkins, H., Green, J., & Ford, S. (2013). Spreadable media: Creating value and meaning in a networked culture. New York: New York University Press.

Johnston, L. (1996). What is vigilantism? *British Journal of Criminology*, 36(2), 220–36.

Karp, D. R. (1998). The judicial and judicious use of shame penalties. *Crime & Delinquency*, 44(2), 277–94, https://doi.org/10.1177/0011128798044002006

Kiefer, M. (2016, November 7). Joe Arpaio no longer "America's Toughest Sheriff". *AZ Central*, https://www.azcentral.com/story/news/local/phoenix/2016/11/07/sheriff-joe-arpaio-arizona-maricopa-county-america-toughest-sheriff/92849258

Kravets, D. (2011, August 2). Mug-shot industry will dig up your past, charge you to bury it again. *Wired*, https://www.wired.com/2011/08/mugshots

Krippendorff, K. (1980). *Content analysis: An introduction to its methodology.* Beverly Hills, CA: Sage Publications.

Lageson, S. (2016). Digital Punishment's Tangled Web. *Contexts*, 15(1), 22–7, https://contexts.org/articles/digital-punishments-tangled-web

Lashmar, P. (2013). How to humiliate and shame: A reporter's guide to the power of the mugshot. *Social Semiotics*, 24(1), 1–32, https://doi.org/10.108 0/10350330.2013.827358

Lynch, M. (2004). Punishing images: Jail Cam and the changing penal enterprise. *Punishment & Society*, 6 (3), 255–270, https://doi: 10.1177/1462474504043631

Makinen, L. A., & Koskela, H. (2014). Surveillance as a reality game. In A. Jansson & M. Christensen (eds), *Media, surveillance, and identity: Social perspectives* (pp. 183–200). New York: Peter Lang.

Maricopa County Mugshots. (n.d.), https://maricopacountymugshots. wordpress.com

Maricopa County Sheriff's Office. (2015a). About: Sheriff Joseph M. Arpaio, http://www.mcso.org/About/Sheriff.aspx

Maricopa County Sheriff's Office. (2015b, February 23). Mugshots, http:// www.mcso.org/Mugshot/#

Martin, W. T. (2014). From the police precinct to your neighbor's coffee table: Limiting public dissemination of mug shots during an ongoing criminal proceeding under the Freedom of Information Act. *Iowa Law Review*, 99(3), 1431–59, http://dx.doi.org/10.2139/ssrn.2255694

Murray, E. (2015, July 13). Vermont police weigh mug shots on social media. *USA Today*, https://www.usatoday.com/story/news/nation/2015/07/13/ police-mug-shots-social-media/30087473

Ohlheiser, A. (2014, January 6). Steven Seagal and Joe Arpaio want to make Arizona no. 1 for vigilante justice. *The Atlantic*, https://www.theatlantic. com/politics/archive/2014/01/steven-seagal-and-joe-arpaio-want-make-arizona-no-1-vigilante-justice/356722

Rockley, A., & Kostur, P. (2003). *Managing enterprise content: A unified content strategy*. New York: New Riders.

Rose, G. (2007). *Visual methodologies: An introduction to the interpretation of visual materials* (2nd ed.). Thousand Oaks, CA: Sage Publications.

Rosedale, R. (2014). A picture says a thousand words: Applying FOIA's exemption 7(C) to mug shots. *St. John's Law Review*, 88(3), 789–823, https:// scholarship.law.stjohns.edu/lawreview/vol88/iss3/6

Rostron, A. (2013). The mugshot industry: Freedom of speech, rights of publicity, and the controversy sparked by an unusual new type of business. *Washington University Law Review*, 90, 1321–34, https://openscholarship. wustl.edu/law_lawreview/vol90/iss4/6

Santos, F. (2012, August 1). When a taste for publicity bites back. *The New York Times*, https://www.nytimes.com/2012/08/02/us/

an-arizona-sheriffs-fondness-for-publicity-may-bite-back.html?page
wanted=all

Schreier, M. (2014). Qualitative content analysis. In U. Flick (ed.), *The SAGE Handbook of Qualitative Data Analysis* (pp. 170–84), http://dx.doi.org/10.4135/ 9781446282243.n12

Shephard, K. (2014). Mug shot disclosure under FOIA: Does privacy or public interest prevail? *Northwestern University Law Review*, 108(1), 343–77, https://scholarlycommons.law.northwestern.edu/nulr/vol108/iss1/8

Sinders, C., & Donovan, J. (2018, Aug. 12). Police departments need to stop posting mugshots on Twitter. *Wired*, https://www.wired.com/story/opinion-police-should-stop-doxxing-protestors

Smallridge, J., Wagner, P., & Crowl, J. N. (2016). Understanding cyber-vigilantism: A conceptual framework. *Journal of Theoretical & Philosophical Criminology*, 8(1), 57-70.

Stern, R. (2016, September 28). Sheriff Joe Arpaio halts public voting for jail "Mugshot of the Day" after website redesign. *Phoenix New Times*, https://www.phoenixnewtimes.com/news/sheriff-joe-arpaio-halts-public-voting-for-jail-mugshot-of-the-day-after-website-redesign-8690032

TMZ. (2015, April 24). WNBA's Brittney Griner wins 'Mugshot of the Day'... On sheriff's website. *TMZ Sports*, https://www.tmz.com/2015/04/24/brittney-griner-wins-mugshot-of-the-day-on-sheriffs-website

Trottier, D. (2017). Digital vigilantism as weaponisation of visibility. *Philosophy and Technology*, 30(1), 55–72. doi:10.1007/s13347-016-0216-4

Vasigh, M. (2013). Smile, you are under arrest: The misappropriation and misuse of mug shots online. *Information & Communications Technology Law*, 22(3), 1–22, https://doi.org/10.1080/13600834.2013.855064

Wise, J. M. (2016). *Surveillance and Film*. New York: Bloomsbury.

Index

About the Team

Alessandra Tosi was the managing editor for this book.

Lucy Barnes and Melissa Pukiss performed the copy-editing and proofreading.

Anna Gatti designed the cover using InDesign. The cover was produced in InDesign using Fontin (titles) and Calibri (text body) fonts.

Francesca Giovannetti typeset the book in InDesign and produced the paperback and hardback editions. The text font is Tex Gyre Pagella; the heading font is Californian FB.

Luca Baffa produced the EPUB, MOBI, PDF, HTML, and XML editions — the conversion is performed with open source software freely available on our GitHub page (https://github.com/OpenBookPublishers).

This book need not end here...

Share

All our books — including the one you have just read — are free to access online so that students, researchers and members of the public who can't afford a printed edition will have access to the same ideas. This title will be accessed online by hundreds of readers each month across the globe: why not share the link so that someone you know is one of them?

This book and additional content is available at:

https://doi.org/10.11647/OBP.0200

Customise

Personalise your copy of this book or design new books using OBP and third-party material. Take chapters or whole books from our published list and make a special edition, a new anthology or an illuminating coursepack. Each customised edition will be produced as a paperback and a downloadable PDF.

Find out more at:

https://www.openbookpublishers.com/section/59/1

Like Open Book Publishers

Follow @OpenBookPublish

Read more at the Open Book Publishers BLOG

You may also be interested in:

The Environment in the Age of the Internet
Activists, Communication, and the Digital Landscape
Heike Graf (ed.)

https://doi.org/10.11647/OBP.0096

 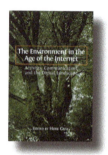

Social Media in Higher Education
Case Studies, Reflections and Analysis
Chris Rowell (ed.)

https://doi.org/10.11647/OBP.0162

Peace and Democratic Society
Amartya Sen (ed.)

https://doi.org/10.11647/OBP.0014

 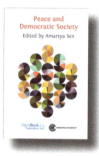